Queering Families

Sexuality, Identity, and Society Series

Series Editor
Philip L. Hammack

BOOKS IN THE SERIES

The Monogamy Gap: Men, Love, and the Reality of Cheating
Eric Anderson

Modernizing Sexuality: U.S. HIV Prevention in Sub-Saharan Africa
Anne W. Esacove

Technologies of Sexiness: Sex, Identity, and Consumer Culture
Adrienne Evans and Sarah Riley

The Story of Sexual Identity: Narrative Perspectives on the Gay and Lesbian Life Course
Philip L. Hammack and Bertram J. Cohler

The Declining Significance of Homophobia: How Teenage Boys are Redefining Masculinity and Heterosexuality
Mark McCormack

Queering Families: The Postmodern Partnerships of Cisgender Women and Transgender Men
Carla A. Pfeffer

Queering Families

The Postmodern Partnerships of Cisgender Women and Transgender Men

CARLA A. PFEFFER

OXFORD
UNIVERSITY PRESS

Oxford University Press is a department of the University of Oxford. It furthers
the University's objective of excellence in research, scholarship, and education
by publishing worldwide. Oxford is a registered trade mark of Oxford University
Press in the UK and certain other countries.

Published in the United States of America by Oxford University Press
198 Madison Avenue, New York, NY 10016, United States of America.

© Oxford University Press 2017

Library of Congress Cataloging-in-Publication Data
Names: Pfeffer, Carla A., author.
Title: Queering families : the postmodern partnerships of cisgender women
and transgender men / Carla A. Pfeffer.
Description: New York, NY : Oxford University Press, [2017] | Series: Sexuality, identity,
and society series | Includes bibliographical references and index.
Identifiers: LCCN 2016025514 | ISBN 9780199908059 (pbk. : alk. paper)
Subjects: LCSH: Female-to-male transsexuals—Family relationships. | Transgender
people—Identity. | Interpersonal relations. | Couples. | Man-woman relationships. | Sexual
minorities' families.
Classification: LCC HQ77.9 .P5155 2017 | DDC 306.874086/6—dc23
LC record available at https://lccn.loc.gov/2016025514

For Maja and Luka

TABLE OF CONTENTS

I went for the first time to a group for lesbian, gay, bisexual, and transgender youth when I was 17 years old. It was the early 1990s, and use of the term "queer" was extremely uncommon. Yet my initial encounter in that youth program and the world that was opened up before me offered the first exercise in *queerness*, as ideas I had once taken for granted were challenged and turned upside down. Most notably, as other youth I met referred to themselves as "family," the conventional conception of family with which I was raised was forever queered. In the lexicon of the day, we referred to other sexual and gender deviants as *family*. Given the hostility so many of us experienced from our families of origin, this reclamation of the term and the concept seemed extraordinarily liberating to me. I have spent my entire life since queering the family concept, constructing alternative forms of relational intimacy and kinship.

I begin with this personal narrative to highlight the significance of Carla A. Pfeffer's timely book, *Queering Families: The Postmodern Partnerships of Cisgender Women and Transgender Men*, not only for the light it sheds on diversity in constructions of family, but also for the visibility it provides to the experience of cisgender women and transgender men in relationships. The initial queering of the family concept among us sexual and gender deviants has given way to more precise formulations of familial queerness. Chosen families have increasingly been recognized as socially and psychologically vital to LGBTQ+ people (Frost, Meyer, & Schwartz, 2016), and the 2015 Supreme Court ruling in *Obergefell v. Hodges* that legalized same-sex marriage across the United States has now provided a new opportunity to queer the concepts of marriage and family. Pfeffer rightly notes that, "While researchers are making considerable progress in including lesbians and gay men in studies of family life, other 'queer' social actors remain relatively absent" (p. X). Her book aims precisely to address this omission in the literature by focusing on the unique experiences of cisgender women in partnership with transgender men.

Pfeffer's book appears at a time of heightened visibility for transgender people, punctuated by the numerous transphobic "bathroom bills" that have arisen to denigrate the lived experience of transgender people by equating them with sexual predators, revealing not just transphobia but also a gross misunderstanding of transgender identity. Interestingly, though, the lens has focused largely on transgender women, and so Pfeffer's contribution is particularly noteworthy, for the voices she captures in this book have been silenced for far too long, even with the recent rise in trans visibility. Pfeffer's book begins the project of representing these relational experiences situated historically at the margins, rarely if ever acknowledged.

With thoughtful engagement with a diverse literature from the social sciences and humanities, Pfeffer highlights the triumphs and tribulations of cis women and trans men committed to an evolving understanding of their intimacies. She reveals the way in which these individuals navigate a shifting taxonomy for social and sexual identity, grappling with their own self-understandings as they and their partners move toward greater authenticity in self-expression. Once identified as lesbians, they may go on to "pass" as a heteronormative couple while experiencing themselves as anything but. The term *queer* best captures the experience of most, as they defy the conventional taxonomies of gender, sexuality, and relationality. But the path to making meaning of these experiences and navigating the ever-shifting discourses of gender, sexuality, relationships, and family is both liberating and challenging. A very novel contribution of Pfeffer's book is its elaboration of this process—of documenting how cis women and trans men in relationships navigate discourses of normativity and their own changing social and biological experiences of gender and sexuality as they evolve. Cis women in these relationships must navigate terrains of both heteronormativity and homonormativity, and Pfeffer details the strategies they use in this process.

Pfeffer's book is an ideal fit for this series, for it considers sexuality and society through the prism of a shifting narrative landscape. It assumes that experiences of gender, sexuality and family are not static but dynamic and constantly evolving. This position resonates well with the idea of *narrative engagement* I and others have used to describe the process of sexual and gender identity diversity in the 21st century (e.g., Hammack & Cohler, 2009), as we witness radical reformulations in our understanding of gender and sexuality, beyond "gay" and "lesbian." The theory of narrative engagement posits that we understand our lives and construct our social worlds with intentionality and authenticity, always in direct reference to storylines that circulate in culture about the meaning of particular identities and concepts. In the case of Pfeffer's book, we see individuals rewriting prior scripts of their own relationships, possible in part thanks to new storylines in our culture that legitimize and validate the transgender experience.

In shining the light on these increasingly common experiences, Pfeffer's book is at the forefront of research on diversity in relationships and family configurations. I expect that her work will provoke more interrogation of queer intimacies—forms of relationality that challenge pre-existing convention and our inherited taxonomies. In so doing, the book contributes to the quest to capture the evolving lived experience of identity and intimacy with fidelity and audacity.

Phillip L. Hammack
Santa Cruz, California
August, 2016

REFERENCES

Frost, D. M., Meyer, I.H., & Schwartz, S. (2016). Social support networks among diverse sexual minority populations. *American Journal of Orthopsychiatry, 86*(1), 91-102.

Hammack, P. L., & Cohler, B.J. (2009). Narrative engagement and sexual identity: An interdisciplinary approach to the study of sexual lives. In P. L. Hammack & B.J. Cohler (Ed.), *The story of sexual identity: Narrative perspectives on the gay and lesbian life course* (pp. 3-22). New York: Oxford University Press.

ACKNOWLEDGMENTS

Financial support for this project was provided by the Andrew W. Mellon Foundation and American Council of Learned Societies through receipt of a Dissertation Completion Fellowship. At the University of Michigan, I am thankful for the considerable financial support provided by grants and fellowships from the Departments of Sociology and Women's Studies; the Rackham Graduate School's Predoctoral Fellowship and One-Term Dissertation Grant; a research grant from the Center for the Education of Women; and a Community of Scholars Fellowship from the Institute for Research on Women and Gender. At Purdue University North Central, work on this manuscript was facilitated through several Faculty Quarter-Time Teaching Reassignments. At the University of South Carolina, work on the revisions and final draft of this manuscript was facilitated through funding and support from the Magellan Program. I am thankful to the National Council on Family Relations for their support through receipt of the Jessie Bernard Outstanding Contribution to Feminist Scholarship Paper Award and to the Sex and Gender and Sexualities Sections of the American Sociological Association for their support through receipt of Distinguished Paper Awards and an Honorable Mention for the Martin P. Levine Memorial Dissertation Award.

I could not have known about the twists and turns, highs and lows, that I would encounter along my path from the day I received my book contract from Oxford University Press to the moment I first held this completed book in my hands. In that span of time, my partner (Maja) and I conceived a child. We reeled from the loss of our home in a massive fire just days after I put the finishing touches on the nursery. We lived in a hotel for a few weeks during the start of a busy new semester and then began building our lives over again, piece by piece, and were grateful that our growing family (even our cats) were safe and sound. Our beloved Luka was born early in 2013 and we were delirious with joy, weariness, and loss of sleep for the next year and a half. We flew 10,000 miles, roundtrip, from Chicago, IL to Zagreb, Croatia to visit Maja's grandmother when Luka was only 6 months old. Maja's grandmother died less than 2 weeks after we returned home and we will always be grateful that she was able to meet her great grandbaby. Our family struggled with health issues. Luka had chronic ear infections for 18 months and finally had surgery to implant ear tubes. For about a year, there was never more than a 2-week period when someone in our household wasn't sick with a cold, ear infection, respiratory infection, or another seemingly countless virus. My mother and both of my grandmothers were also hospitalized during this time and my mother was ultimately diagnosed with a progressive, relatively rare, and incurable disease in early 2014. I have traveled home to Michigan to visit my mom or attend a doctor's appointment with her as much as possible. My maternal grandmother died unexpectedly following a relatively routine outpatient surgery. My mother then faced the daunting task of burying her mother on the same date her mother had birthed her 63 years earlier. Over the span of these past several years, I stopped exercising, my thyroid went wonky, and I gained 100 pounds.

The world kept on turning, I taught 9 courses each year (and 10 during one particularly stressful year), I went on the job market, I accepted a new job, we drove 24 hours (from Indiana to South Carolina and back again) 4 times while looking for a house, we bought a house, and I wrote the first draft of this book. We packed up our stuff and moved to the South, away from our family and friends. Just 4 short months after moving, our new city (Columbia, SC) was struck by a devastating "1,000-year" flood. We were lucky to escape the worst of it. I revised the book and settled into my new position, our new community, our new life. My sister was in a terrible car accident and sustained a life-threatening injury. I flew back home to care for her for a month, emailing final book files to my Editor at Oxford along the way.

All of this simply would not have been possible without the encouraging support and love of so many people. Through the final push of writing the first draft (long days that stretched out into weeks and months over the summer), I often didn't leave my office until 2 or 3 a.m., driving home on winding roads through foggy, dark, Indiana cornfields with bleary, tired eyes. I grew close to the campus police officers and cleaning crew who seemed incredulous that I was still on campus, as I did my best to keep out of their way and not interfere with their work. Facebook became one of my only avenues for connecting with others aside from a once-every-other-week crafting night thanks to our friends (Sarah and Kim McDallen). Maja would bring Luka to my office for dinner visits several times each week during the last months of writing the first draft of this book. He would run through the halls, demand an apple or stickers, and take all of the books he could reach off of my bookshelves, one by one. It didn't escape me how ironic it was that writing a book about partnerships and families meant that my own were profoundly neglected for a time. I carved out weekends as much as possible, soaking up every possible minute with my family. The investments of our energies always involve tradeoffs, some more precious, painful, or irrevocable than others.

Through it all, I am indebted to (and deeply thankful for) my family (Maja Belamaric, Luka Pfeffer-Belamaric, Kelly Pfeffer, Jan Pfeffer, Bob Pfeffer, Vickie Bergeron, and Roy Bergeron); my patient and understanding Senior Editor (Abby Gross), Assistant Editor (Courtney McCarroll), Series Editor (Phil Hammack), and Copy Editor (Cheryl Jung) at Oxford University Press; Kim Greenwell, academic editor and writing consultant extraordinaire; Purdue University North Central former students and colleagues (especially Ginny Borolov, Jane Brooks, Kristi Brosmer, Cheryl DeLeón, Janusz Duzinkiewicz, Cari Gee—undergraduate teaching and research assistant extraordinaire, Mike Lynn, Christabel Rogalin, Rachel Steffens, and Cynthia Zdanczyk); my University of Michigan research and writing group (Laura Hirshfield—special thanks for help with book title brainstorming, David Hutson, Emily Kazyak, Katherine Luke, Zakiya Luna, and Kristin Scherrer); University of South Carolina students and colleagues (especially Shelby Clemmer for working to develop an early prototype of the index for this book); those not already mentioned who offered feedback on earlier drafts, or whose work inspired me or helped shape my thinking around this project (Jonah Aaron, Elizabeth A. Armstrong, Pallavi Banerjee, Cara Bergstrom-Lynch, Amy Brainer, Nicola Brown, Christopher Carrington, Cati Connell, Raewyn Connell, Marjorie DeVault, Aaron Devor, John Elia, Patricia Hill Collins, Sally Hines, Arlie Hochschild, Amber Hollibaugh, Reese Kelly, Anna Kirkland, Betsy Lucal, Karin Martin, Mignon Moore, Alison Moss, Esther Newton, C. J. Pascoe, Minnie Bruce Pratt, Sharon Preves, Carol Queen, Abigail Saguy, Tam Sanger, Kristen Schilt, Steven Seidman, Julia Serano, Eve Shapiro, Pam Smock, Amy Stone, Susan Stryker, Ahoo Tabatabai, Avery Tompkins, Salvador Vidal-Ortiz, Tey Meadow, Jane Ward, Tre Wentling, Laurel Westbrook, and Elroi Windsor); and all those who offered commiseration, joy, comic relief, food, and vital support (most notably Sarah Bane, Melissa Cox, Cheryl DeLeón, Peggy Geeseman, Kate Hershey, Kim McDallen, Sarah McDallen—special thanks for book cover design ideas, Kelly Pfeffer, Christabel Rogalin, and Shannon Saksewski) during these years that have been some of the most trying and wonderful of my life so far.

My family and I have been able to live and work and recover because of the childcare providers, medical personnel, housekeepers, therapists, insurance agents, firefighters, cleaning crews, campus safety officers, and cooks with whom we have worked, and whose services we have utilized and depended upon, over the past several years. We are fortunate even as we are tested. Maja has completed far more than her equitable share of the housework and childcare in these last months of book writing. I am both deeply grateful and ashamed, the only ethically sound combination of feelings under such a circumstance. I owe you big and for a very long time, Maja, and I won't forget it.

The 50 cis women partners of trans men who shared their stories and experiences with me have made this book not only possible, but necessary. I hope that other cis women partners of trans men who read this book might recognize some of their own strengths and struggles and perhaps feel a bit less alone and more a part of an ever-expanding community. When this is not the case, I hope this work inspires more research to include and represent an even broader cross-section of the diverse identities and experiences of not only cis women partners of trans men, but the proliferating landscape of 21st-century partnerships and family forms. There is so much more to be done and I am thankful for the opportunity to contribute to efforts to grow a comprehensive body of knowledge on trans partnerships and families.

Portions of this manuscript have been reprinted or adapted, with permission, from the following published and unpublished works:

REFERENCES

Pfeffer, Carla A. (2008). Bodies in relation—Bodies in transition: Lesbian partners of trans men and body image. *Journal of Lesbian Studies* 12(4):325–345. doi: 10.1080/108941608022781

Pfeffer, Carla A. (2009). *(Trans)formative relationships: What we learn about identities, bodies, work and families from women partners of trans men* (Doctoral dissertation). Retrieved from ProQuest Dissertations and Theses database. (UMI No. 3382326)

Pfeffer, Carla A. (2010). "Women's work?" Women partners of trans men doing housework and emotion work. *Journal of Marriage and Family* 72(1):165–183. doi:10.1111/j.1741-3737.2009.00690.x

Pfeffer, Carla A. (2012). Normative resistance and inventive pragmatism: Negotiations of structure and agency among transgender families. *Gender & Society* 26(4):574–602. doi:10.1177/0891243212445467

Pfeffer. Carla A. (2014). "I don't like passing as a straight woman": Queer negotiations of identity and social group membership. *American Journal of Sociology* 120(1):1–44. doi:10.1086/677197

Pfeffer, Carla A. (2014). Making space for trans sexualities. *Journal of Homosexuality* 61(5):597–604. doi:10.1080/00918369.2014.903108

Pfeffer, Carla A. (2014, August 20). Transgender culture clashes: Social recognition and determining the "real." *Gender & Society Blog*. Retrieved from https://gendersociety.wordpress.com/2014/08/20/transgender-culture-clashes/

INTRODUCTION

Queer Families and Development of the Sociological Imagination

On the very first days of class, I will often ask my students in a course on families to talk to me about what families look like and who and what "counts" as family.[1] We often begin with the United States Census Bureau definition, which asserts that families consist of "two or more people (one of whom is the householder) related by birth, marriage, or adoption residing in the same housing unit."[2] Students generally nod or quietly take notes, but do not seem too off-put by the definition until we begin to consider which types of arrangements would *not* count as family under the Census Bureau's conceptualization. My classes are very focused on discussion and it doesn't take long before students begin to ask and wonder aloud: "Can only one person be the head of the household? What if both people contribute equally?" "What if the couple is gay men or lesbians who cannot get legally married in their state but who have a child . . . do they count?" "Why do you have to live in the same house? What if you have to live in different states or cities because of your jobs?" "What if you have been living together for 30 years, but have never gotten legally married or had kids?"

Indeed, these are all excellent questions and I often find myself hoping that these students might go on to become the next drafters of U.S. Census Bureau policy, full of indignant questions about family forms which the current definition fails to reflect and encompass. In essence, my students are thinking like postmodern family scholars. They understand that formal definitions like these often constrain social and cultural *acknowledgment and representation* of diverse families and fail to reflect their everyday existence in the real world. These students are also responding to tremendous social, economic, institutional, and cultural changes over the past 60 years that have transformed not only families themselves, but also the very ways that we *think* about partnerships, family, and family life.

Long before I became a college professor and a sociologist, I was a student of my own family. Looking from the outside-in, my family structure might not predict my future interest in diverse postmodern family forms. I grew up in a family with a cisgender and heterosexually identified mother and father of the same race (White) who had 2 children when they were well into their late 20s and early 30s and after they legally married with the full support of both of their families. We lived in a rural community 20 miles outside of Detroit in a single-family home with a fenced yard, a dog, and plenty of green grass upon which to play. My father worked in an auto factory and my mother was a full-time stay-at-home mom and homemaker. This is just the sort of family that has been described as "traditional" or "nuclear" by family studies scholars and safely recognized and counted according to official U.S. Census Bureau definitions for quite some time now. Yet it seems that this nuclear family *ideal* has persisted far longer and more widely than the actual nuclear family form ever did.

Long before the appearance of the nuclear family ideal in the 1950s, previous U.S. Census counts included slaves, co-resident farmhands, and household servants as members of households and, hence, families.[3] Agrarian family life necessitated extended family households as each family member contributed in some way to the work of the farm.[4] Even in the 1950s, the nuclear family was more ideological than actual in terms of family structure and preponderance.[5] Flashing forward to the 21st century, the "traditional" nuclear family form is an increasingly rare bird indeed. Much more common is the broad patchwork of single-parent families, cohabiting families, blended families, and marriage after the birth of a child (if at all). Increasingly, we are also seeing interracial families and same-sex families entering the field of broader social and cultural representation with shared though distinct cultural histories of social and legal challenges to their legitimacy and belonging.[6]

TURNING THE LENS AROUND

As the shape and form of our families continue to shift and transform, some court more focused attention and scrutiny than others from social policy makers, researchers, and even the media. It was on the afternoon of April 3, 2008, that I began to realize that I needed to write the book you are holding in your hands. I was working on my dissertation and the television was on, providing the comforting hum of background noise. Oprah Winfrey appeared, announcing that she had partnered exclusively with *People* magazine for an interview with Thomas Beatie, whom the press was dubbing, "the world's first pregnant man."[7] At that time, I had been studying a group of 50 cisgender (nontransgender, "cis" for short[8]) women partners of transgender men over the past 3 years and was excited to see one segment of the trans community covered on a forum that would, quite literally, reach millions of people (HARPO Studies, 2008). Over the next hour, Winfrey interviewed Thomas Beatie and his then-wife, Nancy.[9] Winfrey followed the Beaties to Thomas' obstetrical appointments, peeked into his body through ultrasound images, and offered video vignettes of the Beaties' neighbors and life together in a suburban community in Bend, Oregon.

What I found most remarkable about this hour of television was not so much Thomas Beatie, his pregnancy, his wife Nancy, or even the details of their day-to-day family life. In many ways, their story actually seemed quite mundane. My focus, instead, was drawn to Oprah and her audience. Over the course of the hour, cameras panned and focused for close-ups upon viewers who appeared shocked and bewildered; in many instances, their mouths quite literally agape, slack-jawed, as they stared at Thomas and Nancy and then turned to one another. Their faces mirrored confusion and disbelief. Winfrey explained that Thomas, with his full beard and flat chest, is a female-to-male transsexual who, while attaining social and legal status as a man, retained his reproductive organs (a uterus, ovaries, and fallopian tubes) and was able to become pregnant via assisted reproductive technologies.

Just 2 years later, Winfrey would feature another interview that elicited many of the same audience reactions. In this 2010 episode, lesbian partners Dr. Christine McGinn and Lisa Bortz beamed with joy as they held their infant twins. Again, audience members' jaws dropped when it was revealed that beautiful Christine was a male-to-female transsexual who used to be handsome military officer Chris, and that Lisa had given birth to the couple's biological children using sperm Chris banked prior to gender confirmation surgeries.[10] And it was Winfrey's chin that nearly hit the floor as she watched video of Christine breastfeeding the couples' children (the episode is referred to online as "The Mom Who Fathered Her Own Children"). After these shows aired, Internet chat rooms were abuzz with thousands of comments; their tones ranged from supportive to curious to overtly disgusted and irate. Simply put, many individuals were confused and shocked by these postmodern, queer family forms about which they knew and understood very little, but which must have seemed very strange. These were not the sorts of families with which most of the commenters seemed familiar.

Indeed, these families reflect an increasingly complex contemporary reality that demands nuanced and critical responses, one that a discipline such as sociology might be particularly well situated to offer. Yet sociologists have been largely silent in responding to the public bewilderment surrounding the everyday lives and realities of those who are transgender or transsexual[11] and those with whom they partner and create lives and families.[12] So, in many ways, this book responds to these existing gaps and silences by generating more sociological understandings of queer families in the 21st century.

Sociological perspectives on today's families are critical and potentially transformative insofar as they allow us to shift the focus from dissection of whether particular individuals are "real" men and women, "real" fathers and mothers, "real" husbands and wives, to why we feel so compelled to identify and authenticate the "real" in the first place. In other words, while one of the goals of this book is to offer greater understanding and insight about actual transgender families and their members, I also wish to focus on social responses *to* these families— responses that tell us much about the limitations and barriers these families face on an everyday basis. Sociologists work to uncover just what is at stake in laying claims to "realness" and belonging within foundational social institutions like the family, and seek to show how these claims are far from universal, often shifting across both time and place. In this way, sociological perspectives often urge us to suspend and examine many of our taken-for-granted assumptions.

We are similarly challenged to connect our personal everyday experiences with patterns and trends existing in the broader social world outside our heads and homes, a process that C. Wright Mills[13] described as developing one's "soci-ological imagination." I hope that readers will follow Mills' lead and work to develop their own sociological imaginations while reading about the lives of the cis women partners of trans men I interviewed. As you read, consider the ways in which your own partnership and family experiences overlap and diverge from those you are reading about. Some of you may be challenged by the language that you encounter in this book. For example, at first it may be jarring to read "cis" (short for "cisgender," a term that means "nontransgender") in front of many mentions of "woman" in this text, while perhaps less jarring to read "trans" in front of many mentions of "man." I have purposely marked nontransgender individuals and identities in this text as a matter of fairness and a reminder that carrying such markings often serves the purpose of creating "Others" and us-versus-them dichotomies in the world.

I hope that readers will push past any initial discomfort and perhaps even ask themselves why it is so uncomfortable or jarring to mark the normative, or the taken-for-granted, while it seems relatively easier or less jarring to mark that which is seen as counternormative or exceptional. For other readers, I hope that these stories might speak to you in a different way. For some, these sorts of inten-tional language shifts may offer welcome relief rather than pose uncertainty or discomfort. Perhaps you will recognize your own experiences and perspectives written across these pages, maybe even for the very first time. If, however, what you read here fails to reflect or adequately capture your own reality, I hope this will inspire and convince you of the critical importance of sharing your own unique and valuable stories and vantage points with others, ever widening our conversations and understandings about sex, gender, sexuality, and family in the 21st century.

For those of you who are already quite seasoned in critical analysis and socio-logical inquiry, I also want to be clear about my aims and intentions with this work. In the discipline of sociology, one of the critical questions that scholars are often asked is: What are the theoretical implications and contributions of this work? And, indeed, the theoretical underpinnings of sociology are part of what make it unique and distinct from other disciplines and disciplinary approaches. Yet I have noticed that this focus on theory in sociology has translated to what might be viewed as a disciplinary imperative to always be *doing* grand "Theory" in our sociological work. This imperative is revealed when we consider that one of the most scathing critiques that may be leveled against a peer-reviewed manu-script or monograph in sociology is that it is largely "descriptive." While much of my earlier work has advanced particular theoretical claims, and the present work also develops and moves some of these claims forward, I want to suggest that the *primary* contribution of this book is in beginning to fill existing lacunae at the intersection of sociological scholarship in the areas of sex and gender, sexu-alities, and families by offering analytically descriptive accounts of participant narratives.

In other words, I intend a primary contribution of this book to be its connec-tion to an analytic project Clifford Geertz termed "thick description."[14] The aim of thick description is not to simply present social "facts," but rather to provide extensive descriptions and quotations alongside researcher interpretations and analysis. Descriptive work undertaken with such an approach is always simultaneously analytical and theoretical. Rather than intended to generate grand Theory, however, thickly descriptive projects often advance or challenge particular aspects of existing theories. Through this work, I want to suggest that thickly descriptive work is inherently valuable and necessary in sociology, not as a second best or less ambitious alternative to theory, but as a critical adjunct and antecedent. This is particularly so when relatively little is known about a substantive issue or population.

AN OVERVIEW OF THE PROJECT

The earliest conceptual seeds for this project were sown while I was working on my senior undergraduate honors thesis on lesbians' experiences in psychotherapy.[15] As I interviewed participants for that project, several research participants began to talk to me about how either they, their partner, or a friend were contemplating "transition," or moving from one gendered self-identification to another. They spoke about psychotherapists who were supportive of their identities as lesbians, but who did not quite know what to do when it came to transgender experience and identity, including transition. Several years later, I began my own relationship with a partner (categorized female at birth) who would, over the course of our relationship, come to identify as transmasculine.[16] The experiences and insights that women shared with me several years earlier resonated and I joined in their frustrations over the lack of available resources and information about the experiences of partners of trans men. I decided to begin reading everything I could find about transgender identity and experience—at that time a relatively narrow body of literature comprised largely of biography and autobiography focusing upon transgender-identified individuals.

Tucked within these narratives, as well as across occasional clinical articles focusing on the medical or psychological treatment of those with "Gender Identity Disorder (GID)," were occasional references to the partners of trans people. In many instances, trans people thanked their partners for support during their transition. Yet I could find little to nothing written by the partners of trans people themselves, especially women partners of trans men.[17] I decided to focus my graduate and dissertation work on this understudied community, with which I was becoming more familiar both politically and personally.

I ended up recruiting 50 cis women partners of trans men for the study, which consisted of telephone and in-person interviews that ranged from under an hour to around 3 hours, averaging just over 1.5 hours each. I interviewed cis women across 13 states in the United States, 3 Canadian provinces, and a single participant from Australia. When interviewing participants in person, I selected a location of mutual convenience, which meant that I ended up conducting interviews in some unconventional spaces: everywhere from hotel lobbies and coffee shops to participants' homes and university classrooms and lounges. In some instances, potential research participants asked me about my interest in the research topic and how it had come to be. They were, quite reasonably, leery of researchers whose perspectives and work had been antagonistic and stigmatizing to the trans community.[18] I told these potential participants about my earlier research with lesbian psychotherapy clients as well as my own relationship with a trans-identified partner. In some instances, these disclosures seemed to reassure potential participants and make them more inclined to participate in the research.

I recruited participants by posting notices in LGBTQ community spaces and sending email recruitment materials to those connected to LGBTQ communities. Doing this allowed me to generate a sample that continued to grow larger and larger, like a snowball being rolled, whereby one participant tells other potential participants about the study, who then tell other potential participants. I was able to provide each participant with a payment of $20 as a gesture of thanks for their time and willingness to share their experiences with me. I also asked participants to choose their own pseudonyms for the study if they so desired, in order to maintain their anonymity but also ensure that they would be able to recognize themselves in any future publications.

While my own status as a then-partner of a trans-identified person may have made it easier for some participants to feel comfortable sharing their stories with me, I sometimes found myself needing to work harder as a researcher when these same participants would cut short their responses with phrases like, "you know how it is," or "but I don't need to explain it to you." Because so little had been written about the experiences of partners of trans men, I did not want to generalize my own experiences or perspectives and, instead, wanted to gather as broad, diverse, and rich of a cross-section of women's narratives as possible. This resulted in me frequently asking participants: "Actually, could you tell me a little bit more about how that happened or what it was like for *you*?"

The youngest participant I interviewed was 18 while the oldest was 51, with the average being just under 30 years of age. My participants were almost exclusively White and highly educated, though not exclusively middle-class. Participants reported a broad range of incomes and socioeconomic statuses growing up. For participant pseudonyms, as well as snapshots of demographics connected to my research participants, their trans partners, and their relationships, see Table 1 and Box 1, 2, and 3 in the Appendix.

When people first learn of the project, one of the questions I am often asked is: Why does your study focus exclusively on cis women partners of trans men? In fact, why focus exclusively on women at all? My answer to these questions is threefold. First, I did not begin my study with the expectation of interviewing only cis women partners of trans men. Rather, my call for participants was open to *all* women and I hoped to interview both trans and cis women. The lack of trans women participants in my sample only highlights the need for additional research with this population as their experiences may be quite different from those of the cis women I had the opportunity to interview. Second, existing research suggests that cis women constitute the largest group of individuals partnered with trans men.[19] Targeting the group of individuals most likely to be partnered with trans men made it much more likely that I would be able to recruit a fairly sizable number of participants. Third, just as there are distinctions between the experiences and perspectives of cisgender straight women and lesbians, gay men and straight men, lesbians and gay men (just to name a few groups), it makes sense that the experiences and partnering practices of trans men and trans women might also be meaningfully distinct. My study's focus on cis women partnered with trans men has allowed me to obtain in-depth information about one critical yet understudied segment of the diverse family forms that exist among trans people and their partners today.

As I began studying the experiences of cis women partners of trans men at the turn of the 21st century, I found myself inspired by groundbreaking earlier work focusing on the lives of lesbians at the turn of the 20th century. One of my academic mentors, Esther Newton, kept pointing out the striking overlaps between some of the patterns and trends that were unfolding in my study of cis women partners of trans men and what had been written earlier about lesbian butch/femme relationships. In the novel *The Well of Loneliness* (by Radclyffe Hall), set in the early 20th century, butch protagonist[20] Stephen Gordon insists that her lover, Mary, must take on a male suitor[21] in order to spare Mary from a life of social shame and suffering. In an analysis of this plot twist, Esther Newton writes: "Mary's real story has yet to be told."[22] While Newton is referring to the need to theorize not only butch subjectivities, but femme subjectivities as well, I contend that this argument must be expanded. Indeed, the stories of cis women partners of trans men also have yet to be told. If we consider femme identity and experience as one possible historical precedent for the experiences of cis women partners of trans men,[23] perhaps we might find threads of similarity and difference across their stories and experiences. Minnie Bruce Pratt describes a conversation about whether or not jazz musician Billy Tipton's wife, Kitty Tipton, was aware that he had been categorized as female at birth. Pratt writes:

> Later you tell me of evidence left by other wives, years ago. If the outlaw husband took another lover, sometimes the wife would go to the police and turn her husband in, to be tried, convicted, and sentenced to jail for perversion, the deception of cross-dressing into the opposite sex. Unwittingly, the wife would leave a record, the nakedness of their love between lines in a police report. You say, "But this life is yours and not just mine. You will write a different record of what our life is."[24]

It is my hope that the narrative accounts featured in this book might *begin* to establish just such a record, to expand our understanding of not only transgender communities, but also a broader cross-section of *women's* romantic and family lives more generally.

You will notice that, across particular chapters of this book, I offer insights and quotations not only from my research participants, but also from previously published trans biographies and autobiographies. A critical component of my research included an extensive analytic review of these resources. In this way, I am able to place the perspectives of the cis women I interviewed in dialogue with existing published work focusing on trans individuals and communities. I have been asked why I did not interview both cis women and their trans men partners, either individually or as a couple. The intended purpose of my research was to provide in-depth exploration of the experiences of women partners of trans men that could serve as a necessary intervention in relation to their relative absence across clinical, academic, fiction, and nonfiction (autobiography, biography, and memoir) writing focusing on transgender issues and identity. To broaden the sample to women and their trans partners, in the context of limited time and resources for completing the research project, would necessarily mean restricting the number of women's narratives I would be able to collect. In subsequent projects I intend to interview both partners, but doing so did not fit with the aims and intentions of this initial project.

While I intend for this research on the experiences and perspectives of cis women partners of trans men to expand scholarship on gender, sexuality, bodies, work, and families, it is not without some degree of trepidation that I write. In my experience, even in spaces that are generally deemed welcoming and safe (e.g., among groups of feminist sociologists or scholars), I have found that individuals tend to focus, primarily, on how some of the narratives I discuss seem to reflect and/or reify heteronormativity and/or heteronormative gender practices. And, indeed, they sometimes do. Just as some cis feminist-identified women may find themselves in partnerships and relationships (even with same-sex and/or feminist-identified partners[25]) that seem to reflect and perpetuate gender inequities so, too, do some cis women in relationships with some trans men.

It is also true that we cannot control how others will take up our research findings and reinterpret them for their own analytic purposes. For example, some of my work has been used by trans-exclusionary radical feminists to portray cis women partners of trans men as tragic dupes while trans men themselves are portrayed as self-deluded women who collude with (and reproduce) patriarchy.[26] One of the dangers of this work is that those who wish to paint trans people and their partners negatively may find fodder to do so. Indeed, this work details not only the transformative and empowering aspects of cis women's partnerships with trans men, but also the sometimes-troubling dynamics and difficult issues with which they struggle as well. I hope readers will consider how their own experiences and perspectives both diverge *and* converge with those of the cis women partners shared here. At all times, I hope that the reader will use their sociological imagination, continually employing a contextual approach to understand and interpret the experiences they read about.

Jack Halberstam[27] warns that the ultimate aim of an intensive study of transgender and transsexual embodiments and identities should not be to determine who wins some imaginary prize for the most counternormative, but to establish a body of work that lends to the further description and deeper understanding of these various identities and embodiments. Further, Henry Rubin addresses the hypocritical tendency of some nontrans people to assail trans people with claims of supporting and/or reflecting binary and/or normative gender embodiments: "They do not walk around, as they seem to be asking us to do, without gender identities or legible bodies. . . . They are not called upon to account for the fact that their gender is something they achieved."[28] Part of this project, therefore, is to document the ways in which gender, sexual, and family identities are socially constructed not just among trans people and their partners, but among *all* of us.

POSTMODERN PARTNERSHIPS AND QUEER FAMILIES

We are living in an era of postmodern partnerships and families. But what does this mean, exactly? Postmodern is generally used as an adjective to describe either (a) an amorphously defined historical time period following the modern era or (b) a set of theoretical precepts connected to notions of futurity, technology, and the instability of categories, identities, and other typologies. In reality, these understandings blur together given that both "modern" and "postmodern" are descriptors that are deployed in different ways depending upon their context in architecture, art, literature, or social theory, for example.[29] In the first instance, "postmodern" is primarily a chronologically descriptive term, beginning in the late 20th century and continuing through today. In the second instance, we consider the social and cultural markers of modern and postmodern approaches toward everyday life and culture. Modernism involved the establishment of a basic trust in science and rationality to achieve what were understood to be universal markers of progress, while postmodernism served to fundamentally challenge or unseat the assumptions underlying modernist suppositions of objective reality and "truth."

For the purposes of this book, I ask: How are postmodern partnerships and families different from the modern family forms that preceded them, or from the "nuclear family" ideals I described earlier, including my own nuclear family growing up? Certainly, families like mine existed: they happened and were part of the lived experience and historical record. But were they common? Were they widespread? Were they long lasting? There can be little doubt that families continue to undergo transformations in their membership, form, and structure. Philosopher Shelley Park, in her 2013 book, *Mothering Queerly, Queering Motherhood*, describes the challenging and exciting task of tracing genealogies of queer and postmodern families: "Postmodern families . . . are rhizomatic. . . . There are no unifying traits that necessarily link family members. . . . It is because the postmodern (rhizomatic) family is perpetually in motion that it cannot be captured by any static image."[30]

Postmodern approaches understand social change and change in the institutions and structures of society as processes leading not necessarily to inevitable social progress and betterment, but simply to transformations (or amalgamations, as the case may be) of what existed prior. In other words, postmodern approaches to understanding social life tend to be descriptive rather than prescriptive. This point is one that many view as particularly unsettling insofar as we tend to believe that each generation grows wiser, learns from its mistakes, and creates a better society than the one before: in sum, we tend to hold hope for (and belief in) social progress over social stagnation and, especially, regress. At the same time, however, we tend to hold (falsely) nostalgic views of the past, that partnerships and families were closer and involved spending more time together, that our streets and communities were safer, that life was easier and simpler.[31] One of the outcomes of these nostalgic yet progress-oriented views of partnerships and families is that forms and structures of partnering, parenting, and building families that are seen as nontraditional or different from the past are viewed with suspicion and fear for the well-being of all those involved, from adults, children, and families to society.

In the context of partnerships and families, postmodern approaches suggest that there is no one "right" way to partner or to have a family.[32] Scholars who use postmodern approaches to understand contemporary forms of partnering, parenting, and forming families have noted the rapid proliferation of diverse family forms and, along with this diversification, dynamic responses calling for a return to "traditional family values and morality" and social movements to halt the legal recognition of partnerships and families existing outside of those considered most traditional.[33] For the purposes of this book, I borrow from Mary Bernstein and Renate Reimann's definition of who and what constitutes "queer families":

> We employ the term "queer" families here to signify the diverse family structures formed by those with nonnormative gender behaviors or sexual orientations. The term "family" refers to groups of individuals who define each other as family and share a strong emotional and/or financial commitment to each other, whether or not they cohabit, are related by blood, law, or adoption, have children, or are recognized by the law.[34]

While much scholarship has been dedicated to proving the "normality" or relative health of those partnerships and families considered nontraditional,[35] a key contribution of postmodern approaches involves resistance (or even refusal) toward engaging defensively or providing justifications for alternative definitions of family that challenge normative social institutions and structures.[36]

You will notice that most of the cis women that I interview are not currently parents. Indeed, only 12% of the women I interviewed had ever had experiences parenting and only 2 of my participants were actively parenting small children in their homes at the point of our interview. Being presently childfree does not necessarily mean, however, that the commitments and connections that these cis women have with their trans partners do not constitute "family." Indeed, I will demonstrate the ways in which their connections exemplify just the sort of critical family bonds that Bernstein and Reimann note above. Further, their intentions and discussions around having children or not having children with their trans partners in the future situate them as engaged with powerful discourses, technologies, and social expectations around the family that deserve fuller consideration.

Scholars drawing upon postmodern approaches grounded in cultural critique ultimately seek to reframe existing debates. In this spirit, family scholars utilizing these approaches might ask: Just who gets to count as "normal" and who decides these criteria in the first place? What are the advantages and disadvantages of leading a "normal" or "traditional" life? Are such lives better for individuals, partnerships, children, families, and societies and according to which metrics? Which social institutions, structures, and dynamics are preserved and maintained by adherence to social rules that value the "normal" and "traditional?" Further, which social and cultural possibilities are forestalled through dogged adherence to particular visions of what partnerships and families "ought" to be? Rather than targeting marginal subjects to defensively justify their way of life, in this book I will argue for reframing and shifting our social analysis of identities, partnerships, and families back to the privileged social center and its taken-for-granted assumptions of social and moral superiority.

While feminist scholars of the family have often been at the vanguard of these debates, critiques of tradition, normality, and status quo are not confined to academia. Increasingly, more mainstream cultural discourses have shifted toward a revaluation of nontraditional and postmodern partnerships and family forms. The increasing representation of interracial families, blended families, cohabitation without marriage, childbearing outside of wedlock, LGBTQ families, single parents, chosen families, and extended kinship networks across the mediums of television, commercials, magazines, and film suggest a "new normal" is underway. Importantly, this "new normal" resists oversimplification into any one *type* or *ideal* of partnership or family form.

In this book, I will explore a number of diverse partnerships and families that illustrate the expanding possibilities for familial formation in the postmodern era. I will also outline the structural barriers and growing pains that these individuals and family pioneers sometimes face along their journeys to realizing their partnerships and families. Importantly, a key component of this "queering families" framework will be to suggest that families don't become queer simply by virtue of their constituent membership and their connections to one another. In other words, "queering families" isn't simply an *add queer people and stir* approach. Rather, an aim of this work is to demonstrate how we might render the very notion of "family," often considered the most traditional bedrock of modern civilization, "queer" if we pay attention to the myriad attempts we make to shoehorn, contain, and circumscribe this unwieldy and shape-shifting social institution.

OUTLINE OF THE BOOK

In Chapter 1, I consider the historical overlaps and tensions between butch/
femme lesbian relationships in the mid-20th century and trans men/cis women
relationships in the 21st century, review the existing professional and academic
scholarship on transgender partnerships and families, and offer an extended
discussion of published autobiographical and biographical literatures focusing
on transgender identity, partnerships, and families. In addition to highlighting
what we know about trans partnerships and families, I will also discuss the gaps
in our knowledge that remain left to be filled in.

In Chapter 2, I grapple with the various ways in which partnering with
someone who is transgender-identified upon first meeting, or who engages in
gender transition over the course of the relationship, may affect an individual's own social and personal identities with regard to gender and sexual orientation. The cis women I interview describe shifting self-identifications, most
often from lesbian to queer, in order both to make sense of their own relationships as well as to become culturally intelligible and resist social normativity and invisibility. As such, this chapter illustrates the complicated ways in
which our identities depend upon others and often extend far beyond our own
volition. I also consider intersections of identity and experience, revealing the
ways in which characteristics such as race, ethnicity, body size, age, gender
expression, and nationality may impact both partnerships between cis women
and trans men as well as their social reception and visibility. Focusing on a
subsample of cis women in interracial relationships with their trans partners,
I draw upon Amy Steinbugler's (2012) framework for understanding intimate
racework among cisgender lesbian, gay, and heterosexual relationships to
begin to consider how these relational processes may operate in some transgender relationships as well.

Chapter 3 focuses centrally on cis women's reported household, childcare, and emotional labor within their partnerships and families with trans
men. While a considerable number of studies document the household and
childcare division of labor and emotion work within heterosexual, gay, and
lesbian households,[37] doing so within trans partnerships and families is virtually unprecedented. This chapter details the ways in which cis women's
partnerships and families with trans men are both similar to and distinct
from some of these other family forms. It also highlights transition-related
carework and rituals in order to document this understudied form of
emotional labor.

Chapter 4 focuses upon bodies, sexuality, and intimacy in the context of cis
women's partnerships with trans men. One of the purposes of this chapter is to
refigure the body and sexuality back into sociological work on partnerships and
families. So often absent from critical discussion and analysis, this chapter does
not talk *around* bodies and sexuality or consider them in an abstract way, but
rather features them centrally, highlighting their importance in producing both
personal and interpersonal subjectivity.

In Chapter 5, I consider what it means for cis women and their trans men partners to form "queer" partnerships and families today. Specifically, I discuss choices and negotiations around marriage, monogamy, and parenthood. These negotiations expose broader sociolegal tensions and dilemmas about what it means to be husbands, wives, fathers, and mothers in the 21st century.

Chapter 6 explores the potential dangers and harms associated with being socially recognized and misrecognized by others. In this chapter, cis women describe instances of being welcomed within heterosexual social spaces and how this welcome may, paradoxically, make one feel both unsafe and invisible. Interviewees also recount instances of being misrecognized as heterosexual or having their partners' legitimate membership within LGBTQ spaces questioned and the marginalization and stress that this misrecognition often entails. Despite encountering social stigma, strain, and danger, the cis women partners of trans men whom I interview also discuss powerful processes of social support and community in operation in their lives. I explore these sources and networks of social support for trans partnerships and families, considering how they might be strengthened and broadened.

In the conclusion, I argue for broader definitions and understandings of family in the 21st century that better represent and encompass the diversity of our postmodern family forms. I suggest that the value of this work ultimately lies not only in its contributions to academic scholarship, but in providing detailed accounts of experiences within trans partnerships and families by and for cis women. Finally, I consider how the bonds between and among "biological family" members are often tenuous and contingent, challenging their presumed superiority and "realness." In this way, the work of "queering families" is proposed as an ongoing social project whose momentum is fueled by an ethics of care, solidarity, social justice, and inclusion.

NOTES

1. See Powell, Bolzendahl, Geist, and Steelman's (2010) *Counted Out: Same-Sex Relations and Americans' Definition of Family* for a comprehensive discussion of contemporary American attitudes about which configurations "count" as family.
2. See the United States Census Bureau (no date).
3. Notably, however, during some of the earliest U.S. Census counts (1790 was the first), each slave "counted" only as 3/5 of an actual person for determining Representation for each state, with this de jure fractional personhood persisting from the late 18th century until the ratification of the 14th Amendment in 1868.
4. See Coontz (1992).
5. See Coontz (1992).
6. For a broad overview of historical and contemporary trends in family formation and configuration in the United States, including the rise in interracial marriage, cohabitation, blended families, and same-sex families, see Barbara Risman's (2015) edited anthology, *Families as They Really Are*.

7. See Tresniowski (2008). Nearly a decade before Beatie's announcement, Patrick Califia (2000), a trans man, published a column in *The Village Voice* describing the family that he and his partner at the time (Matt Rice, also a trans man) created after Rice gave birth to their son in 1999. Califia and Rice are no longer partnered.

8. Schilt and Westbrook (2009:1) define "cisgender" as a label describing "individuals who have a match between the gender they were assigned at birth, their bodies, and their personal identity." Some scholars, including K. J. Rawson, have traced the first print usage of "cisgender" to biologist Dana Leland LaFosse in 1994 (Brydum, 2015). As Brydum (2015) notes: "From an epistemological standpoint, the word is essentially a straightforward antonym of 'transgender.' Both words share Latin roots, with 'trans' meaning 'across, beyond, or on the other side of' and 'cis' meaning 'on this side of.' Add the suffix 'gender' onto either word, and both terms emerge as strictly descriptive adjectives."

9. Thomas Beatie gave birth to 3 children from 2008 to 2010. Beatie (2008) published a memoir, *Labor of Love: The Story of One Man's Extraordinary Pregnancy*, detailing his first pregnancy. In spring 2012, multiple Internet media sources (including *Huffington Post*) announced that Beatie and his wife, Nancy, were divorcing after 9 years of marriage following Beatie's revelation on a television show, *The Doctors*, that he and Nancy had separated.

10. While the phrases "sex change" or "sex reassignment surgery/SRS" tend to be commonly used in mainstream discourse, some people within the trans community prefer the phrases, "sex affirmation surgery," "gender affirmation surgery," "sex confirmation surgery," or "gender affirmation surgery," as they more accurately reflect the importance (for some trans people) of aligning the body with one's gender identity and understanding that alignment as confirmation of one's gender identity.

11. Throughout this book, I use "transgender" as an umbrella term that may encompass identities from transsexual to genderfluid. Those who are transsexual generally make hormonal and/or surgical interventions in order to bring their bodies into closer alignment with their gender identity. Those who are genderfluid may adopt modes of gender expression and embodiment distinct from their sexual categorization without taking hormones or pursuing surgeries. Gender fluidity may include adopting and/or moving between certain hairstyles, clothing choices, vocal affectations, and bodily comportments that result in myriad styles of gender expression not easily categorized as male or female or that move between these categories.

12. Exceptions include Devor (1989, 1997); Namaste (2000); Sanger (2010); Schilt (2006, 2010).

13. See Mills (1959).

14. See Geertz (1973). See also Ponterotto (2006).

15. This research was undertaken in 1998 and 1999.

16. My relationship with this partner ended in 2008 and I subsequently dated several other trans-identified individuals until 2009, when I met (and subsequently married in 2014) my cis lesbian-identified partner. I share this information to highlight my researcher role as situated between the emic (observations gleaned as a participant in and member of a particular group) and the etic (observations gleaned as an outsider nonmember of a particular group).

17. Minnie Bruce Pratt's (1995) *S/He* might be considered the lone exception, though it may be argued that Pratt's partner (Leslie Feinberg) did not self-identify as a

"trans man" (but as a "transgender lesbian") and preferred, in general, to be referred to using pronouns such as "she" or "ze."

18. For example, see Blanchard (2005); Jeffreys (2014); Raymond (1979).

19. More specifically, cis women. See Chivers and Bailey (2000); Devor (1993); Lewins (2002).

20. See Hall (1929). Some [see Hale (1998)] have argued for the reclamation of fictional character Stephen Gordon as a trans man rather than a butch lesbian.

21. There is, of course, a feminist critique to be made here of any masculine-identified social subject with the power to "turn over" a feminine-identified partner as if she were chattel.

22. See Newton (1984:575).

23. Not all cis women partners of trans men are femme identified or feminine in appearance, of course. In my sample, 14 of 50 participants (28%) noted their femme self-identification, despite the fact that I did not explicitly ask them for their gender identification beyond cis and trans. Similarly, only 1 of 50 (2%) noted a masculine self-identification. Jane Ward (2010), who has conducted research with this population, also notes the predominance of femme-identified participants among her sample.

24. See Pratt (1995:169).

25. See Carrington (1999).

26. For example, see Jeffreys (2014:114–118) and the following blog post: http://dirtywhiteboi67.blogspot.com/2011/03/50s-housewives-future-of-tmates.html. Also see my writing on this in the Note on Methods in the Appendix.

27. See Halberstam (1998).

28. See Rubin (1998:273).

29. See Nicholson's (1990) *Feminism/Postmodernism* for a more substantive exegesis of the tensions, overlaps, and blurs between modernism and postmodernism, particularly Flax (1990:39) and Huyssen (1990:234).

30. See Park (2013:164).

31. For illuminating insights on (and a corrective to) these trends, see Coontz (1992).

32. See Bernardes (1999).

33. See Barbara Risman's (2015) edited anthology, *Families as They Really Are*. Consider, for example, a vast psychological literature addressing whether or not the children of gay men and lesbians have equivalent behavioral and achievement outcomes as children raised by heterosexual parents. Perhaps even more remarkable is the body of literature attempting to discern whether the children of LGBTQ people are more likely to self-identify as LGBTQ themselves. These inquiries reveal the cultural anxieties that underlie nonheterosexual and noncisgender self-identifications.

34. See Bernstein and Reimann (2001:3).

35. See Steinbugler (2012).

36. For example, see Holstein and Gubrium (1999).

37. For more on emotion work, household labor, and family care work, and how it manifests across a diverse cross-section of families, see DeVault (1991, 1999); Duncombe and Marsden (1993); Erickson (1993, 2005); Frisco and Williams (2003); Hochschild (1979, 1989); Kroska (2003); Minnotte, Stephens, Minnotte, and Kiger (2007); Schrock, Boyd, and Leaf (2008); Yogev and Brett (1985); Zelizer (2005).

GLOSSARY

It should be understood that, as is common with most identity-based communities, the following glossary of terms and concepts is incomplete, contested, and rapidly shifting; there is no universally agreed upon set of definitions for lesbian, gay, bisexual, transgender, and queer (LGBTQ) identity and experience. This glossary is intended to provide a cursory overview of terms and concepts as *I* intend and understand them for the purposes of my research.[1]

Assisted Reproductive Technologies: Also known as "ART," "assistive reproductive technologies," "alternative insemination," and (falling increasingly out of favor due to its linguistic marginalization of some fertilization techniques over others) "artificial insemination." These include a host of reproductive technologies designed to make pregnancy possible in new ways. Some specific techniques include (but are not limited to) the use of gestational surrogates, sperm donation, egg retrieval and donation, intrauterine insemination, intracervical insemination, and in-vitro fertilization and embryo transfer.

Binding: For trans men, wrapping the chest or using a compression garment to flatten chest tissue.

Bottom Surgeries: For trans men, such surgeries may include (but are not limted to) hysterectomy, oopherectomy, metaoidioplasty, salpingectomy, scrotoplasty, and/or phalloplasty. For trans women, bottom surgeries may include (but are not limited to) orchiectomy, vaginoplasty, and labiaplasty.

Cis: An abbreviated form of "cisgender" or "cissexual" (see below).

Cisgender: A term describing nontransgender persons, preferred over "biological man" and "biological woman." This term is used to specifically refer to nontrans people since their identities are often unnamed or taken for granted, unlike the identities of their trans peers, which are most often linguistically marked and face hyperscrutiny.

Cissexual: A term describing nontranssexual persons, often preferred over terms such as "biological male," "biological female," "natal male," or "natal female" since these terms obscure the ways in which both sex and gender involve social construction, as well as the fact that many trans people utilize hormones and surgeries in ways that bring their bodies into biological consonance with categories such as "male" or "female."

Estrogen: The hormone most often utilized by trans women who choose to use supplemental hormones as a component of their transition. Estrogen may be taken in pill form, administered dermally through topical gel or a patch, or injected. In some limited instances, progestagens may be prescribed in conjunction with estrogen.

FTM: "Female-to-Male" or "Female Toward Male." Individuals categorized as "female" at birth, who come to gender identify as a man or on the transmasculine spectrum.

Gender: The vast array of social and cultural constructions (involving bodily comportment, manner of dress, social roles, etc.) that adhere to individuals once they have been placed into a particular sex category, thus marking an individual as a "girl," "boy," "woman," or "man."

Gender Affirmation Surgeries: Also termed "sex confirmation surgeries," "sex reassignment surgeries," "gender confirmation surgeries," "gender reassignment surgeries," "gender alignment surgeries," "sex alignment surgeries," and "genital reconstruction surgeries." Though not uniformly embraced, this term has become increasingly popular as it situates surgeries not as singular or definitive of a transition or a particular sex categorization, but as a constellation of possible surgical interventions that serve as components of some trans people's gender identities and gendered embodiments. Note that gender affirmation surgeries are often not covered by medical insurance and are, thus, not equally accessible for all who may wish to pursue them. For specific types of gender affirmation surgeries of possible relevance to trans men, see "Bottom Surgery" (also "Hysterectomy," "Metoidioplasty," "Oopherectomy," "Phalloplasty," "Salpingectomy," and "Scrotoplasty") and "Top Surgery." Also included are surgeries to modify nongenital/non-chest areas of the body associated with specific gendered embodiments.

Gender Dysphoria: See also "Gender Identity Disorder." Refers to a sense of psychological distress that one's gender identity is not aligned with one's embodiment and/or with how one's sex or gender is perceived by others in the world.

Gender Expression: Refers to one's social presentation of gender in everyday life (through dress, bodily comportment, vocal expressions, etc.). Gender expression may also shift across social contexts depending on perceived safety and risks.

Gender Identity: Refers to one's subjective sense of being a boy, girl, man, woman, androgynous (a blend of the aforementioned), or agender (none of the aforementioned).

Gender Identity Disorder: A diagnostic category that appeared in the *Diagnostic and Statistical Manual of Mental Disorders* (*DSM*) from 1980 to 2012. The category was replaced by "Gender Dysphoria" in 2013 in the fifth edition of the *DSM* as a response to research showing that trans identity, itself, is not a mental disorder, but that social responses to those who are trans may produce anxiety and problems with social functioning. Treatment includes not only psychotherapy, but hormonal and surgical treatments (if desired by a patient) to bring one's embodiment into closer alignment with one's gender identity. While some resist medicalization of trans identity, others maintain that such classifications are necessary in order to establish greater avenues to accessibility of transition-related medical treatments since insurance coverage for such procedures generally requires diagnosis.

Genderqueer: Also termed "gender fluid." An umbrella term for those whose gender identity and/or expression does not normatively align with the sex into which they were categorized at birth and/or whose gender expression may not be static.

Hysterectomy: For trans men, the surgical removal of the uterus.

Intersex: This term replaces the pejorative and medically inaccurate term, "hermaphrodite." It is a category into which individuals are sometimes placed if their sex chromosomes and/or sexual anatomy are ambiguous or are discordant with expectations for how genitals, reproductive organs, secondary sex characteristics, and sex chromosomes most often align.

Labiaplasty: For trans women, surgical construction of labia.

Metoidioplasty: For trans men, the surgical release of the tissues keeping the clitoris (which may enlarge to the size of a micropenis following administration of testosterone) tethered to the body.

Micropenis: For trans men, the enlargement of the clitoris after prolonged administration of testosterone.

MTF: "Male-to-Female" or "Male Toward Female." Individuals categorized "male" at birth, who come to gender identify as a woman or on the transfeminine spectrum.

Oopherectomy: For trans men, surgical removal of the ovaries.

Orchiectomy: For trans women, surgical removal of the testes.

Packing: For trans men, wearing a penis prosthesis or creating the appearance and/or feel of a penis under clothing. These penis prostheses are termed "packers." Penis prostheses that also allow for the passage of urine are often termed "pissers."

Passing: To be socially perceived in accordance with one's own gender identity rather than with the sex into which one was categorized at birth. Some find this term offensive as it conveys a sense of inauthenticity or even deception. Consider use of phrases such as "socially recognized as . . ." instead, since this places emphasis on gender as a social interaction rather than a biological given or right.

Phalloplasty: For trans men, the surgical creation of a penis. Often referred to as a "phallo."

Queer: In the context of sexual identity, this term is often used to describe those whose identities may not be easily classified using other identity terms or categories (e.g., "bisexual," "gay," "heterosexual," or "lesbian"). This term may also be used to indicate the intentional adoption of a more radical or outsider identity as a form of cultural resistance.

Salpingectomy: For trans men, the surgical removal of a fallopian tube or fallopian tubes.

Scrotoplasty: For trans men, the surgical insertion of testicular implants.

Sex: A perceived and/or actual convergence of hormonal, chromosomal, and anatomical factors that lead to a person's categorization, usually at birth, to sex categories such as "male," "female," or "intersex."

Sex Category: Refers to the sex categorization most often registered on a birth certificate—either "male" or "female." Sex category may also be broadened to include those whose sex categorization may not be unambiguously male or female, such as those who may be classified as "intersex."

Sexual Identity: Other terms include "sexual orientation" (which may convey the assumption that this is a characteristic determined primarily by biology) and "sexual preference" (which may convey the assumption that this is a characteristic determined primarily by personal choice or desire). Refers to one's personal sense of sexual attraction and/or sexual community identification (e.g., asexual, bisexual, gay, lesbian, queer). Transgender individuals may hold any of these sexual identities. Sexual identity is based on both one's own gender identity and the gender identity of the person to whom one is attracted.

Sex Reassignment Surgery (SRS): A term that has fallen out of favor as it fails to reflect the fact that surgically mediated transition often requires more than a singular "surgery." This term also tends to overdetermine the dependence of gender identity and social categorization on surgery; see "Gender Affirmation Surgeries."

SOFFA: An abbreviation for significant others, friends, family, and allies (of a transgender or transsexual person).

Stealth: Describes someone who receives recognition for their gender identity across all social situations. For example, when a trans man is perceived, socially, as male all of the time and does *not* identify as female, a woman, or as a trans man.

T: A colloquial abbreviation for testosterone.

Testosterone: The hormone most often utilized by trans men who choose to use supplemental hormones as a component of their transition. Taken most frequently by intramuscular injection (biweekly, weekly, bimonthly, or monthly). May also be administered dermally through daily topical gel or a patch or subdermally through an implant. For some trans women, hormonal treatments may include anti-androgens, to counteract the effects of testosterone.

Top Surgery: For trans men, this may refer to bilateral radical mastectomy (removal of breast tissue) with or without chest wall recontouring or reduction mammoplasty (breast tissue reduction). This surgery may also involve reduction and/or re-placement of nipple and areolar tissue. For trans women, this may refer to breast implantation and augmentation.

Trans: An abbreviated term that refers to "transgender" and/or "transsexual."

Transgender: An umbrella term for those whose gender identity and/or expression does not normatively align with the sex into which they were categorized at birth.

Transition: To bring one's gender expression into closer alignment with one's gender identity. Transition may involve changes in one's style of dress, hair, body comportment, pronoun/name use, legal sex/gender status, social roles, hormones, and/or physical anatomy. Transition should be understood as a process rather than a singular point in time.

Transfeminine: Sometimes used to refer to the expressions of gender identity by trans women. Refers to the spectrum along which trans women express their femininity. Some have critiqued this term as it fails to reflect the fact that trans and cis women also embody and express masculinity and/or androgyny.

Transmasculine: Sometimes used to refer to the expressions of gender identity by trans men. Refers to the spectrum along which trans men express their masculinity. Some have critiqued this term as it fails to reflect the fact that trans and cis men also embody and express femininity and/or androgyny.

Trans Man: Short for "transgender or transsexual man." Individuals categorized "female" at birth who come to gender identify as a man or on the transmasculine spectrum.

Transsexual: A particular type of transgender identity or embodiment. Usually describes an individual who makes surgical and/or hormonal changes to their body in order to bring it into closer correspondence with their gender identity.

Trans Woman: Short for transgender or transsexual woman. Individuals categorized "male" at birth who come to gender identify as a woman or on the transfeminine spectrum.

Vaginoplasty: For trans women, surgical creation of a vagina.

NOTE

1. For an excellent and provocative collection of trans-related concepts and definitions from a critical 21st century perspective, see Currah and Stryker (2014).

Queering Families

1

Trans Partnerships and Families

Historical Traces and Contemporary Representations

Far from being a monolithic group, "transgender" has come to serve in common parlance as an umbrella term comprised of ever-expanding and contested identity categories: femmes, butches, transsexual men and women; those who are intersex, androgynes, and cross-dressers; those who identify as "gender-queer"; those with nonnormative gender expressions; and many more.[1] Aaron Devor[2] postulates that there were 3 distinct waves of trans visibility, disseminated through the media, that allowed individuals to conceive of the possibilities of trans identity for themselves.

According to this historical "wave" theory of trans visibility, the first wave consisted primarily of widely circulated news reports on a trans woman, Christine Jorgensen, in the 1950s. The second wave was comprised of magazine stories on transsexuals in the 1960s. The third wave was marked by the proliferation of news stories on transsexualism and the appearance of trans men and women on talk shows in the 1970s and 1980s. These historically specific accounts of trans people's sources of information connected to transgender identity help us to consider how these information sources and resources continued to shift into the 1990s and the 21st century, affecting the awareness and conceptualization of possibilities of a new generation of trans people, their partners, and families.

Beginning in the late 1980s, anthologies, autobiographies, and biographies, focusing on trans and genderqueer narratives, memoirs, photographs, and poetry, proliferated.[3] Around this same time, a number of documentaries and films also emerged that featured trans-identified people as primary subjects. In the 1990s and beyond, full-length autobiographies tended to have largely transsexuals (those trans individuals who had taken hormones and/or had gender affirmation surgeries) as their authors, keeping the stories of other genderqueer people on the margins of social representation and intelligibility. This early preference for featuring the stories and embodiments of transsexuals may stem from both an insistence on maintaining sex and gender binaries and cultural curiosity (as evidenced through transsexual guest appearances on talk shows) toward what is deemed a fascinating spectacle of gender morphing.[4]

HISTORICAL TRACES BETWEEN BUTCH/FEMME
AND TRANS MEN/CIS WOMEN PARTNERSHIPS

Huddled together under the sprawling "transgender umbrella," we might ask: Are transgender people and partnerships unique to the 21st century or do they have a historical precedent? For example, I am often asked to explain what distinguishes trans men and their cis women partners today from butch/femme lesbian relationships that rose to cultural visibility in the 1950s.[5] The answer is that both types of relationships are complicated, revealing similarities, distinctions, and (in some instances) deep rifts and contention among those who identify as "transsexual," "transgender," "butch lesbian," "femme lesbian," and "queer." As murky and turbulent as these waters may be, it makes sense to wade through to examine both the overlaps and tensions. Doing so often reveals the ways in which identities are culturally and historically situated, forming in relation to and against one another.

Some of the earliest scholarly accounts of females who identified as men or masculine appear in the writing of German physician and neurologist Richard von Krafft-Ebing in his important 1886 work, *Psychopathia Sexualis*.[6] Krafft-Ebing used the term "gynandry" to specifically refer to females who lived as men, while Havelock Ellis referred to this same population as "congenital inverts."[7] Jay Prosser forcefully argues that "among the case histories of sexual inverts, we find our first transsexual narratives."[8] In 1910, sexologist Magnus Hirschfeld coined the term, "transsexual."[9] It has been argued, however, that female-to-male transsexualism was brought into existence in 1949 when a female who identified as male requested hormones and surgery from physician David O. Cauldwell, resulting in the diagnosis of "psychopathia transexualis."[10]

However, Jay Prosser challenges the idea, argued most notably by Bernice Hausman,[11] that transsexuality is a subject identity invented through medical technologies and psychological discourse.[12] Instead, Prosser asks a provocative question: "Was transsexual subjectivity simultaneous with its discursive naming, as absolutist constructionist theories would have it?"[13] Prosser argues that it was not and that, instead, "this naming of transsexuality was, rather, a response to preexisting transsexual identity patterns and, indeed, embodiments."[14] Prosser substantiates his claims by noting examples like Michael Dillon, whom he hails as the world's first trans man to transition using hormones and surgeries. Dillon convinced physicians to prescribe testosterone in 1939, underwent a double mastectomy in 1942, and had a phalloplasty in 1945.[15]

Yet Dillon was not the first patient categorized female at birth to request a double mastectomy in order to have a more masculine chest. Indeed, Magnus Hirschfeld wrote about a similar case in 1922, and a German doctor noted the case of a female patient who underwent "genital masculinization" in 1882.[16] Even earlier, in 1779, a doctor performed surgery on a 7-year-old child, reassigning the child from female to male.[17] Prosser claims that transsexual embodiments and requests for medical interventions certainly preceded the naming of transsexuals as medical subjects in 1949. He writes:

> The discourse of inversion in turn-of-the-century sexology, its medicalization of transgender in the body, provided the significant threshold under which the transsexual as a sex-changeable and indeed sex-changed subject could make his/her first appearance. Sexology's case histories reveal subjects seeking out (and sometimes achieving) somatic transitions before the invention of the transsexual as a discursive subject, before sex hormones and plastic surgery had been decided by clinicians as treatment for the condition—indeed, before the medical diagnosis was written.[18]

Historian Joanne Meyerowitz[19], agrees with Prosser's assertion that people who have crossed sex and gender boundaries have existed across time but have only recently been understood as transsexual subjects per se due to changes that emerged in medical discourses and technologies. Prosser claims that an important failing in social constructionist work on transsexuality[20] is that it often fails to consider the agency of transsexuals as not only subjects constructed *by* medical technologies and discourses, but as subjects who also meaningfully *shape* these technologies and discourses to their own needs, expectations, and desires.[21]

It is a historical fact, then, that some individuals who were categorized as female at birth began making hormonal and surgical changes to their bodies, in order to bring them into closer alignment with the way they saw themselves in the world, long before the 21st century. Indeed, what would now be described as transsexual embodiments clearly seem to predate even the emergence and coherence of "butch" and "femme" as gendered sexual identity categories in the mid-20th century. Not all scholars agree with this assessment, however. For example, Henry Rubin theorizes the emergence of trans men's identity as a distinct outgrowth from butch lesbian identity.[22] He writes:

> The consolidation of a female-to-male transsexual identity was a secondary project of the formation of the revolutionary subject of second-wave feminism, the "woman-identified-woman." This revolutionary subject was created by obscuring important differences between heterosexual women and lesbians. These differences were class-based and gender specific. In forming this revolutionary subject, as with all identity formation, something fell outside of its boundaries. This revolutionary *excess* consolidated itself as female-to-male transsexualism, giving male-identified individuals another subject position to inhabit.[23]

Rubin substantiates his claims by noting that the number of trans men was much lower than the number of trans women prior to the 1970s, at which time this gap began to narrow.

Indeed, Christine Jorgensen, one of the first trans women to gain substantial public notoriety in 1952, was (arguably) not to be followed by trans men counterparts until talk shows began, in the late 1970s, to feature trans men as guests.[24] Still other scholars disagree with Rubin's historical interpretation, insisting that while "the trans man" may have just begun to emerge as a discursive subject in the 1970s, those who were categorized female at birth who sought to live lives as men predate not only a linguistic label, but also the discursive emergence of "butch" lesbian identity more specifically.[25]

Given ideological and political skirmishes over the emergence and distinctiveness of butch lesbianism, female-to-male transgenderism, and female-to-male transsexuality, there have also been a number of contestations over female historical figures who occupied social roles as men. The 2000 film, *If These Walls Could Talk 2*,[26] features a vignette situated in the 1970s that focuses on the efforts of lesbian feminists to feminize, demean, and ultimately reject a masculine character played by Chloë Sevigny. Some viewers claim Sevigny's character ("Amy") as a trans man, while others claim "Amy" as a butch lesbian. This film, therefore, brings to light existing tensions among not only lesbian feminists and butch lesbians of the 1970s, but among butch lesbians and trans men today.[27] Nan Boyd[28] asserts that, while lesbian and transgender communities have each laid claim to various historical figures as "their own," some lesbian communities, especially those that have restricted or limited access to trans women, tend to establish their community parameters through utilization of "birth body" narratives. In this way, the only rightful members of lesbian communities are those whose bodies are designated female at birth. Ultimately, these skirmishes reveal the ongoing boundary work that exists around granting or refusing to grant recognition to individuals based upon their own gendered self-identifications. These tensions over recognition are not limited to communities of lesbians and trans men, however, nor are they always intentional in the way they establish representational exclusions and omissions.

Recognition and Misrecognition

Similarly, scholarly representations of genderqueer historical figures are not always affirming, and some even cross the line into disrespect. Historian Jonathan Ned Katz, in his history of gay and lesbian America, claims Dr. Alan Hart as a tragic lesbian besieged by false consciousness and also describes "passing women" from 1782–1920 as "lesbians," "immoral imposters," and "real women" engaging in a "masculine masquerade."[29] In many instances, potentially trans historical figures are presumed to be lesbian rather than trans.

Diane Middlebrook,[30] biographer of musician Billy Tipton, portrays Tipton as a tragic circumstance of limited employment and social opportunities for women. Jack "Bee" Garland (aka "Babe Bean") was described in various media outlets as "she" or a "woman in male clothing."[31] The character Stephen Gordon, from Radclyffe Hall's *Well of Loneliness,* and Radclyffe Hall "her"self, have been claimed as "mannish lesbians."[32] Brandon Teena has been depicted in the media as a butch lesbian, sometimes referred to by his birth name, "Teena Brandon."[33]

Jack Halberstam[34] analyzes the depiction of Brandon Teena in the mainstream cinematic rendering of the events surrounding his life and death in the 1999 film, *Boys Don't Cry;* Halberstam argues that, in the end, Teena and his cisgender woman partner (Lana) are depicted as "really" lesbians and that Teena is murdered in an instance of homophobic rather than transphobic violence.

Halberstam writes: "Many revisionist accounts of transsexual lives rationalize them out of existence ... and thus do real damage to the project of mapping transgender histories."[35] Each of the aforementioned figures (Billy Tipton, Brandon Teena, Jack "Bee" Garland, Radclyffe Hall, Dr. Alan Hart, and Stephen Gordon) have been (re)claimed as trans by members of trans communities.[36] Indeed, the tragic 1994 murder of the person who has come to be known as "Brandon Teena," has been interpreted, by some, as a central galvanizing force for activism and mobilization among trans men.[37]

While it may be possible that some of the writings about (those who are now often considered) transsexual historical figures misconstrue, conflate, or ignore distinctions between cross-sexual and cross-gender embodiments and identities, it is important that we do not forget that all of these revisionist accounts are historical products of the times in which they were written, generally prior to contemporary trans social movements and their subsequent public discourse. In addition, not all trans-identified people agree that each of these figures was, in fact, "one of their own," or even that anyone, outside of the person in question, can make that determination for the deceased.[38]

Border Wars

There are numerous points of convergence and divergence among those who identify as butch, female-to-male transgender, and female-to-male transsexual in terms of sex and gender embodiments, identity, gender roles, and social roles.[39] Halberstam,[40] arguing against any oversimplified account of trans identity and embodiment, notes the wide variability across trans narratives. As such, there have been a large number of attempts to disaggregate transsexuality, transgenderism, and butch lesbianism.[41] As Prosser asserts:

> The female protagonist of *Stone Butch Blues* moves away from a lesbian origin through somatic transition but without finding refuge in transsexual man. Refusing to close on a transsexual transition, she makes of transition itself a transgendered subjectivity—the movement in between a destination. Feinberg's departure from conventions is symptomatic of a larger political transition underway: the creation precisely of a transgender *movement*—a politics and culture of transition. If transsexual has been conceived conventionally as a transitional phase to pass through once the transsexual can pass and assimilate as nontranssexual—one begins as female, one becomes a transsexual, one is a man—under the aegis of transgender, transsexuals, now refusing to pass *through* transsexuality, are speaking en masse

as transsexuals, forming activist groups, academic networks, transgender
"nations." No longer typically ending at transition, transsexuals are overtly
rewriting the narrative of transsexuality—and transsexual narratives—as
open-ended.[42]

In Prosser's telling, therefore, transgender identity and politics may be conceptualized as an outgrowth of transsexual embodiments. Jacob Hale argues for
a more nuanced understanding of continuities between butches, female-to-
male transgender, and female-to-male transsexual men.[43] Indeed, for Hale, the
only definitive, categorical difference between butches, female-to-male transgender-identified people, and female-to-male transsexuals is self-defined and
self-expressed membership to one of these subject identities. Unfortunately,
arguments between cis and trans activists and theorists carry the potential
for devolving into polemical, circular assertions of "false consciousness" and
"essentialism."[44]

In examining autobiographies and first-person narrative accounts of trans
men, it became clear to me that individuals may sometimes interpret the very
same events and experiences in entirely dissimilar ways, either highlighting
their similarity to, or divergence from, butch-identified lesbians. Mario Martino,
a trans man whose autobiography was published in 1977, writes:

> One area of public ignorance or confusion concerns how the female-
> to-male transsexual differs from the masculine-acting lesbian. I think
> I can clear that up quite easily. In female duos of that type, the partner
> who acts in a sexually aggressive manner may be doing so without any
> desire whatsoever of changing her sex. Proud of being a woman, she
> makes love to another woman who responds to her as a female. Their
> sex life may include mutual masturbation, oral sex, perhaps even the use
> of a dildo or store-bought phallus. Yet the masculine-acting lesbian is
> happy with her femaleness. The lesbian's satisfaction is the woman-to-
> woman contact.[45]

Here, Martino draws boundaries to differentiate not only trans men from lesbians, but also femmes from the partners of trans men. Based on the description Martino offers of butch sexuality, are we to infer that the same catalogue
of sexual practices he mentioned does *not* figure into trans men's sexuality?
Martino's juxtaposition of "female-to-male transsexual" and "masculine-act-
ing lesbian" is important in the context of his argument. In counterposing
these identities, Martino frames butchness as an "act," presumably asserting
his "real" trans maleness as a contrast. Martino also fails to consider that, for
butches, identity as a "woman" may also be problematic.[46] In addition, much of
the work written on butches and femme-butch desire discusses, in rich detail,
the charge of sexual and gender difference between partners in ways that are
not entirely dissimilar from the narratives of trans men who partner with cis
women.[47]

Max Wolf Valerio draws a stark distinction between butch and trans embodiments in the following passage from his 2006 autobiography, where he evaluates butch women after he has been on testosterone for some time:

> All the women here seem softer, rounder, more distinctly feminine, prettier than they were before. Even the butch women ... the women I used to think of as "butch." Sometimes butcher or more masculine than me. They've changed. And I know that they would hate me for thinking this, but I perceive their "womanly" qualities without intending to. Suddenly, their feminine qualities are painfully apparent—in my face. It's an odd surprise. Each time I come here, these changes are more pronounced. Yet I know these women aren't actually changing. My perceptions are. *Can it be I'm beginning to perceive women as men do?*[48]

In this passage, Valerio simultaneously renders butch lesbians feminine and female through the justification that he is now able to perceive this social reality through his insights as not just trans, but as cis male. Mark Rees also draws distinctions between his own male identity and others' butch identity:

> Although I hated wearing women's clothes, it worried me lest I were seen as "horsey" or "butch." Certainly I didn't identify with mannish women and was repulsed by the thought of being classed as one. I didn't want to be seen as a woman, either feminine or "butch." Yet—and this seemed paradoxical to some, especially my mother—I enjoyed seeing others looking feminine and attractive. If however, my gender, my true self, were male, then this is self-explanatory.[49]

The powerful and emotional language here of *repugnance* upon the mere thought of being misrecognized as a butch woman rather than a cis man reveals the importance of maintaining social distance and distinctions between members of these groups.

In contrast, Jean Bobby Noble attempts to narrow the seemingly wide chasm between trans men and butches. In his 2006 autobiography, he writes:

> Who better to occupy the space of *guy* but former lesbians who have walked the streets as women, loved as fierce and sometimes stone butches, and who have come of political age in the context of lesbian-feminism? For me, that's a proud history that does not get left behind in the operating room.[50]

Others suggest that the boundaries between butch lesbianism and trans identity can be quite permeable, though highly contested and policed.[51] More recently, there has been cultural concern expressed within lesbian communities that butches are a "dying breed," becoming an extinct sort of species as so many butches transition to live life as men. While it is likely that such concerns are overstated and contribute to the cultural invisibility of butch women,

I also saw these concerns echoed in my own research. One participant, Emma, told me:

> Sometimes I question, "Where have all the butches gone?" In the 50s and the 60s and the 70s that's what queer women were. It was butch-femme, butch-femme, butch-femme all over the place. And now there's many more trans people, particularly trans guys. And I know I've even come across some suggestive readings or media releases suggesting that trans identity is taking over, that people who have been butch are now trans and where's the crossover and where's the difference and is there a difference?

Yet another participant puzzled when I asked her to describe the differences between butch lesbians and trans men who primarily date cis women. Jodi told me:

> The difference between a trans man and a butch lesbian is . . . it's like how do you describe the difference between green and brown? They're just different and they share some qualities. They're both dark colors but then green kind of feels more grassy and brown feels more like dirt. It's so ambiguous and it's just really hard to define. But it's definitely a Venn diagram.

Ultimately, these sorts of questions seek to define community, membership, belonging, and the "Other." A 2001 study of British and North American lesbian and trans accounts of identity states: "For the lesbians, the social 'other' was heterosexual women and the sexual 'other' was heterosexual men; whilst for the FTMs, the social and sexual 'other' was both heterosexual women and lesbians-as-women."[52] In another sample, trans men reported intentionally modeling their masculinity after cis gay men in order to embody a greater balance of masculine and feminine qualities.[53]

A Queer Kind of Trans?

Sexual orientation in the context of trans self-identification has also been a hotly contested site within and across communities. It is interesting that one of the most outspoken gay trans men, Lou Sullivan, never told his own story in an autobiography despite publishing the biography of another trans man. To date, of all the full-length autobiographies that have been published by trans men, only 1 has been written by a self-identified gay trans man.[54] Writing about Lou Sullivan, Jamison Green notes: "His own identification was with the gay male community, but he didn't make a big deal about it."[55] Sullivan's purported silence, as a gay trans man living with AIDS, and Green's rather casual dismissal of it, deserves more analysis than it has received. Later in his own autobiography, Green writes about a trans support group of which he was a member: "A handful of men from our group had decided that there were too many gay-identified guys joining up, that too many people who looked like lesbians were coming to the meetings. . . .

They began holding their own meetings in another city." Reading between the lines, we might have a glimpse into some of the reasons why Lou Sullivan may have not made "a big deal" about his gay identity during his life.[56]

Matt Kailey offers the following explanation in his own 2005 autobiography:

> While some gay men and lesbians are scared off by any association with transfolk, some, maybe even the majority, of transpeople feel the same way. They identify as straight, have assimilated into the larger mainstream community, and want no association with the "fringe" element that they consider the gay and lesbian population to be.[57]

Aaron James writes a controversial piece about buying a gun as a replacement for the penis he wishes he had. His angry, forceful, and honest narrative expresses not only frustration with the current state of phalloplasty, but at being rejected from trans community on the basis of his gay identity and from cis gay community because of his body.[58] James writes:

> I got a collection of strap-on fuck sticks that is by no means unimpressive, and I hate every goddamn one of them. D'you get it? I gotta *tie a fake dick around my crotch* in order to fuck like the man I'm trying to be, and it pisses me off. *You* try being a fag with no dick, see how *you* like it. And the available surgery *sucks*. I do not want to go through life waving a Frankenstein's Cock at prospective sex partners any more than I wanna spend my life stuffing my underwear full of condoms and hair gel. Am I compensating by carrying a firearm? You better fucking believe I am.[59]

Marginalizing gay trans men has also been a component of academic discourse. One invalidating and pathologizing case study of 2 gay trans men states:

> In genetic females … transsexualism in a heterosexual individual—that is, an individual sexually attracted to phenotypic males—is relatively rare … Most of the reported cases of genetic female transsexuals erotically attracted to phenotypic males appear to have an erotic preference that includes the fantasy or thought of being a gay male.[60]

Chivers and Bailey echo this assertion: "Clinical presentation by nonhomosexual female transsexuals (i.e., gender dysphoric genetic females who are sexually attracted to males) is extremely rare."[61]

Such phrasing not only denies gay sexuality between cis and trans men, it completely obscures consideration of gay sexuality between trans men as well. David Schleifer concurs: "This approach excessively privileges the materiality of the body over the discursive and intersectional strategies that individuals use to negotiate their bodies, selves, and desires."[62] It is also important to note that it is only relatively recently that gay-identified trans men have been allowed to obtain transition services.[63] Raine Dozier[64] discusses the ways in which *failing* to embody and represent hegemonic heterosexual masculinity can result in "gay bashing" for perceived or actual identity as a gay man. In addition, gay trans men are often marginalized or rendered invisible within not only trans, psychological, medical, and academic communities and discourse, but also within cis gay communities as well:

> I soon discovered that calling myself a gay man didn't go over well with one particular population—gay men. Some gay men have become mightily offended when I've called myself a gay man. Ironically, the men who get the angriest with me when I mention that the "gay community" tends to be phallically oriented are the first to insist that I can't call myself a man because I don't have a penis. They go on to tell me that I'm not gay because I haven't had the "gay experience" in my life.[65]

Only recently have researchers begun to consider gay sexual orientation in the context of trans identities.

In his 1997 published work, Aaron Devor reported that a relatively large percentage of trans men moved from female to male partner attraction following their transitions. David Schleifer, in his 2006 article, "Make Me Feel Mighty Real: Female-to-Male Transgenderists Negotiating Sex, Gender, and Sexuality," asserts that such a transition can be explained, in part, by the way in which cis men can validate a gay or bisexual trans man's identity. Dozier[66] also found that some trans men formed gay relationships in order to retain their personally valued identity as "queer," an identity frequently rendered invisible in their relationships with cis women, which were often seen as heterosexual by others, post-transition (these themes are explored in greater depth in Chapter 4).[67] Despite beginning to understand the various types of partnerships that butch lesbians and trans men have had over the past decades, relatively little has been written to date that details the experiences and perspectives of their partners.

Where are the Femmes and the Cis Women Partners?

Butch/femme identity began to proliferate within LGBTQ communities, and become more visible to the mainstream, during the middle of the 20th century. Yet it wasn't until nearly 4 decades after this cultural emergence that academic writing on femmes began to be published, despite the prominence of "femme" as a topic of lesbian feminist debates on androgyny in the 1960s and 1970s. Madeline Davis, Amber Hollibaugh, Eve Lapovsky Kennedy, Biddy Martin, Joan Nestle, and Minnie Bruce Pratt were some of the most foundational and prolific writers about the experience of being a feminine lesbian or "femme."[68] These writings, published largely in the 1990s, often involved concerted focus on delineating all of the ways in which femme lesbians were distinct from feminine heterosexual women, in essence establishing their credibility within lesbian contexts. Writings on femme identity also offered a reclamation of femininity as a potentially empowering embodiment of lesbian identity rather than a disempowering and patriarchal feature of women's lives.

This glut of writing on femme identity in the 1990s informed a body of lesbian-feminist literature that a number of my cis women participants discussed reading as they considered the historical echoes between lesbian femme identity and their own experiences as cis women partners of trans men. As you'll read in subsequent chapters, they discuss their shared experiences of invisibility as queer women, the accusations and fears that they are pawns of patriarchy or only visible and intelligible in relation to their masculine partners, and that their identities and experiences are simply seen as less remarkable or focus-worthy than their masculine partners. Throughout this book, I'll offer consideration of the particular identities, experiences, and perspectives of cis women partners of trans men (some of whom self-identify as femme) so that these accounts may be further compared and contrasted to the existing body of work on lesbian femme identity.

One of the hallmarks of published professional and academic work on trans partnerships and families is that most sources aim for breadth rather than depth, choosing to include perspectives from a sweeping cross-section of the significant others, friends, family, and allies (SOFFAs) of both trans men and trans women rather than focusing on any particular group. One of the advantages of such a focus is that we begin to develop a broader sense of the diversity across these narratives and experiences. Some of the disadvantages, however, are that it can be difficult to discern any patterns, themes, or trends across these narratives and having only a few individuals from each group speak about their experiences can make it difficult or even impossible for patterns to emerge at all. It is also true that if we only have broad overviews of trans people's partnerships, there may be a tendency to assume that the experiences of all SOFFAs are the same.

Minority groups have struggled with these issues of individual and group representation across time. When groups first begin to gain critical attention, they are often spoken about categorically and in generalizing ways, as if they were a monolithic entity (e.g., "people of color," "homosexuals," "the handicapped"). Over time, individuals and groups press for more nuanced representation and characterization, highlighting the diversity that exists within groups. While monolithic representation may have made sense to clinicians, academics, and social commentators in the 1950s and 1960s, gay men and lesbians' self-advocacy had become powerful enough to demand more specific and less stigmatizing representation. Lesbian feminists pointed out that the needs and lives of those within lesbian communities were often quite different from those within gay men's communities.

The AIDS crisis in the 1980s underlined the need for more focused understanding of the particularities of various contingents of queer communities. The Civil Rights Movement illuminated the need to consider not only how the experiences of gay men and lesbians might differ from one another, but also the ways in which sexual identities intersecting with racial and ethnic identities (for example) also produce diverse experiences in terms of one's communities, opportunities, resources, and oppressions. We might say, then, that writing about the experiences of transgender people and their partners and families remains at an incipient place at this time, often poised at the point of singular representation rather than delving into their intricate diversities.

Given the complexity and diversity of trans lives, it is beyond time to move toward greater understanding. As sociologist Viviane Namaste writes:

> English-language scholarship on transsexual and transgendered people is severely limited to the extent that it does not account for how these individuals situate themselves in the everyday social world. . . . Both queer theory and objectivist sociology share a narrow understanding of how transsexuals live in the world . . . by focusing exclusively on the *production* of transsexuality (whether through examination of culture or the medical establishment). . . . Thus rather than asking *what* or *why* questions about transsexuality, I am interested in learning more about how transsexual and transgendered people live in the social, institutional, and cultural world.[69]

Transgender rights activist, Riki Wilchins, further underlines this point:

> No one bothers to investigate the actual conditions of our lives or the lives of those we hold dear. No one asks about the crushing loneliness of so many translives, or about sexual dysfunction. Nor does anyone question why so many of us have to work two minimum-wage jobs and suck dick on the side so we can enjoy the benefits of a surgical procedure theorists and academics are casually debating for free.[70]

Indeed, while academic scholarship on transgender identity and experience began to grow rapidly in the 1990s, the vast majority of this literature focused somewhat atomistically on trans identity and experience, with relatively less written about trans people's experiences in partnerships and families.

TRANS RELATIONALITY: SITUATING TRANS PEOPLE IN PARTNERSHIPS AND FAMILIES

In the following sections, I offer an overview of existing contributions to understanding the partnerships and families that trans people and their loved ones co-create across the following 4 genres: (a) trans autobiography and memoir; (b) significant others, friends, families, and allies' (SOFFAs') representations; (c) professional, clinical, and medical literatures; and (d) empirical and theoretical academic literatures. It should be understood, of course, that these 4 areas overlap considerably. Consider, for example, that much of the empirical and theoretical academic scholarship on trans identity, partnerships, and families has been authored by individuals who are trans or SOFFAs themselves. In the following sections, I offer an overview of major themes and findings from each of these 4 broad genres contributing to knowledge about trans people, their partnerships, and families.

Trans Autobiography and Memoir

Trans people (and, to a much lesser extent, the SOFFAs of trans people) have told their own stories[71] through autobiography, memoirs, and (less commonly) fiction. The publication of trans autobiographies skyrocketed in the 1990s.[72] In addition to the proliferation of books, videos and documentaries[73] featuring the lives and experiences of trans people have also been produced at an ever-expanding rate since the late 1990s. While these autobiographical accounts and documentaries tended to focus, by definition, upon the author's subjective identity, life experiences, and transition, it was not unusual for them to also briefly highlight a trans person's partner or the families they were working to co-create. In this way, these literatures and documentaries offered some of the first glimpses into the lives of partners of trans people. One of the primary limitations of these glimpses, however, was that they were both peripheral and indirect. Rarely did partners of trans people at this time have a platform from which to speak in any depth about their lives and experiences from their own unique vantage points.

In his 2004 autobiography, Jamison Green reports on an alarming case of marginalization of trans men by members of their trans men's community due to their family and parenting choices:

> In 1999 Matt Rice, an FTM[74] who had been rather public, announced to the community via email that he had stopped taking testosterone in order to conceive a child and that he had given birth to a son, whom he and his partner Patrick Califia, another FTM, planned to raise together. Instead of congratulations and good wishes, he was vilified on numerous Internet lists for bringing embarrassment upon those of us who regard ourselves as men because "men do not have babies." A flood of vitriolic messages berated Matt and Patrick, and some even wished the child dead.[75]

These narratives revealed the challenges some trans men and their partners encountered, even within their own communities, when trying to engage in everyday activities that many others take for granted such as marrying, working, having children, and maintaining friend and family connections. Thomas Beatie, a controversial figure across both cisgender and transgender social circles, broke new ground in 2008 with the publication of his book, *Labor of Love: The Story of One Man's Extraordinary Pregnancy*. In the book, Beatie detailed not only his journey to fatherhood, but also the relationship that he had with his wife Nancy and the struggles they encountered as they worked to grow their family.

One of the central themes of trans autobiography often involves negotiating the loss of connection to (and support of) families of origin and choice. Marc Angelo Cummings, a trans man, described losing the support of his family in the process of transitioning: "A transgender world is a lonely world. We cry in silence, hiding our scars, our imperfections. We die everyday [*sic*], as we get buried by our families, who swear never to speak to us again."[76] Transgender activist Riki Wilchins concurred: "Loneliness, and the inability to find partners, is one of the best-kept secrets in the trans community . . . When we find partners, they must be willing to negotiate the ambiguity of the terrain."[77]

In one 2008 edited anthology, Tracie O'Keefe and Katrina Fox[78] offered articles from 25 authors about their experiences in romantic partnerships, all written from the perspective of a trans/genderqueer-identified man or woman. In another edited anthology published in 2011, Morty Diamond[79] presented first-person narratives from 29 trans and/or intersex-identified writers. While brief (the narratives span just 3 to 8 pages each), the accounts offered insights into sex, love, and relationships. Many of the narratives presented explicit discussion of sex and sexuality that were markedly distinct from the sanitized and disembodied discussions of trans sex and sexuality most common to the clinical and professional literatures. None of these narratives, however, featured insights directly from the partners of the trans and intersex writers. Across these narratives, central themes included challenges connected to finding community and support for building and maintaining romantic and family relationships. Further, authors frequently reported experiences with marginalization and stigma across both cisgender and transgender communities.

Significant Others, Friends, Families, and Allies' (SOFFAs') Representations

In addition to a large body of autobiographical work on transgender identity and experience, a growing body of biographical, documentary, and photographic work produced by the SOFFAs of trans individuals also sought to represent trans lives, experiences, and families. Andrew Solomon,[80] for example, devoted a lengthy chapter of his 2012 book, *Far from the Tree: Parents, Children and the Search for Identity*, to exploring the experiences of trans kids and their cis parents (as well as some trans parents and their cis kids).[81] Inspired by her own experiences as the mother of a child who transitioned later in life, Mary Boenke[82] edited the collection *Trans Forming Families: Real Stories about Transgender Loved Ones*. The book, first published in 1999, offered very brief vignettes, most only a few pages long, from the SOFFAs of trans men and women. Largely focused on the SOFFAs of trans women,[83] narratives from the partners of trans people came from just 7 individuals whose collected experiences take up fewer than 25 pages of text.

With very few exceptions, therefore, research and writing on trans people's romantic relationships has been almost uniformly one-sided (the trans partner's perspective on the relationship). While I hoped I would stumble across a number of in-depth, article- or book-length narratives written by women partners of trans men while working on my dissertation from 2003 to 2009, I was disappointed to find not a single example.[84] Helen Boyd, the cis woman partner of a trans woman, has written 2 books[85] about her experiences of being partnered with someone who first identified as a cross-dresser and, later, as a trans woman.[86] Boyd discusses the challenges of being a partner of someone who is a member of a maligned and often misunderstood group. She also drew upon feminist politics and theory to consider the ways in which some forms of cross- dressing may pose challenging dilemmas with regard to stereotypes about women and femininity. As Boyd's partner moved from cross-dressing toward transitioning to live as a woman, Boyd discussed feelings of anger, loss, even betrayal. One of the ways in which she coped with her own feelings and sense of isolation, as gender became the central focus of her relationship for a time, was by creating an online support group for partners in similar positions. Boyd's texts and online support network became major social support resources for cisgender women partners of transgender women.

In 2014, partners Diane and Jacob Anderson-Minshall published *Queerly Beloved: A Love Story Across Genders*, a co-authored memoir. Diane[87] is a cis woman and Jacob is a trans man who was lesbian identified when the couple first met over 20 years ago. I present an extended overview of this text as it stands as one of the few precedents to the book you are now reading.[88] Using a format that is relatively novel within this genre, Diane and Jacob each tell their own story, with their narratives volleying back and forth across the entirety of the book. Diane details feelings of fear, excitement, and loss as she discusses what it was like for her as her partner transitioned. Diane notes the importance of online support and information communities (YouTube, Google, blogs, and message boards) during the earliest stages of her partner's transition, for both herself and her partner.

Interestingly, Diane describes her role in Jacob's transition as not solely supportive, but also a catalyst for her own concerns about living in an uncertain liminal space, or limbo. Despite her enthusiastic support, Diane discusses cloaking her fear and concerns, sometimes locking herself in the bathroom or car to cry in private. Diane also attempts to steer her partner's transition in particular ways, describing her encouragement of her partner becoming a certain *type* of man (one who engaged in "manscaping," for example, a metrosexual aesthetic practice her partner quickly rejected). Diane's attempts to shape her partner's transition reveal a desire to contribute to a process that may feel otherwise unwieldy or out of one's direct control.

Diane also details her struggles about what Jacob's transition will mean for her own identity and career as (at that time) a relatively high-profile lesbian in the lesbian publishing industry. Diane discusses a period early in her partner's transition where she over-disclosed to strangers and was defensive about her lesbian identity even as she began to try on labels like "bisexual" and "queer." Diane describes the process of Jacob becoming "duller"[89] as he transitioned, in both emotional and physical terms. Diane even details how her partner touches her body differently since beginning transitioning. She reasons that testosterone's skin-thickening properties may mean that his rougher touch is due simply to not being able to feel as he once did. And while Diane does not write about it herself, Jacob describes how he must be particularly cautious when he displays anger because Diane reacts in a visceral way to his embodied expressions of anger as a man.

Diane discusses frustration as the focus of her life became Jacob's gender and transition for a period of their life together. As Diane writes: "The first few months of Jacob's transition were so much about him that I hardly had time to deal with my own emotions. I felt like I couldn't show any disappointment, denial, or concern either to him, our family, or the outside world."[90] She also writes about the challenge of feeling the need to put up a strong and unequivocally positive front around friends, families, and strangers who were initially unsure or unsupportive with regard to her partner's transition. She describes becoming fiercely protective of him and ensuring that others did not misrecognize her partner as lesbian, especially during the first year of Jacob's transition.

Diane experiences loneliness and isolation as she is increasingly misperceived as heterosexual and realizes that she is no longer always immersed in "women's space" as her partner is no longer a woman and she finds herself alone in locker rooms and other sex-segregated spaces for the first time in decades. As she loses recognition as a lesbian, Diane describes accessing heterosexual privilege for the first time. Street harassment directed toward her and her partner suddenly stops once her partner begins to be recognized as a man and the couple has access to legally recognized marriage. Despite these structural and institutional privileges, Diane describes facing acceptance from some family members and rejection from others (for example, her own mother does not attend her wedding to Jacob).

Jacob writes about the importance of affirming Diane's lesbian identity, pointing to the fact that sexual identity is not reducible to the gender identity of one's current partner. Diane also writes about the experience of increasingly being drawn to trans men and possibly even cis men, in a way she was not earlier in her life. Both Diane's and Jacob's writings urge the reader to consider what it means to be a "real" man or woman. As Jacob writes:

Essentially, the question is, what makes someone the sex that they are. What makes a man a man? Is it a penis? A certain level of testosterone? XY chromosomes? Certain experiences? Behaviors? Values? I'm an XX boy. My chromosomes still say I'm female, but my hormone levels and appearance indicate that I'm male. Am I a real man? If a man loses his penis to accident or disease does he cease to be a man? If I haven't had bottom surgery, does that mean I'm not a man, but if I've had the surgery I am one? Is it having the money or access to medical care that determines whether or not I'm *real*?[91]

Diane and Jacob describe deflecting others' curiosity about what lies underneath Jacob's clothing and having to grapple with intrusive questions about genitals that people would never consider asking a cisgender person, all ostensibly part of this project to discern one's "real" sex.

The concluding chapters discuss Diane's and Jacob's attitudes toward monogamy and nonmonogamy, as well as their attempts to become parents, and their experiences as proctor/foster parents to teenage boys. They also outline struggles with a foster program that forces Jacob and Diane to remain closeted—not about their sexual identities, but about Jacob's gender identity and history. This book clearly fills an important gap in the autobiographical trans genre, substantively drawing in the first-person perspectives of a cis woman partner of a trans man for the very first time. As you continue to read this book, I think you may notice some considerable overlaps between the central themes of this sole existing memoir of a cisgender woman partner of a trans men and the cisgender women partners of trans man I have interviewed.

One of the latest contributions to the genre of autobiographical and biographical works from trans people and their partners is *Love, Always: Partners of Trans People on Intimacy, Challenge & Resilience*, a 2015 edited collection by Jordan Johnson and Becky Garrison.[92] This collection marks the first time that all of the authors are the *partners of* trans people. Though the narratives are brief (each contribution is between 2 and 9 pages), each partner has the opportunity to share a piece of their story and experience from their own unique perspective. The authors span a range of genders, ages, races, and sexual identifications, though the editors reveal that most are cis women. Because the narratives are presented individually and the editors are not conducting research with their contributors, we know relatively little about each author, their partner, or the ways in which members of the group of authors are similar to or different from one another. Indeed, that is not the intended purpose of the book. Instead, we are offered brief vignettes into the lives of 50 partners of trans people, who choose to share their thoughts on intimacy, challenge, and resistance.

Maggie Nelson's *The Argonauts* (2015) also deserves mention here. Nelson, an award-winning critic and poet, offers autobiographical vignettes from her life and queer family, with focus on her trans partner's (Harry Dodge) transition as well as the way in which becoming a mother transformed her sense of self. Described as "autotheory," Nelson utilizes a poetic narrative structure that blends personal experience with theoretical insights in a way that does not always proceed chronologically. In this memoir, Nelson touches upon subjects connected to transition-related aftercare (and how it relates to and diverges from others undergoing similar procedures but for different reasons), challenges of shifting identity and social perception when a partner is trans, the importance and meaning that underlie caring for others, and offers brief glimpses into what it is like to create one type of queer family today.

Moving beyond the narrative and textual, other possibilities for conceptualizing trans families and their contours include photographic and filmic representations.[93] In 1999, Peggy Gillespie[94] edited a collection of photographs by Gigi Kaeser that includes portraits of trans parents and their families. Images of families are accompanied by narrative vignettes from members of those families. Importantly, these brief narrative vignettes and photographic portraits offer some of the very first representations of the experiences of the partners of trans individuals. Mariette Pathy Allen's (2003) collection is powerful insofar as it situates trans people directly within communities and activism, highlighting trans social movements against transphobic violence, exclusion, and inequality. The book also includes photographic representation of trans people with families of choice and biology, intimate and extended, engaging in everyday activities such as attending school events, painting, protesting, taking a bath, gardening, dancing, and sitting around on the couch.

More recently, Sara Davidmann's (2014) work, which combines both narrative vignettes and photographic representations, offers particular insights into the diversity and forms of trans partnerships. Moving even farther beyond the binary, Davidmann's work includes partnerships that are often ignored or obscured (such as triads, for example). Filmic representations of trans partnerships and families include, for example, *The Aggressives*,[95] *Boys Don't Cry*,[96] *Normal*,[97] *Southern Comfort*,[98] *Soldier's Girl*,[99] *Transamerica*,[100] and *Trans Entities: The Nasty Love of Papí and Wil*.[101] Just this brief selection offers representations centering on trans men, cis men, trans women, cis women, genderqueer people, and their partnerships with one another. This sampling also includes documentaries (including docuporn[102]), made-for-television movies, and mainstream motion pictures based on both fictional and nonfictional accounts of the experiences of trans people, their partners, and families.

The 2006 documentary *Transparent*[103] is a film focusing on the challenges and rewards of trans men giving birth and raising children, but does not include these trans men's partners, even when the men were raising children with a partner. In this instance, partners are rendered invisible both as partners and as parents. More recently, Amazon Studios released an online streaming video series also titled *Transparent*,[104] starring Jeffrey Tambor[105] as a trans woman struggling to come out to her wife and children. Of the relatively few film and textual resources produced at this time that do offer insights into trans partnerships and families, many offer a fairly bleak picture, reflecting the power of social stigma, structural transphobia, and lack of resources. Trans individuals across these resources frequently report losing partners as a result of their decision to transition, being denied custody of their children, or children rejecting them upon learning of their decision to transition.[106]

Professional, Clinical, and Medical Literatures

During the late 1990s and early 2000s, medical doctors, psychologists, and social workers began to publish clinical and professional literature focusing on trans people and, in some cases, their partners and families, at an accelerated rate.[107] Some texts, especially those written by clinicians (e.g., social workers and psychologists), have focused on providing support and resources to assist SOFFAs and other clinicians with understanding their trans loved ones, colleagues, and clients.[108] Relatively little research, however, has explored the social resources available to trans people and their partners in terms of providing support to enable the formation of strong relationships, families, and communities.[109] It was not until quite recently that these literatures paid much attention to transgender issues at all. Indeed, a recent content analysis[110] of 10,739 articles published in peer-reviewed marriage, couple, and family therapy journals from 1997–2009 revealed that only 9 of these articles (or less than 1% of the total sample) substantively pertained to transgender issues.

Further, until relatively recently, the scholarship that existed on transgender identity and experience focused almost exclusively on trans women. Much of this work derived from case studies of gender clinic patients who underwent gender affirmation surgeries. The scholarship that emerged from these case studies was focused, primarily, on clinical assessments, medical treatments, and psychotherapy options for those considered mentally ill on the basis of their "gender identity disorder."[111] One of the common features of much of the early clinical literature on trans identity and relationships with trans individuals is that it tended to repeat a narrative trope that had come to serve a gatekeeping function with regard to accessing transition-related medical services (including hormone prescriptions and referrals for gender affirmation surgeries). In this narrative, trans people discussed being "born into the wrong body."[112]

Hormone therapies and gender affirmation surgeries were thus conceptualized as curative for the seeming failings of nature. Viewing trans identities as stemming from physiological rather than psychological causes was a crucial turning point in the shift from psychiatric to medical treatments for what came to be known as "gender identity disorder."[113] Transsexuality, in particular, went from being understood as a sexual fetish rooted in Freudian understandings of arrested psychosexual development to a medical disorder. Harry Benjamin,[114] an endocrinologist and sexologist, developed the "Standards of Care for Gender Identity Disorders" in 1979.[115] These standards offered treatment protocols[116] for psychological and medical professionals working with trans clients and created pathways by which trans individuals were able to access hormone therapies and referrals for gender affirmation surgeries.

The standards generally required trans people to obtain 1 letter from a mental health professional in order to obtain hormones and/or breast/chest surgeries and letters from 2 different mental health professionals in order to obtain genital surgeries. These letters could only be obtained by undergoing a prescribed regimen of psychological counseling sessions and adhering to certain behavioral protocols.[117] Moreover, some trans people reported that conformity[118] to medical and psychological care provider expectations became increasingly necessary in order to obtain the required letters from these professionals. Trans people in many cases learned to craft narratives that followed a predictable and heteronormative trajectory of gender crosstypical behaviors and preferences in childhood and adolescence, feeling one was born into or "trapped" in the wrong body, and sexual desire for members of the same sex while feeling that these desires were heterosexual (because of one's cross-gender identification).

These expectations for the provision of care meant that many trans people had to cloak their own histories, feelings, sexual desires, and relationship experiences while presenting a heteronormative transsexual narrative if they wished to use legitimate medical channels to access gender-affirming hormones and surgeries. Over time, mainstream understandings of trans identities and experiences became somewhat limited to this normative trope and perhaps even shaped how trans people understood or would come to understand themselves and their experiences.[119] More recently, trans people and their loved ones have begun to publicly challenge and resist these normative cultural tropes and expectations about what it means to be trans.[120]

Existing clinical research on trans people and their partnerships has attempted to assess the stability of these relationships, often using grief and death response models to conceptualize family members' reactions to transition.[121] In a study of 22 trans men and their cis women partners, Fleming, MacGowan, and Costos found that these relationships tended to be "stable and enduring."[122] In a study by Lewins,[123] a sample of 55 trans women and 14 trans men are compared to explain perceived differences between these groups in terms of relationship stability. From a sample of 6 trans men, Lewins concludes the following:

> It is a reasonable inference that FTMs' relationships with women are more likely to be stable because both parties were socialized as girls and then as women. As women value, more than do men, the expressive properties of relationships and, correspondingly, place less stress on the importance of physical qualities, this wider pattern helps to explain the, arguably, counter-productive nature of FTMs' relationships. Despite the anatomical disadvantage of not having a naturally functioning penis for sexual intercourse, FTMs' relationships with women are the most stable category.[124]

Clearly, the author assumes that having a "naturally functioning penis" is a central defining feature of a stable romantic relationship.

In a study by Chivers and Bailey,[125] examining the sexual orientation of trans men, the authors twice report that "homosexual FTMs" (the authors' way of referring to trans men partnered with cis women) desire "very feminine partners."[126] Mark Rees reports on a *Canadian Medical Journal* article that proclaimed:

> The partners of female-to-males are normal heterosexual women, not lesbians, and see their lovers as men, in spite of the lack of a penis. The partners were feminine, many had had earlier relationships with genetic males and often experienced orgasm with their female-to-male partners for the first time. The report stated that these relationships were stable and long lasting and that the transsexuals made good parents of any children their partners had.[127]

Fleming, Costos, and MacGowan[128] determined that the "ego development" of trans men and their cis women partners was virtually indistinguishable from that of cis men and their cis women partners, which the authors submitted as proof of their normality. Kockott and Fahrner[129] report on the exclusive heterosexuality of trans men in their study, and their tendency to be in stable relationships that are sexually satisfying.

Research conducted on romantic relationships between trans people and their partners is generally quite limited. The vast majority of clinical studies before 2008 or so that do include the partners of trans people tended to focus on the cis women partners of cross-dressing individuals categorized as male at birth or on the cis women partners of trans women.[130] Authors writing in clinical journals during this time period often reveal biases and assumptions such as: "It was assumed that FTMs, unlike MTFs, were largely, if not exclusively, sexually attracted to females."[131] Chivers and Bailey[132] assert the extreme rarity of gay trans men, likely an artifact of gatekeeping practices wherein gay trans men learned not to share this aspect of their identity with clinical professionals if they wished to access prescriptions for hormones and approvals for transition-related surgeries.[133]

Such assertions stand in stark contrast to Devor's findings[134] that approximately 40% of post-transition trans men in his sample were sexually interested in men and approximately 20% had acted, sexually, on this attraction.[135] In terms of thinking about sexual orientation, Matt Kailey makes the following statement:

> "Gay," "lesbian," "straight," and "bisexual" are labels, not orientations. And the interesting thing is that these labels are applied based not on the gender a person is attracted to, but on the gender of the person feeling the attraction. As a female, I was considered "straight." As a male, I'm considered "gay," My sexual orientation, which is to men, hasn't changed. My label has changed because my own gender has changed. My label has nothing to do with who I'm attracted to. It has everything to do with who I am.[136]

Attesting to the possibility for trans people to hold a broad diversity of sexual orientations, Kenagy and Hsieh write: "FTMs can be heterosexual, bisexual and gay."[137] In another study of trans men considering gender affirmation surgeries, among 27 trans men in the sample, only 63% identified as heterosexual.[138] In a study of trans men who gave birth to their child, the sample consisted almost exclusively (except for 1 participant) of gay trans men.[139]

Some clinicians have also advanced troubling etiological frameworks for trans identity that situate it as psychopathology, a sexual fetish, or perversion. Sexologist Ray Blanchard's highly controversial notion of "autogynephilia" among trans women (which has also been supported by psychologist J. Michael Bailey[140]) suggests, for example, that some trans women are best understood as sexual fetishist men whose primary sexual attraction is not to another person, but to the thought of themselves as physiologically female. This body of research on "autogynephilia" is not without critique. For example, Talia Mae Bettcher[141] identifies logical errors riddling theories of "autogynephila" as she simultaneously considers the undertheorized ways in which *all* of our sexualities largely depend upon the erotic charge of thinking of not only others, but of *ourselves* as particularly gendered beings in relation with and to other particularly gendered beings. Jamie Veale,[142] a psychologist, has conducted research that similarly fails to find support for Blanchard's theory.

Despite the ways in which some clinical research has been pathology focused, other clinical research is increasingly focused not on trans people's presumed pathology, but on the need for greater social support for trans people, their partnerships, and families. In this way, contemporary clinical research increasingly designates pervasive ignorance, stigma, and discrimination as the primary limitation and challenge faced by trans people and their partners. Suggestions to address these issues include better professional training on trans and trans family issues for clinicians of all stripes as well as the need for broader social awareness, education, and activism around trans issues. More recent research on trans issues also considers the particular challenges that trans people and their partners face throughout the process of transition. Some of the common themes highlighted across these literatures include: (a) shifts in sexual identity for trans people and their partners;[143] (b) relationship uncertainty;[144] (c) inclusion of partners in transition-related decisions;[145] (d) social and familial reception of trans people and their partners;[146] (e) potentials for social/familial stigma, violence, and discrimination,[147] and; (f) social resistance and activism.[148] More recent attempts also aim to gauge the size and demographics of the trans population,[149] as well as to document relationship dissolution rates among this community.[150]

A growing number of resource guides and manuals exist for parents seeking resources on raising children who may be trans.[151] Sociologist Tey Meadow writes about the contemporary shifts underway as some parents become increasingly supportive of children who express trans identity and of efforts to transition at ever younger ages, with some parents even serving as facilitators and liaisons with medical professionals.[152] A number of texts also consider the experience of cis children growing up with 1 or more trans parents.[153] Common features of these texts include discussion of the dynamic shifts that often surround realization that a family member is trans-identified and challenges to acceptance as the family member seeks to gain recognition for their gender identity. Some of these challenges pivot upon role shifts and the anxieties that these shifts might trigger in a family context. Indeed, a trans person whose identity shifts from male to female assumes not only the social role of woman, but also possibly that of daughter, sister, aunt, mother, and wife. Family members of trans people, therefore, often face transitions of their own, from mother of a son to mother of a daughter, or from knowing and loving one's brother to coming to know and love one's sister.[154]

Parental transitions are described as particularly challenging for some children as the roles of mother and father are so deeply gendered in our culture. Therefore, shifts in gender identity mark shifts in family identifications, roles, and processes that may be quite challenging. This is especially true given that gender transitions of parents often involve simultaneous challenges to (or uncertainty around) both parental role (as mother or father) and spousal/partner role (as wife or husband). Because we live in a culture that views both trans identity and same-sex relationships as "alternative" and counternormative, the children of trans parents must often negotiate new understandings of not only their trans parent, but of their parents as a unit. For example, in the case of a cis heterosexually married set of parents wherein the father transitions to living as a woman, does the child now have lesbian parents and 2 mothers? Will the parents remain together or will a gender transition mark the end of a no-longer-tenable relationship? Longitudinal research on these sorts of family transitions remains virtually nonexistent.

Empirical and Academic Literatures

Until the turn of the millennium, scholarship on the romantic relationships of transgender people and their partners was much more commonly produced by clinical professionals in active practice (such as doctors, psychiatrists, social workers, and psychologists) who were often able to draw their patients and clients into convenience samples for their research studies. Around 2000, however, transgender partnerships began to emerge as a topic of empirical inquiry among non-clinical academics as well as pre-professional scholars in training to become clinicians. Over the first decade of the new millennium, a spate of masters' theses and doctoral dissertations[155] on the topic suddenly appeared thanks to the growing cultural visibility and awareness surrounding transgender identity. During this same time period, graduate training programs seemingly first began to consider the study of these partnerships legitimate as well.

In an interesting historical shift, while much of the published research in clinical literatures had focused on trans women and their romantic partnerships, academic scholarship at the turn of the millennium increasingly attended to trans men and, later, their romantic partnerships. Because the cultural visibility of trans men's identities was slower to develop, this is not necessarily surprising. From the 1990s onward, there was also a seeming rise in the number of butch-identified lesbians who began to self-identify as men and began taking testosterone and having surgical procedures to bring their masculine gender identities into closer alignment with their physical embodiment and social perception by others as masculine or as men. Because college campuses were often sites where trans men transitioned, it makes sense that those within the academic context would begin to take not only social but also scholarly notice. Those writing dissertations on the experiences of trans people's partnerships often discuss, in methodological appendices or the introduction to their work, having close social connections to trans people and their partners, or report going through the experience of transition alongside a trans partner. Upon learning that very little knowledge existed at the time, scholars have been inspired to contribute to a growing body of knowledge and information about these processes and partnerships.

A common thread across much of this early literature is that the majority of partners of trans people included in the samples of such studies were White cis women, as were the majority of researchers conducting the studies. As such, it should be noted that much of the existing scholarship on trans partnerships, at this incipient stage, is not representative of the entire, diverse community of trans people and their partnerships. Across this admittedly limited research, one of the most consistent themes to emerge is the way in which a trans partner's transition may affect a cis partner's sexual identity. Cis women heterosexually partnered with men who later transitioned often spoke about being recognized as a heterosexual and then having that recognition fall away or come into question as their partners transitioned. Was there an expectation that one would now self-identify as a lesbian? What might it mean if one did not generally experience attraction to other women, yet remained with one's trans woman partner? Cis women partnered with trans men grappled with similar (though reversed) questions.

In many instances, trans men had been previously identified as butch lesbians and the partnership between them had been recognized as lesbian. Yet once a partner transitioned, could a cis woman partner still claim identity as a lesbian? If she did, would she and her partner be welcomed and accepted within lesbian spaces and communities? Would such an identification fail to recognize her partner as a man? Would the rest of society see her as a lesbian or would she slide into invisibility as a heterosexual woman? These questions about identity and community are echoed across the academic literature on partners of trans people.

Another early query involved legal recognition for trans partnerships as individuals sought legal changes in sex-marker designations from male to female or female to male. For those who were legally married, would their partnership retain this legal recognition? For those who were previously deemed unable to legally wed in some states because they were a "same-sex couple," would this change once their partner's sex marker was legally changed? Of not insignificant concern are the financial costs often associated with medically facilitated transition, much of which remains unsubsidized by medical insurance for many if not most people.[156] Other questions related to identity and shifting family roles and concerns over who would be seen as a wife, husband, father, or mother.[157] Coming out to friends and family was a topic that emerged as central not only to trans people, but to their partners as well, who were often seen as buffers in managing difficult disclosures. Affording expensive transition-related medicines and medical procedures was reported as an area around which trans people and their partners sometimes struggled.

Renegotiating sexual intimacy was also described as challenging. Pre-existing sexual norms within couples (such as who was generally the one to initiate sex; who was seen as the more dominant or passive partner; which body parts were centrally involved in sexual interactions and which were off limits; what were the words used to describe various sexualized parts of the body; and shifting sexual attraction, desire, and libido) often transformed over the course of a partner's transition in ways that could be challenging to each partner. A consistent theme across these early narratives is that trans people and their partners rarely had access to others or to ready-made communities who shared their struggles and could provide support. Instead, trans people and their partners learned that they would have to build such sources of support, knowledge, and community from the ground up.

Tam Sanger's (2010) *Trans People's Partnerships: Toward an Ethics of Intimacy* addresses both trans men and women's partnerships utilizing in-depth interview data with 37 individuals, both trans men and women and their men and women partners (some of whom are trans as well). Sanger's book represents the only published text, prior to this book, that offers a monograph-length exploration of trans people's partnerships from an academic perspective. Utilizing a Foucauldian analytic framework centered around the notions of governmentality and ethics, Sanger argues that there is a certain freedom inherent to occupying subject positions outside of sociolegal recognition, given that recognition usually entails regulation of various types.[158] For example, as cis gay men and women have fought for the legal recognition of same-sex marriage, gaining mainstream cultural approval has seemingly necessitated advancing particular normative frameworks, such as the belief that individuals are born gay and would never willingly choose such a path, that gay and lesbian couples are just like everyone else (usually referring to cis heterosexuals), and that gay and lesbian couples are monogamously pair bonded.

Even if the everyday lives of individual gay and lesbian people do not map neatly onto these normative discourses, it is these very discourses that made the sociolegal recognition of same-sex marriage stretch from unfathomable to contemporary reality. Moreover, these discourses and frames hold the power to shape everyday practices, ultimately producing the normative social subjects they seek to recognize. As such, Sanger calls for expanded possibilities, an ethic of intimacy that exceeds the limits of formal contemporary sociolegal recognition of partnerships. For example, Sanger's ethics of intimacy would make space for those who are polyamorous, bisexual, BDSM-identified,[159] asexual, or who choose to engage in sexual practices deemed "risky" (such as barebacking, for example) by some social institutions. In this way, Sanger's work calls for an expansion of the cultural imaginary around gender, sexuality, partnerships, and families. In so doing, she remains aware that such a call may be accused of being "utopian."

Rather than defend her vision against such a claim, Sanger doubles down and urges sociologists to work toward developing more utopian visions in sociology as an intervention against becoming stuck in what society *is* rather than imagining possibilities for what it might *become*. Failure to generate new possible imaginaries in both mainstream society and the discipline of sociology is not, Sanger argues, a commitment to being a realist or some objective science project, but evidence of a lack of hope. In this way, Sanger calls for a reinvigoration of sociological utopian theorizing with the intent of generating a broader vision of possibilities for intimate relationships and partnerships in the 21st century.

In many ways, this book may be said to be an extension of such a call insofar as it engages, in depth, with the everyday intimate relationships, partnerships, and families of trans people and their cis women partners as they interact with, conform to, and resist existing social structures, norms, and institutions. The subsequent chapters will offer insights into the whys and hows of these complicated processes as they suggest that postmodern partnerships are not mere potentialities, but are already unfolding in the everyday lives of people in kitchens, doctor's offices, schools, courts, and bedrooms all across the land. Moreover, the chapters will highlight the enduring constraints of social systems, institutions, and structures as utopian ideals are sometimes realized and sometimes abandoned.

The research that informs this book is one effort to begin to offer greater depth and specificity to studies of trans partnerships and families without endlessly spinning in theoretical circles. If representations can be thought of as illustrations, we have had only line drawings of trans partnerships and families; it will take some time to begin coloring in these images and perhaps even learning to redraw some of their contours. In the next chapter, I will begin some of this "coloring in" process by discussing how the cis women I interviewed met their trans partners and how their own identities are shifting, transforming, and being challenged as a result of these unions.

NOTES

1. See Bornstein (1998, 1994); Feinberg (1999); Girschick (2008); and Nestle, Howell, and Wilchins (2002). It should be noted, also, that not all individuals I have just situated under the arc of the "transgender umbrella" may wish to be classified in this way. As such, while definitions such as these may offer a useful heuristic, transgender identification is highly complex and replete with tensions between self identification and social categorization.
2. See Devor (1997).
3. For example, see Allen (2003); Ames (2005); Blank and Kaldera (2002); Brown and Rounsley (1996); Cameron (1996); Cromwell (1999); Cummings (2006); Devor (1989); Diamond (2004); Green (1999, 2004); Hansbury (2005); International Foundation for Gender Education (1988); Kailey (2005); Kane-DeMaios and Bullough (2006); Khosla (2006); Kotula (2002); Link and Raz (2007); Middlebrook (1998); Namaste (2000); Nestle (1992); Nestle, Howell, and Wilchins (2002); Noble (2006); O'Keefe and Fox (2003); Pratt (1995); Rees (1996); Rubin (2003); Schofield (2008); Scholinski (1997); Sennett (2006); Sullivan (1980, 1990a, 1990b); Valerio (2006); Volcano and Halberstam (1999).
4. See Ames (2005); Gamson (1998); Kailey (2005); Khosla (2006).
5. See Kennedy and Davis (1993).
6. See portions translated and reprinted in Stryker and Whittle (2006:21–27).
7. See Devor (1997:29–30).
8. See Prosser (1998:10).
9. See Bockting in Bullough, Bullough, and Elias (1997:48–49).
10. See Prosser in Stryker and Whittle (2006:40–44).

11. See Hausman 1995.
12. Henry Rubin's (2003) historical account of the emergence of transsexual men differs substantially both from that of Hausman (1995) and Prosser (1998). Rubin's account centers upon the tensions that have developed between butches and FTMs, tensions that Halberstam (1998; in a phrase borrowed from Gayle Rubin) terms, "border wars." According to Henry Rubin's "genealogy of a specifically FTM subject position," the sexological discourse of inversion seeking to understand and explain female bodies that did not conform to normative sex, gender and sexuality imperatives, branched into at least 2 distinct categories of identity and embodiment by the 1970s: lesbian and FTM transsexual [see Rubin (1998:266)]. This distinction separated those with non-normative sexual object choices from those with incongruent sex and gender expression.
13. See Prosser (1998:9).
14. See Prosser (1998:10).
15. See Prosser (1998:10) and Kennedy (2007).
16. See Prosser (1998:141).
17. See the case of Dr. Thomas Brand's patient, as discussed in Warren (2014).
18. See Prosser (1998:10).
19. Historian Joanne Meyerowitz (2002), author of *How Sex Changed: A History of Transsexuality in the United States*
20. Such as that by Hausman (1995).
21. Donna Haraway's (1985) writing on the cyborg may be useful to consider here, as she cautions feminists against drawing artificial distinctions between science and nature, bodies and machines, subjects and objects, and the natural and the artificial in a social world that is, increasingly, formed co-constitutively through and among all of these forces. See also Schleifer (2006).
22. The non-substantive and dismissive way in which FTM transsexuals are mentioned in Janice Raymond's (1979) scathing "feminist" critique of MTF transsexuals in *The Transsexual Empire: The Making of the She-Male* also suggests FTM transsexuals' relative invisibility at that time. See also Valerio (2006).
23. See Rubin (2003:63).
24. See Devor (1997); Gamson (1998).
25. See Prosser (1998). In response to the question of whether or not FTM transsexuals have always existed, across time, Devor (1997:35) answers: "probably."
26. See Coolidge (2000).
27. See Nataf (1996) for a primer on debates between cis lesbian feminists and trans men.
28. See Boyd (1999).
29. See Katz (1976:209–210).
30. See Middlebrook (1998).
31. See Sullivan (1990a).
32. See Newton (1984).
33. See Hale (1998); Lee (2001); see also Muska and Olafsdottir (1998).
34. See Halberstam (2005).
35. See Halberstam (1998:293).
36. See Califia (1997); Cromwell (1999); Green (2004); Hale (1998); Lee (2001); Morris (2002); O'Hartigan (2002); Prosser (1998); Sullivan (1990a,1990b).

37. See Green (2004); Hale (1998). Also of note, as a point of cultural comparison, is that in her *Sexualities* article, Farquhar (2000) traces lesbian identity in a "post-lesbian world," gathering data from lesbians in the UK (between 1994 and 1995) about identity policing and what being a lesbian means and does not mean. Noticeably absent is any mention, whatsoever, of trans men or trans identity. This absence may suggest that the perceived rifts and "border wars" between butch lesbians and trans men developed post-1995, or that it was perhaps slower to develop in the UK than in the US.

38. See Hale (1998). Similarly, we must also not fail to consider the danger of imposing contemporary constructs, understandings, and readings onto historically prior subjects in ways that are decontextualized, falsely construing them as transhistorical.

39. See Halberstam (1998); Rubin (1992).

40. See Halberstam (1998).

41. See Khosla (2006); Namaste (2000); Prosser (1998); Valerio (2006).

42. See Prosser (1998:11).

43. Hale refutes Prosser's interpretations and accuses him of employing a "binary, totalizing methodology." See Hale (1998:340).

44. See Roen (2002).

45. See Martino (1977:218).

46. See Newton (1984); Rubin (2003).

47. See Blank and Kaldera (2002); Burana, Roxxie, and Due (1994); Munt (1998); Nestle (1992); Pratt (1995).

48. See Valerio (2006:145).

49. See Rees (1996:14).

50. See Noble (2006:85).

51. See Hale (1998); Lee (2001); McCauley and Ehrhardt (1980); Rubin (1998)

52. See Lee (2001:356).

53. See Dozier (2005).

54. See Kailey (2005).

55. See Green (2004:28).

56. See Green (2004:77).

57. See Kailey (2005:97).

58. A potential critique of this narrative is that it evokes the stigmatizing discourse of trans men as pathological, emotionally unstable characters with penis envy.

59. See Nestle, Howell, and Wilchins (2002:126).

60. See Dickey and Stephens (1995:439).

61. See Chivers and Bailey (2000:259).

62. See Schleifer (2006:60).

63. See Schleifer (2006).

64. See Dozier (2005).

65. See Kailey (2005:87). Note, also, the similarity of this argument with Michigan Womyn's Music Festival defenses that trans women should not be admitted to the festival because they have not had the experience of adolescent girlhood. It is unclear how these arguments might shift as trans individuals begin transitioning earlier. Prepubertal transitions would seriously challenge many of these arguments.

66. See Dozier (2005).

67. See Pfeffer (2014a) for a related discussion of cis women partners valuing and wishing to retain their identities as "queer," even when socially misrecognized as heterosexual when with their trans men partners in public spaces.
68. See Hollibaugh (1997, 2000); Kennedy and Davis (1993); Martin (1996); Nestle (1992). See also edited collections by Harris and Crocker (1997) and Munt (1998).
69. See Namaste (2000:51, 56).
70. See Wilchins (1997:22–23).
71. It is important to note that published autobiographies are not necessarily representative of the broad spectrum of trans identities and experiences and, as some critics [see Ames (2005)] have noted, published autobiographies in the 1990s and 2000s, in particular, tended to follow a somewhat formulaic pattern with regard to presenting a "born into the wrong body" narrative that finds resolution through transition and subsequently "finding" one's "true" self. Postmodern scholars have been particularly critical of these narrative tropes as they: (a) align with medical and psychological professional gatekeeping practices connected to access around hormones and gender affirmation surgeries; and (b) advance the notion that the self is a pre-extant entity outside of social construction.
72. For a more comprehensive overview of the literature focusing on trans narratives, see Ames (2005); Pfeffer (2009).
73. Some examples include: "You don't know dick: Courageous hearts of transsexual men" [Cram (1997)]; "Gendernauts" [Treut (1999)]; "Southern comfort" [Davis (2001)]; "Venus boyz" [Baur (2002)]; "The aggressives" [Peddle (2005)]; "TransGeneration" [Simmons (2005)]; "Transparent" [Rosskam (2006)]; "She's a boy I knew" [Haworth (2007)]; "Against a trans narrative" [Rosskam (2008)]; "Becoming me: The gender within" [Watson (2009)]; "Cruel and unusual" [Baus, Hunt, and Williams (2012)]; and "Trans" [Arnold (2012)]. Examples of feature-length films focusing on transgender individuals, based on adaptations of real events, include: "Boys don't cry" [Peirce (1999)]; "Soldier's girl" [Pierson (2003)]; and "Beautiful boxer" [Uekrongtham (2004)]. Examples of more mainstream releases with fictional accounts of trans lives and experiences include: "Ma vie en rose" [Berliner (1997)]; "Normal" [Anderson (2003)]; and "Transamerica" [Tucker (2005)].
74. "FTM" is an acronym meaning "female-to-male," a synonym for "trans man" and designating those individuals who move from female sex categorization at birth to living (and identifying as) a trans man or man in the world.
75. See Green (2004:143).
76. See Cummings (2006:40).
77. See Wilchins (1997:120).
78. See O'Keefe and Fox (2008).
79. See Diamond (2011).
80. See Solomon (2012).
81. For additional narratives focusing on mothers of trans kids, see Pepper (2012).
82. The book is now in its third edition.
83. One of the relatively fewer stories focusing on trans men and their families is written by Loree Cook-Daniels, a cis woman partnered with a trans man (Marcelle). Cook-Daniels describes that Marcelle gave birth to the couple's son, Kai, noting that Marcelle's pregnancy was horrific for him, physically, psychologically, and emotionally. In a tragic postscript to her story, Cook-Daniels reveals that Marcelle later committed suicide.

84. Minnie Bruce Pratt's (1995) *S/He* might be considered the lone exception, though it may be argued that Pratt's partner (Leslie Feinberg) does not necessarily self-identify as a "trans man" and prefers, in general, to be referred to using pronouns such as "she" or "ze."

85. See Boyd (2003, 2007).

86. There are a number of articles and texts written by the cis women partners of cross-dressers who were categorized male at birth. Some of these cross-dressing individuals retain their identity as men, while other transition and identify as women. See Dixon and Dixon (1991); Rudd (1999, 2000).

87. While it is generally my practice to refer to individuals using their last names, I switch to first names here in order to distinguish between partners who share a last name.

88. Minnie Bruce Pratt's (1995) *S/He* might be considered an exception here, though it may be argued that Pratt's partner (Leslie Feinberg) did not self-identify as a "trans man" (but as a "transgender lesbian) and preferred, in general, to be referred to using pronouns such as "she" or "ze."

89. Anderson-Minshall and Anderson-Minshall (2014:101).

90. Anderson-Minshall and Anderson-Minshall (2014:108).

91. Anderson-Minshall and Anderson-Minshall (2014:156).

92. See Johnson and Garrison (2015).

93. Photographic representations of individual trans people can also be found in Allen (2003), Cameron (1996), and Marcus (2011).

94. See Gillespie (1999).

95. See Peddle (2005).

96. See Peirce (1999).

97. See Anderson (2003).

98. See Davis (2001).

99. See Pierson (2003).

100. See Tucker (2005).

101. See Diamond (2007). See Steinbock (2014) for an extended discussion of *Trans Entities: The Nasty Love of Papí and Wil.*

102. The genre of "docuporn" is a type of "reality porn" that utilizes narrative and nonsexual documentary footage in an attempt to draw the viewer into the lives of the performers. It generally involves graphic depictions of sexual acts interspersed with scenes of the actors talking about their lives and experiences or sharing nonsexual scenes from their everyday life with the viewer. In some instances, docuporn is reality-based (depicting performers who are partners in their actual everyday lives); in other instances it is fictive.

103. See Rosskam (2006).

104. See Soloway (2014).

105. One of the critiques made of this and other trans-focused media productions is that they most often cast cisgender actors to play transgender characters, despite the notable emergence of talented trans actors over the past decade.

106. See Green (2004); Hines (2006); and the 2006 documentary, "Transparent."

107. Clinicians writing about trans men prior to this time were not unheard of, but certainly not as numerous. See Benjamin (1966) and Stoller (1975) for some of the earliest discussions of trans men from a clinical standpoint.

108. See Brown and Rounsley (1996); Leli and Drescher (2004); Lev (2004); Zamboni (2006).
109. See Kenagy and Hsieh (2005) for a counterexample.
110. See Blumer, Green, Knowles, and Williams (2012).
111. See Benjamin (1966); Ellis and Eriksen (2002); Lothstein (1983); Strassberg, Roback, and Cunningham (1979).
112. See Ames (2005).
113. Gender Identity Disorder was listed in the *Diagnostic and Statistical Manual of Mental Disorders* from 1980 to 2012. In 2013, this diagnostic category was removed and replaced with "Gender Dysphoria."
114. See Benjamin (1966).
115. The Harry Benjamin International Gender Dysphoria Association (HBIGDA) Standards of Care (SoC) were replaced in 2006 by the Standards of Care for the Health of Transsexual, Transgender, and Gender Nonconforming People by the World Professional Association for Transgender Health (WPATH).
116. These protocols were considered to be nonbinding, but this generally meant that psychological and medical professionals could choose whether to use them or not, not that trans people could choose not to follow the protocols and still be assured that they would receive desired services from their psychological and medical care providers.
117. One of these protocols involved passing the "real-life test," wherein a person who has not yet received any type of hormones or surgery is required to live and work for 6 months while presenting in the gender with which they identify. Critiques of this protocol rightfully focused on the impossibility of such a task for many trans people and the physical, psychological, emotional, and material dangers such a requirement presented for the trans patient [see Serano (2007)]. The "real-life test" requirement was dropped for hormones in 1981, but many practitioners providing care to trans people still follow these protocols for care. The International Bill of Gender Rights (IBGR) was first adopted by the International Conference on Transgender Law and Employment Policy, Inc. (ICTLEP) in 1993. This statement stipulates that trans people should be able to make their own choices about hormones and surgeries on the basis of informed consent, not through required psychotherapy sessions or passage of psychological and/or medical professionals' tests. Some medical professionals now offer hormone and surgical services grounded in patient informed consent alone rather than requiring letters from psychological and medical professionals.
118. See Ames (2005); Serano (2007).
119. There are interesting parallels here with trends across gay and lesbian identities. For instance, "homosexuality" was once considered a psychological illness or a sexual fetish or perversion. In the late 1960s and early 1970s, gay and lesbian rights activists and organizations began to push for the de-pathologization of homosexuality. Since the 1980s, we have seen an advancement of "born this way" explanations for gay and lesbian identities with concomitant adherence and advancement, by lesbians and gay men themselves, to these explanatory frameworks. Alongside these biologically based etiological explanations have come advances in mainstream social acceptance of gay and lesbian rights [see Powell, Bolzendahl, Geist, and Steelman (2010) for an overview of these trends].

See Grzanka, Zeiders, and Miles (2016); Sheldon, Pfeffer, Petty, Feldbaum, and Jayaratne (2007); and Walters (2014) for discussions of the ways in which "born this way" etiological frameworks for understanding homosexuality may not, ultimately, be liberatory.

120. See Mock (2012) for a discussion of these trends.
121. See Emerson (1996).
122. See Fleming, MacGowan, and Costos (1985:47).
123. See Lewins (2002).
124. See Lewins (2002:84).
125. See Chivers and Bailey (2000).
126. See Chivers and Bailey (2000:261, 269).
127. See Rees (1996:59).
128. See Fleming, Costos, and MacGowan (1984).
129. See Kockott and Fahrner (1988).
130. See, for example, Brown (1998); Cole (1998); Erhardt (2007).
131. See Lewins (2002:79).
132. See Chivers and Bailey (2000).
133. See Vidal-Ortiz (2002) for additional information about the intersections between trans men's gender, sexuality, and pragmatism around accessing regulated medical technologies.
134. See Devor (1997:508).
135. Cromwell (1999) and Schleifer (2006) also present evidence to contradict claims of near-universal heterosexuality among trans men.
136. See Kailey (2005:86).
137. See Kenagy and Hsieh (2005:205).
138. See Rachlin (1999).
139. See More (1998). This relatively high percentage is likely due to the possibility that heterosexual trans men who wish to become parents may often rely on a cis woman partner to give birth, and that identity as a gay trans man may limit possibilities for legal adoption.
140. Radical feminist theorists (e.g., Bernice Hausman, Sheila Jeffreys, and Janice Raymond) have also discounted trans identities through various arguments. One argument is that all gender is dangerous and should be eradicated [e.g., Jeffreys (2014)]. Under this understanding, transsexuality is understood as anachronistic clinging to (and reproduction of) harmful social artifact. Other radical feminist arguments suggest that trans identity involves encroachment upon gender-segregated social spaces understood as "safe" and free from sexist oppression. The most radical of the radical feminist critiques assert that transitioning constitutes the ultimate rape of women's bodies via bodily mutilation (in the case of trans men) and appropriation (in the case of trans women) facilitated through technological and medical pathways [e.g., Raymond (1979)]. For a pointed critique of trans-exclusionary radical feminist approaches, see Stone (1991).
141. See Bettcher (2014).
142. See Veale (2014).
143. See Alegría (2010); Alegría and Ballard-Reisch (2013); Joslin-Roher and Wheeler (2009).

144. See Samons (2009).
145. See Bischoff, Warnaar, Barajas, and Dhaliwal (2011); Nuttbrock, Bockting, Hwahng, Rosenblum, Mason, Macri, and Becker (2009).
146. See Nuttbrock, Bockting, Hwahng, Rosenblum, Mason, Macri, and Becker (2009).
147. See Alegría and Ballard-Reisch (2013); Joslin-Roher and Wheeler (2009).
148. See Tompkins (2011) for an academic/empirical exploration of the role of cis partners of trans-identified people as allies and activists. This resource contains insights of use to clinicians, academics, and laypersons alike.
149. See Flores, Herman, Gates, and Brown (2016); Meier and Labuski (2013); Rosser, Oakes, Bockting, and Miner (2007).
150. See Meier and Labuski (2013).
151. See Brill and Pepper (2008); Brown and Rounsley (1996); Lev (2004).
152. See Meadow (2011). See also Pepper (2012).
153. See Hines (2006); Howey and Samuels (2000).
154. It is important to note, however, that in some trans families, trans parents and their children retain the social role labels (such as "dad" or "mom") they have always used, though this may spark confusion for those outside the family who, for example, see an ostensibly male person being called "mom." For a compelling memoir on the intersections between trans identity, experience, and families that is co-written by a mother and her trans son, see Link and Raz (2007).
155. See Brown (2005); Mason (2006); Nyamora (2004); Pfeffer (2009); Sanger (2007); Tesene (2011); Tompkins (2011). Gurvich (1991) was an early exception, though this work misgenders trans women, as was common during the time in which it was written, by referring to trans women married to cis women as "transsexual husbands."
156. See Lenning and Buist (2013).
157. See also Faccio, Bordin, and Cipolletta (2013); Whitley (2013). For a cross-cultural example that runs counter to existing trends for sexual identity shifts among cis women partners of trans men found in the U.S., see Theron and Collier (2013).
158. See also Taylor (1992).
159. "BDSM" refers to the practices of bondage, discipline, dominance, sadism, sado-masochism, and submission.

Identity Shifts, Recognition, and Intersectionality in Trans Partnerships and Families

In this chapter, I propose that gender and sexual orientation are sometimes fluid beyond our own volition and that queer people may strategically manage these (mis)recognition processes to gain access to particular social and material benefits of social group membership. Further, I consider the ways in which various aspects of identity may intersect in the lives of cis women partners of trans men. The following sections detail specific pathways and processes that cis women described following and using as they met their partners, formed unions, and managed their own and partners' identities and others' perceptions of them.

HOW THEY MET

One of the first questions couples are often asked by others is: "How did you meet?" The answers to these questions become part of the narrative threads with which people weave the stories of their lives and relationships. When I asked cis women how they met their trans partners, more than 1 out of every 5 told me that their initial meeting was facilitated through the Internet. My interviewees talked about meeting their partners through Craigslist posts, online social networking sites that were particularly popular in the early-to-mid-2000s (such as Friendster and MySpace), LGBTQ discussion boards, and online dating sites. One of the hallmarks of postmodern partnerships is the increasing frequency by which they are technologically facilitated and mediated.[1] Trans community development has been catalyzed through the advent and proliferation of the Internet and virtual social networks across the world.[2] Now, trans people and their partners with access to computers and Internet technologies can find information, resources and community on websites, listserv, email, blogs and chat rooms. Tucker Lieberman[3] writes: "I'd never knowingly met any kind of queer individual in person. I thought I was the only female-to-male in the world until I got an Internet connection to prove otherwise."

In a study of cyber community support among trans men, the authors assert: "Today, [FTMs] can enjoy feelings of solidarity with the virtual community of FTMs that were not available to transsexuals even in the recent past."[4] The documentary, *Gendernauts: A Journey across the Great Gender Divide*, also explores the powerful effect the Internet has had in shaping and developing trans communities. Those able to access these resources can, privately and anonymously, do any or all of the following: determine costs of hormones and various surgeries; read tips about the best and worst (as well as most affordable and most costly) mental and physical health care providers; research surgical transition procedures; find support groups in their local area; engage in activism on behalf of their communities; research laws pertaining to sex, gender, and sexuality; lobby legislators for more trans-progressive policies; find, organize, and/or contribute to research conferences on trans issues; research potential employers and their policies related to gender identity and expression; find legal representation; meet potential partners; purchase sperm for alternative insemination; raise money for transition hormones and surgeries; plan travel to gender clinics and/or surgical centers; buy testosterone on the black market or price it out with a prescription; find trans-inclusive pornography; research the history of trans identity and experience; research the effects of testosterone injections or estrogen administration; view photos of "top" and "bottom" transition surgeries; find any type of clothing and shoes, binders (elastic bands, belts, or bandages to flatten chest tissue), pissers (devices that facilitate urination through a prosthetic penis while standing up), packers (materials to place in the underwear to give the appearance and, in some cases, "feel" of a penis while clothed), penis prostheses (designed with enough rigidity to allow for penetration during sex), pumps (suction devices used to enlarge the clitoris/micropenis), and much more.[5]

This is an enormous change from the 1980s, when Lou Sullivan was typing out a how-to resource manual for trans men—many of whom had never met or corresponded with another trans man in their own lifetimes. Sullivan's manual gave advice on how to dress, comb your eyebrows, cut and style your hair, effect male postures and body language, bind one's breasts, "pack" to give the appearance of a penis while dressed, use men's restrooms, modify vocal pitch, and translate women's clothing and shoes sizes to men's sizes. A later section of the manual discussed transition, noting all of the hormonal and surgical options for trans men available at that time. Resources for the partners of trans people, however, remained at a fairly incipient stage of development, confined largely to online support groups, YouTube channels, email listserv, and early social media groups.

In addition to meeting one another online, the cis women I interviewed often discussed meeting their partners at colleges and universities, often in connection to LGBTQ social and/or activist campus groups and organizations. One interesting trend that I noted was that, for 5 of the cis women I interviewed, the relationship they had with their trans partner was their first queer relationship and, in some of these cases, their first romantic relationship *ever*. One of the central concerns that often emerges through both virtual and land-based mutual support groups is how partnering with a trans man may impact one's own sexual identity and sense of self and social intelligibility.

Some of the cis women I interviewed told me that they worried about losing their lesbian identity or community once their partner transitioned to male.[6] Others were excited or saddened about the possibility of being perceived by others as unremarkably heterosexual when in public with a partner who is socially recognized as a man. Nearly all those I interviewed told me that that their own identities had been called into question or foregrounded, either by themselves or others, through their partnership with a trans man. It is simply not possible to consider the sexual identities of cis women partners of trans men without attending to the ways in which these cis women engage in management and negotiation of these identities on a daily basis.[7] The following sections explore some of the specific strategies the cis women I interviewed used to manage their identities personally, interpersonally, and socially.

NEGOTIATING IDENTITY: SOCIAL "PASSING" VERSUS "(MIS)RECOGNITION"

I learned that a critical component of the daily lives of cis women partners of trans men involves being both hypervisible and invisible, being recognized and/ or not recognized, as a rightful member of the particular social identity groups with which they most closely identify. For trans men and their cis women partners, these meaningful social recognition processes often include (sometimes unintentional or even undesired) social "passing" with regard to gender and sexual orientation. The concept of "passing" has a rich yet contentious history[8] and a problematic aspect of this history is the way in which the notion of "passing" reinforces the existing social status quo. Consider, for example, the notion of racial "passing" during the first quarter of the 20th century in the United States. At that time, several southern states enacted the "one-drop rule," which stipulated that a person was Black if they had so much as a single Black ancestor (i.e., 1 drop of "Black blood") in their lineage.[9]

As such, those individuals who appeared unremarkably White to others could still be accused of "passing" for White and accessing privileges to which they were deemed not legitimately entitled. It is clear that in order to establish the illegitimacy of a group, you must also establish the legitimacy of another. In the case of race, individuals might have identical skin tone, hair color, and eye color. Yet if it could be established that one of them had a great great uncle who was Black, that individual could no longer legitimately self-identify as White and could now only hope to "pass" (illegitimately) as White. What is often erased in considerations of social "passing" is the tremendous extent to which racial intermixing occurs in actual social practice and the resulting ways in which lines of demarcation between Black and White (to name just 2 groups) are increasingly blurred.[10]

The concept of "passing" with regard to sex and sexuality tends to operate in a similar though distinct fashion. We cannot understand what someone means when they say that someone is "passing" as a man or a woman or "passing" as heterosexual or queer unless we believe that only some people hold a legitimate claim to maleness or femaleness, manhood or womanhood, heterosexuality, or queerness. Using these assumptions to reinforce the existing social status quo, we come to believe that only certain individuals legitimately "belong" to various groups of gender and sexual identity, while others may only hope to "pass" into relatively inauthentic membership as (often tragic) "wannabes."

In the postmodern era, lines of demarcation between sex, gender, and sexual identity are becoming increasingly blurry. As Queen and Schimel[11] write:

> Postmodern thought invites us to get used to the Zen notion of "multiple subjectivities"—the idea that there is no solid, objective reality, that each of us experiences our reality subjectively, affected (or influenced) by our unique circumstances. This mode of thought encourages overlapping and sometimes contradictory realities, a life of investigation and questioning as opposed to essentialism's quest for the One Truth, the innate quality, indubitable facts on a silver platter, the answer to everything.

With the advent of hormone replacement and supplemental therapies, gender affirmation surgeries, and sex and gender transition occurring earlier in the life-cycle, our sexed and gendered embodiments become increasingly fluid. I argue that we need to shrug off dusty notions of "passing" to consider alternative frameworks for thinking about social identity and belonging. For example, sociologist and gender theorist Raewyn Connell suggests that it would be more useful for us to turn to the concept of "recognition" (in lieu of "passing") when considering the lives and experiences of people whose identities are often contested by those who wish to maintain the existing social status quo.[12]

Consider, for example, a trans man who walks into the Department of Motor Vehicles (DMV) in his town, seeking to renew his driver's license. If, upon seeing the bearded man standing in front of her, the clerk notices the "F" on his existing license and begins to laugh, noting out loud that she will also be sure to correct the obvious "clerical error" on his official documentation, this recognition of his identity as a man holds both social and legal implications. Once his driver's license is "corrected" with a simple letter change from "F" to "M," he is suddenly granted legal access to a number of social institutions that may have been previously inaccessible. More simply stated, he has now gone from the gender identity of a man to the social and legal status of a man, at least as far as the DMV worker and his driver's license are concerned. He has been recognized as a man. If he is partnered with a cis woman, he may now find it easier to access legal "opposite sex" marriage without much question in some states or counties that do not require applicants to supply a birth certificate.

He may now find it more difficult or even impossible to travel internationally as his legal documents, physical appearance, and flesh or prosthetic body parts under his clothing may reveal what are seen as inconsistent sex and gender markers, raising Transportation Security Administration (TSA) suspicions of identity fraud. All of these are hefty social consequences revolving around a single letter F → M. Of course, it is possible for this scenario to also work in other directions. Consider, for example, the experience of Belinda and her trans partner. Belinda told me:

> I can remember just going into a doctor's office with him before he even came out as trans ... and him showing his health card and them telling him that he was trying to [commit] health fraud because there was an "F" on his card and his name was androgynous.... We both got really upset. We basically just argued with the woman.... She accused him of trying to use my health card because I was clearly a girl and he was a boy and she was like, "Are you trying to use her health card? Is this her health card?" And he's like, "No, this is my health card." And she's like, "Well, why does it say 'female' on it?" and made it into a big thing. And we just basically stood there and argued with the woman ... getting really frustrated and angry.

In this instance, Belinda's partner has essentially "passed," or been recognized socially as a man, with consequences for access to health care resources given the fact that forms of identification had not yet been changed at that liminal point in the gender transition process. These vignettes reveal the ways in which social systems and structures render sex and gender binary and static when, in many people's actual lives, they are often experienced in a less binary and more fluid way.

When individuals refer to someone "passing" as a man or "passing" as a woman, the social meaning-making that is taking place lies at the thorny intersections of sex and gender categorization, expression, attribution, and identity.[13] The concept of passing also relies on juxtaposed notions of conscious, intentional, deceptive "dupers" and presumably natural, authentic, deceived "dupes."[14] Nevertheless, "passing" is often held as the gold standard of "successful" transsexualism, particularly by medical establishments; as such, "passing" is often conceptualized as emblematic of normativity or a desire to *be* normative.[15] Analyses of "passing" in racial and class contexts, however, adopt a more nuanced lens that views "passing" as a potentially pragmatic (though fraught) strategy for accessing and attaining regulated social, material, and legal resources, and consider the personal, interpersonal, and sociopolitical effects and consequences that the use of such strategies may involve.[16]

While "passing" may grant reprieve from the social stigma and potential danger of ambiguous gender expression, as well as access to social and material resources granted only to particular group members, these reprieves and access are often tenuous, context-specific, and revocable. Trans men who must always "pass" in ordinary social situations may live in fear about the consequences of being involved in a serious accident during which the removal of clothing (or, in some cases, the accessing of identification records indicating legal sex and/

or gender status) would seriously impair their ability to be unambiguously recognized in accordance with their gender identity. The concept of "passing" may be further illuminated by focusing on those ordinarily granted "natural" and unquestioned status within particular identity categories. Jean Elson,[17] for example, presents a compelling exploration into cis women's experience of identity post-hysterectomy and whether or not those who undergo this surgical procedure are still considered (and consider themselves) "women" or not, reaching the equivocal conclusion of "Yes, No, Maybe,"[18] probing and destabilizing the supposedly "natural" and essential links between female biology, gender identity, and social perceptions of which bodies rightfully constitute "woman."

In my gender in society classes, I routinely ask students if they have ever had a test to determine their own sex hormone levels (some have) and genetic karyotype[19] (most have not). If they have not, I inquire about why they feel so confident in their own assessments of themselves as "purely" male or female. I also propose various thought exercises to ask students to consider if a man who loses his penis and testicles in an accident is still a man, or if a person born with an XY sex chromosome pattern and a vagina[20] is a woman. Students quickly come to recognize that essentialist belief in the "naturalness" of sex binaries are part of the way in which we socially construct not only gender, but sex as well.

Sociologist and gender theorist Raewyn Connell's[21] notion of "recognition" offers a productive conceptual framework for thinking about the juxtapositions between one's body, subjective identity, social group memberships, and social appraisals of all of these. Following Connell, we would do better to supplant our biologically essentialist notions of "passing" with the more sociological notion of "recognition." By doing so, we might come to consider and recognize that trans people's efforts to "pass" occur not when living in accordance with their subjective gender identities, but as they attempt to live within gender identities normatively corresponding to their *sex assignment* (the assignment of a person, at birth, to "male" or "female" based on bodily signifiers such as presence of a penis or vagina) and/or *sex categorization*[22] (the everyday placement of a person into social categories such as "girl," "woman," "boy," or "man").

In other words, many trans men do, indeed, "pass" for much of their lives . . . as girls or as women. They often report struggling within bodies and social identities that do not feel like "home" until these efforts become untenable, at which point some take further steps to bring their bodies and social embodiments in line with their gender identity. Indeed, nature seems to provide the original prototype for transsexuality in the myriad forms of natural bodies that are produced and then systematically altered. Surgery on intersex infants and children erases naturally occurring somatotypes in the service of neatly reinscribing binary sex categories and incidentally demonstrating the social constructedness of not only gender, but of sex as well.[23] Indeed, perhaps transsexuality would be seen as natural if these other bodily manifestations of sex diversity were not so methodically erased by surgeons each and every day.[24]

I suggest that we need to take Connell's notion of "recognition" a step farther to propose that *mis*recognition is another critical process shaping the experiences and lives of those within partnerships and families with transgender and transsexual people. In other words, it is not only being recognized in accordance with your gender and sexual identity and/or legal status that matters, but people's *mis*recognition of those identities often carries significant implications for our everyday lives as well. Despite the potential for social recognition and misrecognition processes to make daily lives more difficult for trans people, their partners, and families, they also hold the potential to grant access to limited resources and even to disrupt the social status quo.

Let us consider one of my interview participants who was told that her parents would no longer help her pay for college once she came out to them as lesbian. Two years following her coming out and her parents' pronouncement of nonsupport, this same cis woman partnered with a trans man and began to self-identify as queer, but did not disclose this information to her parents. She brought her partner home one weekend to meet her parents and they confided that they were thrilled that she had finally come to her senses, gotten through a rough "phase," and was now dating such a fine young man. In this instance, while the trans man was recognized as a man, his cis woman partner was misrecognized as heterosexual, and there can be little doubt that each of them may now be afforded privileges and opportunities (such as being welcomed into the family and financial help from her parents to pay for college) that they otherwise may not have received without this recognition and misrecognition. Note that these outcomes depend largely on the social perceptions and judgments of others rather than any concrete "reality" that supposedly exists out in the world somewhere. We act in accordance with our assumptions and perceptions.

Through my research with cis women partners of trans men, I learned that our gender and sexual identities are always about more than our own personal choices, autonomous desires, and the people to whom we are attracted and with whom we choose to partner. Rather, our gender and sexualities are *interpellated* by others every day. Interpellation is a term and social process most often linked to philosopher Louis Althusser. According to Althusser's notion of interpellation,[25] we are "hailed" into being by others, often simply by presuming that another's call is directly addressing or recognizing us. In this way, our investments in others' presumed "hailing" of us holds a great deal of power in determining who we are, what our life choices and possibilities may be, and who we may become.

For example, on a street somewhere, someone is whistling loudly, a "cat call." A woman on the street may (or several women on the street may) hear this whistle. The whistle may make one woman feel excited or that she is beautiful and desired while another woman may feel ashamed, nervous, or possibly even afraid. Still another woman may feel a mixture of these emotions. The fact that she is not the only woman on the street or that the whistling may not be directed toward her specifically (or possibly even anyone) does not ultimately matter.

What matters is if any of the women change the way they dress, the way they walk, or the route they take in order to court more or less future attention as a result of the initial action of the stranger's whistling. Similarly, the whistler might observe the target of their whistle and adjust their own behavior based upon their assessment of the recipient's response. If she smiles, the whistler may presume that the action of their whistling was desired and engage in this behavior more frequently, or perhaps even feel justified to approach the woman more directly. The fact that her smile may have expressed her discomfort, nervousness, or fear (rather than delight) is of no consequence to the whistler when it comes to driving his or her subsequent behavior. If she is deaf and never heard the whistle, but is coincidentally smiling at a pleasant memory, that is also irrelevant to the whistler; the whistler's course of action still proceeds in the direction of his or her assessment of the situation.

Through speaking with cis women partners of trans men, I came to consider how (mis)recognition by social others also has both quotidian and remarkable effects on the ways in which we see and understand both ourselves and our partners. Moreover, these sexual identity social interpellation and (mis)recognition processes are not without social and material consequences that structure our opportunities, challenges, social memberships, and life possibilities. Because of this, I wanted to learn more about how the cis women I interviewed both understood themselves and were understood or interpellated by others.

"QUEER" WAS A BETTER IDENTIFIER FOR ME

While researchers are making considerable progress in including lesbians and gay men in studies of family life, other "queer" social actors remain relatively absent.[26] It sometimes seems as if scholars who produce what has come to be known as "queer theory" have failed to recognize the everyday lives and realities of the individuals for whom "queer"[27] is more than grounds for intellectual debates within small, academic circles. Because of these limited and limiting discussions, the social processes by which people come to take on personal *identities* as "queer" remains relatively understudied and sometimes misunderstood.

When I asked the cis women I interviewed to describe their own sexual identities, they often spoke about these identities in relation to their partner's gender identity, rhetorically asking: "What does that make me?" We have identity categories for women who are attracted to and date women (lesbian), women who are attracted to and date men (heterosexual), and women who are attracted to and date both women and men (bisexual). But what is the term that we use to describe women who are attracted to and date transgender men? Does the "transgender" adjective preceding "men" change the way in which we understand sexual attraction and identity, or the way individuals understand their own sexual attractions and identities?

One of the cis women I interviewed, Martha, told me that she personally struggled with issues connected to identity in her relationship with her trans partner:

> I thought of myself as a dyke and then now I'm with someone who identifies as a man and I'm thinking, how do I identify now? I'm not a lesbian. . . . I'm not really perceived as queer by many other people right now. And it really messed with me for a while. What am I? Who am I? Not that I didn't know who I was, but what identity should I give to people? A lot of times I'd try to adopt my identity as my own and it doesn't matter what other people think. But it's hard not to judge myself by other people's judgments.

Having difficulty figuring out how to self-identify was often described as not only an internal struggle, but an interpersonal one as well. Tiffany said: "People are wondering what your sexuality is. . . . I get asked on surveys and things like that and I really don't know what to put."

Another participant, Linda, refused her friends' and family's calls to put a label on her relationship with her trans partner: "All these people would go, 'Oh, what does that make you now?' And I would say, 'Happy and in love. That's all.' I didn't see why anything else has to matter." For those cis women I interviewed who self-identified as lesbian or who had done so in the past, they reported facing challenges around how to identity, their sense of community, and other people's expectations about their lives and choices. Polly told me:

> If you're a lesbian, everybody works so hard to accept it. They accept it, then you fuck them up by being with a trans guy. And then they're like, "Okay, next she's going to go to men." That it's just this form of evolution . . . and you're just graduating in this progressive chain of eventually getting to the pinnacle of the "real" man. I sort of feel like people see it as this progressive growth into being fully, Freudianly, "correctly" socialized to heterosexuality.

Cis women partners of trans men described facing persistent challenges in actively negotiating their own (and their trans partner's) shifting identities across a variety of personal, interpersonal, and social contexts. One of the ways in which this negotiation manifested for many participants was through language and determining how they would self-identify, with regard to sexuality, in the context of their unique relationships.

Just over half of the cis women participants in my study self-identified as "queer" at the point of our interview and about 65% described their relationship with their trans partner as "queer." In another study focusing on 20 cis women (current and former) partners of trans men, while 30% of the sample self-identified as "queer" prior to their partner's transition, 70% assumed some variant of this label following their partner's transition.[28] In nearly half of the relationships that cis women talked to me about, their own sexual identity was different from their partner's sexual identity. In the majority of these instances, interviewees described their own sexual identity as "queer"[29] or "lesbian,"[30] while they described their trans partner's identification as "heterosexual" or "straight."[31] Less frequently,[32] cis women self-identified as "lesbian" while their trans partner was said to self-identify as "queer." According to the cis women I interviewed, over 60% of their trans men partners were perceived as men in social spaces either "always" or "almost always." When in public together, therefore, many of the cis women I studied reported being frequently (mis)recognized as part of a fairly unremarkable heterosexual couple.[33] Several participants also described instances in which clerks "corrected" sex designators from "female/f" to "male/m" on their trans partner's paperwork or in computer records systems, remarking about how there must have been an "error in the system," upon seeing the trans man in front of them.

But it was not solely verbal cues that indicated to the cis women I interviewed that strangers were "reading" or recognizing their trans partners as men. Nonverbal indicators that their trans partners were being socially "read" as men and/or that the couple was being "read" as heterosexual included the check being consistently handed to one's trans partner at restaurants and other service establishments, other men giving a head "nod" when passing one's trans partner on the street, being smiled at by older persons when holding hands with one's trans partner in public,[34] and not being scrutinized when in sex-segregated public spaces (such as restrooms).

It would be easy to assume that being (mis)recognized as heterosexual in public might be a welcome relief for those cis women who had experience dealing with social discrimination or public harassment upon being perceived as lesbian. Yet being (mis)recognized as heterosexual was described by the women I interviewed as personally and socially problematic, particularly insofar as they feared being (mis)recognized as "heteronormative" by social others. Heteronormativity emerged as a "bad word" among most of my participants, but what does that term even mean? For the cis women I interviewed, being heteronormative meant fulfilling stereotypically gendered "roles"[35] in their relationships, endorsing majoritarian ("just like everyone else") politics, and not being seen as queer or politically radical. These were most often not social encounters they felt good about or found validating. Instead, they described feeling invisible and misunderstood when they were assumed by others to be heterosexual rather than queer.

Calling oneself "queer," was described as a fraught (though sometimes powerfully political) solution to the fact that current language and terminology doesn't carve out a particular space for their identities, partnerships and families:

> Before my ex partner ... I had been sort of actively claiming that I wasn't straight ... and I was very comfortable telling people that. But I also come from a small town and the options there were very much "gay," "lesbian," "bisexual" or "straight." I didn't feel that any of those fit me. So, I started saying to my friends and to whoever else, "Well, I'm not straight." But that's as far as it went.... I hadn't had any other partners that would actually

complicate that at that point.... But [once I met my trans ex partner], it just made sense for me to think about identifying as "queer" and that felt comfortable.

Sage's narrative walks us through her process of coming to self-identify as "queer." She considers sexual orientation self-identification labels in the context of her own life, coming to the conclusion that none of the existing labels accurately "fit." She first chooses a new identity category rooted in *dis*identification with an existing identity category ("not straight"). Later, a new relational context (partnering with a trans man) serves as the impetus for self-identifying in yet a new way: adopting an identity label ("queer") that was not part of the original range of self-identification choices of which she was aware and/or that were available to her.

Another participant, Rachel, echoed some of these same themes:

I thought you could only pick "gay," "straight," or "bi"; but I feel like "queer" is more accurate. Because I think "gay" implies one polarity and "straight" implies another and it doesn't include a grey area of people having a flexible self-identity.... So, I felt like "queer" was a better identifier for me. Plus, I feel like "queer" carries with it a political component more than just like the middle-class gay people who are now, like, you see on TV and everything. "Queer" implies still active, still moving to make the world a safer and better place for people.

For Rachel and others, choosing to self-identify as "queer" may serve as a conscious and intentional social indicator of a political stance that explicitly resists or rejects normativity in order to imagine a different or transformed social landscape. When asked what identifying as "queer" meant to her, Ani told me: "I needed a language for *not* being heteronormative." Eliza talked to me about how mainstream visibility of partnerships between cis women and trans men had allowed her to consider alternate identity labels for articulating her own partnership. As Eliza told me: "I was reading something about Michelle Tea and Rocco Kayiatos[36] and they identified themselves as a 'queer straight couple' ... and I'm like, 'Okay, that's us!' " Living in a postmodern era means that transgender people and their partners are becoming increasingly visible and accessible as role models through online resources and social media.

Each of these experiences stand in stark contrast to some scholars' call for a "post-queer study of sexuality,"[37] or claims that the term "queer" exists primarily to symbolize a departure from sexual identity categories.[38] Rather, the cis women I interviewed told me that "queer" was one of the few, if not the *only*, sexual identity terms that did not overly constrain or threaten the relationships they have with their trans partners. Identifying as "lesbian" carried the possibility of invalidating their trans partner's identity as a man, while self-identification as "bisexual" was also an untenable choice for some because it could introduce identity and relationship insecurity as trans partners were left to ponder: Is my partner attracted to me and recognizing me as a man or as a woman? Only 2 participants self-identified as "heterosexual" in my study, with most cis women telling me that they placed strong value on their connection to (and membership within) LGBTQ communities.

QUEER DILEMMAS

While many of the cis women I interviewed spoke to me about just how much they valued their queer identities and how invisible they felt when these queer identities were not seen by others, others were more skeptical of the ability for "queer" to fully and specifically encompass their sexual identities. The phrase "queer umbrella" has been used to explain how the term "queer" has become an identity category that encompasses a broad arena of nontraditional gender and sexual identities. However, a dominant theme that emerged even among participants who did choose to self-identify as "queer" was the worry that "queer" can become *so* all-encompassing, as a catchall identity, that it may be in peril of becoming an *empty* social category.

Joshua Gamson[39] describes this tendency as the "queer dilemma." While "queer" as an identity label may be particularly appealing to those for whom other categories (such as heterosexual, lesbian, or bisexual) feel overly restrictive or inappropriate, for others this very openness or fluidity may, paradoxically, feel quite confining. As Polly told me:

> I could say I'm queer but I also am not so sure I want to signal that identity either because I feel sometimes queerness is a little irresponsible because it's just so overused that it becomes sort of meaningless. I don't even know what people [are] trying to indicate to me when they say that. So, I don't know if I feel comfortable saying it. . . . I think my sexual identity doesn't have a particular proclivity or erotic choice that has anything to do with a pre-existing terminology. . . . So, I feel like in my life I slide myself into the term that worked mostly to make *other* people understand me, not necessarily because I feel like it really is an adequate description of who I am.

For Polly, "queer" serves as a social identity category into which she reluctantly places herself for the purposes of becoming socially intelligible to *others* rather than from a felt sense of its personal resonance or "fit." Polly's narrative thus highlights the critical importance and paradox of social recognition with regard to queer identities. How we *feel* matters, but often not nearly so much as how we are perceived and categorized. Polly comes to adopt a label that makes her socially recognizable and interpretable to social others. This label, however, fails to fully encapsulate or accurately describe the specificity of her particular partner choices and desires.

Amber offered another example of the limitations of "queer" as an identity signifier. She told me: "'Queer' is such a vague term. If you say you're queer then people will often just assume that, if you're a girl, then you're a lesbian . . . But

I date men so I don't want to . . . be just kind of lost in the queer umbrella. If you're going to look at me and want to know what box I go in, put me in the right one." For Amber, then, "queer" is a category that renders her attractions to cis men invisible. Rather than being overly all-encompassing, she finds it overly restrictive and exclusionary in the context of her own attractions and desires. Both Polly and Amber articulate the paradoxically constraining power of a seemingly "umbrella" identity category such as "queer."

Cis women and their trans partners must often work to (re)define their identities, as individuals and in relationship to one another, in ways that both challenge and extend existing language and social categories. Furthermore, the rising visibility and media presence of partnerships between cis women and trans men, particularly via the medium of the Internet, contributes to the emergence of queer cultural communities through which language and support may be continuously developed, challenged, and shared.[40] The Internet emergence of a new linguistic identity term, "queer-straight" (which 2 participants in this study used to describe their relationship with their trans partner), may be one way in which language is being innovated and developed out of existing frustrations over the potential lack of specificity and meaning with "queer."

In addition to negotiating language and identity classification systems, the cis women I interviewed reported marked and sometimes painful discrepancies between how they see and understand themselves and how they are seen and understood (or not) by others in their social communities and contexts. Two themes that frequently emerged for cis women partners of trans men were actually flip sides of the same (mis)recognition coin: being (mis)recognized (or "passing") as unremarkably straight in both queer and nonqueer social spaces and becoming invisibly queer (i.e., no longer being recognized as a rightful member of the queer community) within queer social spaces. Clearly, (mis)recognition, or being seen and not seen, by various communities is a powerful social process that critically informs, validates, and invalidates personal identities and group memberships. So, just how do cis women negotiate these processes?

RESISTING NORMATIVITY

One of the strategies cis women talked to me about revolved around not wanting to fall into patterns with their partner that might be interpreted as normative or reflecting the status quo. Some cis women voiced this intention directly to their trans partner, as in the case of Emma who spoke of a conversation during which she reportedly told him: "I am a feminist and I don't want to be a housewife. . . . That's not who I am and that's not who you're going to be in a relationship with." Some cis women and their trans partners shared in the desire to reject and resist normativity. As Mel told me:

> It's kind of nice to be different from the mainstream sometimes. So, it's kind of nice how that can automatically set you apart say at work or something

like that. It sort of puts an automatic flag above your head that says, "I challenge norms," which I embrace. And there's a bit of that that I feel isn't there
when . . . I use male pronouns [for him] and [we] pass as straight.

According to Sage: "It sort of is a little disturbing to both of us, as individuals and
together, to think that we might fall into sort of a heterosexuality, a heteronormative pattern. Being queer, interacting as queer, presenting as queer, and being
queer in the world is something that's really important to both of us."

In a similar vein, Belinda explained: "We both say that it's a queer relationship. Neither of us are interested in passing as a straight couple or having people
believe that we're a straight couple." The majority of cis women I interviewed
told me that they had been (mis)recognized as heterosexual by strangers. I argue
that this group of cis women's vocal resistance to being socially (mis)recognized
as anything but "queer" holds the power to shake up normative assumptions.
They trouble notions of what a "heterosexual couple" is *like*. My interviewees
frequently resisted being seen as "normal," because they viewed being "normal"
as antithetical to their deeply held feminist and queer self-identities. Of course,
their resistance may ultimately be limited given that opportunities to correct the
social (mis)recognition of others do not always readily present themselves, may
be unsuccessful, may be resisted by one's partner, or may be unsafe in certain
social contexts.

Some of the cis women I interviewed, particularly those who self-identified as
"queer," told me that they more often judged *themselves* to more strongly reject
or resist normative practices and politics than their trans partners. This makes
sense if we consider that being recognized by others as male often depends upon
appearing hypermasculine or supporting traditional masculinity and heterosexuality.[41] In other words, trans men (like cis men) often gain social recognition of
their gender identities as men when engaging in stereotypical social behaviors
associated with "being a man."[42] Younger cis women (those who were under 35
years of age) more frequently worried that their relationships would be (mis)rec-
ognized by others as heterosexual than the older (those at least 35 years of age) cis
women I interviewed.[43] This makes sense if we consider that younger participants'
feminist views were most likely to have been informed by Third Wave feminist
politics which emphasize individual and even radical forms of self-expression.

EMBRACING NORMATIVITY

Despite the fact that participants most frequently identified themselves (and their
relationships) as "queer," and distanced themselves and their relationships from
characterization as "heteronormative," a vocal minority made statements that
could be interpreted as reflecting heteronormativity. Older cis women reported
desires for heteronormativity more often than those who were younger. Those
cis women who reported that their trans partners were perceived socially as male
"always" or "almost always" were most likely to report performing traditional

enactments of gender in their relationships (like doing more of the household or emotional labor in their family; see Chapter 3 for more on this) and to report that their trans partner embraced normativity or was "traditional." Cis women were also more likely to report performing traditional enactments of gender in their relationships when their partners were trans-identified when the relationship began and then transitioned over the course of the relationship (as opposed to those whose relationship began as lesbian or those who were with partners who had already completed most of their transition by the time the relationship began).

When I asked Ellia how she would describe the type of relationship that she has with her partner, she responded: "We're just a straight couple. He's my fiancé, we're getting married, we're just a straight couple." Pay close attention to the sort of words that Ellia uses here to describe her relationship: "straight," "he," "fiancé," "married," "straight," "couple." Ellia's use of the phrase, "We're *just* [my emphasis] a straight couple," twice, might be an indicator of her awareness that, without defending the normativity of her partnership, her relationship may be quite unlikely to be seen by others as "just a straight couple." While Ellia aligns herself and her partnership with unremarkable normality, Margaret offers another perspective. Margaret explicitly distances her family from *the need* to be radical or counter-normative altogether: "One of the first conversations we ever had was about kids, how many we wanted, and what the time frame was and we aligned completely. . . . Sometimes, when you're *super* radical, you get to *not* be radical! And I want our kids to have one set of parents with one last name."

Margaret's conceptualization is interesting and provocative; it suggests that privately held queer identities (which may be socially invisible and/or hidden, particularly in the context of family life) remain socially radical. Furthermore, it suggests that, based on this internally held queer identity, it is possible (and perhaps even acceptable) to access certain privileges and normative institutions that do not challenge or erode the "queerness" of these privately held queer identities. Margaret acknowledges and resists normative understandings of family as she casts herself in the part of "*super* radical" and talks to me about the negotiations and deliberations in which she and her partner have engaged with regard to having and naming children. This possible future that Margaret envisions allows her to transform normative ("*not* radical") practices of having and naming children into a "*super* radical" enterprise of queer family building.

The cis women in my study also talked to me about engaging in family dynamics that some might describe as traditional or even conservative. In many of my participants' views, however, these dynamics may be considered playful, a form of resisting the traditional and conservative through conscious performance.[44] According to Rachel:

I think he had this fantasy . . . which I don't think exists for anybody anymore. But, in his head, part of becoming a man was becoming a *Leave it to Beaver* dad. Like coming home and mom has dinner on the table and whatever else is happening. But it turns out he cleans house more than I do and he cooks more than I do. So, I think, at this point, our relationship is

undefinable by present terms; so, I would just say, "queer." It's just different.
It's different than anything available.

Eliza offered another example that paralleled Rachel's, but she also considered the
importance of other people's possible perceptions of her queer family dynamics:

> We're both very sort of intrigued by '50s décor and roles and all that sort of
> stuff. . . . Sometimes I'm concerned that other people might not quite get it and
> that they might think that we're really espousing these very traditional roles. . . .
> I don't want to be the passive wife. . . . I'd much rather be the tough wife.

For some of the cis women I interviewed, acting in ways that might seem normative is something they and their trans men partners do despite their concerns
about *not* wanting to be (mis)recognized by others as traditional or unremarkably heterosexual.[45] I wondered, then, why some cis women or their trans partners might pursue these strategies for blending seamlessly into the social status
quo. In the next section, I explore some of their reasons.

NORMATIVITY, BOREDOM, AND SAFETY

Psychologist Nicola Brown[46] describes "sexual identity renegotiation" as a central
challenge faced by cis women partners of trans men. When providing accounts
of their experiences in social spaces, the cis women in my study sometimes discussed how being (mis)recognized as unremarkably heterosexual was something
that their trans partner loved, while their own feelings remained more ambivalent or even conflicted. As Frieda discussed:

> [My partner] definitely was into the whole idea of us passing as a straight cou-
> ple, so nothing queer really fit into our everyday lives or relationship because
> his main priority was passing as a man and that I should look like a woman
> so we can pass as a straight couple and he can blend in. So, he encouraged
> me to look more feminine and to have my hair long and things like that . . .
> [but] I wanted to shave my head and . . . pierce things and . . . do things that
> normal, boring, feminine, straight women didn't usually do and they didn't
> fit in with what he wanted. . . . I kind of felt guilty or selfish if I tried to dress
> the way that I wanted. . . . When we were going out together, I tried to look as
> feminine and as boring as I could so we could pass as a normal, boring couple.

Polly offered a very similar description of her experiences, one that was even
more focused upon challenges connected to reinterpreting her own identity, the
social perceptions of others, and social group memberships:

> I think I'm still trying to sort out what it means *not* to be a lesbian. There is
> a nice *recognition* [my emphasis] when you're walking down the street with

your girlfriend and you're holding hands and see another lesbian and they see you as a lesbian and it's like you feel like you're all in the same club. So, I miss that. . . . I just sort of feel like this level of boringness. I guess I have to say I definitely got off on the transgression of having men look at me and then kissing my girlfriend. And now it's like I have men look at me and then I kiss him and it's like, "Big whoop." . . . It's just not the same charge. So, I think I miss that. I miss some of that transgressive sort of fucking with people's heteronormative assumptions and now I'm just like basically following the script and it feels a little weird. It's not quite as fun. [I miss] the performativity of being gay. . . . Sometimes it's scary and you don't do it. So, I definitely don't miss being scared.

Margaret echoed this desire to not disappear into the woodwork:

I liked having an externally [visible] lesbian identity because it was pretty much the only radical thing left about me. When I was in high school I went to a very, very preppy private school and everyone wore their Abercrombie and Fitch and I wore black leather zip-up boots, a leather jacket, black jeans, and heavy metal t-shirts. I was radical. I got a tattoo when I was 14. I got piercings. I was hardcore. And I smoked and I partied and I was tough. And then slowly as a professional, and as an adult, transitioned out of a lot of those vestiges of my radical self. So, all I really had left was, "Yeah! I eat pussy! That makes me radical!" Now I don't. So, now I'm straight and not radical.

For Frieda, Polly, and Margaret, whenever their trans partner was recognized by others as a man, it became much more likely that their own queer identities would be erased. This created the paradoxical situation of gaining access to certain social privileges associated with heterosexuality, while simultaneously losing access to (and recognition by) the sexual minority communities with which they strongly identified.

Furthermore, all 3 describe "passing" or being (mis)recognized as heterosexual as "boring," or "not radical," highlighting the power of visibly queer social identities to feel both exciting and transgressive. Why would anyone want to be perceived as boring and usual when they could be perceived as exciting and unusual? Namely, safety. Polly's concluding remark, alluding to the danger associated with being socially perceived as lesbian, highlights another pragmatic aspect of being (mis)recognized as heterosexual: the reduced threat of physical and sexual violence directed toward those who are read as more visibly queer.

Violence isn't necessarily directed at people because of their actual sexual *identities*. People rarely fly into a homicidal rage simply by hearing someone say, "I am gay" or "I am lesbian." Rather, violence tends to be enacted following outrage over one's personal assessment that norms of gender or sexual conventions are being transgressed or that one's own assumptions or perceptions about another person's gender or sexual identity may have been mistaken. The practice of "closeting" was developed by LGBTQ communities, in large part, as a self-preservation mechanism, to avoid triggering just these sorts of perceptions among others who might be incited to rage over their own inability to cope with gender and sexual identity ambiguity and transgression. The cis women I interviewed were no strangers to walking these sorts of tightropes: wanting to be seen and recognized in accordance with their experiences and identities, but understanding that this recognition may sometimes carry dangerous consequences.

Most cis women who reported being (mis)recognized as part of a heterosexual couple, by family, friends, or strangers, acknowledged the privilege that that (mis)recognition entails, while simultaneously expressing discomfort with this privilege and bemoaning the inevitable tradeoff of losing social recognition as queer. Margaret told me: "I have mixed feelings about it. Sometimes I really like passing. There's a real social benefit to it; it makes it a lot easier." Veronica said:

> It makes me feel safe in the world. It makes me feel really invisible and that's something he and I both deal with a lot. We don't like the invisibility factor. We're always looking for ways to be visible and to educate others. So, maybe that's the only way because I don't really know how much we can walk down the street wearing shirts that say, "We're not so straight!"

When I asked Maya, who had just had a baby, to discuss how she felt she and her partner are perceived by others, she responded: "It's annoying because we get such privilege everywhere we go. . . . My mother's like, 'Thank God!' And I provided her a grandchild, so I'm 'normal.' In some respects it's good and in other respects I wish *everyone* had that."

Eliza, who is legally married to her trans partner, stated: "With family . . . there's a thing in the back of my head that wonders if it's so easy for them because now we're a 'straight couple.' It's almost less explaining for them to do in the future. Sometimes it's a mixed blessing." The stories the cis women I interviewed told me also revealed a keenly developed consciousness of the way queer people experience the sometimes-marginalizing gaze of nonqueer people, poignantly highlighting the disjuncture between self-identification and social (mis)recognition. One of the most painful social interactions that cis women talked to me about involved becoming invisible to the communities that often mattered the most to them.

"ANOTHER BREEDER[3] COUPLE INVADING"

The cis women I interviewed described the experience of losing access to, and social recognition within, queer communities as they became "invisibly queer."[47] Margaret said:

> When I see lesbian couples with a baby, I smile at them and have this moment of like, "What a cute couple with a baby." And [my partner]

and I have this experience together because, at one point, he had been externally identified by others as a lesbian. So, we have this moment of, "Oh, another queer couple with a baby!" But [lesbian couples] ... don't see that we're having this moment of camaraderie like, "Yay, you did it, we're going to do it!" They see us as like, "Oh, those straight people are looking at us."

Maya offered a similar story: "We can go anywhere and not have people looking at us except when we're in [a gay neighborhood] and then it's like, 'Oh, another breeder couple invading.' And I just want to wear rainbow flags everywhere I go so I can prove that I belong in this community."

Lilia also spoke to me about the not-uncommon experience of having her queer identity made invisible by others within the queer community: "My lesbian friends ... [are] like, basically, 'Oh, so you turned straight.' ... [But] I don't consider this a straight relationship since he's very queer.... I can see how it's straight in some contexts. But it's queer. His experiences of growing up as a woman [are] what makes it queer." Disappearing into the background of queer communities within which cis women formerly found support and recognition *as* queer was described as quite painful. Many cis women participants described being (mis)recognized as heterosexual as not only personally invalidating, but as alienating from queer communities of social support and belonging (read more about this in Chapter 6).

The cis women partners of trans men whom I interviewed faced challenges of marginalization from queer communities—not only from social distancing, exclusion, and (mis)recognition by others within LGBTQ communities, but sometimes as a result of their trans partner's wish to disassociate from these communities to reinforce their own social recognition as a man. Belinda spoke to me about losing her connection to lesbian community when her partner disengaged from it:

It was tough for me as someone who had just kind of come out as a lesbian. I remember wanting to do lesbian things and go to lesbian bars and that kind of stuff. And I remember a switch in him where he was like, "No, I'm a straight guy." And I think that was hard because there was this community that I was trying to get involved with that suddenly didn't work with his identity.... I didn't really know that there was the option of him saying, "I'm queer." I just figured that's what happened when someone became trans. You were a lesbian and now you're straight.

Belinda talked about the limited and often limiting nature of social models of identity in the context of transition. Belinda was unaware that there were other ways (than "straight male") for trans men in relationships with cis women to identify, and that these different identifications (if embraced by her partner) might generate alternate possibilities for *her own* identity and membership to social communities.

The cis women I interviewed provided an excellent example of the ways in which our identities often extend far beyond our own self-identifications and labels. Our identities are also deeply social, dependent upon others' acknowledgment or rejection of our belonging. In the following section, I consider some of these tensions in how the social aspect of our identities have consequences in the everyday lives of cis women partners of trans men.

INVISIBLY QUEER

Susan used to identify as lesbian prior to her relationship with a trans man. At the point of our interview, she was no longer partnered with a trans man. Her voice was filled with emotion as she talked to me about distinct dilemmas she now faced as the former partner of a trans man: "I lost my community. . . . You lose the lesbian community and you really don't get anything else. . . . And the partners' [of trans men] community; you're only a valid member of that as long as you're in your relationship, which has nothing to do with *you* and everything to do with *him*." For Susan, successfully carving out a space in the queer community often depended upon someone else's identity or perceived social status. Susan's experiences of being pushed out of lesbian community spaces upon partnering with a trans man was not uncommon. Rather than operating along explicit cut-and-dry practices of inclusion and exclusion, many cis women described more subtle social practices in which their rightful membership within lesbian community spaces was challenged or brought into question once they began relationships with trans men or once a previously lesbian-identified partner began to move away from that identity and transitioned to living as a trans man.

Ani discussed another challenge in her relationship with a partner who socially identified as a "man" rather than as a "transgender man": "It's a lot easier to be able to [say]: 'Yes, I'm queer, I'm dating a *trans man*', as opposed to, 'Yes, I'm queer, I'm dating a *man*'. People won't ask you to justify yourself in the same way. . . . Your sexuality clearly relies on your partner." Ani's partner's gender identity and recognition by social others as a man meant that her own queer identity was frequently made invisible, rendering her unremarkably heterosexual in the eyes of social others, including queer social others.

Nearly 30% of the cis women I interviewed self-identified, unprompted, as "femme," meaning that the actual number of femme-identifying and/or feminine-appearing cis women with whom I spoke is likely higher than 30%. Researchers have described the ways in which cis femme-identified women partners of trans men frequently experience a grieving process in connection to the perceived loss of their queer femme visibility.[48] Further, many of the participants in my study discussed how others' recognition of their queerness often relies upon their connection to a partner who embodies female masculinity in a visible and culturally intelligible way. For example, Teresa told me:

> I think as a femme ... I don't feel like I've ever been seen as queer when I've been by myself. I think so often in my history of dating people that the people that I dated would make me visibly queer. So, it's really interesting when the person I'm dating makes me *invisible*. And so, I don't gain any visibility as a lesbian or as someone who is queer when being out in public with [my trans partner] the way I would with past partners. So, that's really, really hard. However, in a way it sort of feels almost liberating because now I and only I am responsible for my queer visibility. ... I think that it's sexism, honestly, that femmes are seen as invisible beings when really we're radically queer in our own right and we're just never given that credit.

As Teresa describes, femme-appearing/identifying cis women partnered with trans men, therefore, may face particular barriers with regard to being recognized as a member of the communities to which they belong and with which they identify.[49]

As discussed in Chapter 1, these narratives echo earlier writings on lesbian butch and femme genders as socially intelligible identities around which communities materialized and organized.[50] Narratives like these also emerged as a striking empirical converse to Adam Isaiah Green,[51] who finds some members of the LGBTQ community identifying as "gay but not queer." These experiences of resisting queer invisibility among the cis women in this sample are shared by some individuals in other undertheorized and often invisible identity and social groups. For example, cisgender "opposite sex" partnerships wherein 1 or more partners is bisexual or queer identified, or partnerships that include at least 1 individual who is intersex.[52] Yet trans and intersex couples may face challenges that non-trans, non-intersex queer people in "opposite-sex" partnerships encounter less frequently, such as accessing legal marriage and having children. Of course, queer invisibility may also hold pragmatic potential for some queer people in terms of accessing regulated social and material resources.

Queer invisibility was of particular concern and consideration to many of the femme-identified cis women I interviewed.[53] Cis women talked to me about the ways in which queer femininities may not only be rendered invisible within both queer and nonqueer cultural spaces, but the ways in which they may also be explicitly devalued within some queer communities relative to queer androgynies and queer masculinities.[54] As Belinda told me:

> Basically within the lesbian community I was like completely made fun of. I used to have people make fun of me for carrying a purse and looking "too girly" and, "Oh you're not *really* gay." Just those kinds of comments. So, that was really hard for me when I was coming out because I just wanted to be taken seriously you know. ... So, my response to that [when I first came out] was to kind of change to become *less* feminine, change my body posturing and the way that I dress and cut off all my hair and that kind of stuff.

Another participant, Lily, spoke about how enactments of femininity felt anything but "natural" to her:

> It isn't 100% natural for me because I was raised kind of gender neutral. My toys were kind of ugly and I played with plastic animals and not Barbies. It's not 100% natural for me to act "like a woman." But I want to because I think it's cool. I had to learn what the hell base coat was when I was 25. I walked up to the makeup counter and was like, "Show me how to use these products. I don't know what they are or what they do at all." I'm not talking about makeup for special occasions. . . . I didn't even know how to apply mascara. It was this thing mom did in front of the mirror every morning that made me late for school. I just had no idea.

These narratives exemplify some queer cis women's experience of living in the liminal (in-between) space of insider/outsider with regard to both queer and nonqueer communities. Another compelling experience that cis women spoke to me about was their trans men partners asking them to change their gendered embodiments to appear *less* queer. Because identities are often socially read in relation to one another, if a cis woman is "read" as lesbian by others, her trans partner may be more likely to be read as lesbian as well. Because of this, some cis women reported that their trans partners requested that they grow or keep their hair longer, wear skirts or dresses, wear makeup, or shave their legs and underarms. These sorts of requests chafed against the queer and feminist subjectivities of many of my participants; some eventually consented to their partner's requests and others did not. Among those who mentioned these requests, most had trans partners who were fairly early in their transition process, a time during which being perceived by others as a man is often most tenuous.

Jane Ward[55] suggests that the sidelining of the power and transgressive potential of femme identity among cis women partners of trans men may be an artifact of their primary social status within trans communities as allies and supporters of their partners, one of the forms of "gender labor" in which they engage. Among my interviewees, some of the strategies that self-identified femme participants described for rendering their queer identities more recognizable included adopting unique hairstyles and hair colors, wearing rainbow jewelry and other LGBTQ pride symbols, dressing in vintage clothing, and obtaining visible tattoos and piercings, engaging in counter-normative embodiment practices with the intention of visually signifying their queer identities.[56] The cis women I interviewed were also quick to note that femme is not synonymous with weak or incapable. As a participant, Rachel, told me: "Even if I'm wearing a dress and heels I can still be tough or fix the air conditioner if it's broken; because my boyfriend's certainly not going to do it." Participants' narratives revealed the impact of being rendered invisible or an outsider not only in terms of one's own queer identity and relationship, but also in determining the parameters of in-group/out-group social membership itself.

CHASING IDENTITY LABELS

Some of the women I interviewed talked about having a general sexual preference that trended toward attraction to trans men specifically. As participants noted, there simply is not a widely recognized sexual identity category that specifically describes those individuals who are primarily attracted to trans men and/or trans women. While some individuals and groups have advanced terms such as "transsensual," the term has not really advanced to the point of becoming part of the lexicon, even within most LGBTQ communities. Further, some suggest that a sexual preference for dating and partnering with trans individuals is simply a fetish. One of the euphemistic terms to describe individuals (especially, though not exclusively, cisgender individuals) who tend to prefer trans people as sexual and/or romantic partners is "tranny chaser."[57]

Avery Brooks Tompkins, examining[58] trans-focused social media and conferences, generates a critical analysis of the "tranny chaser" label. Tompkins queries what effect the "tranny chaser" label may have on trans and trans-allied communities and social networks. Tompkins finds that the "tranny chaser" label generally assumes that the person being so labeled fetishizes trans identities and embodiments. Yet the subjects of Tompkins' analyses (cisgender women partners of transgender men) consistently refute such claims, arguing that erotic, affective, and romantic preference for trans partners does not insinuate fetishization of the trans identities or embodiments of said partners.

There was, however, a slippery slope as many individuals in Tompkins' study asserted that a hypothetical exclusive or intentional preference for trans partners *would* indicate fetishization or a troubling focus on an aspect of identity that some trans people, themselves, may not wish to have placed at the foreground. Tompkins postulates that the "tranny chaser" label has emerged, in large part, due to (a) the limited lexicon for expressing trans-focused desire in contemporary cultural discourse, and (b) a denial of the erotics of transness within trans community. Tompkins argues for a sex-positive revaluing of transness that does not require the denial of desire for transness, trans people, and trans embodiments, noting the potential of trans-produced, trans-focused, and trans-affirmative pornography to serve as a potential cultural model for such a revaluation. Tompkins further asserts that critical dialogues between cis and trans people around the "tranny chaser" label must occur so that truly exploitative or fetishizing relationship dynamics may be disentangled from those that are not.

IDENTITY AS A POLITICAL CHOICE

The experiences of cis women partners of trans men allow us to consider the complex social identity processes at play not only when social actors make *sex and gender* attributions, but when they make *sexual orientation* attributions as well. The cis women I interviewed often vocally asserted their self-identification as queer. Yet in many instances, these cis women's accounts focused on being (mis)recognized by both queer and nonqueer social others as unremarkably heterosexual. Which of these accounts of their sexual identity is "true?" These findings prompt consideration of how the social effects of (mis)recognition processes (e.g., being able to access regulated social institutions and social membership within particular groups) are powerfully structuring, perhaps even largely determinant, of social group membership. So, just how might we make sense of the following narrative from Martha, which is so emblematic of many of the responses that I received?

> I don't like passing as a straight woman. I would feel like I wasn't visible at times. And same with him, that he wasn't visible. . . . Both of our identities were very blurred; and that's a tough thing when so much of who we are is about other people perceiving us. . . . I like my queer identity and that's what I want people to see. So, it was tough when I knew that wasn't being seen.

Much of the thrust of the mainstream lesbian and gay social movement over the past several decades has focused on protesting and bringing greater public awareness to discrimination against lesbians and gay men as well as their exclusion from various social institutions and privileges, such as legally recognized marriage.[59]

In calling for expanded rights and inclusion, mainstream lesbian and gay social movements have largely centered upon crafting a politics of sameness and respectability that stand in stark contrast to the *oppositional* politics of activist groups of the late 1960s through the early 1990s such as the Gay Liberation Front, ACT UP, and Queer Nation.[60] Further, many of these more recent efforts depend largely upon appeals to the biological/genetic etiology of sexual orientation and gender identity (transformed into a pop culture anthem and rallying cry in 2011 through Lady Gaga's song, "Born This Way"). Couching demands for inclusion, equality, and freedom from discrimination within a framework of biological determinism consistently compels the following presumably rhetorical defense of these demands when they face social opposition: "In the context of such social discrimination and exclusion, why would anyone *choose* this?" Yet queer narratives and self-identifications provide evidence against the counterfactual claim that no one would choose queerness if given such an option, just as they simultaneously recognize and explicitly *value* queer identity and queer culture per se. They also reframe the issue of "choice" to consider that choosing to self-identify as queer is not synonymous with choosing social (mis)recognition, exclusion, and discrimination.

Rather, the cis women I interviewed often discussed their queer sexual politics as being deeply rooted in challenging existing social norms, speaking out against discrimination aimed toward those who transgress, and advocating for greater social equality and inclusion regardless of gender or sexual identity. Many of the cis women I interviewed for this project, in their outspoken self-identifications as queer, fissure normative assumptions of both mainstream lesbian and gay and heterosexual cultures as they raise their hands in response to the now-familiar social refrain: "Who would *choose* this?" As such, these cis women's claims assert a queer identity that poses challenges, inside/out, to the logics of both mainstream lesbian and gay social movements as well as normative cultural ideology, despite the persistent social and structural challenges they face when doing so.[61] As Michael Warner writes: "The preference for 'queer' represents, among other things, an aggressive impulse of generalization; it rejects a minoritizing logic of toleration or simple political interest-representation in favor of a more thorough resistance to regimes of the normal."[62]

In following sections, I further explore examples of the ways in which the experiences of the cis women partners of trans men I studied broaden existing understandings of contemporary partnerships and families. In particular, I will consider some of the diversity that often exists within these queer partnerships and families in order to trouble the misconception that partnerships between cis women and trans men are a monolith. Despite the fact that I examined only 1 type of transgender family in my research (cis women partnered with trans men), these partnerships and families exhibited considerable diversity with regard to differences between partners across the areas of age, educational attainment and socioeconomic status, feminist self-identification, body size and ability, and race and ethnicity.

Diversity Within and Across Trans Partnerships and Families

There were, on average, about 2 years age difference between the cis women I interviewed and their partners, with a range in age difference between partners from 0 to 11 years. When there was an age difference, the cis women I interviewed tended to be older than their partners. Cis women reported higher educational attainment than their trans partners.[63] Of the cis women providing complete data on socioeconomic class origins for both themselves and their trans partner,[64] most reported that they and their partner were of a similar social class growing up.[65] But when cis women did report that there was a discrepancy in social class status growing up, they tended to report that their own socioeconomic status was lower[66] than that of their trans partner. Cis women were also more likely to self-identify as feminist than their trans men partners.[67]

While most participants did not describe differences in body size or ability levels between themselves and their trans partners, when they did it was most often they who were considerably larger than their partner. The cis women I interviewed who self-identified as disabled were more likely to report being in a partnership with a trans partner who also self-identified as disabled. While most of the cis women (90%) I interviewed were White,[68] just over a quarter[69] described partnerships with trans men whose race or ethnicity was not the same as their own. While I discuss the ways in which the experiences of trans people and their partners are shaped by and through many of these demographic characteristics across each of the chapters in this book, in the following sections,

I provide a more in-depth focus across several of these critical areas of intra-couple diversity to consider the ways in which such differences may shape queer partnerships and family life.

Age

Perceived and actual differences in age between partners was a notable trend across my interviews. Of the 50 cis women I interviewed, 16 (32%) reported an age difference between themselves and their partner that exceeded 5 years. When there was an age difference that exceeded 5 years, it was most often (63% of the time) the cis partner who was older than her trans partner. When I asked Tabitha if the 9-year age difference between her and her partner was ever something they discussed, she said:

> I bring up the age thing a lot. I think it made me kind of insecure and stuff. . . . He was talking about how in the past he has been with people who fetishized him because he's trans or because of he's a person of color and he's [playfully] like, "You just fetishize me because I'm so young," and I was all, "It's always something!"

The potential for age disparities to affect a partnership extended beyond the couple, and some of the cis women I interviewed talked to me about how age differences between partners could be disparaged by friends or family as well.

As Tabitha mentioned: "I think some of my friends just thought that he was a lot younger than me and didn't have too much to offer me and I was kind of just 'making do' with someone." When I asked Tabitha to reflect on stereotypes about people with younger partners and to consider if there are particular advantages to having a younger partner, she said:

> I don't identify as mommy who's into like a little boy or anything like that but I think sometimes . . . we go out and I think I would sometimes order for us and things like that. He's got a lot of energy and stamina. You know [younger people] have innocence and naïveté and they're not totally jaded at all in the world; which is nice for someone who is . . . to see the world through their eyes.

Other cis women I interviewed worried that, at times, their romantic partnership did assume a maternal dynamic, especially at the beginning of transition. According to Selma:

> I told him the other day, "Sometimes I feel like you are such a 14-year-old and I'm your mother." For a long time he was Peter Brady. That time of change, he hated that. He would laugh and he would say something and crack his voice. So, our thing around our house is, "We're growing a boy!"

His voice has really, really dropped. . . . So, when he gets up in the morning we now have Barry White. Broadening of his shoulders, his face. . . . His features look more masculine to me. Maybe a roughening of the skin. There's a little baby, pre-pubescent mustache still. He's not a hairy person. I don't think he comes from hairy people. He's really kind of disappointed that there's not a little bit more there. But it's really funny; I've talked to other partners of trans men that are much farther along in their transition and they go, "Oh my God you're going to get so sick of hearing about every new follicle." And we're at the point now where he's like, "Look, honey, I've got more fuzzies on my butt!" It's really cute. He's completely adorable. But I just kind of go, after a while, "Yes, dear, I see that."

Celebrating a trans partner's budding body hair growth after beginning testosterone was often likened to celebrating puberty. But because this event was being experienced anachronistically, it could feel to some cis partners as if they were a parent celebrating with an adolescent, which evoked an uncomfortable maternalism for some, especially when it was exaggerated by actual or perceived age differences.

In addition to actual age differences between my participants and their partners, the former frequently spoke about others erroneously *perceiving* that their trans partner was much younger than they actually were. Especially during early transition, before the development of facial hair, many trans men appear younger than their chronological age given their shorter (relative to cis men) average height, smaller hands, and rounder faces. For some cis women partners of trans men, this meant that they were sometimes rendered invisible as a partner and, instead, assumed to be a friend, sister, or even mother in some instances. Veronica told me: "I think the only reason that we actually get stared at sometimes is because we both look so young. [My trans partner] looks about 13 and a lot of trans-guys do. I'm 21 but I look 16 so we look a little weird in a bar." As Lily described a former partner: "He probably looks like a young boy because he's very short, shorter than me, and has such delicate features that he probably passes, but as the wrong age. He's 22 and he probably looks like an 11-year-old boy." Nina concurred: "He is really young looking. I mean people definitely think that he is not old enough to be driving when he drives a car. And that's something that he really can't control, looking like a really young guy."

Belinda told me that her 21-year-old partner "reads like an 18-year-old gay boy." Ani offered a similar assessment to describe her 21-year-old partner: "He passes as 15, but he does pass. I worry that strangers perceive us as straight but I feel like that won't happen truly for a while partly because he looks so young. So, it's kind of like he looks a little bit young, and I look a little bit dykey, so I feel like people look at us and they see something queer even if they can't necessarily put their finger on it." As Lilia (whose partner was 24 years old) noted, a trans partner's perceived age could shift through choices that he makes to shave or not shave: "He kind of looks like this 16-year-old boy. But when he has a beard, he definitely looks older and he definitely looks male." Another interviewee, Lily, told me that her partner's acne flares, a common symptom of testosterone administration, could also give him the social appearance of a younger person.

Finding acceptance for one's partnership among friends and family was mentioned as a potential issue when partners were considerably older or younger than one another. Amber, who is 8 years younger than her trans partner, told me:

> It was an issue to our friends I guess more so than it really was us. I didn't know he was that old when I first met him and then when I found out it was kind of . . . not a shock but it was just like a step back, "Oh he's really cute but I can't date someone that old." But we talked about it and we decided that we really didn't care. It was just our friends that would make comments every once in a while that would tease him or tease me about it. . . . My mother knows and she was more bothered by the fact that he was [much older than me] than the fact that he was FTM. . . . She was like, "Well, we just won't tell your father. I'm okay with it, I guess, but we just won't tell your dad." Now my dad knows and he doesn't really care. They've met him. It was more so in the beginning and now we're just kind of over it. It was just how were other people going to react to it? It didn't really bother us so much.

In some instances, however, being considerably older than one's partner, and being an older couple in general, was seen as granting particular advantage.

Donna, who is 7 years older than her trans partner, spoke to me about how being older grants her and her partner stability across a number of areas in their lives, something that many younger couples in her social networks struggle to attain. I asked Donna to describe some of those areas of strength and stability:

> Money for instance. We are just older, more stable, more financially stable, even though we're both very working class. We're also both very responsible financially so we just have money in a different way or can save money in a different way. Stability of relationships . . . again, we're just enough older that we kind of got it that this was going to probably be the one that we would live out our lives in this relationship. So, the commitment is there. I don't have to worry about him going away and he doesn't really have to worry about me going away.

Drea also talked to me about differences that she perceived between her own situation, and those of younger trans couples. While Drea is 7 years younger than her partner, the fact that her partner is older meant that the couple tended to lean toward social support networks that consisted largely of older participants, which could be challenging to find:

> For some reason, here a lot of them are very young. . . . And they're just not that coordinated in anything at that point in their life. I'm 28 and he's 35.

I just don't have anything in common with an 18-year-old. It's kind of like just because someone might be trans doesn't mean they're going to have anything else in common with you.

Kendra found herself on the flip side of this age-related support dilemma in trans community spaces:

It's hard finding support as a partner of a trans person. And especially being young, I kind of find that some of the support groups that I have found kind of almost discount my experience. I think that some of the people that I've interacted with thought that because I was young ... it wasn't important that I was there ... or that any advice that I had to give was discounted because "What does a 21-year-old have to offer to us?"

In this way, both actual and perceived age differences between partners held the power to highlight the ways in which age matters in affecting whether trans people and their partners will be recognized as partners and the sorts of access they may have to regulated social groups and resources as well (read more about this in Chapter 6).

Educational Attainment and Social Class

On average, the cis women I interviewed had higher educational attainment than their trans men partners. Around 60% of the cis women I interviewed had a Bachelor's degree or higher, while just under 50% of their trans men partners had reached this level of educational attainment. These educational differences were most stark when examining postgraduate educational attainment. More than 25% of the cis women I interviewed had earned master's or doctoral-level degrees, as opposed to just 13% of their trans partners. Potential contributors to these differences include cis women in my sample being more likely to be White and older than their trans men partners, reflecting existing age and race discrepancies in educational access and attainment, which also intersect with socioeconomic status.

Although usually mentioned only when discussing the high economic cost of transition, there is a remarkable lack of academic theorizing around social class and trans identity. Hansbury[70] has developed a taxonomy of transmasculine identity driven by age, race, education, and class-based distinctions among men. In essence, Hansbury's work prompts consideration of transmasculine identity along a spectrum rather than as a monolithic entity. According to Hansbury's taxonomy, trans men may be broadly classified into 3 groups: *woodworkers*, *transmen*, and *genderqueers*.

Woodworkers—so-named because they tend to want to "blend into the wood-work as men"—disidentify from their history as girls or women and are often described as conforming to essentialist notions of sex and gender. Woodworkers tend to constitute the oldest group and are described as mostly working class with little to no college education. Members of the group categorized as transmen are in the middle age group and generally described as more educated and with a higher socioeconomic status, relative to woodworkers. Members of this group identify as men, but as a particular type of man distinct from the experiences of cis men. While they wish to be recognized as men in the world, they are often comfortable discussing their history as girls or as women. Finally, those described as genderqueers are classified as largely social constructionist when it comes to understandings of sex and gender and may disidentify with categories such as "man" or "woman" altogether. Genderqueers are described as the youngest group, comprising those who are mostly White, college educated, and middle to upper class.[71] Among the trans partners of the cis women in my study, classifications spanned across all of these possible ranges, with genderqueer classification being the least common and transmen being the most common. However, cis women explained that their trans partner's ability and desire to be recognized as a cis man, a trans man, or as genderqueer was not necessarily static across either time or social context, an important consideration that many taxonomies fail to consider.

One of the class- and race-based critiques that often emerges from within trans communities is the rather exclusive nature of membership to certain categories of trans identity. For example, given the relatively high costs of gender affirmation surgeries, alongside the fact that most insurance companies do not offer these medical services as a covered benefit, only a select group of trans individuals, disproportionately White and middle class, tends to have access to gender affirmation surgeries. While surgeries tend to exclude many trans men from access to specific forms of trans embodiment, the high cost of other trans-related products may be inaccessible as well. Jay Sennet, for example, offers a cartoon drawing of a prosthetic penis with a price tag on it that reads, "$59.99." The accompanying caption states: "I guess you could call it penis envy."[72] This cartoon, though humorous, highlights the differential access (on the basis of class) to products that may enable various trans embodiments and identities.

Trans communities might benefit from an analysis similar to that conducted by Kennedy and Davis,[73] on working-class lesbian identity from 1930–1960, in order to discern if rifts within and across particular subsections of LGBTQ communities might be largely inflected or produced by class differences. As Raine Dozier notes:

> Not all FTMs gain social status by being perceived as men. It is a common assumption, bordering on urban legend, that transitioning brings with it improved status, treatment, and financial opportunities. However, having a paper trail including a previous female name and identity can severely compromise job prospects, especially in a professional position.[74]

While gender transition may not be a guarantee of future professional and economic success, we do know that interpersonal and economic security are critical to overall well-being. As Katherine Rachlin notes: "The outcome research indicates that satisfaction with life after gender transition is more likely when individuals have solid professional lives, good family relationships, good social support networks, and are emotionally stable."[75]

The cis women I interviewed discussed various ways in which socioeconomic differences between themselves and their partners, or between their class status as a couple and those of other individuals and couples, could present challenges interpersonally and in terms of developing community support networks. As Lynne discussed:

> I think there were times with [my trans partner] that issues of class would come up because I grew up middle class and he grew up working class. I think there were things that I took for granted, as far as money and stuff would go, that were a constant struggle and issue for him. And I think that a lot of times I would want to do things that involved money and, for me, it wasn't an issue because I grew up with this feeling that money would be there. But for him, he didn't grow up with that. So, at times there would be issues like I wanted to do something that cost a certain amount of money and he wouldn't want to do that. And it wasn't necessarily that he didn't have the money then. It was just this perception that it might not be there later.

Sage also spoke to me about the impact of her and her ex-partner having very different social class origins and experiences:

> He has always been working class or poor.... That's always been something that he's been very aware of and that has really shaped his own experiences. And, for me, while I can really respect that and while we could have discussions about that, it wasn't part of my own history and my family history. Since I was in a relationship with him I have come to terms with the fact that my family is fairly well off and I'm really fortunate.... I've been aware that I have privilege and ability to do whatever as it relates to money or financial stuff. I've been really aware of my privilege but I hadn't really been comfortable with it and I hadn't really thought about it a lot.... And so that was hard for me at times because I definitely felt sort of guilty ... like class guilt ... because I always had my parents' financial support if I needed it.... So, there definitely were tensions there where my past partner was very aware that my family didn't struggle with money.

For both Lynne and Sage, then, having a higher social class status than a trans partner could present challenges or tensions between partners as trans partners considered their relative economic disadvantage and cis partners acknowledged or grappled with relative class privilege.

Yet this was not the only possibility. When a differential in social class status existed between partners, the cis women in my sample tended to report lower social class status growing up relative to their trans partners. Economic social class status differences, however, could be attenuated by educational attainment. As Eva told me:

> I grew up working class and my partner grew up upper middle class. But we were both sort of creating independent lives as firmly middle class, educated people. And everything having to do with trans issues we approach from feminist theory. I don't know, we're sort of bourgeois in that way. And then we would meet these other people and, at the time, we were living in a really working class city, and then so the other trans people that we were meeting, that wasn't appealing to them. That wasn't necessarily the language that they spoke.

Other cis women I interviewed, who had a lower socioeconomic status growing up relative to their trans partner, were cognizant of the ways in which their partner's economic privilege could provide expanded possibilities around options for gender transition. Gail spoke about having a wealthy trans partner and how his transition experiences were starkly different from those with fewer material resources: "If you have a ton of money you can change your gender pretty quickly."

Other participants spoke to me about how their social class status meant that their world view and political focus may be different from mainstream trans or feminist politics. When I asked Julie to describe her level of feminist self-identification, she offered an answer that highlighted the importance of attending to the ways in which identities are always intersectional:

> Since I'm not a middle-class American, sexism is not an oppression I tend to focus on very much. I see it all the time and I call people on it because there are so many women around me. But I actually tend to put more effort and take more risk around calling people on their racism than sexism because racism sort of indirectly impacts me more since all anti-immigrant policies are actually just racist policies. What I'm saying is that my immigrant and queer identities are more important to me and affect me more, therefore I identify that way. . . . My entire community is pretty much middle-class, White, queer Americans . . . most of them very strongly identify as feminists . . . [but] I don't focus on that oppression much except for as a subset of all my social justice values.

These narratives demonstrated the diversity that exists not only between the cis women I interviewed and their trans partners, but among cis women and trans men as well.

Feminist Self-Identification

While the cis women I interviewed described many different ways of being feminist or relating to feminism, most had been strongly influenced by "Third Wave" feminist politics emphasizing free will, performativity, individuality, and choice.[76] For some cis women, like Julie, their feminist ideals were also strongly inflected by a broader human rights and social justice frame. As with many of the areas I asked about, participants' relationship to feminism wasn't necessarily static across their lives. For example, Anna told me that she had a rather "up and down" relationship to feminism over the course of her life:

> I came to a point in my life of feeling really sort of annoyed with what I thought was the racial and class bias of the feminist movement overall and the sort of limited vision of who women were or what they could be. So, I went through a period of time, like when I was 18. I started to call myself a feminist and then a dozen years later, or maybe 15 years later, being like, "I'm not a feminist!" because I didn't want to be associated with what people thought that was. And maybe in the last 10 years [I] kind of came back around to, "Well I just need to make that word mean what I believe it is or should be." So, for me, being a feminist is much more about human rights and kind of empowerment of people; not just women, but of everybody. Everybody having equal access to healthcare, to housing, you know? Those kinds of things. So, it feels like it's some of that awareness of the need for everybody to have that access that came out of an original understanding of the lack of access that *women* had, but then grew beyond that.

This growing *beyond* the constraints of understanding feminism as a politics rooted solely in gender and gender equality formed the core of a number of participants' narratives about their feminist self-identifications. This was particularly true of those participants who reported higher levels of education, particularly at the graduate level.

Not all of the cis women I interviewed, however, strongly identified as feminist. Indeed, some reported that their trans partners were more aligned with and supportive of feminist politics than they.[77] When I asked Amber if she self-identifies as feminist, she told me:

> I think it's great for those who want to do it really hardcore and want to believe in it. I mean, I've taken women's studies classes and when you're in the class it's really easy to get caught up in it and really believe. But then when you get out of the class and you still want to put on high heels. Like where does that put you? Am I contradicting everything I just learned? I think it's great. I do believe in a lot of it, I just don't have it written on my shirt. I don't go out preaching it. . . . I guess I just am not really hardcore about it.

I next asked her: "What about your partner, do you think he would self-identify as feminist or not?" She said: "He's got a lot more respect and would probably be more open as feminist than I would be. That might be just because he's older and understands it more and has more life experience with it. . . . He's got a lot of respect for women and women's issues."

Amber was 19 years of age at the time of our interview; like several of the youngest participants in my study, she reported being more disconnected from feminist politics or self-identification as a feminist. This did not mean, however, that their trans partners were similarly disconnected or did not self-identify as feminist, particularly when these partners were older or had completed some college education (Amber's partner, for example, was 27 years of age and had completed 3 years of college at the point of our interview). In addition to age and feminist self-identification, another characteristic that marked some cis women as different from their trans partners was body size and ability.

Body Size and Ability

While most of the focus on bodies tends to fall onto trans people whenever they are part of a conversation, the cis women I interviewed spoke to me about other embodied differences between themselves and their partners, often having nothing to do with trans embodiments per se. One of the differences that Tabitha spoke to me about, in intersection with other areas of difference between herself and her partner, was body size. As Tabitha told me:

> I definitely got more comments with my partner who is a lot younger than me, a lot smaller than me, and isn't White. I'm sure we look like a very odd pair. . . . I think outsiders would see some punk-rock woman in her late 20s/ early 30s, with a bunch of tattoos, tall, fat, with, I don't know, probably like just some 14- or 15-year-old [appearing] Black or Latino boy and just think, "Huh. That's kind of an odd pair." But, hey, what are you going to do? I think at first I felt a little unsure about being with someone so tiny. He probably weighs at least half of my weight if not less. And then I just didn't care anymore. And it's sort of nice to feel over that now and if it came up with someone else it wouldn't feel as weird because I've already been through that and realized that it didn't really matter. He's a chubby chaser, which was another reason I felt kind of comfortable with him. I mean in some ways it's kind of problematic for someone to have a fetish but, I don't know, it can also be just kind of like a breath of fresh air too when you feel like a lot of people are kind of discriminating against bigger people. So, I don't know. It's fine by me. I don't really care.

Anna discussed her thoughts about the fact that she is in an interracial relationship and also a relationship in which partners have different body sizes.

I asked her how she thought strangers likely viewed her partner and her when they walk down the street together. She told me:

> Well, certainly on the surface, on the sort of walking down the street being a man-woman kind of thing, it's fitting into everybody's notion of the, you know, general social norms. Yet there's a hundred ways that it doesn't. So, most obviously and most visibly actually in terms of us being an interracial couple but also I'm really large. I'm a fat woman. And I'm aware all the time of all the ways that socially there's pressure on men to not acknowledge their attraction to large women. And that he's totally like . . . if he's aware of that, he doesn't show that at all. He's like, "I love you. I think you're beautiful and I want everyone to know it." So, I'm like always aware of that being outside of conventional norms.

Some of the fat cis women with whom I spoke talked to me about their concerns about fat-admirers or "chubby chasers" and the possibility of being sexually fetishized. They sometimes drew parallels between these concerns and, as discussed earlier in this chapter, other people's assertions that cis women who are sexually attracted to, or partnered with, trans men must be "tranny chasers."[78]

Like body size, not much empirical work has been conducted on disability and trans identity. Notable exceptions to this research gap at the intersection of disability, trans identity, partnerships, and families appear in the work of Eli Claire,[79] a trans man with cerebral palsy, and Joe Samson,[80] a self-identified fat "other-gendered boy." The disabled cis women I interviewed were much more likely than nondisabled participants in the sample to report instances of struggling with poverty and homelessness. In some instances, cis women who were disabled spoke about partnering with trans men who were disabled as well. Defying stereotypical assumptions linking disability with helplessness, participants spoke about managing their everyday lives in ways that were strategic and revealed the importance of interdependence.

In one instance, when a cis woman was unable to attend to a series of physical tasks due to her chronic illness, her trans partner completed those tasks on her behalf. Later, when he found himself in need of medical care, she was able to provide that support for him. While each of the partners' chronic health conditions placed certain limits on their lives and induced additional stressors, they were also described as bringing the couple closer together and serving as a shared identity that brought awareness and knowledge that those without these conditions generally do not have.

I asked a cis woman whom I interviewed, Josie, who identified as fat and disabled, if she felt that there were any areas of convergence or divergence between her experiences as a fat disabled person and her partner's experiences as a trans person. She said:

> I think there are in terms of some of the dynamics of living in a body that doesn't necessarily fit into what you're told your body should be. Like you

just have to relate to your body in a different way. That has a lot of space in it for imagination and recreating and redefining. And also I think that there are some kind of contrasts that could be almost in conflict. I think a lot of my process around empowerment around being a fat girl is acceptance and being like, "This is my body. This is what it is." And the same with disability. Being like, "This is what it is and my power in this is to accept and incorporate it into the fullness of who I am and keep moving." And for the people that I know who have gone through some kind of physical transition around gender, it's different than that. It's "I'm changing my [body] so that I can be more comfortable in the world," and that's hard for me.

Josie's experiences highlighted the potential areas of convergence and divergence that disabled people, fat people, and trans people may experience in relation to their bodies and identities. While some struggles may be shared or aligned, others remain quite distinct. In the following section, I provide more extended consideration of an additional site of potential difference between the identities of cis women and their trans men partners that some participants discussed: race and ethnicity.

Race and Ethnicity

While 90% of the cis women I interviewed were White, their partners were less likely to be so (77%). More than a quarter of the relationships that the cis women I interviewed described were identified by them as interracial or interethnic. While many women spoke about the enriching aspects of racial and ethnic diversity within their relationships, others discussed particular challenges they faced. Lilia (who identifies as White, Native American, and Black) told me that she feels "isolated" in her identity as a woman of color dating a White trans man and that she has not encountered many others like her in the LGBTQ community who share this experience. She said:

There's all these dynamics. There's gender dynamics, race dynamics. For me, as a Black woman to be dating a White man is very specific. And also, me as a mixed woman with light-skin privilege to identify as a Black woman and to be dating this White man. What does that mean? Who is approving of that? Who is frowning upon that? And it's something I don't feel like I can discuss with everyone.

Lilia also noted concerns that circulated in her family and community: "It would be like, 'All the good women are being taken by White men.' Mostly though it was, 'All the good men are being taken by White women.'" Some participants spoke to me about within-group differences with regard to naming practices. For example, Anna told me that her trans partner (who is Black) self-identifies as "gay," but not in the same way that some White trans men tend to take up this term. Rather than being attracted to and dating other men, for Anna's partner being "gay" meant being attracted to (and dating) cis women while having a personal history of being seen by others as a woman who dates other women.[81] These differences in how language is used and understood may further complicate the shifting identities that many cis women have reported across this chapter, particularly as these identities are understood or recognized by others outside the relationship.

An important trend emerged among some White cis women I interviewed. It was fairly common for White cis women to tell me they had nothing to report upon with regard to race or racial dynamics in their relationships, even among those who reported being in a current or former interracial relationship with a trans partner. This absence of critical analysis around race may speak to the cultural prevalence of "colorblind" approaches to contemporary race relations. Amy Steinbugler refers to the practices through which those in interracial relationships navigate issues connected to race in their partnerships and families as "intimate racework."[82] Steinbugler, focusing on interracial lesbian, gay, and straight couples (all of whom are presumably cisgender), discusses the strategies and techniques that partners use to manage racial difference in their relationships when embedded in a society in which racial inequalities are persistent and rife. She explores these strategies and techniques as everyday iterative practices across social situations as well as within one's own partnership and families. Steinbugler's work challenges the notion that interracial relationships are evidence for colorblindness or racial neutrality in postmodern partnerships and families. Instead, Steinbugler demonstrates the particular forms of intimate labor in which those in interracial relationships often must engage around race and racial politics in these partnerships and families.

In Steinbugler's study, she found that same-sex interracial couples tended to become invisible in public spaces, while heterosexual interracial couples became hypervisible. In my research, similar trends emerged, though they were also filtered through the lens of gender attribution and contained a temporal dimension. For some cis women who were with their trans partner prior to his transition, and who were once seen as a same-sex interracial couple, they reported experiencing the shift from invisibility to hypervisibility following their partner's transition and the public (mis)recognition of them as an interracial heterosexual couple.

Indeed, the cis women in interracial relationships with trans men whom I interviewed described engaging in many of the same types of intimate racework that Steinbugler outlines in her study of cisgender couples. Some of the White cis women I interviewed went out of their way to assure me that they were not the sort of White person to take a noncritically conscious approach toward race and racial relations. Some cis women of color in partnerships with White trans men spoke about their partners' involvement in antiracist activism, while others described their White trans partners as relatively clueless about race and racial inequalities, often making jokes about this cluelessness or minimizing it with humor. Some of the cis women with whom I spoke, most often those who were White and in partnerships with trans men of color, told me that race was simply not an issue in their partnership or that race had no impact on their interactions with their partner.

These sorts of "colorblind" approaches might indicate relative lack of aware-ness of racial inequalities and discrimination, a belief in the racial exceptional-ism of one's partner, or perhaps even "racial fatigue," as Steinbugler terms it: the experience of simply becoming exhausted from constantly dealing with race and race issues in one's life. Not all of my participants, however, were able to take comfort or reprieve in such "colorblind" approaches. One participant, who identified as Black, recounted a conversation she had with a White LGBTQ com-munity member friend of her White partner's who had asked her to come to an event at a local bar: "'Bless your heart for not seeing me as a brown person, but I'm not going to that redneck bar with you. Are there any other Black people there?' 'No. Why? I don't see you as Black.' 'Well, you don't, but the guy over there with the rope does.'" Other cis women in interracial relationships described feeling either invisible or hypervisible as a couple, depending on social context. Not infrequently, the cis women I interviewed discussed the salience of their interracial partnerships in the context of their relationships with their own and their trans partner's family of origin. Some cis women described mediating these relationships not only to help their or their partner's family better understand trans issues, but to assist them in navigating race issues as well. In some families, the importance of transgender identity fell away somewhat as racial differences rose to the forefront.

In other instances, racial or ethnic differences between partners were described as a catalyst for personal consciousness raising as well as political action and activism around race. Nina described her father's race/ethnicity as White and mother's race/ethnicity as Colombian. Personally, she self-identifies as White and Latina. Nina told me that her trans partner identifies as White. She said:

> In the same ways that we both identify as feminist, we also identify as peo-ple who look White but try to live in antiracist ways. So, [me] being some-one who doesn't identify totally as White has come up in our relationship and is part of our lives in terms of him validating that and knowing what that means to me, knowing how we are different. And also me understand-ing that there are a lot of things about him that are very different from other White guys that I have dated because his parents are immigrants and so race is present in terms of us being pretty self-conscious people about it in general and then being really talkative about his experience as a White person and my experience as someone who is biracial.

Terry (who identifies as Black) told me that her trans partner (whom she describes as White) has "good politics" around race, but that she had encountered many White individuals in the queer community whose politics were not aligned with her own. As she said:

> The queer community, the queer youth of today that are going around screaming about tacking [LGBTQ liberation] onto civil rights. Are they really ready to sacrifice what the first civil rights people were willing to

sacrifice? I really don't think they're ready for that. I hate to say these things because they're so general, everybody's different, but as a single loud voice it's like a legacy that they're talking about tacking themselves onto, a centuries-old legacy. And that pisses a lot of Black people off. It pisses a lot of people in the Civil Rights Movement off. They see some kid kicking around with purple hair and stretchers in their ears and they shift to their parents and they're like middle class Bob and Sue Smith and they're like, "Who the fuck are you? How dare you step up and say this to me that 'It's just like civil rights, we know what it's like.' Kiss my ass!" And that's the general picture that people get. That's what they see, these suburban refugees that are in college. That's my favorite oxymoron: oppressed college dykes. Really? Bless your heart.

In this instance, Terry takes issue with White, middle-class members of the LGBTQ community who draw overly simplistic analogies to the Civil Rights Movement (and its strategies and gains) to advance LGBTQ rights. An interesting component of this analysis is that Terry is quite literally marking her own experiences and political perspectives as distinct from others with whom she might be regularly grouped together (cis women partners of trans men), demonstrating the importance of not viewing this group in an overly simplistic way.

Just as cis women partners of trans men are not a monolithic group, neither are their trans men partners. Anna (who identifies as White) told me that her trans partner (who identifies as Black) does not always feel that his own experiences and perspectives are reflected among trans men more broadly. For instance, Anna told me that her partner often told her that "White guys have a dick thing," to contrast his own disinterest in bottom surgery with his perception of White trans men's relatively greater interest. Anna also discussed her awareness that particular treatment options, with regard to medically facilitated gender transition, are not equally available or accessible to all trans men. Indeed, race can play a critical role in determining availability, access, and outcomes when it comes to psychotherapy, hormone use, and transition-related surgeries and prostheses.

Intimate interactions connected to sex, bodies, and romance, which are described in greater depth in Chapter 4, were a particular site that could highlight complex intersections between sex, gender, and race. As Tabitha, a White participant,[83] told me when thinking about her Black and Latino trans partner: "I had a drawer full of dicks and they were all White-person-flesh color and I wouldn't ask him to use one on me because I just thought that might be seen as offensive." Some of the cis women I interviewed talked to me about cultural anxieties surrounding interracial intimacy as they have surfaced in their own interracial partnerships and families.

Anna, a White cis woman, told me that her mother (her father is deceased) is not aware that her partner is trans and was quite relieved when she married him. She told me that her mother is much less happy, however, about the fact that her husband is Black. Anna said that it is probably a good thing that her father is no longer alive since she assumes that he, too, would be quite upset that she

married a Black man. In this instance, Anna and her partner enjoy heteronormative privilege given that her mother recognizes her trans partner as a man, but
they do not benefit from the racial privilege that many monoracial trans couples
may enjoy and take for granted.

For other cis women I interviewed, ethnocultural differences translated to distinct family experiences between partners, made more stark when each partner
interacted with the other's family. Ellia (who identifies as Latina and whose partner identifies as White) told me:

> As far as family goes, it's been my experience that Latino people are very
> family-centered. And so I have my immediate family, my extended family,
> my second cousins, and we're all very close-knit. And I noticed with his
> family, and with a lot of other [White people] ... I hate to generalize but
> this is something that we've noticed in our relationship ... is they don't
> really communicate a lot. So, like, when we were going to tell our fami-
> lies [about our relationship] he told his immediate family and let it slowly
> trickle down to like an aunt and an uncle. And I told my mother, an aunt,
> another aunt, a couple of my cousins, because they're all so close. And so
> that's a big difference. And also, my family is very loud. . . . I guess just fam-
> ily involvement would be the big thing. His immediate family is very, very
> close but that's so weird to me to see the outlying family isn't.

Given that our own families often serve as the first socializing agents for what
families are like, encountering family dynamics and patterns that are distinct
from those with which one is most familiar can be a simultaneously illuminating
and jarring experience.

The cis women I interviewed spoke to me not only about how race and ethnicity may shape family dynamics and patterns, but also about how race and gender
intersect and are "read" or recognized on the body by social others. Bella, who is
White, spoke to me about her multiracial (Asian and White) trans partner and
how his racial and trans identity intersect when it comes to social perceptions as
well as their identity as a couple together in public. She said that, as her partner
transitioned, he did not develop much facial hair, and she noted that smooth
facial skin was relatively more common among Asian men than men of other
races. In this instance, we are prompted to consider how gendered embodiments
may also be racialized in particular ways, which carries implications for whether
and which trans men will be recognized as men and within which contexts. The
cis women I interviewed also detailed their struggles to find communities of
social support when members of those communities often had backgrounds considerably different from their own. I asked Nina to talk to me about what finding
community looks like for her:

> That looks like just trying to connect to people ... trying to meet people
> who know the differences between various Spanish-speaking cultures. That
> is a big part of it. It is just like being somewhere and if I don't pass as White

then sort of the discussion around like, "Well, what kind of not-White are you?" I haven't met that many Colombian people outside of Colombia, so I'm really trying to take advantage of being around people who are familiar with the culture, who are immigrants, whose parents are immigrants. And I've still met just a handful of biracial or multiracial people. It is something I am still struggling with and working on; like "What is the connection there?" For me, at this point, it is about staying connected with having conversations with my mom around her past, keeping in touch with relatives, and just trying to connect to whoever I can where I am at.

While maintaining connections with others was an important goal and strategy for obtaining social support and a sense of well-being and safety, participants described discrimination as a particular threat to their, their partner's, and their family's well-being and safety.

When I asked Charlene (who identifies as White) about any experiences she or her partner (who identifies as Canadian Aboriginal) have had with trans-related discrimination, she told me that he encounters racial discrimination far more frequently than trans discrimination. While it might be assumed that transitioning from female to male necessarily involves moving from an oppressed to a privileged social status, such analyses often fail to consider how intersections of race and gender produce differing social locations. In sociological studies of transgender men, some Black individuals who transition from female to male report facing additional employment-related discrimination[84] and may be perceived as dangerous or violent by others,[85] consonant with virulent racial stereotypes about Black men. Sociologist Raine Dozier[86] notes that Black trans men have discussed how, rather than becoming "gender traitors" for accessing male privilege, they often experience diminished social status and power when they transition. One of Dozier's research participants states:

I am a Black male. I'm the suspect. I'm the one you have to be afraid of. I'm the one from whom you have to get away, so you have to cross the street, you have to lock your doors. You have to clutch whatever you've got a little closer to your body ... It's very difficult to get White FTMs to understand that ... [As a Black person], if I go into a store, I am followed. Now I am openly followed; before it was, "Oh, let's hide behind the rack of bread or something so that she won't see us." Now it's, "Oh, it's a guy, he's probably got a gun; he's probably got a knife. We have to know where his hands are at all times."[87]

To date, there are no published, full-length autobiographies of Black trans men. Of the 4 trans autobiographies published by men of color,[88] all but 1 of the authors[89] are mixed-race and are often (mis)recognized, socially, as White.

Three films that do substantively engage with Black trans identities are the 2003 production, *Venus Boyz*, focusing on the life and performance art of Dréd Gerestant; Daniel Peddle's (2005) documentary, *The Aggressives*; and Kortney

Ziegler's (2008) documentary, *Still Black: A Portrait of Black Transmen*. In an anthology of trans experience, Wyatt Swindler[90] writes:

> Young Black men manage to be both the epitome and the antithesis of masculinity: all that is feared and coveted of manhood. I have known these things since I was a young boy. In order to survive I've memorized the expectations and limitations of Black masculinity. I have been hurt, silenced and terrorized by what it means to be a Black man. After so many years of wanting to gain unqualified acceptance into the world of Black men, I am realizing that I have much to learn about what it means for me to be one.

In a powerful poem, Imani Henry discusses the echoes between historical and contemporary forms of White racist oppression, potentials for subverting racism, joining together in solidarity as Black trans men, and frustration at having these dreams thwarted by the everyday realities of oppression, murder, suicide, racism, sexism, and transphobia. The end of the poem, however, is still hopeful in its fierce yet gently loving plea for nurturing community among Black trans men.[91] Gavriel Alejandro Levi Ansara, discussing the limits of hegemonic embodiments of masculinity, writes: "In stereotypical Western Anglo (which isn't my culture anyway), if masculinity was a requirement of belonging to the man club, my Dad and all of my male relatives would be kicked out."[92]

Bobby Jean Noble offers a framework for thinking about how gender and racial privilege and oppression operate intersectionally. Noble writes:

> For White trans men in particular, an active anti-racist practice is imperative. That we transition into a masculine identity is not enough; we must also self-consciously and willfully embody an anti-racist, anti-White supremacist politic at the same time ... When we think we're seeing FtM trans-sexual male privilege, I suggest that what we're actually seeing is Whiteness modifying masculinity to give it power. If, for instance, transgendered "women" of colour transition into FtM trans-sexual masculinity, we'd be quite remiss to suggest that this FtM is transitioning into a privileged gender position in our culture. There's absolutely no way that we can say, in good conscience, that a trans-sexual man of colour has more power than a White, born-female, heterosexual feminist, can we? So, if I have more power as a White trans-sexual man than I had as a trans-gendered and extremely masculine lesbian, is it not my Whiteness that is articulating power through my gender? ... It seems to me that these criticisms, then, of FtM trans-sexual men are bound within non-intersectional models of thinking identity within White supremacy, which tells us more about the anxieties of Whiteness or tells us a great deal about the limitations of our theoretical paradigms.[93]

Squires and Brouwer[94] consider the deployment of parallel "passing" tropes across both racialized and gendered discourses. In their study, Squires and Brouwer examined media sources to determine and analyze discussions of "passing" in the context of both racial and gender identities. The authors noted the ways in which racial passing was often confounded with class passing; while gender passing was often confounded with sexual orientation passing. In both contexts, "passing" was construed as deception rather than a legitimate means to obtain resources among those individuals and groups systematically denied access to these resources. Those who passed were also constructed as "traitors." In both contexts, those who "fell for" the passing person's "deception" were described as "dupes."

What these sorts of characterizations of the motivations and intentions of socially disempowered people and groups often fail to consider is the way in which these very same behaviors and actions may be alternatively conceptualized as strategic, pragmatic, and culturally adaptive. Indeed, "passing" or receiving cultural recognition as White, middle-class, cisgender, or heterosexual may be thought of as one of the most basic cultural survival strategies in the context of unequal and normative societies. In the next chapter, I attend to another understudied yet vital component of partnership and everyday family life for cis women partners of trans men—division of household and emotional labor and care work around the process of transition.

NOTES

1. See Shapiro (2010).
2. See Cromwell (1999); Gauthier and Chaudoir (2004). See also Eve Shapiro's (2010) *Gender Circuits: Bodies and Identities in a Technological Age* for a more substantive discussion of the interface between gender and technology.
3. In O'Keefe and Fox (2003:104).
4. See Gauthier and Chaudoir (2004:393).
5. See Gauthier and Chaudoir (2004).
6. See also Devor (1997); Feinberg (1993); Green (2004); Kailey (2005).
7. For additional discussion of the sexual identities, relationships, and identity management processes of women partners of trans men, see Brown (2005, 2009, 2010); Harvey (2008); Joslin-Roher and Wheeler (2009); Nyamora (2004); Pfeffer (2008, 2009, 2010, 2012, 2014a); Ward (2010). For an overview of existing work on cis women partners of trans men, see Franklin (2014).
8. Studies of "passing," and the social accomplishments of sex and gender, have a long, revered, and contentious history in sociology, particularly among symbolic interactionists and ethnomethodologists. See Denzin (1989); Goffman (1976); Kessler and McKenna (1978); Rogers (1992); West and Zimmerman (1987); Zimmerman (1992).
9. See Harris (1993).
10. For further critiques of the concept of "passing" with regard to race and class, see Calavita (2000); Harris (1993); Johnson (2002); Kennedy (2002); Ong (2005).

11. See Queen and Schimel (1997:21).
12. See Connell (2009).
13. For further discussion of these and other concepts, language, and terminology related to transgender identity and experience, see Pfeffer (2010); Vidal-Ortiz (2008); Wentling et al. (2008).
14. See Serano (2007).
15. As reviewed by Connell (2009).
16. See Calavita (2000); Harris (1993); Kennedy (2002); Ong (2005).
17. See Elson (2004).
18. See Elson (2004:172)
19. Karyotype refers to the exact chromosomal content of cells. Using staining techniques, it is possible to determine the chromosomal makeup of cells in the human body, including one's sex cells.
20. Swyer Syndrome is the medicalized term for an example of this particular intersection between chromosomes and embodiment.
21. See Connell (2009).
22. See West and Zimmerman (1987:133).
23. See Preves (2002, 2003).
24. See Fausto-Sterling (1992, 2000) and Kessler (1998).
25. See Althusser (1971).
26. As Biblarz and Savci (2011:489) note, for example, "academic research on transgender people and their family relationships is almost nonexistent."
27. Sociological scholarship on queerness has been, in large part, devoted to assisting sociology in: (a) tracing the historical roots of; (b) considering the influence of; (c) assessing the commensurability of sociological theory with; and (d) catching-up with; queer politics and/or the "queer turn" in the humanities. See Duggan (1992); Epstein (1994); Gamson and Moon (2004); Green (2002, 2007); Moon (2008); Namaste (1994); Plummer (2003); Seidman (1994, 1995, 2001); Stein and Plummer (1994); Valocchi (2005). The 1994 publication of the 6-article symposium on "Queer Theory/Sociology" within *Sociological Theory* was groundbreaking. It marked the first (and only, as of this writing) time that a mainstream peer-reviewed publication in sociology offered a collection of scholarship focusing explicitly on the interface between queer theory and sociology, an interface that Epstein (1994:188) describes as steeped within mutual "suspicion" and "misrecognition." It was also a symposium that was not without critique, some of which was more memorable for its vituperative and dismissive tone than its engagement with the substantive content of the work of the authors [e.g., Oakes (1995)]. The relative absence of queer-identified social subjects makes some conceptual sense in the context of the epistemological foundations of queer theory, which are often rooted in challenging and deconstructing subjectivity and identity itself [Gamson (2000); Green (2002); Green (2007); Seidman (1994)]. Yet Stein (1997) notes that existing classificatory systems of sexual identity, reflecting binary sex and gender categorizations of "heterosexual," "homosexual," and "bisexual" are remarkably inadequate when describing people's experiences.
28. See Brown (2010).
29. n=12 (20%).
30. n=6 (10%).

31. n=20 (33%)
32. n=5 (8%).
33. Verbal evidence participants provided in their accounts of these social encounters included others using words like "sir," "bro," "boyfriend," "husband," "dad," and "father," as well as pronouns such as "he" and "him" when referring to their trans partners, and using words/pronouns such as "Miss," "Mrs.," "Ms.," "m'am," "girl," "girlfriend," "wife," "mom," "mother," "she," and "her" when referring to the participants themselves.
34. Some participants, who had been with the same partner prior to his transition, found this form of social exchange particularly salient as they noticed very different reactions from older persons when engaging in public hand holding with the same partner. Prior to transition, when their partner was reportedly "read" as female and the couple was "read" as lesbian, they recalled older individuals staring at them while not smiling, whispering, avoiding eye contact, and not returning smiles.
35. Participants themselves used the term "roles" (e.g., "1950s housewife role") to describe the enactments of traditional wife/husband and mother/father family dynamics as they understood them.
36. Michelle Tea and Rocco Kayiatos are queer public figures. Michelle Tea is a cis woman who is an author, poet, and organizer of feminist and queer literary and spoken word events. Rocco Kayiatos is a trans man who is an artist, activist, educator, and entertainer. His stage name as a rapper and hip-hop artist is "Katastrophe." Tea and Kayiatos are no longer romantically partnered.
37. See Green (2002:537). See also Ghaziani (2011) for a discussion of post-gay collective identity.
38. See Green (2002, 2007).
39. See Gamson (1995).
40. See Shapiro (2004).
41. See Connell's (1987) writing on "hegemonic masculinity."
42. See Brown (2009); Connell (1987); Pfeffer (2010); Ward (2010).
43. As I have written earlier [Pfeffer (2010)], these patterns likely reflect the influence of Third Wave feminist and queer politics in the lives of cis women under 35 years of age in my sample.
44. See Pfeffer (2012) for more about these trends.
45. For more on this see Brown (2009); Pfeffer (2010, 2012); Ward (2010).
46. See Brown (2009).
47. See Brown (2009) for a discussion of similar experiences among another sample of cis women partners of trans men.
48. See Nyamora (2004) and Brown (2009).
49. For more on this, see Brown (2009); Joslin-Roher and Wheeler (2009); Nyamora (2004); Ward (2010). See Hutson (2010) for more on how queer visibility is often culturally synonymous with social perceptions of female masculinity and male femininity.
50. Some of this earlier work includes Kennedy and Davis (1993); Krieger (1983); Ponse (1978); Taylor and Whittier (1992).
51. See Green (2002).

52. See Alexander and Yescavage (2003); Ault (1996a, 1996b); Burrill (2001); Preves (2002, 2003); Tabatabai and Linders (2011); Wolkomir (2009).

53. This articulated invisibility also stands in marked contrast to theorizing around femme identity, which marks it as politically transgressive (and even transgender) in its own right [see Hollibaugh (1997, 2000); Levitt, Gerrish, and Hiestand (2003); Munt (1998)].

54. For more on these trends within LGBTQ communities, see Cogan (1999); Kennedy and Davis (1993); Levitt, Gerrish, and Hiestand (2003).

55. See Ward (2010).

56. See also Pitts (2000) for more on how queer people work to embody their queer identities.

57. As mentioned earlier, in the endnotes for Chapter 6, the term "tranny" is hotly contested within trans community and often considered a term of disrespect too stigmatizing and steeped in marginalization and violence to be effectively reclaimed at this point in history, particularly by those who are not members of the group most targeted with this term as an epithet: trans women.

58. See Tompkins (2014). Tompkins employs digital ethnographic and participant observation methods.

59. For an overview of these efforts, public and structural responses to them, as well as academic critique, see Brake (2012); Corvino and Gallagher (2012); Heath (2012); Kimport (2014); Richman (2014); Stacey (2011); Stone (2012); Walters (2014).

60. See Duggan (2002); Ward (2008).

61. For a more extended discussion of cis women partners' expressions of agency and "normative resistance" in the context of limiting social structures and institutions, see Pfeffer (2012). For an earlier extended discussion of "queer by choice" frameworks, see Whisman (1996). For a more recent discussion of the cultural imperatives driving limited "born this way" approaches to sexual identities, see Walters (2014).

62. See Warner (1993:xxvi).

63. Among the women, 59% held at least a bachelor's degree, with 26% holding a postgraduate degree; among trans men partners, only 49% held at least a bachelor's degree, with 13% holding postgraduate degrees.

64. 60% of women provided complete information for both themselves and their partner(s).

65. 57% of women providing complete data reported that their socioeconomic status was the same as their partner's.

66. 27% of women providing complete data reported that their socioeconomic status was lower than their trans partner's, while 16% reported that their socioeconomic status was higher than their trans partner's.

67. 93% of women self-identified as feminist while 77% reported that their trans partner also self identifies as feminist.

68. 45 participants self-identified as White, 3 as multiracial, 1 as Black, and 1 as Latina.

69. n=14 (28%); of the 15 trans men partners who were not described as White among the reported sample of 61, 11 were described as multiracial, 1 as Asian, 1 and Black, 1 as Native American, and 1 interviewee reported being unsure of the race of her partner (and did not want to speculate) in 1 instance.

70. See Hansbury (2005).

71. See Hansbury (2005).

72. See Sennett (2006:39).

73. See Kennedy and Davis (1993).

74. See Dozier (2005:309).

75. See Rachlin (2002:14).

76. See Pfeffer (2010). For more on Third Wave feminism see Henry (2004), Heywood and Drake (1997), and Reger (2005).

77. For more about trans people's perspectives on feminism, see Scott-Dixon (2006).

78. See Thompson (2014). Also, it should be noted that use of the term "tranny" is hotly contested within transgender communities and politics. In particular, because the term has been primarily deployed as an epithet against trans women, reclamation of the term by others within the trans movement (for example, trans men or cis women partners of trans men) is offensive and fails to recognize the particular and ongoing pervasive discrimination against trans women [see Serano (2013)].

79. See Diamond (2004).

80. See O'Keefe and Fox (2003).

81. See Daniel Peddle's (2005) documentary, *The Aggressives*, for consideration of other terms and modes of self-identification used by some trans masculine people of color.

82. See Steinbugler (2012)

83. All racial and ethnic categories used herein were provided through the self-descriptions of participants.

84. See Schilt (2010).

85. See Dozier (2005); Ziegler (2014).

86. See Dozier (2005).

87. See Dozier (2005:310).

88. See Cummings (2006); Khosla (2006); Martino (1977); Valerio (2006).

89. See Cummings (2006).

90. In Diamond (2004:67).

91. In Diamond (2004).

92. In Diamond (2004:91).

93. See Noble (2006:27).

94. See Squires and Brouwer (2002).

Queering Family Labor

Managing Households, Relationships, and Transitions

In the past 2 chapters, I have provided an overview of what we know about transgender partnerships and families across a broad array of sources, the particular histories of transmasculine identities and partnerships with cis women, discussion of the identity management and negotiation processes of cis women partners of trans men, and consideration of the diversity that exists among and between cis women and their trans men partners. In this chapter, I turn to focus on the sorts of work that cis women report doing on behalf of their partners, households, and families.

A critical contribution of sociologists of the family has been demonstrating just how gender and gender expression often matter when structuring and accounting for everyday family chores and tasks.[1] The work of pioneering sociologists revealed that there is often a striking disconnect between what people say they do, what they actually do, and how they describe the distance between these, creating what Arlie Hochschild termed "gender strategies" and "family myths."[2] For example, Hochschild observed an interesting "upstairs-downstairs" phenomenon in her research with 50 nontrans heterosexual couples.

Among the 50 cisgender women married to cisgender men she interviewed for her book, *Second Shift: Working Parents and the Revolution at Home*, Hochschild noticed that they tended to tell her that they were responsible for the "upstairs" of the house (which generally included the kitchen and cooking, cleaning bathrooms, vacuuming, and mopping) while their cisgender husbands were responsible for the "downstairs" (which encompassed the garage, taking out the garbage, and lawn and car maintenance). Describing the division of household labor in this way allowed this group of cis women, including those who were feminist identified, to maintain the illusion that their work was divided pretty much down the middle in an equal way, distinguished primarily by location: "upstairs" or "downstairs." However, in comparing reports of the actual labor performed by cis husbands and wives, the "upstairs" tasks for which cis women held primary responsibility included tasks that were completed with much greater frequency, and tended to take more time to complete overall, than the "downstairs" tasks to which their cis husbands attended.

One might assume that if heterosexual cisgender couples divide household labor in gender-stereotyped ways that result in cis women getting the shorter end of the stick,[3] one of the advantages of being in a gay or lesbian relationship would be that such divisions would simply vanish and an egalitarian division of household labor would prevail.[4] Christopher Carrington, in his book, *No Place Like Home: Relationships and Family Life Among Lesbians and Gay Men*, showed us just how wrong such an assumption could be. Rather than having perfectly equal divisions of labor in their household, Carrington found that the same-sex couples he studied also tended to divide work in ways that reflected the existence of gender roles in their relationships.[5] In other words, being in a same-sex relationship is not synonymous with being in a same-gender relationship. Some partners in the same-sex relationships Carrington studied identified more with tasks and roles that could be described as gendered in feminine ways while others identified more with those that could be classified as masculine.

The sorts of gender strategies and family myths that these partners created together often worked to shore up a partner's gendered self-expression in ways that might help them face less social discrimination in the world outside their homes. For example, within lesbian households, feminine partners who performed a greater share of "upstairs" tasks often exaggerated a more masculine partner's contribution to these "upstairs" tasks when in the presence of others. Carrington reasoned that such maneuvers could serve the purpose of buffering social stigma directed toward what might be seen as conformity to stereotypes about lesbians (as masculine) or gay men (as effeminate).

In her study of Black lesbian stepfamilies, Mignon Moore[6] found that cis women who had given birth to their children reported completing the majority of household labor, but that undertaking these tasks connoted higher status within these relationships. Moore's work challenged a taken-for-granted assumption within feminist studies of the family (most of which focus on White and middle-class heterosexual cisgender families): that egalitarian division of household labor and childcare is desirable and perhaps ideal. Through careful examination of the everyday family arrangements and particular sociohistorical context of a sample of lower-income Black lesbian stepfamilies, Moore proposed that assuming greater responsibility over household labor is associated with greater authority across the areas of financial control and childrearing practices, each of which translates to greater relative power within the structure of the relationships and families she examined.

While the work of these sociologists of the family provides an excellent base from which to better understand the division of household and emotional labor among heterosexual, lesbian, and gay households *without* a transgender member, there are no similar studies of households *with* a transgender member. Does the division of labor within households comprising cis women and trans men most closely resemble the heterosexual cisgender couples Hochschild studied, the gay or lesbian cisgender couples that Carrington studied, or perhaps neither?

I decided to ask the cis women participants in my study a broad array of questions related to the division of labor in their homes.[7] Out of the 61 relationships cis women spoke to me about, 38 of these involved living together and experience with dividing household chores and responsibilities. I asked these cis women to describe the division of chores and responsibilities in their homes, from cleaning toilets to taking out the garbage, childcare to maintaining automobiles (when relevant), and shopping for groceries to sending out birthday cards to extended family members. I was also open to learning more about forms of household and emotional labor performed by cis women partners of trans men that may be somewhat unique to this population and therefore not described in existing research on gender and the family.

HOUSEHOLD AND EMOTIONAL LABOR AMONG CIS WOMEN PARTNERS OF TRANS MEN

I was interested in learning not only how cis women felt about the way that various forms of work were divvied up in their homes and in their lives, but also the way they described (and even rationalized) these tasks and divisions. For the sake of simplicity, I draw from Carrington and group the 20 types of household labor I asked my interviewees about into 4 broad categories: (a) feeding work (cooking, grocery shopping, and knowledge of partner's tastes and preferences); (b) house work (bathroom cleaning, decorating, dishes, dusting, floor care, garbage, home repairs, laundry, lawn care, tidying, and window cleaning); (c) kin work[8] (scheduling and attending doctor appointments; child care; maintaining correspondence with family members in the form of calling, sending cards and buying gifts; pet care; and transition-related care); and (d) consumption work (car care, driving, and paying bills). It is important to note that some of these tasks might reasonably fit under more than a single broad category. For example, we might consider making doctor appointments for one's family member to be not only a type of kin work, but also a type of consumption work as well. Similarly, grocery shopping might be considered both feeding work and consumption work (see Appendix Table 2).

I have published findings from this household labor aspect of my research in the *Journal of Marriage and Family*.[9] While I encourage readers to take a closer look at that article, I do not wish to simply rehash those findings in this chapter. Instead, I will share the results of some additional data analyses I have conducted on the housework configurations reported by the cis women in my study who lived with their trans partners.[10] As a group, these cis women were highly educated and largely self-identified as feminist. They described general familiarity with decades of feminist scholarship on nontransgender heterosexual families attesting to both historical and contemporary gender imbalances in division of household labor. In their comments, they expressed knowledge that cis women in heterosexual relationships, both historically and today, tend to perform relatively more of this work than their cis men partners and that one of the central goals of feminism is reducing this gap between the work cis women and cis men do in their homes each day. Perhaps it is unsurprising, then, that many cis women in my study, when asked to describe the division of household labor in their own homes, frequently began this conversation by telling me that the division was roughly equal across a broad number of the various types of household labor about which I asked them. After all, this is the answer we would expect of someone whose politics and personal experiences are perfectly aligned.

However, as revealed in the previously discussed work on lesbian, gay, and heterosexual cisgender couples, such perfect concordance between ideologies, ideals, and behavior seems to be more often the exception than the rule across many different types of partnerships and families. When I pressed cis women in my study to elaborate on the specific household tasks that they and their partners perform in their queer families, some potential inequalities began to emerge. Cis women reported roughly equal division of labor for many tasks related to house-work and consumption work (e.g., bathroom cleaning, car care, driving, and tidying). Cis women reported performing a greater share of *all* feminine-typed tasks generally connected to feeding work and kin work as well as "upstairs" house work tasks (e.g., dishes, dusting, and laundry). Cis women who reported that the division of labor in lawn care, car care, floor care, garbage, and/or driving was *not* equal were more likely to note that their trans partner performed the bulk of these masculine-typed "downstairs" tasks. Cis women who reported that the division of labor in managing bills was *not* equal were more likely to note that they (cis women) performed more of this generally masculine-typed task.

In addition to asking cis women about a variety of individual household tasks and responsibilities, I also asked them to offer an overall assessment of the division of domestic labor in their homes. Despite offering a fairly clear assessment (through discussion of individual tasks) that cis women tended to complete the bulk of this labor, reports of which partner did the most work overall were fairly evenly divided between (a) the cis women themselves doing most of this work, (b) the cis women's trans men partners doing most of the work, and (c) both partners splitting the work equitably. One of the noticeable differences between cis women who reported that they were responsible for the majority of the house-work, and cis women who reported that their trans men partners were perform-ing most of those tasks, was that cis women in the former group more frequently offered percentage estimations of the perceived labor division in their homes, while cis women in the latter group rarely did so. Further, the percentages among cis women who claimed to do less than their trans men partners revealed a nar-rower difference between these numbers, reporting about a 20–30 percentage point gap compared to the 20–70 percentage point gap reported among cis women who described doing the majority of this work.

In other words, the cis women in my study reported divisions of household labor that roughly mirrored those reported in published studies of cisgender heterosexual households, with cis women reporting primary responsibility for feeding and kin work as well as the majority of house work tasks and report-ing that their trans men partners held primary responsibility for stereotypically masculine-gendered forms of labor like taking care of lawns, home repairs, and the garbage. Some of the ways in which reports from the cis women I studied differ from reports from cis women in relationships with cis men are that the cis women I interviewed reported that their trans partners took primary responsibility for tasks such as bathroom cleaning and floor care (especially vacuuming), each of which are generally stereotyped as "women's work." Further, the fact that the cis women in my study more frequently reported being in charge of managing the household bills is another way in which this group's reports tended to differ from those of cis women in relationships with cis men. These findings are particularly compelling when we think back to Mignon Moore's[11] work, which revealed that among Black lesbian stepfamilies, partners who held primary responsibility for managing household bills could be said to hold positions of relative power within their families.

Caring for Children

Only 2 of the cis women I interviewed (Maya and Polly) were actively raising young children in their homes at the time we spoke with one another. Maya was a new mother and, for our interview, she invited me into the apartment in which she, her husband, and their newborn daughter lived. We sat next to one another on the couch and talked for nearly 2 hours, during which time Maya intermittently nursed her little one, who was pink-cheeked, quietly cooing, and seemingly content. I asked Maya to talk to me about the process of bringing their daughter into the world. She stressed the importance of using an anonymous sperm donor:

> It was very, very important to [my husband] that [he] be the father and that there would be nobody else that could claim fatherhood over [our child]. . . . We didn't want to have to deal with the legal issues of having a known donor, as well as just dealing with any kind of emotional tie between the donor and [our child].

Maya became pregnant on a third round of intrauterine insemination performed by a doctor: "I found out I was pregnant on National Coming Out Day and it was very exciting and then it hit me like a brick, 'Oh my God, we're having a baby!'" Maya and her partner dealt with the roller coaster of pregnancy complications, a traumatic birth experience, and a delivery wherein their baby struggled to take her first breath. I asked Maya to talk to me about how she and her partner divided both household labor tasks and childcare tasks. She told me:

> I guess we divided it to what we know. . . . Like I hate taking out the garbage so [my partner] does that and that's kind of a traditional, the-man-does-the-garbage kind of thing. He kills the spiders. Literally. He put up the crib. He's much more traditional. We have some traditional gender roles because I'm not very handy and he is. He is definitely stronger than I am. I will put a nail

in the wall; it's not like I can't do things, but he's better at it so he, by default, just does it. In terms of baby care, he does everything except feed her [Maya was breastfeeding at the time], and even then he feeds her a bottle occasionally. I go back to work on Thursday and, at that point, he'll be taking 2 weeks off work to care for her full time. I would say he does 50% of child care other than feeding when he's home. So, we definitely both nurture her. In terms of other household stuff, it's just according to the things that we like to do and those things tend to be gender stereotypical. Except for the cooking, he does the cooking.

Maya also spoke to me about the ways in which typical divisions of labor within the home often break down or transform during times of personal or medical transition or crisis. Maya laughed when I asked her who usually does the dishes in her home, gesturing toward the sink piled high with dishes:

If you look in our sink, no one does the dishes very often. We used to have a rule that whomever doesn't do the cooking does the dishes; however, he does the cooking and since I went on bed rest I wasn't really able to stand and do the dishes, so he's been doing both for a while. And since I've been doing the nursing, and [our daughter] does a lot of nursing, he's been doing the dishes also. I'm recovering from childbirth, so lately I haven't been doing a lot of dishes. I should probably start. If I'm cleared by the doctor to go to the gym, I guess I can do some dishes.

Maya described similar temporary transfer of household task responsibilities around laundry, noting her restrictions around lifting during a medically imposed period of bed rest and following a C-section.

Maya's family, therefore, reflects some traditionally gendered divisions of household labor yet reverses others (such as Maya's trans partner being the one to do the cooking). A particularly postmodern component to this ebb and flow of daily housework, and one that resonates across diverse family forms, is that over time certain household tasks are being performed less frequently or even not at all. Indeed, family scholars have noted a downward trend, since 1965, in the total amount of time spent performing housework.[12] While housework tasks are consuming less of the "budget" for family care tasks, the amount of time families invest in childcare has been steadily increasing over this same time period. And while men's time contribution to childcare has tripled since the mid-60s, women still perform the vast majority of this labor within postmodern families.[13] Among the cis women parents I interviewed, these trends were playing out in their everyday lives and queer families as well.

Polly, who was actively parenting young children with her trans partner in their home, was raising 2 daughters under 10 years of age. She was the natal mother of both children, who had been conceived and born during a prior relationship. She estimated that, in her current relationship, she was responsible for about 70% of the childcare responsibilities and talked about the variety of often taken-for-granted tasks that such care involves:

> So, it's just like putting them to bed, making sure they have everything for school, coordinating all their school trips, and when they need their bathing suits and all that stuff going to meetings with their teachers, helping them to do their homework, making sure they do their music lessons, taking them to different activities or play dates, watching their friends, feeding them, making their lunches in the morning. All those tasks. But it's also just the psychic energy of dealing with their emotional needs and that's the part that seems to be the most sapping of energy. And just all the worrying about them, you know? And then also coordinating for the not-so-distant future. Like what are we going to do during this break and what sort of vacation are they going to do and visiting family. They're very involved with my parents, so making sure they get to see them enough. And coordinating different types of social engagements for them, soccer games, and they take an acrobatics class. And then also like meeting with my ex to kind of see how they're doing and checking in about that. So, it's sort of like there's the labor of it and just how time consuming it is to do child care and child rearing. And it's hard to sort of quantify how much time is given to that.

This litany of iterative tasks and scheduling that Polly describes is just a small part of an unpaid labor calculus whose metrics are often shifting and uncertain. It may be possible to calculate just how many minutes are spent each week driving in a car ferrying children to various extracurricular and school-related activities. But how does one tally the minutes spent planning visitation schedules with one's ex, the hours invested with worry about how children are adjusting to a new family configuration, or figuring out how to coordinate transportation for 2 children who need to be in 2 different places at the very same time?

Arlie Hochschild and Marjorie DeVault[14] described these tasks as "emotional labor," unpaid and often unrecognized forms of work that tend to accrue largely to women in our culture. Future research would do well to explore the parenting practice of a broader diversity of trans parents and their partners to ascertain whether parenting labor in these families tends to be distributed similarly to that among cisgender parents, or if these divisions of labor are more flexible, egalitarian, or even gender counter-normative. While some research does document the parenting practices of trans people,[15] this research often utilizes very small sample sizes and focuses on trans parents who have transitioned later in life, often when their children are relatively older. Moreover, much research on queer families, in general, approaches the measurement of children's outcomes as if children's subsequent development of LGBTQ identities is necessarily negative, revealing the cisnormative and heteronormative biases of much family studies research.[16] As trans people transition earlier and earlier, with some maintaining their reproductive capacities,[17] it will be important to explore partnering, parenting, and family possibilities across the areas of household labor, childcare, and emotional labor. In the next section, I will document a form of emotional labor and kin work that may be more particular to the partners of trans people and that remains largely undocumented in research literatures on family labor.

Transition-Related Kin Work

My conversations about the domestic and emotional labor of this group of cis women were not solely focused on housework and childcare. Indeed, these conversations prompted me to consider: Just how might the forms of domestic labor in which cis women partners of trans men engage extend *beyond* those most frequently measured and discussed by sociologists of the family? Are there some forms of emotional work, kin work, and family labor that might be more specific to cis women partners of trans men, or at least a common part of their experience that often goes unexplored? Here, I wish to consider a form of kin work that has not received much attention previously: work surrounding a partner's transition.[18] Some of the cis women I interviewed described performing aspects of what Jane Ward has termed "gender labor,"[19] work people do to affirm or validate the gender of themselves and/or others.

One of the most striking examples of this form of labor was cis women's work in connection with the surgical components of a partner's transition.[20] Nearly all of the cis women I interviewed had partners who had had or were planning to have "top surgery." Top surgery is the phrase used for the removal of breast tissue (through liposuction or bilateral radical mastectomy with chest wall recontouring), most often performed as an outpatient procedure.[21] A considerable number of cis women also described participation in what may be described, from a sociological perspective, as "rituals" surrounding their partner's top surgery. Social scientists understand rituals as critical cultural markers, symbolic or ceremonial rites of passage that mark transition from one milestone or era to another.[22] I came to see the various work that cis women performed to help mark their partners' transitions as rituals that were important not only for their partners or for themselves, but often for their queer families, and larger communities as well.

Ellia described feelings of sadness surrounding her trans partner's impending top surgery, realizing that her partner's body was about to be radically transformed. One of the ways that she coped with her sadness was by photographically documenting her trans partner's body prior to surgery: "We just took some Polaroids and I made a little secret book that we have." Ellia was not the only cis woman I interviewed who told me about commemorating a trans partner's body by taking photos before surgery. Lea reported a similar experience: "The night before surgery, I got this fascination with like photographing his chest. I took all these photographs. We had been photographing different stages of his transition. . . . I had a weird sense of mourning about it." Lea described this sense of mourning as "weird" because her partner's chest had been an area of his body that was relatively off-limits throughout his transition. Gail, who told me she had never seen her partner's bare chest prior to just before his top surgery, told me:

> He's an artist . . . so it was sort of like kind of a performance in a lot of ways. We did this thing where we had a goodbye-to-your-tits party and we actually had a ceremony. But it was also kind of about art because he wanted to document it all and take pictures and stuff. We took a bath together, there were like a million candles all around. His friend was there too and she took some pictures for a minute and then we were just in the bath tub and said goodbye to the tits.

Gail described her emotional reaction to this ceremony as "intense."

The work involved in ceremonially marking a partner's bodily transition, before or after surgeries, was something that other cis women talked to me about as well. Josie described how her partner had drainage tubes at his incision sites after top surgery and that he collected and saved some of the blood from these tubes. She told me: "[My partner] had this weird doll with these giant boobs who had a name. I can't remember it, but I feel like it had something to do with boobs. And we buried the doll and poured some blood in there." Mel described an even more elaborate ceremony and ritual that involved friends and a "farewell to breasts" party: "We had a fun boob party where we sort of said goodbye to them with a bunch of our friends. We had a topless party and everyone was here. It was a really fun night. We made it quite a conscious goodbye and letting go and thanking and honoring process." Party activities and features included making and painting plaster casts of everyone's chest (including her partner's, the guest of honor), body painting and "breast prints" made by leaning against sheets of paper after painting one's breasts, cookies in the shape of breasts, the infamous "pencil test" wherein attendees placed various objects, from pencils to soup cans, under their breasts to see what they could hold before the objects fell to the ground, and a truth-or-dare game involving breast-related questions connected to, for example, attendees' memories surrounding their first training bra.

As with earlier chapters, I want to draw parallels here to published literature on the experiences of trans identity. This literature often speaks to the emotional, psychological, and social importance of marking bodily changes related to transition and considering embodied connections to the experiences of others. In one story, a trans man (Aaron Link) and his mother[23] weave their stories together about their family's chest scars. Link's brother has one from a heart operation he had when very young, Link's scar is from his top surgery as part of his transition, and his mother's is from a mastectomy necessitated by breast cancer. Both Link and his mother discuss the ways in which these scars, etched across their bodies, unite their family through stories and reminders of pain, struggle, strength, and future possibilities. Link notes: "In 1995 I start taking testosterone. There are no pictures of people like me. I look and look through books of gender theory, autobiographies of heroic transsexuals who won't let anybody take their picture, and medical literature."[24] The photographs that many cis women partners described taking at their partner's request (and with their consent) begin to fill this gap or absence and allow trans people to generate images of themselves and their bodies over which they have greater control.[25] So, too, does the proliferation of social media, Internet-facilitated social networks, and audiovisual communication possibilities in the 21st century. These postmodern inventions have ushered in previously unimaginable possibilities around the dissemination of resources and support.

Some of the cis women I interviewed described organizing parties and events to help raise funds for a trans partner's top surgery given that insurance most often does not cover these procedures, and costs generally range from around $6,000 to $9,000. For those couples with merged finances, or who were working mutually toward particular financial goals, affording surgeries could be challenging. Many participants used "we" quite frequently when I asked them to talk to me about their partner's transition. I told Donna that I noticed she had been using "we" a lot when describing her partner's transition and I asked her to reflect on that a bit. She said:

> As a couple, and as a committed couple, we [laughter as she realizes she's used the word again]. . . . It's a financial commitment and it's one that we both kind of had to be okay with. It *was* a "we" thing. It had to be, because he wasn't doing it by himself. We just planned it. He did all the calling as far as the surgery and everything but we had to plan the money, borrow the money. Some of it was borrowed, some of it we had in student loan help. So, it was very much a partner decision.

Terry reported managing many of the day-to-day details surrounding her partner's surgical transition: "I had most of the conversations with the surgeon because where [my partner] worked, he couldn't make those phone calls and I could. So, the first time he actually spoke with the surgeon was when he met her face-to-face. He already knew who he wanted to go to and I called and found out what [information] they needed to see if his insurance would handle it." Learning about and documenting transition-related surgeries and procedures could be a time-consuming, and consuming in general, task. As Frida described it: "Yeah, if it wasn't the whole finding doctors and, 'When is your doctor's appointment?' and 'Oh, this new book just arrived at the book store, I'll go pick it up for you', then it was about school and art and a photo exhibit and, 'Let's put that together.' Yeah, it was always something about him."

Many cis women described extensively using and poring over Internet sites dedicated to hormonal and surgical transition, alternately describing fascination, horror, fear, uncertainty, excitement, and worry as they contemplated their own trans partner's body transforming or meeting a surgeon's blade. Cis women described scouring the Internet for information about how to administer testosterone injections; transition-related surgical procedures and techniques; surgical results photos; caring for surgical incision sites, dressings, and drainage tubes; under which circumstances insurance will cover hormones and surgeries; dosing and schedules for postsurgical pain medications; postsurgical physical activity restrictions; potential surgical complications; and what to expect as a partner's body changes in response to testosterone or as he recovers from surgery.

EXPLAINING INEGALITARIAN DIVISIONS OF HOUSEHOLD AND EMOTIONAL LABOR

Like the respondents in Hochschild's and Carrington's studies, the cis women I interviewed often provided explanations for reported unequal divisions of household, emotional, and kin labor—particularly if those inequalities seemed to reinforce normative or stereotypical gender roles for men and women. Many of the cis women in my study, most of whom were college educated and self-identified as feminist, drew upon the postmodern notion of "gender performativity"[26] when I asked them to account for unequal divisions of labor in their households. A number of cis women told me that they and their trans partner enjoyed (re)enacting kitschy gender scenes or "roles" like the one Ellia described:

I will take on the role of housewife or whatever and a lot of the time it's this tongue-in-cheek sort of thing. He'll be like, [low and gruff voice] "Get me a beer!" and I'll put on an apron and run off into the other room, [high and lilting voice] "Here ya go dear!" It's very sort of playful. Again, it's the *performance* of gender instead of really taking it all that seriously. And I'd say in some ways they're [gender roles] inherently flexible because they aren't typical presentations of gender. But at the same time ... they are flexible and they're not because we have sort of, I think, eased into certain roles in terms of who sort of has the upper say. And certain decision making that has to do with food or whatever, that's me. The kitchen is my kitchen and all this sort of stuff and that's very gendered. But sometimes, I don't know.

Describing her own preferred aesthetic, Kyla told me that in her ideal world, "I would be dressed up and looking very typically like your '50s domestic housewife with pearls, the dress, and the apron. I love feeling and looking that way." In a similar vein, Martha remarked:

I'd often cook dinner and I would clean the house while he was gone. I'd take care of his animals. . . . I definitely took on a role. And we would joke about it often that I was the housewife and that I was doing my duty as a woman. We would joke around about that a lot. And that's actually something that I enjoy doing. In a way, I do like domesticity. I enjoy keeping house for someone and for myself and cooking meals and serving food to people. So, that wasn't anything forced but it was just ... it was amusing to both of us because we were taking on these very specific, gendered roles. Here we are trying to fight against this just in being who we are. But we also were taking on some of these roles that are gendered. But we were able to create them and make them more specific to who we were, I feel.

When I asked Martha to say more about what she meant by that she said:

Well, it wasn't just about being a woman for me or being the housewife, it was something I *enjoyed* doing. And because we were able to joke about it too, it was fun. It never felt forced or anything. And I didn't feel like I was playing in to any role that I was supposed to be doing because I was the female of the couple.

I found the discussion of gender performativity interesting as it urges us to consider when and how conscious performance serves a parodic purpose, with the potential to render taken-for-granted gender roles more salient. On the other hand, it also prompts us to question when and how performances of gender inequality, when repeated often enough, simply become another example of gender inequality rather than parody. I also wondered why the gendered performances that cis women described seemed to conform to such a narrow script. None of the cis women I interviewed described their trans partner donning an apron and doting after her as she languished on the couch, demanding beer. Why were many of these gender performances so predictable?

But then I began to ask a different question: Why would they *not* be predictable? The Third Wave feminist ideals and politics that many of the cis women I interviewed were drawing upon stress choice, individuality, performativity, and autonomy around body projects and personal aesthetics. One of the primary ways to engage performativity is to appropriate normative cultural practices and aesthetics with the intention of resignifying their meanings and power dynamics. Despite engagement with Third Wave feminism and having a partner who is transgender, the cis women I interviewed still live lives and have relationships in the same world as everyone else. So long as we continue to believe that certain household and family tasks are feminine and others are masculine, and we develop explanations that attempt to neutralize the stigma of being associated with a gendered task that is not normatively connected to our gendered identities, why would we *not* expect to see these same patterns and trends echoed in the queer family relationships that cis women have with trans men?[27]

Cis Women Partners Mediating Social Gender Judgments

One of the reasons we might strongly anticipate normative enactments of gender within trans families stems from the perilous nature of gender attributions and social recognition. Because many trans men, particularly those early in the transition process, may not receive consistent social affirmation of their gender identities, being recognized *as* men often serves as a powerful validation of one's gender identity as a man.[28] As sociologists Laurel Westbrook and Kristen Schilt[29] theorize, determinations about other people's gender are context-dependent and, increasingly, moving away from being solely or even primarily reliant on biological characteristics such as chromosomes or genitals.

Indeed, in many social spaces, the criteria used to determine whether a trans man will be socially "read" as a man depend largely on whether or not a social space is gender integrated or segregated. In gender-integrated spaces, as most public spaces are, strangers will tend to rely on "cultural genitals,"[30] physical and interactive social cues that people believe indicate a person's sex (and therefore gender), such as hair (especially the presence or absence of facial hair), shape of chest and hips, vocal pitch or tone, how someone moves or takes up space, what someone is wearing, and the activities in which they are engaging. Because the cis women partners of the trans men I interviewed were cognizant that their partner's ability to be recognized in social spaces in accordance with their gender identity was consequential and possibly even a matter of personal safety, they often spoke to me about particular efforts to mediate these social encounters in ways that would protect their trans partner from gender misattribution and misrecognition.

For example, I asked Eliza whose responsibility it was to walk the dog that she and her partner had. She responded that she was the one to usually do it and offered the following explanation: "Just as a disclaimer for that, a lot of that is based around the fact that for morning walks and evening walks my partner doesn't have his binder on and doesn't feel comfortable [walking around in public]. I keep joking that after T and T [testosterone and top surgery], it's his responsibility to walk the dog!" So, while Eliza was clearly working to protect her trans partner from potential gender misrecognition in public spaces, she was also deeply cognizant that the outcome of such a decision may be an inegalitarian division of household tasks and responsibilities, at least for a time. The cis women I interviewed sometimes expressed discernible discomfort with their own responses when they did express what could be perceived as inegalitarian divisions of household labor, particularly when those divisions were organized in ways that were seemingly gender normative. After asking several questions about pet care in which Polly noted that it was her trans partner who bore primary responsibility for those tasks, Polly told me: "You're making me feel very guilty!"[31]

Cis women also sometimes described a trans partner's reluctance to engage in telephone conversations. One of the effects of testosterone administration is deepening of one's voice. Some trans men have very deep voices after years of taking testosterone, while others find that their vocal pitch ends up somewhere in a mid-range, particularly in the early stages of testosterone administration. As such, verbal exchanges serve as a potential site where the gender identity of trans men may be misrecognized and put to social test. Cis women partners of trans men described sometimes serving as mediators in these social exchanges in order to help their partner avoid potential social scrutiny and challenges to his gender identity. As Drea told me about her partner: "He absolutely hates the telephone. Anything he can do to not use it. If we order food, I'm always the one who has to order it, even if he's paying for it. It doesn't matter. I'm almost always the one who has to do the phone stuff." Tiffany described occasionally making doctor's appointments for her partner:

> He hasn't legally changed his name and it's difficult having an obviously female name and call up a doctor's office with an obviously male voice and ask for an appointment. So, sometimes, just for the ease of things, I call because they're not going to question me if I call with a female voice and ask for an appointment for [someone with] an obviously female name. So, sometimes it's just the easiest thing.

In each of these instances, cis women described taking on additional responsibilities and tasks in order to shield their trans partners from the very real possibilities of social misrecognition, confusion, and hassles.

After presentations of some of these data, I have been told (at academic conferences, on job interviews, in the classroom) that cis women partners of trans men seem to have relationships and families that are more reminiscent of Ozzie and Harriet than utopic visions of postmodern gender performance, queer families, and liberation. I often find myself wondering about the questioner's (most often cis women's) personal relationships. It would seem that many people believe that partnerships with transgender people must involve (or perhaps *should* involve) transcendence of normative gender socialization and regulation. Many seem shocked that cis women partners of trans men become so deeply invested in their partner's hormonal and surgical transitions, serving as unpaid and untrained nurses who administer testosterone injections and attend to dressings and drainage tubes at surgical incision sites.

Yet what are the alternatives? Placed in social context, the surgical and hormonal aspects of transition for trans men are largely outpatient procedures: bimonthly intra-muscular testosterone injections and bilateral radical mastectomy with chest wall contouring. Home care for these procedures is now considered standard. While caring for a partner who is recovering from major surgery or critical illness can be a physically and emotionally exhausting experience, it is one that many (if not most) individuals will likely face in their lives. Indeed, in this postmodern moment, medical care is increasingly devolved to family members (most often women) and the home.[32] Provision of such care certainly required additional unpaid labor from many of those with whom I spoke. Despite the fear, anxiety, and exhaustion that often accompanied this provision of care, especially while simultaneously juggling work, school, and other family responsibilities, most of the cis women I interviewed told me they felt deeply honored to be a critical part of their partner's transition process.

This chapter has highlighted some of the diverse forms of household labor, childcare, and transition-related kin work in which cis women partners of trans men engage, noting parallels and distinctions to forms of labor in which other groups of cis women engage in the context of their partnerships and families. While these forms of unpaid labor are often sites of family discord and tension, they also contribute to the fabric of day-to-day family life. Moreover, this chapter renders visible various forms of queer family labor that often go unnoticed and understudied because it often happens behind closed doors and is considered private and mundane. In the next chapter, I turn to another area of partnership and family life that is also understudied and often considered too private to explore from an academic perspective, yet is rarely dismissed as too mundane for critical inquiry: sex, bodies, and sexuality.

NOTES

1. Family scholars have also examined intersectional identities and differential outcomes and opportunities for various group members. For example, Damaske (2011) attends to intersections of gender and class as they shape the paid employment and unpaid family labor in which women engage.
2. See, for example, Carrington (1999); DeVault (1991, 1999); Hochschild (1979, 1989); Oakley (1974).
3. See Hochschild (1989).
4. While the household labor gap has begun to narrow [Kan, Sullivan, and Gershuny (2011)], women in heterosexual relationships report on the continuing existence of the "second shift" within their relationships [Bianchi (1995); Kamo (2000)] no matter if they are married or unmarried and living together [Bianchi, Milkie, Sayer, and Robinson (2000); Smock (2000)]. In fact, some research demonstrates that men's contribution to household labor may actually decrease when moving from cohabitation to marriage with the same partner [Gupta (1999)] or when their female partner earns more than they do [Bittman, England, Sayer, Folbre, and Mattheson (2003); Greenstein (2000)], though some more recent research [Sullivan (2011)] challenges the scope of these findings.
5. See also Gabb (2004).
6. Indeed, some researchers [Blumstein and Schwartz (1983); Kurdek (2001, 2006, 2007)] *have* found evidence for the minimization of domestic inequalities within same-sex partnerships. See Biblarz and Savci (2011) and Patterson (2000) for overviews of research on family labor among same-sex couples.
7. See Moore (2008, 2011). Moore's findings also resonate with work by Deutsch, Kojot, and Binder (2007), who assert that evaluations of egalitarian divisions of household labor must approach the very concept of egalitarianism as one that is fluid and open to multiple interpretations.
8. For a more extensive discussion of the concept of kin work, see di Leonardo (1987).
9. Pet care is listed as a form of "Kin Work" rather than "House Work" as the majority of people tend to see their pets more as members of their family than as objects or possessions [Powell, Bolzendahl, Geist, and Steelman (2010)]. Further, house work tends to pivot upon people's relationship with and to inanimate objects, while kin work pivots upon their relationship with and to other sentient beings.
10. See Pfeffer (2010).
11. About 62% of the relationships women reported involved cohabitation, or living together, at one point or another.
12. See Moore (2008, 2011).
13. See Bianchi, Milkie, Sayer, and Robinson (2000). It should be noted, however, that the overall hours that cis men spend in performing household labor slowly but

steadily increased from 1965 to 2000 and plateaued thereafter, according to Pew Research Center data.

14. See Pew Research Center Social and Demographic Data (http://www.pewsocial-trends.org/2013/03/14/chapter-5-americans-time-at-paid-work-housework-child-care-1965-to-2011/)

15. See DeVault (1991, 1999); Hochschild (1979, 1989).

16. See Lev (2010) for an excellent overview and critique of these hidden biases in research on LGBTQ families. See Sabatello (2011) for a discussion of strategies for promoting the rights of transgender families using advancements in science and the legal system.

17. See Vanderburgh (2012) on the need for childbirth professionals to develop greater cultural competency around the identities and birth/family care needs of trans people and their partners. See Henig (2014) for mainstream coverage of some of the challenges that pregnant trans men face.

18. See Hines (2006).

19. For notable exceptions, see Brown (2005); Mason (2006); Nyamora (2004); Pfeffer (2009); Sanger (2007); Tompkins (2011); Ward (2010).

20. See Ward (2010).

21. For those interested in reading more about the household labor and emotion work reported by women partners of trans men in this study, see Pfeffer (2010).

22. For additional discussion of women partners' involvement in postsurgical after-care for these largely outpatient transition-related surgeries, see Pfeffer (2010).

23. See Turner (1969).

24. See Nestle, Howell, and Wilchins (2002).

25. See Nestle, Howell, and Wilchins (2002:88).

26. So, too, does photographic work by Mariette Pathy Allen (2003), Loren Cameron (1996), Jana Marcus (2011), and Del LaGrace Volcano [in Halberstam and Volcano (1999)].

27. Similarly, Iantaffi and Bockting (2011) find, in a large sample of trans partici-pants, high levels of practices that could be classified as heteronormative. In other words, that this trans sample was similar to most cis samples from their respective populations.

28. While Connell (2009) describes the social processes whereby individuals make gender attributions for trans people as one of "recognition," I (see Pfeffer 2014a) broaden and extend this framework to consider how people make gender and sex-uality attributions for all people, terming this process "(mis)recognition," while Westbrook and Schilt (2014) term their framework for how people make gender attributions "determining gender." A shared feature across all of these analyses and frameworks is their central focus on identity attributional processes that establish and reify normative assumptions about the way that sex, gender, and sexuality "should" align.

29. See Westbrook and Schilt (2014).

30. See Kessler and McKenna (1978).

31. An alternative explanation of Polly's exclamation is that she simply felt guilty to be doing so little of the pet care, not that her guilt was in recognition of the potential gender-typing of such a household task.

32. See Glazer (1990, 1993) and Guberman, Gagnon, Côté, Gilbert, Thiviérge, and Tremblay (2005).

4

Partners Negotiating Bodies, Sexuality, and Intimacy

When we consider what it means to be in a postmodern partnership, the body and sexuality are primary sites for illustrating the ways in which meanings are often fractured and reconfigured. In the 21st century, hysterectomies, mastectomies and mammaplasties, phalloplasties and vaginoplasties, testosterone and estrogen injections, limb prostheses, implantable insulin pumps, stem cell transplants, and pacemakers, to name but a few embodied medical interventions, quite literally reshape the contours of interpersonal interactions and bodies both inside and out. Flesh and bone meet silicone and surgical steel as sutures dissolve and staples are removed, leaving traces of scars stretching across skin as family members weave stories that bring meaning to their experiences. Medical technologies are recontouring bodies and life possibilities to a greater extent than ever before. Trans men's embodied transitions highlight our increasing ability to transform our bodies in the 21st century using these medical technologies. In this chapter, I consider some of the specific ways in which trans embodiments are shaped, made possible, and limited using existing medical technologies. I will also consider the ways in which trans men and their cis women partners engage in sexual practices that transcend the body's literal contours and limits, reconfiguring possibilities for gender, sexual relationships, and identities.

Trans sexuality and partnerships have become the focus of a number of relatively recent texts published outside of academia. Miranda Bellwether's[1] inaugural zine, *Fucking Trans Women (Issue #0)*, broke ground by centering trans women's perspectives and experiences around sex and sexuality, including instructional guides on actual sexual practices. The quarterly print zine, *Original Plumbing*, edited by Amos Mac and Rocco Kayiatos, debuted in 2009 and expanded to the Internet in 2010. *Original Plumbing* features first-person accounts and photography of the lives and experiences of trans men, including focus on sex and sexuality (Mac and Kayiatos, 2009). Morty Diamond's[2] edited volume, *Trans/Love: Radical Sex, Love & Relationships Beyond the Binary* and Tracie O'Keefe and Katrina Fox's[3] edited volume, *Trans People in Love*, each make contributions to featuring the voices and experiences of trans people and their partners as they discuss sex and relationships. Tristan Taormino's 2011 edited volume, *Take Me There: Trans and Genderqueer Erotica* centers on explicit narratives about trans sexuality. An expanding genre of trans-focused and trans-affirmative pornography has also emerged through Handbasket Productions, Morty Diamond Productions, Pink & White Productions, S.I.R. Video Productions, and T-Wood Pictures, to name just a handful.

In academic scholarship on LGBTQ sexualities, however, "trans" too often remains present in acronym only,[4] with very real consequences both in terms of excluding actual trans people and their everyday lives and producing incomplete and partial scholarship.[5] When trans sexuality does appear within academic scholarship, it often focuses on forms of sexuality considered problematic, pathological, and/or connected to health risk (e.g., trans sexual labor or theoretical and empirical work on "autogynephilia," as discussed in Chapter 1). Academic approaches to trans sexualities[6] are well situated to deconstruct and perhaps even reframe how trans sexualities are understood and represented. One of the challenges of approaching sex and sexuality from an academic perspective is that academics have a tendency to shy away from topics and language considered "crass." In many instances, the very materiality and corporeality of sex and sexuality are extracted and transformed into dry academic prose.

Notably, careful consideration of the ways in which various embodiments and sexual interaction may play critical roles in partnerships and families seldom appears in books focusing on partnerships and families.[7] This is despite the fact that partnerships and families are often initiated through processes of sexual attraction and are not infrequently rocked to their foundations by sexual incompatibility, boredom, communication issues, loss of attraction, and infidelity. Sociologist Kevin Walby writes about the importance of studying sex and sexual practices from academic perspectives: "[We] must start with bodies coming together, their parts and fluids, the interactions between bodies and the meanings produced therein."[8] It is my hope and intention that this chapter does this as it also responds to the very last line of Joshua Gamson's review of more than a decade of sociological texts in the area of LGBT issues: "LGBT sociology books, you might say, could use some more sex."[9]

I argue that we must broaden these critiques to include embodiment and sexuality as vital and necessary components of more holistic studies of partnership and the family. While positive sexual relationships are often considered integral to the health and well-being of partnerships,[10] family studies research rarely includes substantive discussion of the forms and dynamics of these sexual practices themselves. By cloaking these practices under the guise of privacy and propriety, researchers may miss important opportunities for better understanding family inequalities, sources of joy and communication, and sources of stress and strain in family life. In a sense, refocusing on sex and sexuality holds the power to queer studies of postmodern partnerships and families.

While sexuality among cis women and their trans men partners has rarely been explored by academic researchers,[11] glimpses of sexually intimate relationships have been gleaned through published narratives from trans men and their cis women partners within autobiographies and anthologies about trans experience. Trans man Marcus Rene Van,[12] for example, discusses the intricate ways in which identity is partially co-constructed and validated with a partner through sex and sexuality:

> In the bedroom I need a woman who sees the man I am and treats me that way. It's difficult to be with a partner who is not understanding of transgender lovers. Even though I bring a strong sense of self-awareness to any sexual encounter, if a partner does not relate to me as male, it's hard to connect. I need a woman who can respect what I am. My trans sexuality is the mental and physical pleasure existing in the same space. It's a fragile world, constructed on beliefs and acceptance, and mirrored in a partner's gaze. This is not to say that it is all a mind game: that undercuts the fact that the connection between partners is visceral and real. Our worlds are connected at some place that reaches beneath the surface. When she says, "You have a shaft," I believe her, and feel myself getting mini-hard on her fingers. Never mind that my dick is enclosed in the folded skin of labia.

Through sexual interaction and language, trans people and their partners generate possibilities beyond the contours of flesh, rendering the meanings of this flesh mutable, a postmodern sexuality of sorts.

As Carol Queen and Lawrence Schimel write:

> "Pomosexual" ... describes the community's outsiders, the *queer* queers who can't seem to stay put within a nice simple identity. ... Pomosexuality challenges either/or categorizations in favor of largely unmapped possibility and the intense charge that comes with transgression. It acknowledges the pleasure of that transgression, as well as the need to transgress limits that do not make room for all of us.[13]

Minnie Bruce Pratt offers one of the few published explicit articulations of the ways in which sex, gender, and sexuality interface:

> In my groans of pleasure from your cock, perhaps some would say I have betrayed womanhood with you, that we are traitors to our sex. You refusing to allow the gestures of what is called masculinity to be preempted by men. Me refusing to relinquish the ecstasies of surrender to women who can only call it subservience. Traitors to our sex, or spies and explorers across the boundaries of what is man, what is woman? My body yawns open greedily for what you are not afraid to give me.[14]

While sexual interactions that validate each partner's gender identity are critical for the health and well-being of most relationships in general,[15] sexual partnerships with trans people may highlight the inability for binary notions of gender to make sense for all bodies and identities. Minnie Bruce Pratt writes: "Sometimes I hold you, brushing my hand over the silky stubble of your hair and say, 'You're my girl, you're my boy'."[16] Pratt also recounts her response to the question, "Is he your husband?" from a social acquaintance, supplying the response: "Yes, she is."[17]

While much has been written on trans men's experiences of their bodies,[18] scholarship on partners' experiences of their trans partner's body is relatively rare. Moreover, few sources discuss the ways in which body transformations during and after gender transition may affect not only intimate sexual and non-sexual interactions between partners, but the way a partner feels about their own body as well. Despite glimmers of evidence that language and sexual interactions play some role in validating the identities of both trans and cis people in relationships, little mention is made in the research literature about these interactions and possibilities. The effects that supplemental hormones and gender-affirming surgeries may have on the partners of trans people, in terms of their relationships, are also rarely discussed.[19]

Sex and sexuality are generally considered fundamental components of most romantic relationships, yet there remain palpable silences around cis women's embodied experiences of sexuality with trans men partners. In this chapter, I want to challenge these silences by offering open and frank accounts, from the cis women I interviewed, about how considering transition and trans embodiment is critical for understanding sexual relationships between trans people and their partners. Simultaneously, I also wish to be cautious and to acknowledge how tender discussion of these components of everyday family life and experience can be given the cultural context of exploitation and sensationalism around trans bodies and sexuality.

There is an inherent tension in this chapter. A frequent refrain from within trans communities is, "Don't ask me about my junk!"[20] Quite simply put, many people view trans bodies (especially genitals) and sexualities as if they were public property. The motivation for the questions often seems to derive from the belief that it will be easier to classify and categorize a trans person if their interlocutor knows more about what lies underneath a trans person's clothing and how it figures into sexual interactions with others. While it would be in very poor taste, indeed, to ask a relative stranger about their genitals and how they use them, trans people field these sorts of intrusive and reductive demands for information with shocking regularity. My intention in this chapter is not to feed or justify prurient interest in trans embodiments and sexualities. Rather, it is to take trans embodiments and sexualities seriously and to begin to more seriously consider their interactional dimensions as well. I also hope that portions of this chapter might serve as a primer for building knowledge about some forms of trans embodiment and sexualities that may reduce ignorance and intrusive questioning around these topics. Across this chapter I urge consideration of trans embodiments and sexualities not as spectacle or farce, as they are too often constructed in media and popular discourse, but as key sites of personal and interpersonal struggle and innovation, processes that should resonate with many readers regardless of their own embodiments and sexualities.

WHAT WE KNOW ABOUT TRANS SEXUALITIES AND EMBODIMENTS

Bodies in Transition

Intramuscular injection of testosterone (often referred to as "T") is the most common method among trans men for administering hormones. Usually, shots are self-administered every 2 weeks, generally in the buttock or hip area. In some instances, topical testosterone may be used instead of (or in addition to) intramuscular injections. New implantable forms of subdermal testosterone allow for less-frequent testosterone administration and slower, more consistent release. Once the effects of testosterone become evident, they are often quite striking. Facial and body hair growth accelerates within just a few months; but it may take several years for some trans men to grow a full beard, and many will never do so (just as many cis men do not). After years of testosterone administration, some trans men may experience a receding hairline, an indicator of male-pattern baldness. Menstruation usually stops within just a few weeks or months, but may take up to 6 months for some. Acne may develop within weeks of starting hormones and usually tapers off after several years on testosterone.

Deepening of the voice and increasing muscle mass generally begin within 6 months. Almost immediately, some trans men report increased sex drive, particularly as the clitoris begins to enlarge.[21] The clitoris may grow up to 2.5 inches after several years of testosterone administration. The skin "roughens" within the first several months. Some cis women I interviewed who had been with their trans partner prior to the beginning of his transition spoke to me about how they perceived a shift in their partner's scent as well. Some described this shifting scent as located primarily in the skin, while others mentioned urine, and/or genitals. Fat re-distribution often occurs over the first several years, with fat shifting from the hips and thighs to the torso and "squaring" off facial features. Some of these changes are permanent (voice deepening, clitoral growth) while others (such as menstruation) may return to their pre-transition state if hormone administration is discontinued.[22]

In addition to these physical changes, some cis women I interviewed also described emotional and cognitive changes in their trans partner that they sometimes attributed to testosterone. In the autobiographical literature, some trans men report becoming more easily angered or moody, particularly as their shot begins to "wear off" during the end of the second week. Others report a decrease in emotionality and tearfulness—a steadying of emotions. Some claim that their thinking becomes more linear and logical. It is difficult to assess whether these perceived changes are largely physiologically or socioculturally motivated, and some trans men assert that these changes are often overstated or even mythical. As one of my interviewees, Selma, stated: "You hear about testosterone rage and it's such a myth. And it's kind of how we always thought; if you had an anger issue before, you're probably still going to have one that is exacerbated now if you don't have good anger management skills."

Possible short- and long-term complications of testosterone administration include the development of "saggy" or pendulous chest tissue (in those who have not had "top" surgeries); edema (fluid retention); weight gain; acne; polycythemia (an overproduction of red blood cells); phlebitis (inflammation of the veins, particularly in the leg); changes in liver function; hypertension (high blood pressure); elevated levels of triglycerides and cholesterol; increased risk for cardiovascular disease; and increased risk of ovarian and uterine cancers upon long-term administration of testosterone without oopherectomy and hysterectomy (surgical removal of the ovaries and/or uterus).[23] In addition to these potential risks, trans men sometimes face added discrimination when seeking medical care to prevent or treat these side effects or other health concerns. The documentary, *Southern Comfort*,[24] details the last years in the life of Robert Eads, a trans man who died from ovarian cancer that several doctors refused to treat because of his identity as a trans man.

In light of the profound physical and psychological changes that trans men often report, many describe entering into "a second adolescence." Not only may this period *feel* like a second adolescence for many, but (as discussed in Chapter 2), it is important to remember that some trans men may *look* like or be socially perceived as teenagers even when they are in their 20s, 30s and even 40s. Matt Kailey writes in his autobiography:

There's nothing like going through a second adolescence in middle age. Male puberty is a curious thing that's best undertaken by someone with a lot of youthful energy, exuberance, and resilience . . . someone, say, 13 or 14 years old. But if you missed it the first time around, intramuscular injections of pharmaceutical testosterone can re-create the experience so realistically that you can almost picture yourself in the middle school cafeteria preparing for a food fight.[25]

In my research, I find that the youthful masculine appearances of many trans men may also affect the way in which their partners are viewed in the world.

The cis women I interviewed spoke to me about social *mis*recognition of a considerable age difference between themselves and their partners. Trans men are often socially perceived to be younger than they actually are, especially if their facial hair is either shaved or not well developed. Trans man Lou Sullivan, in 1980, published an article entitled, "How to look 30 when you ARE 30." Sullivan writes: "The biggest problem when going female-to-male is that a 30-year-old female, when cross-dressed as a man, can end up looking like a 14-year-old-boy."[26] The effect of this social *mis*perception of youth means that in many couples consisting of trans men and cis women, cis women are often perceived as much older than their trans partners. In some instances, cis women even spoke to me about being misrecognized as their partner's mother, a decidedly unsexy prospect for most.

In another autobiographical work, Max Wolf Valerio describes some of his experiences upon beginning testosterone: "My energy is like a teenage boy's—moving, pacing, shifting in my seat, speaking in wild bursts. I'm inter-rupting people in conversation, suddenly overcome with bolts of enthusiasm—I can't hold back! I feel more confident, expansive, cocky. It's a pounding-on-the-chest kind of feeling, a swagger, a strut."[27] Mark Rees describes himself as "more like a gawky adolescent than a man nearing thirty."[28] Mark Angelo Cummings writes in his autobiography: "I went through puberty at 39 years of age. Like a teenage boy, my voice cracked with every syllable I spoke."[29]

Jamison Green describes this period in his autobiography as a wondrous, though difficult and lonely period:

> I now felt faced with rebuilding my relationship with the entire world. I had no one to guide me through what was turning out to be a new adolescence composed of the physical changes and social adjustments necessitated by becoming a visible man. . . . [There was a] problematic difference between my chronological age (mid-forties) and my biochemical age as I recreated myself (late teens). There weren't many other transmen I could talk with, since "community" didn't really exist then.[30]

This "adolescent" stage, while exhilarating for some, is described as a fairly hell-ish period of indeterminacy for others.[31] For many trans men, the effects brought about by testosterone, and their ability to be recognized, socially, as men, was enough. Others, however, determine that they wish to pursue "top" and/or "bot-tom" surgeries as a central component of their transitions.

Bleeding Like a Man

Given the large proportion of cis women in the study whose partners were tak-ing testosterone, some interviewees spoke to me about the various excitement and challenges they and their partners experienced as their trans partner's body transformed upon testosterone administration. While testosterone administra-tion at sufficient doses generally ends menstruation, trans men must often find a correct dose for their body, which may take several months. In the interim, it was not uncommon for trans men to menstruate. Further, some trans men do not experience complete cessation of menses even following long-term testoster-one administration. As Jodi told me: "He feels betrayed by his body whenever he does bleed."

Ellia spoke to me about the ways in which menstruation could serve as a criti-cal and undesired mark of female embodiment for her partner during the earli-est stages of his physical transition:

> The first month [he was on testosterone] he had a full on period and that was horrible for him. He was not like hysterically crying, but noticeably very dis-turbed and very upset. He called his endocrinologist and said, "What the hell is going on? I need this to stop!" Because she had started him on a very low

dose of the [testosterone topical] gel. And then the next month, he didn't tell me he had his period. He didn't have a full-on period, but he was spotting and he was uncomfortable about that and he didn't say anything. But I noticed he wouldn't let me touch him, so I figured it out through that. And that was very hard for him. He was going through this, "I'm a man. Why do I have my period? I can't have my period. That's such a female thing to have. I can't go into the men's restroom and change my tampon." And luckily it stopped after that. He hasn't had it since. Thank God because it was very difficult for him.

Ellia was one of a number of cis women who told me that her trans partner was uncomfortable buying or being seen with menstrual supplies such as pads and tampons until *after* he no longer menstruated himself: "In the past he was never really comfortable buying that stuff but now he is." Similarly, Martha told me:

He was very uncomfortable having tampons around. One time we were out in public and he had his "thing" and he came up to me and he whispered, "Do you have something with you?" And I said, "Yeah," and pulled a tampon out of my pocket and handed it to him. We were on the street. And he got very upset with me. He said, "You can't ever do that. Don't ever do that again. If I need you to hand me something like that, we go somewhere private and we do it. But you don't ever do that." So, it was a very private thing for him.

Exchanges such as these could be particularly challenging to the cis women I interviewed as interactions between partners that had been accepted and even mundane at earlier points in their partnership were suddenly filled with tension or entirely unacceptable, sometimes without their conscious awareness that a shift was underway or necessary.

Some cis women talked about how they and their partners co-created a language around menstruation that felt less linked to the feminine or female. Some of the terms used for menstruation itself included "Fred," "bleeding," "leaking," "manstrual cycle," "manstruation," "my thing," "TMS" [for "testosterone male syndrome"], and "my boy." Terms for tampons and other menstrual supplies included "evil Ts," "diapers," and "those things." Not all cis women reported that their trans partner was uncomfortable menstruating. For example, Samantha told me: "He's really like okay with himself. He knows that he's male and even bio guys bleed. It has no sort of bad connection in his brain." While cis women were generally not taken aback by transition-related shifts in their partner's menstrual cycle and his reaction to it, some reported relatively greater challenges around their trans partner's transition-related shifts in sexual attractions and desires.

Identities in Transition

An unanticipated finding in my research was that a considerable number of the trans partners of the cis women in my study became sexually interested in other men, either cis or trans, over the course of their relationship. Cis women often made sense of this development as an outgrowth of a testosterone-driven pubertal developmental phase. Some cis women considered the possibility that a trans partner's new attraction toward other men may be a way for some formerly lesbian-identified trans men to retain their self-identification as same-sex attracted or "gay" rather than disappearing into heterosexuality. Yet other women spoke about the potential for sexual relationships with other men to provide the ultimate validation of a trans man's identity as a man. While some women described a partner's new sexual interest in other men as a phase and something that did not concern them very much, other partners expressed some fear or trepidation. As Selma, whose partner had developed sexual interest in other men, told me:

> The odds are against us that our relationship survives, especially when you were in that relationship pre-transition. They're not favorable. On pretty much every article, and every news show, and things that I've seen, there are very few couples that survive intact 5 or 6 years down the road.[32] And I'm fearful about that. There is so much in question. It's very much a puberty, a time of growth, exploration, experimenting. And for me, what I've decided and am comfortable with [is], "Okay. I will help you explore these things. And you'll do them with my knowledge and my understanding' ... in hopes that that makes us that much stronger. Because if it doesn't, there was nothing else I could do anyway. But I worry about it. I'm very ambivalent ... because I wouldn't have wanted to miss this journey, not a step of it. It's been my honor, it really has. And still there are days that I think, 'I can't believe it's me you picked to walk by your side.' And I amaze myself at my level of understanding and how easy it comes to me to just go with the flow with every new adaptation.... But also to think *you* might be what's sacrificed in the end for all of your understanding and all of your support and everything.... I wouldn't have missed the trip, but I think that I'm not alone when I say that I think a lot of partners have an underlying insecurity. Will it still be me that they want?

Concern that a trans partner's desire to sexually experiment with other men might not just be a phase, but something more permanent, was mentioned by a considerable number of the cis women I interviewed whose partner had developed such attractions. In other instances interviewees spoke about, being cruised by gay men was reportedly desired by their trans partner not because of reciprocated sexual attraction or interest, but because it confirmed and validated that they had been socially "read" as a man by someone considered an expert in, well, men.[33] Nina told me:

> Around a lot of young gay guys his age, they definitely think he is gay.... This [gay] guy was just shocked to find out that he had a girlfriend. Like, "You seem like you should have a boyfriend." We were [in a gay neighborhood]

a couple of weeks ago at this mostly gay boy bar. Gay men communities definitely read him as being a fag, which is fine with him. . . . Depending on what sort of group we are in, we get read really differently.

Some of the emotions and feelings interviewees mentioned experiencing upon recognizing that their trans partner was being cruised by gay men included indifference, annoyance, sexual arousal, fear, humor, invisibility, and anger.[34] In the following sections, I consider not only shifting sexual desires, but shifting sexual embodiments as well.

SEXUAL EMBODIMENTS AND SATISFACTION

Bottom Surgery

While the vast majority of the cis women I interviewed reported that their trans partners were taking or wanted to take testosterone in the future,[35] and had had or wanted to have top surgery in the future,[36] a much smaller number had had or wanted to have bottom surgery in the future.[37] In a blended study with 74 trans men participants, Kristen Schilt and Elroi Windsor[38] found that, among their sample participants, transition tended to focus primarily on aligning gender identity with outer social appearance and, for many, had little if anything to do with surgically altering genitalia. Indeed, very few sample respondents reported having genital surgeries and phalloplasty was particularly rare. Further, many of Schilt and Windsor's participants reported that as they were increasingly socially recognized as men by others, the self-reported importance of having a surgically constructed penis diminished. In another study of 25 trans men, by Williams, Weinberg, and Rosenberger,[39] how comfortable trans men were with their bodies was impacted by partners' comfort with, and acceptance of, their body as male no matter its particular contours.

The trans men in each of these studies held sexual identities across the spectrum that, in some cases, shifted as they transitioned. Their reported sexual practices also sometimes shifted or were reinterpreted depending upon the gender and sexual identities of their partner(s). Trans men described generally fulfilling sex lives with partners across the sex and gender spectrum, prompting reconsideration of phallocentric assumptions about gendered embodiment and sexual satisfaction. Schilt and Windsor draw upon these findings to develop a sociological theory of "sexual habitus," the constellation of sexual practices and potential sexual partners with which and whom one engages across time. They note that the sexual habitus of the trans men in their sample often shifted during transition, from one set of sexual practices to another, and that the gender of one's sexual partners could also shift. Williams, Weinberg, and Rosenberger[40] develop a theory of trans sexual embodiment, wherein gender and sexual embodiments develop in ways that are loosely, moderately, or tightly coupled. The desire for bottom surgery often depended upon the strength of these couplings between gender and sexual embodiments, as well as upon the gender of one's sexual partners.

In mainstream representations of sexuality between cis men and women, penetrative sexual intercourse involving a penis and vagina is often considered the hallmark of sexual interaction. One might assume, then, that not having a flesh-and-blood penis would be considered an essential *lack* that trans men experience and one that derails sexual intimacy between trans men and their cis women partners. Not so, according to most of the cis women I interviewed. Sage told me: "He absolutely does not [want bottom surgery] at all.... He's just really not interested in having any sort of phallus attached to his body." As Jodi noted, not having a flesh-and-blood penis might even open up greater possibility for a broader range of sexual embodiments and interactions: "Sometimes we call them his 'peni' because we have a couple different ones." Mel said: "[My partner] doesn't really have an interest in having his own penis or feel a lack at not having one and I don't really feel a need for him to have one either." As Lily explained:

We both think phalloplasty is stupid.... [My partner] had to get used to the cognitive dissonance of having a brain that didn't fit the body.... Finding out that there were FTMs that didn't physically transition and were so productive and were happy and everything? [We felt like] that might work just because the options aren't tremendously amazing ... the surgery options. It's really more about getting to live the kind of life that [my partner] wants rather than being able to look in the mirror and flex a penis or something.

When discussing how they or their partner felt about the possibility of having bottom surgery, cis women mostly reported disinterest given the cost, poor results[41] with regard to appearance and sexual function, long recovery times, and high complication rates.

As Amber told me:

He says now that at this point in time he doesn't feel any form of bottom surgery is necessary. He's content with himself right now ... he already feels like a male so he doesn't think that spending more money and getting something that may or may not be useful ... like it won't function properly.... Is it really going to make him any more content or any more male? He's content for the time being with just what he has.

Concerns about phalloplasty are also reported across the autobiographical literature of many trans men. Mark Rees, discussing his decision not to have phalloplasty, writes:

Were the surgery (both for sex and micturition[42]) safe, and the constructed phallus sensitive, aesthetically pleasing and functional, then it would be a different matter, but with the present situation in this field I believe that it is wiser to make the best of what one has got. For me, the price is too high. Many people have ended up worse off than before, some even to the point of suicide. I do not want to be one of them.[43]

A British study[44] compared 40 trans men who underwent phalloplasty with a group of 23 trans men who had been approved for the surgery but had not yet had it. In a comparison of these groups, it was shown that the postoperative group was more depressed and had lower relationship satisfaction.[45] However, once a decision is made about various transition-related surgeries, postoperative regret among trans men, opting for either "top" or "bottom" surgery (or both), has been reported at exceedingly low rates.[46]

The literature on transition-related surgeries primarily focuses on the experiences of White trans men and most researchers do not discuss the risk of surgical complications in both "top" and "bottom" surgeries among darker-skinned men, who may face greater risks for developing keloids and more extensive scarring.[47] The costs of transition surgeries also prove prohibitive to many of those seeking them, particularly among those who are unemployed or working-class, populations in which trans men of color may be disproportionately situated.[48] As Mark Angelo Cummings, born in Havana, Cuba, writes about his thoughts surrounding the possibility of transition surgeries: "I could never afford the surgery, this was something they did in another country."[49] In the autobiographical literature from trans men, widely-varying reported surgical costs ranged from $5,000 to $200,000, with most costs generally not covered by insurance.[50]

Among the cis women I interviewed, many discussed conversations they and their partner had about the possibility of pursuing bottom surgery. Donna said:

> Well, he has no interest because it's not a very good surgery. Like, nobody is getting very good results. You know, if you could just plop a good one on there. Yeah, great; that would be great! But to lose a part of an arm or thigh or whatever other body part is, you know, way so not worth it to him. Especially since we obviously know how to negotiate sex without the penis. And all that is fairly straight up.

June offered a similar assessment:

> I guess his transition will never come to an end. But as for [not pursuing] bottom surgery: for one it's the costs and two it's the end result. Right now, trans men's surgeries, for the most part, don't appear to look like a non-trans man's penis. Nor do they guarantee that it's going to work. So, for [him], he's not willing to give up what he has now for something that won't be aesthetically pleasing or sexually pleasing to him.

Jodi went so far as to describe current surgical results of phalloplasty as "horrifying" and "disappointing," while Rachel used the term "creepy" and Toby "disgusting" to describe their partners' assessments of the typical results of phalloplasty at that time (between 2005 and 2007).[51]

Given the perceived state of phalloplasty outcomes and cost at the time I conducted interviews,[52] a number of cis women discussed their trans partner's intention of not having phalloplasty at that time and either leaving the possibility open for future phalloplasty (when it becomes cheaper and more effective) or other types of bottom surgery (such as metoidioplasty, defined below). As Judy said: "He's talked about bottom surgery; no immediate future on it. I think he's going to wait until medicine advances until he messes around with the sexual organs. I know he doesn't want to do the phallo." Other cis women discussed alternatives to pursuing phalloplasty. Lea said: "I think [bottom surgery's] great for the person who wants [it]. I think it's fantastic if that's what they need. I'm of the thinking that interchangeable parts is fine and [my partner] feels the same way right now. He's looking at it very medically. This is a lot of work right now for something that's not perfected." Across the autobiographical literature from trans men, some have written about the feeling that without both "top" and "bottom" surgeries, they are not "complete."[53] Despite this, most studies of trans men consistently find low rates of bottom surgery among sample participants.[54]

In a small German study of trans men following phalloplasty, the number of reported orgasms had increased, general and sexual satisfaction were both high, and the frequency of reported sexual encounters increased by 100%.[55] In one review of studies on trans men's transition surgeries, there was an 80% overall reported satisfaction rate.[56] Phalloplasty is not the only (or even the most common) type of "bottom surgery" considered by trans men. Metoidioplasty, which is often abbreviated as "meta" or "meto," is a surgery that capitalizes on testosterone's ability to enlarge clitoral tissue. Following clitoral enlargement, metoidioplasty involves untethering clitoral tissue from a relatively flattened position on the body by severing ligaments that surround this structure and then moving it forward, creating a micropenis. The micropenis is capable of erection and ranges in length from 1–3 inches, on average. In some instances, the urethra is extended and rerouted so that the trans man may urinate from their micropenis. Some trans men also elect scrotoplasty, which involves the surgical construction of a scrotum below the micropenis.

Metoidioplasty is much more common among trans men than phalloplasty given that the procedure is less complicated, requires less time for recovery, generally preserves sexual sensation, and does not require the use of stiffening rods for erection.[57] The largest complaint with the surgery generally involves the "micro" aspect of the penis or its inability to become as rigid as some trans men would prefer. Unlike discussions of phalloplasty, for cis women whose trans partners pursued metoidioplasty, outcomes were generally described more positively. As Margaret told me: "He had metoidioplasty with urethral lengthening and testicular implants . . . He had incredible results like virtually in probably a year post-op it would be hard for a doctor, on a quick glance, to recognize that he was not born the way that he now looks."

The Place of the Penis

Many cis women described how synthetic penises, strap-ons, and dildos had become a critical component of sexual interactions with their trans partner and one of the ways in which sexual interactions contributed to the co-construction of gender and sexual identities for both themselves and their partners. In some instances, use of a synthetic penis was a part of sexual interaction that had shifted over the course of the relationship between a cis woman and her trans partner, a shift that was welcomed in some instances and not so much in others. Emma told me:

> The way that our sex life looked did drastically change to the point where we were first together as two women and both of our bodies were completely open to one another. And even the sexual acts that we did, initially, we didn't have any of the sex toys in our life. And then that started to become part of our sex life and then it got the point where 9 times out of 10 our sex ended up being about intercourse.

Frieda spoke to me about the intercourse-focused sexual experiences she had with an ex partner. She said:

> [My partner] was very much stone[58] and didn't want to be touched in any particular way because he didn't enjoy his breasts or his cunt or anything like that. He wanted to ignore it and hope that he could just wake up with a penis and it would all go away and with a flat chest. So, there was no enjoying any of that. So, basically sex was very one-sided and it was very much about the strap-on and a lot of talking and imagination and getting him to believe where he was. I was bored. The whole time, he would ask me stuff, and I'd be like how many times can I describe it? And, "Oh yeah, your penis inside me feels so good! Oh my God." Yeah, I was very bored. I was describing these things that were supposed to feel so amazing, but they didn't. It was about strap it on, get it in, get on top, get it in kind of thing but the whole imagination thing so that he can get off and then he can roll over and go to sleep. I don't remember very many orgasms or anything like that. I don't remember too many times when he concentrated much on me. I'm sure there were times and I'm sure that we did have some great times, but I'm having difficulty recalling them.[59]

Narratives like Frieda's were stark in their assessment of some trans partners becoming very sexually self-focused and intercourse focused, especially during the earliest stages of transition. In partnerships where cis women perceived this to be the case, they often reported feelings of detachment.

Willow, who was currently partnered with a trans man at the point of our interview, talked to me about difficulties she had feeling connected with her partner during sexual interactions:

When we have sex there's this sense that he *needs* it, in his own body and his own head. I feel left out of the picture. I feel like I could be a doll, a prop, something else. And he doesn't know how to have really joined sex. We're not having sex because I get cold, I don't get aroused, and if I don't get aroused, it's like I'm a cold fish. And when we have good sex it's really good. He thinks that I just want to be fucked and it's not all I want. I want intimacy.

Rachel talked to me about challenges around feeling sexually connected to her trans partner when their primary sexual interactions involved her trans partner penetrating her with a prosthetic penis:

When we first met he wanted to use a strap-on all the time and, at first, it was fine and then it started to, for me, feel more like a barrier than a connector. I felt more separated from his body than brought closer to him. And I didn't know how to express this to him but it was starting to get really frustrating for me. . . . Every once in a while, that is fine; but as far as that being every single time we had sex. It was really starting to fuck with my head a little bit and I didn't know how to talk to him about it. He had always referred to it as part of his body, so I didn't want him to feel like I was rejecting him. . . . I feel like it's blasphemy for me to say in some ways. . .but it doesn't have a heartbeat. . . . I know some people can say it feels the same and they see that as a part of their partner's body; I just can't.

These descriptions are remarkably reminiscent of some heterosexual cis women's accounts of unsatisfying sexual experiences with cis men. The common feature of each of these types of accounts seems to be primary focus on men's genitals (however they might be configured) and a relative lack of attention to intimacy, sexual communication, and women's sexual pleasure.[60] Nicola Brown[61] found similar trends in her study of 20 cis women partners of trans men. It is important to note, however, that the focus on penis-vagina intercourse that a number of cis women across each of these samples discuss could be artifactual and compensatory; as mentioned earlier, many trans men and cis women report increased focus on penis prostheses and intercourse near the beginning of transition, when trans men are becoming accustomed to their shifting sociosexual embodiments. This focus may shift over time as trans men and their partners communicate and as trans men gain increased nonsexual social recognition as men by others in their lives.

Certainly, not all of the sexual relationships with trans partners that cis women described employed the frequent use of a prosthetic penis and not all cis women I interviewed felt negatively toward them. As Maya reported:

[My partner] prefers not to use a dildo in either direction. I like the sensation and so when I asked for it, it's tricky; because sometimes when I ask for it, it reminds him that he doesn't have something he really wants to have.

He starts thinking that I'm feeling like I'm missing out and then he's reluc-
tant to use it. Even though I say that I'm perfectly happy with the parts that
he has. But he doesn't have an 8-inch cock and the cock feels a lot different
than his hand. It's a different feeling. I tried to convince him that it's just the
feeling that I'm looking for, not that I feel like he's not whole. He feels like
he's not whole. So, usually it doesn't work if I specifically and directly ask
for it. Usually I have to kind of beat around the bush, pardon the pun. But
I indirectly ask for it and make suggestions and whatever.

Maya's discussion here about her partner not having an "8-inch cock" is interesting as it prompts consideration of the cultural anxiety surrounding penis
length and size among *all* men, not only those men who are trans. A thriving
consumer industry of products and surgeries for extending the length and size
of cis men's penises seems to suggest that many cis men, too, simply do not feel
"whole" with the genital appendages with which they were born. I think we can
usefully draw some parallels here between cis and trans men and perhaps even
better understand why so many cis men have a difficult time accepting trans
men as "real" men.[62] If jockeying for "real man" status among cis men is often
tied to contests over which member's member is most robust, then trans men
will often (though not always) come up short, particularly those who do not
pursue phalloplasty.

Even without surgeries like phalloplasty and metoidioplasty, however, the use
of testosterone often radically transforms trans men's genitals. Clitoral tissue,
after months to years of regular intramuscular testosterone injections (and, in
some cases, topical clitoral administration as well), usually grows; measuring,
on average, from 1–3 inches in length. As Selma told me: "I cannot see him as a
girl. It's like impossible. And so I don't see any of his parts as a girl either. I don't
see any of his parts as female." Nina concurred: "His genitalia looks really different now [after testosterone]. It is much more about giving him blowjobs like I
would give some other non-trans guy a blowjob." Cis men's flaccid penis length
is, on average, 3.61 inches, with an average erect length at 5.16 inches.[63] Further,
a small percentage of cis men are born with a "micropenis" that is quite similar
to the average size of many trans men's penises. As such, the size and sexual
function of some trans men's flesh and blood penises can be said to approximate
those of some cis men's, challenging simplistic or essentialist biological notions
of which biological traits or individuals constitute the group of "real" men. In
one study[64] of cis men who experienced a prostatectomy (removal of the prostate) as a treatment for prostate cancer, sexual functioning (the ability to have
or maintain an erection) was not significantly related to men's quality of life or
emotional distress despite the fact that they reported a high degree of erectile
dysfunction, overall, following their surgeries. In other words, even among cis
men, the penis and its sexual function need not make the man or determine the
quality of his life.

Perhaps even more noteworthy for the purposes of this book, among the partners of the cis men in the study[65] (most of whom were cis women), it was not their

partner's sexual *functioning* that was most predictive of their own quality of life, but their own level of sexual *satisfaction*. Given existing literatures on orgasm rates and sexual satisfaction among cis women, there is much evidence to believe that a penis (its presence, absence, or functionality) are of far less concern and relevance than partner communication, sexual openness, and knowledge about female orgasm (including the need for direct or indirect clitoral stimulation). It is possible that, among cis heterosexual couples facing an issue like erectile dysfunction, being compelled to generate an expanded set of sexual activities may result in greater and/or more consistent sexual satisfaction for women. In addition to considering the power and importance of new sexual repertoires, the critical importance of the development of new language was also described by participants in my study.

New Embodied Sexualities and Lexicons[66]

Cis women who were uncomfortable shifting their vernacular for body referents and sexual behaviors from those typically associated with the female or lesbian (e.g., "breasts," "clit," "dildo," "strap on," "vagina," "eating out," "go down on," "finger") to the (trans)male or heterosexual (e.g., "chest," "dick," "cock," "front hole," "bonus hole," "blow job," "fucking," "hand job"), often reported sexual tension and arguments between themselves and their trans partners. Not all cis women, however, reported challenges around developing a new lexicon and behavioral repertoire around sexuality. Tabitha discussed how she felt that her prior sexual experiences with both cis men and women had better prepared her for sexual interactions with her trans partner. When I asked her about the language she uses to describe her trans partner's genitals and the sort of sex in which they engage, she told me:

> I guess I would say "cock" for "clit" and I mostly just say "blow job" for "going down on" him because that was pretty much like what I would do. I kind of realized at that point that I was able to give the best tranny[67] boy blow job you can. I think it's good to have experience being with both women and men because it's kind of like a combination of going down on a woman and giving a biological guy[68] a blow job.

Given that many cis women also described sexual interactions with their trans partner that involve penises that are synthetic rather than flesh and blood, I also wanted to get a sense of the way in which cis women and their trans partners related to these prosthetic penises.

What sorts of language did they use? Did they relate to a prosthetic penis as an extension of their partner's body, as an object, something between these, or in some other way entirely? The intersection between synthetic body parts, flesh and flood body parts, and flesh and blood body parts that have transformed in response to testosterone administration, meant that cis women often

worked to develop and define their language around their trans partner's body.[69]
Cis women spoke to me about how their language choices for their partner's
anatomy would sometimes shift depending on context. For example, as Lynne
explained: "I think if we needed to talk about something involving his vagina,
we would say that. I mean if he got a yeast infection or something we would use
that word ['vagina'] if it was absolutely necessary to be used. But never in bed. In
sexuality, we would never use that word."

In addition to generating terms for body parts that might shift depending
on context, cis women also spoke to me about working to develop descriptive
terms that (a) differentiate between a partner's synthetic and flesh and blood
penis(es), and (b) capture the sexual hybridity of some trans genitals. As Eliza
described: "Basically [the prosthetic penis] is his cock. For his body, we'll refer
to it as 'mini-peen' or 'mini-penis' or 'micro-penis.' I once tried to come up with
a term that would sound both like 'cock' and 'clit' and the best I could come up
with was 'clock'. So, sometimes we joke about that . . . Oh and 'clenis' also doesn't
work [laughing]." Ellia talked to me about how the sorts of language one uses to
describe a trans partner's body could shift across time. I asked Ellia what sorts of
words she used to refer to her partner's chest (before top surgery) and flesh and
blood genitals. She said:

> If we were dirty talking and I called [my partner's chest] anything feminine,
> that would sort of kill the mood. Not outwardly, but you could just tell . . .
> whoops! So, I didn't really know how to deal with that at first. . . . I just call
> [my partner's flesh and blood genitals] "penis" even though it's not a typi-
> cal penis. People will call it a "dicklet" or "weenis," so we'll joke about it
> like that. But in a sexual context, it's just "penis," "dick," stuff like that . . .
> all male.

Samantha told me that she and her partner have adopted the use of the word
"crotch" to refer to everything below her partner's waist, as it is one of the few
unisex terms that exists to refer to genitalia. Despite existing gaps in sexual lexi-
cons, cis women and their trans partners are clearly at the vanguard of new terminology for trans sexual embodiments and its broader cultural dissemination.
This inventiveness of trans men and their partners when developing a lexicon
around trans sexual embodiments may also be linked to a broader constellation
of inventiveness: the establishment of queer sexual imaginaries.

Trans Embodiment and Queer Sexual Imaginaries

In the late 1990s, some femme-identified women began to publish essays on their
butch partners transitioning. I read these essays prior to interviewing cis women
partners of trans men and was struck by the ways in which the experiences that
many described keyed on developing a sexual imagination with the power to
transform experience and co-construct gendered identities. In one of these

essays from the late 1990s, Robin Maltz[70] ponders what femme partners' identities and sexualities will come to mean as their butch partners transition:

> One of a femme's areas of sexual expertise is her ability to transform a stone butch's body through acts of imagination, so that a stone butch never risks being "womanized." A femme knows how to masculinize a stone butch's body; a phallic length of silicon is not a dildo or a sex toy but a butch cock, and a chest is a chest, not breasts. If a trans man no longer needs masculine validation from a femme but rather by passing as a male, by body alteration, by blending into heterosexuality, is a femme still a femme? Or is she a significant other (a term for the partner of an FTM) who witnesses the gender/sex transformation instead of participating in an ongoing process of imaginatively re-creating gender? The transitions of butches to FTMs have left some femmes in the lurch. Do they follow their lovers into passing anonymity?

As first explored in Chapters 1 and 2, Maltz's queries raise important questions to consider in terms of the identities of the cis women partners of trans men. If they are feminine, are they femmes? Are they gender-normative? Are they cisgender? Are they heterosexual? Are they something different altogether?

One of my participants, Lilia, spoke about the ways in which her sexual relationships with some butch lesbian and trans men partners were both similar and different:

> I feel like a lot of times when we're having sex it's just about [my trans partner] pleasing me, which is frustrating. And I've been with a butch woman before who was not really into me touching her and she got pleasure from my pleasure sort of thing. But I don't know if [my trans partner's] really into that so much. I think he wants pleasure himself, which I want to give to him, which is hard.

In this instance, Lilia speaks about having similar sexual experiences with both butch and trans men partners. Yet she views the sexual desires of her butch and trans partners differently. Similarly, in both mainstream and lesbian cultures, sex involving a prosthetic penis is often described as "strap-on sex" and involves the use of what many describe as a "dildo," yet many of the cis women I interviewed described imaginatively adapting and inventing sexual language and practices in order to forge more direct connections between synthetic and flesh and blood genitals. In other words, while both butch lesbians and trans men may be employing the use of the same prosthetic penis, the meanings around that prosthetic penis may be quite different.[71]

As Emma told me about sex with her trans partner, "It tended to not be a 'dildo'. It tended to be … mainly the word 'cock' was used." Drea said: "He's gotten to the point over the last couple years where he doesn't actually use the strapping-on [harness] part of it. So, he keeps his underwear on and, for him, it's more preferable so he doesn't feel like he's having 'strap-on' sex. He doesn't feel like he's a big dyke having sex with a dildo. He can feel like it's more a part of him, against his skin." According to narratives like those offered by Emma and Drea, there are ways in which harnesses and terms like "dildo" *code* for lesbian sex. As such, some trans men and their cis women partners have adapted sexual language and practices that allow them to develop a stronger sense of connection with trans genitals (flesh and blood and synthetic), and to forge conceptual and behavioral distinctions between trans and lesbian bodies and sexual practices.[72]

Ellia talked to me about the language she uses to describe sexual interactions between herself and her partner that, on occasion, involve the use of a prosthetic penis:

> I just experimented with it sexually. . . . I would just treat it like a male penis or talk about it like that or instead of saying anything I would say, "blow job" and that hit right on, so I knew. . . . We both just view it as an extension of his body. Like I don't treat it any different. I don't act like he can't feel it. I just treat it like it's a penis, like "hand job," "blow job," like it's a full on and that's how he'll view it. It depends if we are using a strap on. . . . I mean we don't really like stop and take the time to differentiate. If it's there, it's a penis. If it's not then he just has a smaller penis and we have to do different stuff with it. . . . Before [top] surgery, we would use it more . . . not even for penetration, but just like gender play.

Ellia's descriptions were interesting as they suggested that top surgery could sometimes be sufficient for coding the body as male, consistent with other studies of trans men which demonstrate high rates of top surgery and low rates of bottom surgery.[73] After top surgery, Ellia's partner tended not to use a strap-on as often in their sexual interactions. In any case, the use of a prosthetic penis was treated as an extension of Ellia's partner's trans body. Tiffany offered further insights into how a prosthetic penis may be viewed as an extension of a trans partner's body: "There have been times that he's taken it off and set it on his desk and it's almost unnerving to me that it's not touching his body. It's definitely something that's his. He left if behind once and it seems very strange to have this thing in my room and not have him here. . . . It's like a foreign thing to me when it's not on him." In this way, prosthetic penises apart from a trans partner's body could seem eerie, a postmodern marker of queer sexual disembodiment.

As some of the previous narratives have alluded, whether or not a prosthetic penis was viewed as an extension of a trans partner's body or as an object could also depend on whether or not a harness or strap was used. As Nina described:

> Sometimes it is an extension, depending on how wears it. If he uses an actual harness or if he has it in boxer briefs, that changes it as well. With a harness . . . just a harness and no pants over it or anything . . . I can actually feel the leather and the metal. [Then] it's something that is harder to connect to as part of him. I'm distracted by something cold or something hard that doesn't feel good. So, when he's wearing a harness but is wearing something over it,

or he's not using a harness and [has it in] boxer briefs or tighty whiteys, it's more comfortable for him and so it's more relaxing for me. But it's also, physically, a lot closer to him than having leather between us ... [Then], I don't think about him penetrating me with a strap-on; it's definitely just *him*.

Eva described her partner's synthetic penis and flesh and blood genitals as united: "a fantasy dick." She told me: "As he took on more of a trans identity, we started to see it more as part of his body." As Drea relayed: "When you're using alternative terms and stuff for some part that is not *clinically* the case, obviously you're using some sense of alternate thinking, imagination, whatever you want to call it because you know, *clinically*, that's not the case."

The cis women I interviewed frequently used the term "it" to refer to both prosthetic and flesh and blood penises in connection with their trans partner and his body. This language did not seem indicative of any sort of discomfort around using more descriptive, explicit, or graphic language around sexual practices or organs. Indeed, the cis women I interviewed generally described, in much greater detail than I had initially anticipated they would, their sexual practices with their trans partners. Rather, cis women seemed to use the term "it" in absence of a pre-existing and well-established lexicon around trans sexual embodiments and practices.

Before interviewing cis women partners of trans men, I conducted an exhaustive review of the existing scholarly, autobiographical, and biographical literatures connected to trans identity and experience. I was struck by the following sexuality narratives from a trans man and his cis woman partner:

A transsexual male friend gives a class a discussion on his surgery. Afterward, a student inquires whether he can successfully have sex like a man, and he responds, "Yes, I can penetrate my lover and we can have simultaneous orgasm." Months later I read a sex piece by his lover in a national bisexual magazine. Unsure what to make of his one-inch penis, she devotes only a sentence or two to it, instead concentrating the bulk of the piece on his penetration of her with his fingers and how she can tell his absolute maleness from the deep, relentless way he fucks her for hours.[74]

I found this story intriguing not only because it reveals the discursive limits of representing trans *sexuality* but, also, because it challenges our understandings of boundaries between the "types" of sex in which various configurations of bodies and identities generally engage. It also highlights potential disjunctures between the subjective experience and narration of sexual experience among partners participating in the very same sexual interaction.

Another narrative on sexuality that struck me came from Sonya Bolus:

Sometimes I have to trick you. We pretend you are fucking me, so you don't have to think about what I am doing to you. I make my body available to you as a distraction. Sometimes I use words: "Let me suck your dick." Whether I go down on a dildo or a cunt, I am sucking your dick. I see it. I feel it.

I know it. We both believe in this absolutely, and there is a shift from role play into another kind of reality.[75]

In her powerful description, Bolus highlights how the discursive power of words can translate the "reality" of not only individual bodies, but the way in which these bodies exist in relation to one another. Bolus also situates herself as subject, agent, and guardian of "the real." In a postmodern sense, we might conceive of these ways of sexually relating to and with trans people and their bodies as transmogrification, an extension of queer gender and sexual imaginaries.

Sexual Communication, Body Dysphoria, and Negotiating Sexual Boundaries

Many of the cis women I interviewed reported high levels of satisfaction with the sexual relationship they had with their trans partner. When issues were reported with regard to sexual intimacy, most often they were described as connected, in some way, to a trans partner's gender-related body dysphoria, particularly among those with trans partners who were early in their transition.[76] Gender-related body dysphoria can be understood as a negative view of one's own body when it fails to reflect one's own gender self-image or identity, or is socially misrecognized by others.[77] According to the cis women I interviewed, one of the potential consequences of gender-related body dysphoria was reduction in sexual reciprocity between cis women and their trans partners. Some (though not all) cis women reported that their trans partner was uncomfortable with his chest, before or in the absence of top surgery, being looked at, touched, or orally stimulated. Some cis women also described a trans partner's discomfort with being the recipient of certain forms of oral or penetrative sex.

Cis women discussed negotiating sexual boundaries with their trans partners and how developing a sense of which forms of sexual touch and interaction were comfortable and uncomfortable could feel not only challenging, but at times paralyzing and personally demoralizing. As Ellia explained:

I would feel uncomfortable. Because, to me, I am very proud of my body. I like to talk about my breasts, touch them. I'm just very connected with myself. So, I was so uncomfortable; I couldn't understand why, if he was a woman, why can't I touch your breasts? Why is that so uncomfortable? Why does it make you awkward to talk about? Eating [him] out, that was so weird. I felt uncomfortable, at first, like I was doing something very wrong, like I was bad in bed. Like I was doing something so wrong. Then I realized later that it wasn't me. And that [realization] took a long time ... I wasn't bad in bed. It was nothing to do with me. Those were his body issues. . . . Once he started to get hairy and once the hormones, the testosterone, I guess essentially raised his sex drive, then he actually wanted sex, wanted me to touch him, wanted to orgasm. That was just something that he said that he had never experienced in his life. I was so happy and amazed. To not be able to touch him sexually was a huge source of frustration and made me . . . feel horrible … And I would still feel like I know it's him, I know it's him, but I still feel like it's me.

Like Ellia, Kyla spoke to me about how her trans partner's gender-related body dysphoria could make her doubt, at least for a time, her own sexual skill or attractiveness:

All of a sudden [my partner] was [like], "I hate this body. I can't wait to start T and get my surgery," and "Don't touch me." . . . At first I thought, "Jeez, I'm not attractive to him anymore." I took it personally because, with this medication I'm on, I've gained 20 pounds since I met him 6 months ago. And so at first I thought, "I'm just not attractive to him anymore and too ugly." . . . I thought about it and it dawned on me that maybe it wasn't that he wasn't attracted to me, but that he wasn't attracted to him. So, I asked him and he . . . said, "Yeah, I hate this body." . . . So, at the suggestion of a couple of the groups that I am a part of, online, we had a very, very serious, nervous . . . it felt like we were teenagers . . . this nervous game of "good touch/bad touch" . . . that was effective. . . . And he [now] reaches orgasm without feeling betrayed by his body.

Sexual negotiations could be stymied by the aforementioned absence of a general, widely agreed-upon vocabulary to describe a trans partner's body and erogenous zones.

Martha described some of her and her partner's tense conversations around this very issue:

I'd say, "cunt" every so often. 'Cause, for me, that's actually a word that I've adopted for myself. That's how I refer to my body parts. And I would use that and he'd say, "No, don't use that word." And I'd ask, "Why?" And he said, "Because that's a female word." And I'd say, "Well, what do you want me to use?" He said, "I don't have a word for it. I don't need you to call it anything." So, I never had a language to talk about it. I would call it his "chest." I would say "chest," that was easy enough. But anything below the waist, I didn't have a word for it. And he never offered me anything and we really never talked about it. So, for a year and 8 months it felt horrible. I wanted to talk to him. I wanted to ask him what he wanted me to do and where. But I didn't know what to call it. And it was really frustrating.

Michele talked to me about struggling around communicating about sex and bodies with her trans partner. Michele expressed these sentiments in long pauses, with emotion washing over her face and her voice quivering at times:

Sexual acts like oral sex on my partner: no more. Penetrating my partner's body with my hands or touching my partner's genitals: no more of that either. No more contact with his breasts. We're having real problems around how to have sex. . . . He hasn't himself fleshed out enough other vocabulary, quite frankly, regarding his body. . . . This is one of the things that we're trying to work on is him being able to tell me what . . . he's really looking for. [I worried that] he no longer finds me attractive for whatever reason, that he's interested in someone else and doesn't know how to tell me about it. . . . [I wish] we could have spontaneous sex, that we could have quickies . . . that it just be far less fraught, that we both felt far more comfortable in expressing sexual excitement, having sex, initiating sex, that sex itself have more variety, that there be less negotiation and trauma.

When I asked her if she had found support from other partners of trans men around these issues connected to sexuality and negotiating sexual boundaries and language, she told me about an unhelpful interaction she had with a member of an online support group:

One of the first things I said was, "Our sex has gone in the toilet and I don't know what the fuck to do." Somebody wrote me back on email and told me how to give a blow job. And I was pissed beyond belief because I give a very good blow job, actually. That's not the problem. If crude mechanics were what were at stake here, that wouldn't be a problem. It is the inability of our partners to be connected to their bodies, to feel comfortable in their bodies, to feel sexual desire at all, to not feel a sense a shame around that. And it is discouraging to me that every single trans partner that I have spoken with struggles with this issue. People who have been in relationships for 10 years, 5 years, a year and a half, 2 years. For all of us it is a huge issue.

This disconnect between identity and embodiment was, as many of the other disconnects and tensions cis women described, often (though not always) time-limited and most common during early transition. For many, these disconnects lessened over time, allowing trans men and their partners access to a broader repertoire of sexual behaviors, language, and new ways to sexually connect.

Penetrating Myths and Realties

Given that most of the trans partners of the cis women in my sample had not pursued bottom surgery, and did not have plans to do so in the future, *physiological* possibilities for sexual interaction generally included "vaginal"[78] penetration of one's trans partner. But how might a physiological possibility translate (or not) to the actual sexual practices that occur between partners? In our culture, all forms of being sexually penetrated are generally coded not only female, but feminine. Indeed, even among cis gay men, those considered the "receptive" partner are more likely to be stereotyped or characterized as female or as feminine.

I wondered if the sexual practice of being penetrated must *always* gender code as "female," "woman," and/or "feminine." If not, how did the cis women I interviewed communicate with their trans partners around the issue of vaginal penetration? Just over half of the cis women I interviewed told me that vaginally[79] penetrating their partner was off-limits or very rare. Lilia told me: "[My partner] is extremely adamant about not wanting to be vaginally penetrated. Penetrating vaginally is not an option. I would probably get physically blocked [and my partner] would probably panic. It would probably take [my partner] months to trust me again physically if I tried to do anything like that." Selma concurred, remarking that she had no sexual (and often visual) access to what her partner referred to as his "girl bits," which included his chest and genitals.

It was not uncommon for cis women to tell me that vaginal penetration was something that was permitted early in their relationship with their trans partner, but waned or was no longer permitted as the relationship (and, often, a partner's transition) progressed.[80] In some instances, the decision to discontinue vaginal penetration was made on the basis of this act not fitting with a trans partner's (or the couple's) conceptualization of what constituted the sorts of sexual interactions that people or couples *like* them had. In other instances, vaginal penetration was described as something that became less pleasurable for trans men as testosterone administration decreased the amount of lubrication their bodies produced, making vaginal penetration uncomfortable (or even painful).

Some cis women spoke about mourning the loss of being able to vaginally penetrate their trans partner as a form of sexual interaction. Susan reflected on the last time that she penetrated her trans partner and how special it now seems to her after realizing that it is unlikely to happen again: "I didn't get a chance to say goodbye as weird as that sounds." Robyn told me: "He's fine with his body compared to most other trans people that I've been hearing about. A little bit [of penetration] is okay but it has to be exactly the right thing because otherwise it's like you know it will make him freak out but other than that he's fine with me touching him anywhere." Determining the line between "exact right thing" and "freak out" could be a tricky and dangerous line to tread for some of the cis women I interviewed.

Lea spoke to me about how vaginally penetrating her partner was often part of a sexual dynamic whose negotiation could be opaque, ultimately leaving her self-doubting and frustrated. She said:

> Pre-transition there were periods of more openness and availability [with regard to vaginal penetration], so I feel sad. It's an interesting dance. It has to do with his mental state. It has to do with negotiations that could be going on 6 hours beforehand. It could be negotiations at the moment, too– "Yeah I feel okay." It's very iffy; you know, I never know exactly. Sometimes I can go into a situation thinking that [vaginal penetration is] okay and then something is triggered or something is changed and then it's not. It stinks. You start to wonder what's wrong with you. You try not to because

you think, "Well, that person's having their issue." But you can't help it. And when sex stopped completely for a while, I was devastated. I just couldn't figure out what was wrong with me. And he tried his best to say, "It's not you." But in my mind I kept saying, "Well, it has to be me; you were fine before."

Eva described a similar experience:

We really developed a lot of sexual issues because I didn't know how to relate to his body anymore ... His biological body was out ... It basically got to the point where I wasn't really sure how to fuck him anymore or what kind of relationship to have to his body in terms of me giving him pleasure. It made me feel very helpless and I felt extremely guilty and I felt like a really bad partner.

For this particular group of cis women, (re)negotiating sexual boundaries could be, in many ways, a guessing game. As such, communication was consistently mentioned as key to developing and maintaining a satisfying sexual relationship with one's trans partner.

Not all cis women described being restricted from penetrating their trans partner vaginally, or feeling that not vaginally penetrating their partners was a personal loss. In fact, feelings of frustration or loss with regard to penetrating one's trans partner vaginally were much more common among cis women who were with their trans partner prior to his transition and who had already established a sexual repertoire that often shifted during and/or after transition. For cis women who met their trans partner during or after his transition, penetrating their trans partner vaginally was something some never assumed would be part of their sexual relationship. As Margaret discussed:

It didn't even occur to me that that [penetrating my partner vaginally] was something that would have been possible. It just never happened. It was not acceptable. It was a conversation we had the first time we had sex. "Is there anything you don't like?" ... He said, "Let's pretend that things that aren't supposed to be there aren't there...." It was a complete nonissue.... It couldn't have been less of a nonissue. I have no desire to do anything with anyone who is not interested in that being a part of them and I didn't experience a loss around it. There's nothing to lose.

Narratives about sexual practices from cis women illustrated the degree to which these practices (and expectations around them) could be mediated by the stage in transition at which partners first met. These narratives also demonstrated remarkable diversity in terms of the emotional responses participants had to engaging (or not engaging) in specific sexual acts.

While a slight majority of the cis women I interviewed reported that receptive vaginal penetration was generally not a sexual practice in which their trans partner engaged, this majority was very slim indeed, and more common among those whose partners were earlier in transition. What this meant was that the reported prevalence of receptive vaginal penetration among the trans men partners of cis women I interviewed was considerable, and perhaps even more so than one might presume. Just under half of the cis women I interviewed told me that they did penetrate their trans partner as part of their sexual relationship. The ways in which these sexual interactions were coded through language varied widely across participants. For Anna and her partner, the language and behavior of vaginal penetration took the following form: "He totally likes to be fucked and wants to be fucked. And that's what he's calling it when it happens. He'll be talking fairly sort of graphically while it's happening. He's like, you know, 'Put your hand in my pussy'." According to Anna's report, her trans partner having a "pussy" and enjoying being "fucked" in that "pussy" is not at all inconsonant with his self-identification as a man. Anna and her trans partner, therefore, engage in consciously queer postmodern reconfigurations of the assumed and taken-for-granted relationships between sex, gender, bodies, and sexual practices.

These reconfigurations, however, were often not without sensitive verbal and nonverbal communication between partners. Many cis women described that touching their trans partner's body sexually, especially below the waist, often involves complex negotiations. Lilia said:

> I usually do not touch him between his legs unless he takes my hand and puts it there. In general that's how most of it goes. And I don't feel free enough to do it on my own. It's hard to know what he wants. I've asked him to tell me and he's like, "Okay," but he hasn't done that. He does show me and sometimes takes my hand and puts it there. I also feel like it depends on his mood. I'm still timid about what I can do. First of all, it's hard to know how to please someone in general, regardless of how they identify. Even with a woman; at first it's hard to know. I feel awkward and clumsy giving them a hand job. [Penetration] feels intense. It feels like a privileged act. It makes me feel closer to him but it also makes me feel like, "Am I doing it right? Is it the right way?" When you're focusing on that, it's harder to focus on the sexiness of it all.

The reported prevalence of receptive vaginal penetration among a considerable proportion of the trans partners of the cis women I interviewed might be considered remarkable or unexpected given the predominance of binary and dualist thinking that surrounds the body and sexuality (such as men do not have vaginas and being sexually penetrated means being a woman). Further, it might be considered a departure from historical configurations of some versions of butch/ femme sexuality wherein "stone butch" partners remained entirely or nearly entirely sexually nonreceptive.[81]

Yet as trans people become more visible in society, they and their partners may develop a broader sense of the diversity of sexed and gendered bodies in ways that similarly broaden the palette of sexual behaviors and interactions considered personally appropriate or desirable. Ann Cvetkovich's[82] writing on ways in which trauma shaped the discourse and everyday lives of butch-femme dynamics and sexuality prompted me to consider other possibilities for conceiving of stone butch and trans men's sexual identities and embodiments. Cvetkovich postulates that touching, being touched, and being untouchable have been integral components of butch-femme sexuality and that it makes sense to consider these aspects in relation to experiences of trauma including sexual assault, physical brutality, discrimination, oppression, and degradation. In part, "stone butch" sexuality has been connected to sexual untouchability.

However, is it possible that some trans men, particularly those with stone butch histories, emerge from transition sexually touchable in ways they never were before? Perhaps, in some contexts, sex and gender transition can serve to heal or reconfigure traumas that are written onto the stone butch body and psyche. This is not to assert that transitioning represents some sort of evolutionary telos for stone butches, but that, for some, transition may allow for alternative postmodern subject positions and queer embodiments of sex, gender, and sexuality.

It is also useful to consider the potential slippage across identity categories and embodiments. As many of the narratives from the cis women I interviewed revealed, identities and embodiments are often complex. Consider, for example, Donna's discussion of her trans partner's embodied masculinity prior to his transition:

> He was socially perceived as male before he even started to transition. So, he just always identified as male. He dressed very male, wore clothes that really hid his figure, and just had a real male energy. So, until he opened his mouth ... he even had a little mustache and a beard before testosterone ... he just looked male. As a child, he had figured out how to get around using female language about himself ever. So, that's just a lifetime habit that he was already in. So, it's certainly something I had noticed.... What his face would do if you called him a lesbian.... I said, "Why do you always do that with your face when I say..." And he's like, "Eh, that's too girly of a word." And then I got where I would just watch all that language. He had already figured out how to be a butch and a dyke without being a lesbian.

Joan Nestle discusses how she learned that many of the butch contributors to her 1992 edited volume about femme-butch desire later transitioned to living life as men in the world. While Nestle and others have articulated sadness over what is sometimes viewed as the abrogation of butch identity through transition, she urges critics not to dig their heels into the ground: "We can stand on old ground, protecting 40-year-old borders, or we can throw open the gates and see what lies ahead in new thinking, new organizing, new narratives, new intersections between political, cultural, economic, and gender-sex struggles."[83] The cis women I interviewed shared narratives that attest to these new personal and political possibilities for their queer partnerships and families.

One of the most visible examples of shattering normative assumptions around the ways in which sex, gender, and sexuality correspond and align exists in the world of pornography. Buck Angel is a trans man and adult-film star who often bills himself as "The Man with a Pussy." Angel's film repertoire frequently includes penetration of his vagina[84] by cis and trans men and women. The existence and growth of pornography featuring trans people was explicitly mentioned as one of the sources contributing to broader understandings of trans embodied diversity and sexuality among the cis women I interviewed. As Rachel told me:

[My partner has] become more and more comfortable with what he's got and accepting like, "I get pleasure from this so I shouldn't be ashamed of it." And he started watching tranny[85] porn which, I think, has really really helped him because he sees other guys just like, "This is my body and I'm having fun and I'm celebrating . . . this is what I look like and it doesn't matter." And I think that that's helped him like, "Oh, they're [trans porn actors] sexy. I can be sexy too!"

In research focusing on language and sexual embodiment, Elijah Edelman and Lal Zimman[86] suggest that rather than experiencing particular genitals (e.g., a "vagina") as limiting one's ability to self-identify as a man, trans men's genitals may be reconfigured through language (e.g., as a "bonus hole") as not only adequate, but as an aspect of *exemplary* and perhaps even "value-added" manhood in the context of postmodern neoliberalism.[87] This potential for the sexual lives of trans men and their cis partners to resist or challenge perceived social limits was not contained to the areas of language, embodiment, or even sexual practices themselves. Indeed, the very structure of some of the relationship types that cis women reported tested these limits as well. In the next chapter, I consider some of these relationship configurations and the queer family forms they introduce.

NOTES

1. See Bellwether (2010).
2. See Diamond (2011).
3. See O'Keefe and Fox (2008).
4. Several notable exceptions to this general trend include: Nicola R. Brown's (2010) "The sexual relationships of sexual-minority women partnered with trans men: A qualitative study" in the *Archives of Sexual Behavior*; Aaron Devor's (1997) *FTM: Female-to-Male Transsexuals in Society*; Tam Sanger's (2010) *Trans People's Partnerships: Toward an Ethics of Intimacy*; David Schleifer's (2006) "Make Me Feel Mighty Real: Gay Female-to-Male Transgenderists Negotiating Sex, Gender, and Sexuality" in *Sexualities*; Jaye Cee Whitehead's (2013) "Sexuality and the Ethics of Body Modification: Theorizing the Situated Relationships among Gender, Sexuality, and the Body" in *Sexualities*; and Colin J. Williams, Martin

S. Weinberg, and Joshua G. Rosenberg's (2013) "Trans Men: Embodiments, Identities, and Sexualities" in *Sociological Forum*.

5. See Moore (2013).
6. See the special 2014 "Trans Sexualities" issue (Volume 61, Issue 5) of the *Journal of Homosexuality* for more scholarship across a variety of academic disciplines and methodological approaches (Pfeffer 2014b, 2014c).
7. An important exception to this general trend is Blumstein and Schwartz (1983), *American Couples: Money, Work, Sex*. See also Schwartz, Serafini, and Carter (2013).
8. See Walby (2012:10).
9. Gamson (2013).
10. It should also be noted, however, that such assertions may be used to marginalize or pathologize those who are engaged in intentionally asexual partnerships.
11. See Bishop (2016) and Brown (2010) for notable exceptions.
12. In Diamond (2004:54).
13. See Queen and Schimel (1997:20, 21).
14. See Pratt (1995:117–118). The inclusion of this quotation was made with some degree of trepidation given important distinctions between butch lesbian and trans men's self-identifications. See Chapter 2 for a more extended discussion of the points of convergence and divergence between butch/femme lesbian partnerships and partnerships between trans men and cis women.
15. See Dozier (2005).
16. See Pratt (1995:80).
17. See Pratt (1995:96).
18. See Devor (1997); Williams, Weinberg, and Rosenberger (2013).
19. See Kailey (2005).
20. "Junk," here, is generally used as a euphemism for "genitals."
21. See Williams, Weinberg, and Rosenberger (2013) for a study of the sexualized embodiments of a sample of 25 trans men. Findings include reports of increased sexual urgency and qualitative differences in the experience of orgasm following administration of testosterone.
22. See Devor (1997) for a comprehensive overview of the embodied effects of transition among trans men.
23. See Hansbury (2005).
24. See Davis (2001).
25. See Kailey (2005:49).
26. See Sullivan (1980:8).
27. See Valerio (2006:19).
28. See Rees (1996: 9).
29. See Cummings (2006:407).
30. See Green (2004:31–32).
31. See Devor (1997); see also the documentary, "You don't know dick: The courageous hearts of transsexual men" [Cram (1997)].
32. In a study by Devor (1997), nearly 50% of relationships that trans men began with cis women prior to transition ended. Meier and Labuski (2013) report similar rates for relationship dissolution.
33. See also Schleifer (2006); Williams, Weinberg, and Rosenberger (2013).

34. It is interesting to consider that, despite the great deal of media and community concern over HIV and HIV transmission rates among trans women, trans men who have sex with other men (including cis men) are often not mentioned as a high-risk population. While this group remains understudied, some research evidence points to an increased risk for HIV rates. For example, see Rowniak, Chesla, Rose, and Holzemer (2011). Yet none of the cis women I interviewed, even those who were aware of their partner's sexual interactions with other men, mentioned any concern about possible HIV contraction or transmission. Additional research on the actual and perceived HIV contraction and transmission risk of trans men who have sex with men while partnered with cis women is necessary. So, too, is research into the perceived and actual risks of HIV contraction and transmission among cis women partners, as well as sexual behaviors and practices of this group.

35. 92% of trans partners were reportedly either taking testosterone (n=42) or wanted to take testosterone in the future (n=14).

36. 97% of trans partners had reportedly had (n=23) or wanted to have top surgery in the future (n=36).

37. 43% of trans partners had reportedly had (n=5) or wanted to have bottom surgery in the future (n=21).

38. See Schilt and Windsor (2014).

39. See Williams, Weinberg, and Rosenberger (2013).

40. See Williams, Weinberg, and Rosenberger (2013).

41. This was especially so at the time during which interviews were conducted (between 2005 and 2007). As time has passed, more effective surgical techniques have been developed.

42. Micturition is the medical term for urination.

43. See Rees (1996:150).

44. See Barrett (1998).

45. But not to a statistically significant extent, and this study has obvious methodological flaws regarding comparison groups and possible confounds in terms of excitement and transitional adjustment periods.

46. See Rachlin (1999).

47. See Dozier (2005).

48. See Roen (2001) for additional discussion on the ways in which transgender theory and embodiment may contribute to (and reflect) the marginalization of people of color.

49. See Cummings (2006:11).

50. See Cummings (2006); Kailey (2005); Green (2004); Khosla (2006).

51. For a more up-to-date and neutral view on contemporary phalloplasty techniques, possible complications, and outcomes, see Rashid and Tamimy (2013).

52. Between 2005 and 2007.

53. See Cummings (2006); Khosla (2006); Martino (1977); Valerio (2006).

54. In Williams, Weinberg, and Rosenberger's (2013) study of 25 trans men, only 2 trans men in the sample reported having bottom surgery.

55. See Lief and Hubschman (1993).

56. See Gauthier and Chaudoir (2004).

57. See Whittle (2000).

58. "Stone" refers to a sexual preference or identity wherein a person prefers not to be touched by another sexually. Instead, their sexual pleasure derives primarily from giving sexual pleasure to another.

59. Frieda's candor likely stemmed, at least in part, from the fact that she was recollecting on an ex and a former relationship (rather than one in which she was presently invested). This distance and hindsight, perhaps, allowed her to unabashedly articulate complaints that would likely be tempered or more diplomatic among cis women in an ongoing relationship with a trans partner.

60. See Brown (2010) for another sample of cis women partners of trans men discussing sexual interactions and feelings about sexual penetration using a penis or penis prosthesis.

61. See Brown (2010).

62. See Boucher (2011) for an extended discussion of trans men's embodiment practices and notions of the "real."

63. See Veale, Miles, Bramley, Muir, and Hodsoll (2015).

64. See Perez, Skinner, and Meyerowitz (2002).

65. See Perez, Skinner, and Meyerowitz (2002).

66. For additional discussion on language around trans sexual embodiments, see Brown (2010); Williams, Weinberg, and Rosenberger (2013).

67. It should be noted that use of the term "tranny" is hotly contested within transgender communities and politics. In particular, because the term has been primarily deployed as an epithet against trans women, reclamation of the term by others within the trans movement (for example, trans men or cis women partners of trans men) is offensive and fails to recognize the particular and ongoing pervasive discrimination against trans women [see Serano (2013)].

68. It may be useful here to trouble the concept of a "biological guy." Indeed, if what is meant are relative hormone levels and body structures, some cis men may not have all of the markers of being a "biological guy." Consider, for example, the instance of a cis man with highly pronounced fatty breast/chest tissue (gynecomastia) or who no longer has a penis or testicles as a result of illness or injury. Is such a cis man still a "biological guy?" What about a trans man who is taking testosterone and has a full beard, deep voice, and is perceived by most strangers as a man. Is this trans man not a "biological guy?" If he undergoes top and bottom surgery, is he now a "biological guy"? If we decide that genes should determine what differentiates "biological guys" from the rest, would this not necessitate genetic testing for all? Is reliance on such biologically essentialist/determinist notions of personhood likely to result in clearer or muddier distinctions?

69. See Brown (2010).

70. See Nestle, Howell, and Wilchins (2002:163).

71. It is also possible that this distinction is false or misunderstood. Some might argue that stone butch sexuality, while often focusing on femme partners' sexual pleasure, does not imply a disconnection from one's own sexual self or a purely other-directed sexual desire.

72. See Chapter 2 for a more in-depth discussion of the boundary work that often occurs between butch/femme lesbian and trans men/cis women identities and sexualities.

73. See Brown (2010); Devor (1997); Pfeffer (2009); Williams, Weinberg, and Rosenberger (2013).
74. See Wilchins (1997:171).
75. See Bolus in Nestle, Howell, and Wilchins (2002:113–114).
76. I have written more extensively elsewhere [see Pfeffer (2008)] about the potential for body-related gender dysphoria to impact some women partners' own body image as well as sexual and nonsexual intimacy between partners. See Brown (2010) for a discussion of factors affecting reported sexual satisfaction for cis women partners of trans men, and Williams, Weinberg, and Rosenberg (2013) for factors related to sexual satisfaction among trans men themselves.
77. See Atkins (1998) for an overview of body image issues among various segments of the LGBTQ community.
78. While I use the terms "vagina" or "vaginal" here in order to distinguish this type of sexual penetration from others (such as oral or anal), trans men and their partners have developed other terms to describe this anatomical structure; examples include "front hole" and "bonus hole," for example [see Edelman and Zimman (2014)].
79. It is important to note that the term "vagina" may not be used by all trans men and their partners to name this part of their or their partner's body.
80. Brown (2010) reports similar trends among her sample of cis women partners of trans men.
81. See Leslie Feinberg's (1993) *Stone Butch Blues* for a fictionalized account of stone butch identity.
82. See Cvetkovich (2003).
83. See Nestle (2002:9).
84. In interviews and press materials, Angel frequently uses the word "vagina" to describe his own anatomy.
85. As mentioned earlier, the term "tranny" is hotly contested within trans community and often considered a term of disrespect too stigmatizing and steeped in marginalization and violence to be effectively reclaimed at this point in history, particularly by those who are not members of the group most targeted with this term as an epithet: trans women.
86. See Edelman and Zimman (2014).
87. See also Williams, Weinberg, and Rosenberger (2013).

5

(Re)producing Trans Families

Accessing Social, Legal, and Medical Recognition and Technologies

Heteronormativity has been conceptualized as a "charmed circle"[1] within which privilege, opportunity, and freedom from social stigma are conferred to those conforming to particular social rules and regulations. Some of these rules and regulations, for example, dictate that opposite-sex, normatively gendered individuals monogamously pair.[2] Chrys Ingraham defines heteronormativity as "the view that institutionalized heterosexuality constitutes the standard for legitimate and prescriptive sociosexual arrangements."[3]

Stevi Jackson describes heteronormativity as "shorthand for the numerous ways in which heterosexual privilege is woven into the fabric of social life, pervasively and insidiously ordering everyday existence."[4] Under such pervasive heterosexual privilege, relational configurations and identities falling outside these compulsory parameters are often rendered socially invisible.[5] In the current neoliberal sociopolitical environment, even those who form same-sex pairings may follow proscriptively normative behavioral patterns, enacting what may be termed "homonormativity."[6] Both heteronormativity and homonormativity are concepts founded upon the actual and/or perceived gender and sexual identities of social actors.[7]

Trans people, their partnerships, and families, however, throw our social identity taxonomic classification systems into wonderfully perplexing disarray, ripe for sociological inquiry. What makes a particular couple "same-sex" or "opposite-sex?" Is it the genetic karyotype[8] of each partner relative to the other? This is unlikely, since most of us will live our entire lives never truly knowing our genetic karyotype, let alone those of our partner(s). Is it the relative levels of sex hormones in each partner's body? Hormone replacement and supplemental therapies allow us to control these presumably natural variations, which we know exhibit greater statistical variation *within* sex categories than *across* them.[9] Then it must be the genitals, reproductive organs, and secondary sex characteristics of each partner, right? Modern medicine increasingly allows us to remove and construct these somatic features in dizzyingly variable amalgamations.[10] Further, most of us go through our everyday lives only *presuming* what lies beneath the clothes and skin of the majority of social others.[11] Then it must be the legal status of each partner: whether there is an "M" or an "F" on their birth certificate, passport, and/or driver's license. Wrong again: as yet, no federal policies exist on the designation of sex status on legal documents, and state policies on whether or not birth certificates and other legal documents may or may not reflect a literal "sex change" vary widely and inconsistently, as do the policies indicating which hormonal and/or surgical procedures provide necessary grounds for requesting that such changes be made.[12]

While these ambiguities and inconsistencies may be confusing, they also open up possibilities for remarkable social transgression and transformation. For instance, the medical, legal, and social realities of some trans peoples' lives, in this historical moment, make it possible for them to choose whether they wish to enter into either a "same-sex" or "opposite-sex" legally recognized marriage or civil union with the very same partner.[13] It is possible, therefore, that some of these relationships may face accusations of being either heteronormative or homonormative, depending both upon how partners conceive of their own identities and relationship, as well as how they are perceived by social others. Given the complexity of social identity in the context of transgender and transsexual lives and partnerships, it makes sense to further consider how these identities are relationally formed, particularly attending to the work required to construct, produce, and reproduce these identities.

As explored in depth in Chapter 2, one of the ways in which cis women negotiate the process of being with a trans partner is to adopt the sexual identity label of "queer," a term that, I argue, is paradoxically freeing and confining, and an identity category that is, borrowing from historian Joan Scott's[14] assessments of the categories of "man" and "woman," at once overflowing *and* empty. It is overflowing insofar as it can best represent the messy (and potentially radical) indefinability of these cis women's identities when partnered with a trans man. It is empty as its deployment, as an all-encompassing umbrella identity, obscures the complex differences among the subjects by which it is constituted, just as it fails to reflect any *particular* cultural, relational, or identity politics. In earlier chapters, I have touched on some of the ways in which the queer partnerships and families that cis women form with trans men appear similar to and distinct from their cisgender lesbian and heterosexual counterparts across the areas of identity (Chapter 2), household labor and emotion work (Chapter 3), and sexual intimacy (Chapter 4). In this chapter, I offer a lens into how these postmodern partnerships and families alternately resist and reflect existing mainstream and academic understandings of the very forms and structures so often considered emblematic of partnerships and family life; marriage, parenting, and monogamy.

NORMATIVE RESISTANCE AND INVENTIVE PRAGMATISM

First, I want to outline dimensions of the 2 major strategic processes that emerged in analyses with regard to cis women's negotiations of agency (cis women's own personal identities and desires) and structure (the sorts of institutions, systems, and structures that operate in the world). I term these strategic processes "normative resistance" and "inventive pragmatism." While the conceptual chart in Appendix Figure 1 visually outlines these strategic processes and their constitutive components, my intention here is not to generate a pure typology. Indeed, as I will describe in this chapter, many cis women in my sample employed strategies of both normative resistance and inventive pragmatism, visually represented in the overlap between the 2 spheres, in their negotiations of structure and agency.

"Normative resistance" is a set of strategies that cis women partners of trans men employ to negotiate social systems, structures, and institutions. Normative resistance refers to conscious and active strategies and actions for making life choices distinct from those considered most socially expected, celebrated, and sanctioned. Recall that the majority of cis women reported that their trans partner was socially perceived as male most of the time. A considerable minority (nearly 30%) of cis women I interviewed self-identified as "femme," and all of the cis women in my sample reported being perceived by social others as a woman all or most of the time. As such, many cis women reported being frequently misperceived as part of an unremarkably heterosexual couple when in public with their trans partner. This stood in contrast to the self-identification of the majority of cis women in the sample as "queer."

Given this tension and discrepancy between personal and political identity and social perceptions, some of the cis women I interviewed described specific strategies for managing and resisting social misrecognition as unremarkably heterosexual and reasserting their identity as "queer" or counternormative. Their strategies for normative resistance spanned across 4 primary areas. Cis women reported resisting (a) marriage, (b) parenthood, (c) monogamy, and (d) queer invisibility. In the following 4 subsections, I will briefly discuss and provide examples of each of these forms of normative resistance in the queer partnerships and families of the cis women I interviewed. While normative resistance was one approach cis women described for making their identities and relationships personally and socially intelligible, they also detailed inventive ways in which they sometimes embraced what might seem like normative behaviors and identities for pragmatic purpose.

"Inventive pragmatism," as I term it, entails active strategies and actions that might be considered clever manipulation (or "workarounds") of existing social structure in order to access social and material resources on behalf of oneself or one's family. Recall, once again, that many cis women reported being socially perceived as an unremarkably heterosexual couple most of the time, which stood in contrast to their majority self-identifications as "queer." Despite this discrepancy, some cis women described inventively manipulating such misrecognition in order to access regulated social institutions, resources, and technologies. Cis women's strategies for inventive pragmatism spanned across 3 primary areas: accessing (a) legal marriage, (b) legal parenthood, and (c) reproductive technologies. In the sections that follow, I detail the various strategies of normative resistance and inventive pragmatism my interviewees described using in their queer partnerships and families.

STRATEGIES OF NORMATIVE RESISTANCE

Resisting Marriage

"Opposite sex/heterosexual" marriage and parenting are often regarded as primary bastions, symbols, and institutions of heteronormativity, heteronormative practices, and/or heteronormative privilege.[15] Further, "same-sex/gay" marriage rights and parenting have recently taken center stage and become a primary goal of what some consider "homonormative" mainstream politics.[16] Cis women in partnerships with trans men often face the unique circumstance of being able to choose between "heterosexual/opposite sex marriage," "gay/same-sex" marriage, or no marriage at all with the very same partner (dependent upon a trans partner's legal sex status and personal gender identity, and the couple's legal geographic residence). As Tabitha described it: "In a way I think it's kind of an amazing loophole. The Christian right hasn't figured it out yet."

Despite the existence of such a "loophole," approximately 25%[17] of the cis women I interviewed expressed antimarriage sentiments, lack of interest in marriage, or situated their support of marriage as far *less* personally or socially important than other issues and causes. I consider this interface between agency and structure in the lives of cis women partners of trans men one of the forms of "normative resistance"[18] in which they frequently engage. For example, as Trixie stated:

> I'm not really into the idea of gay marriage. If that is something that any gay person wants, I'll definitely support them in that, that they should be able to have whatever they want. It's just not what I want. My idea of living my life successfully has nothing to do with assimilating to that kind of heterosexist ideal of a man and a woman as a unit with children. . . . When I think about pressing gay or queer issues, marriage is never one of them. It's not in my agenda to show the public or the world that I'm just like them.

Trixie makes it clear that her notion of what it means to be queer involves anti-assimilation personal life choices, and that she views accessing marriage as an assimilationist choice that she resists and ultimately rejects.

Emma articulated another perspective on marriage—namely, that even as it expands to "same-sex/gay" couples, it remains exclusionary in other ways:

> In Canada [same-sex marriage is] legal everywhere, but it's still exclusive in that sometimes people of certain migration can't get married or it's the financial thing and they can't get married and religion plays a lot into marriage. So, neither of us wanted to get married in the very traditional sense of

going to church or otherwise. We talked about getting married if we wanted the legal benefits with each other . . . [but] we didn't want to play into that because it wasn't where our politics lie.

These expressions of politics and agency centered around resisting, opposing, and decentering marriage are a key component of much queer theory and social activism, which critiques social imperatives to marry, and the very linkages between state-sanctioned marriage and regulation of social and material resources.[19] Toby told me that she and her partner are able to legally marry as an "opposite sex/heterosexual" couple where they live, yet have chosen *not* to marry as an extension of their political and ideological beliefs:

Neither of us have ever been particularly fond of the institution for anybody. I've always been adamant about it and harassed my heterosexual friends when they say, "We're getting married!" And I'm like, "Why?! Why are you joining this private club that I'm not invited into?! Would you join a club that Jews were not allowed to join, that Black people are not allowed to join? Well, you're doing the same thing."

Cis women who self-identified as "queer" were more likely to express antimarriage political beliefs, and to report that their trans partner was more interested in marriage than they. Cis women from the western United States (particularly California) were more likely to hold antimarriage sentiments than those from other regions of the United States or Canada.

Resisting Parenthood

Participants also expressed normative resistance in the form of eschewing parenthood or expressing the desire for their queer partnerships and families to remain childfree. Nearly half (44%) of the participants I interviewed told me that they were either not interested in becoming a parent now or had no specific plans to become a parent in the future. Among those not expressing a desire or plans to parent, this was conveyed as indifference, conflict, and (in some cases) active resistance to normative ideals and celebration of new possibilities connected to being childfree.

For example, when I asked Jodi if her decision not to become a parent had been a difficult one for her, she told me: "No. Actually, I celebrated by going and getting a huge tattoo piece. . . . I will not be having babies from this body; it would ruin my tattoo! Part of the symbolism in the tattoo . . . represents an empty womb." Jodi's tattoo exemplifies another critical aspect of normative resistance in transactions between agency and structure, constructing new rituals to signify, and quite literally mark on the body, important life choices that disrupt and diverge from the socially normative and celebrated ideals of having children as key to both womanhood and family. As Tabitha told me: "I'm starting to feel a little bit like an aberration. I'm 33 and I'm not interested in kids. . . . I'm on my own queer path now and that's my focus." The choices that participants had made and intended to make about their marital and parental status were sometimes informed through and against intrusive inquiries from their families, friends, and acquaintances.

Rachel said: "I know I never want to be pregnant because I think it sounds awful and I also feel really strongly about not further expanding the population. . . . I want to be a professor, so I have a lot of school ahead of me. . . . I don't want to compromise my desire to teach to have a child." When I asked Rachel, whose friends and family do not know that her partner is trans, if she had received questions or comments from them about her choices around parenting or marriage, she told me:

> My whole family loves [my partner]. . . . He's every parents' dream so every-one's like, "When are you getting married, when are you getting married?" Well, first of all, we live in Ohio, so even if we wanted to [get married], legally we couldn't. His birth marker isn't changed; he hasn't had surgery yet. So, we just kind of try to play it off right now as like solidarity with our other friends who are gay until they can get married. We feel wrong doing it. . . . But my family doesn't understand it. . . . They'll ask me, "Why are all your friends so gay?" and "Why does it matter what they can do and what they can't do?" And it's like, "Well, they really matter to me." [I'll be] talking to other women in the mall and they'll be talking about birth control or whatever. . . . And they were like, "Do you want kids?" And I was like, "No, not really." And they said something about birth control and somebody looked at me and was like, "Oh, what pill do you take?" I was like, "I don't take that shit. It's poison," and didn't even think about it in a heterosexual context. I don't have to think about getting pregnant. They do all the time and they all looked at me like, "So, you guys use condoms all the time?" . . . And it was like, "Oh, shit." I wasn't even thinking. . . . And people like (a) don't want to accept that I don't want children regardless of who I'm with and (b) they're like, "Well, what would you do if you did get pregnant?" And it's like, "That's not a prob-lem." "But what if it was, what would you do?" . . . I just say, "I'm really, really careful," and I try to add an air of mystery.

Reasons for not desiring to become a parent were varied and included one's own or a partner's infertility, physical and/or mental health problem(s), lack of economic resources, desire to prioritize education and/or career, advancing age, citizenship status, not enjoying children, wishing to preserve one's autonomy and indepen-dence, and conflict with one's partner over reproductive and parenting options.

Resisting Monogamy

Partnering is a social-relational practice that may be particularly "queered" and destabilized when considering the lives and experiences of the cis women

I interviewed. Cis women talked to me about relationship configurations that differed in striking ways from the monogamous relationships generally considered normative and expected in our culture. For those who chose to talk about the structure of their sexual relationship, 40% of the relationships with trans men that cis women talked to me about were described as polyamorous (not strictly monogamous) at one point or another over the course of the relationship. This figure does *not* reflect reported infidelities that occurred across the relationships but, instead, captures the proportion of the sample that engaged in consensual,[20] negotiated polyamory/nonmonogamy (or "open relationships").[21]

Cis women from the Western United States and Canada reported the highest rates of nonmonogamy in their relationships, while those in the Midwest and Northeast United States reported the highest rates of monogamy. Though the number of cis women actively raising children in their homes with their trans partner was very low (n=2), both of these cis women reported having a monogamous relationship with their trans partner, despite the fact that one of these participants self-identified as polyamorous. Future research on trans families might investigate how raising children intersects with politics and practices of monogamy and polyamory.

Queer-identified cis women and cis women younger than 35 years of age were more likely to report practicing nonmonogamy in their relationships than those who were lesbian identified or older than 35 years of age. For younger, queer-identified cis women in particular, then, forming an open relationship structure with a trans partner may serve as one way in which this group engages in social innovation to keep their relationship and queer families counter-normative, though they may present the semblance of normative in the public sphere. Moreover, it may be a strategy of resistance for maintaining a personal and community-based "queer" identity in the context of being perceived by many social others as unremarkably heterosexual.

Robyn discussed that, among her community of queer-identified individuals, polyamory is not only common, but perhaps even necessary for being "truly" queer: "I know a lot of people who have been in open relationships because it's kind of like people are expected to be in open relationships … it's kind of the norm. You're supposed to be in an open relationship because, otherwise, that's like oppressive." Ellia offered a similar perspective: "The more people we meet in life it seems like people are very into open relationships. A lot of the queer community that we've been meeting lately, they all seem to be in open relationships." Study participants discussed numerous types of polyamorous relationship configurations and varying degrees of negotiation between partners regarding the contours of sexual and/or romantic relations with others outside of their primary relationship.

The polyamorous relationship configurations described by a sizable portion of respondents challenge conceptualizations of these relationships and queer families as simply "heteronormative," insofar as heteronormativity is predicated upon individuals establishing intentionally exclusive, monogamous pairings.[22] These polyamorous relationships further differed from normative ideals given that the configurations described (duos and triads) reflected a broad spectrum of various gender identities and expressions. For example, a considerable number of cis women in open relationships with trans men told me that their trans partner was engaged in another relationship with a man (in some cases trans and in others cis).

In the context of these relationships, some of the cis women I interviewed told me that their trans men partners were generally perceived by others as unremarkably "gay." Nearly 30% of the cis women in my sample described instances in which their trans partner was presumed to be a cis gay man by strangers when in physical proximity to other men. In another scenario, a participant in an open relationship described her relationship with a trans woman who was not always socially perceived as a woman, discussing how their relationship was variously perceived as lesbian or as unintelligible (hence "queer"). In some cases, cis women described the power of these relationships to socially recuperate their own (or their partner's) otherwise-invisible queerness. These reported experiences highlight shifting relational, context-dependent, and nonstatic possibilities for sexual identity and its social (mis)recognition

A considerable minority of cis women partners of trans men explicitly discussed their open relationships as a conscious form of resisting normativity (as well as a critical aspect of some queer identities and relationships) and countering others' social (mis)perceptions about the presumed heteronormativity of their relationships. These relationship configurations also parallel emergent postmodern trends toward open relationships, even in the context of legal marriage, among other segments of the LGBTQ population.[23] Yet I would urge caution in assuming that polyamory is always reflective of greater equity and flexibility within partnerships. As some sample participants noted, decisions to enter into particular relationship forms are always bound up in various interpersonal power dynamics. For example, Lynne told me: "When we first met he wanted to be monogamous and I said okay and then in the middle he started to want to be nonmonogamous and I said okay. But really [nonmonogamy] was very difficult for me and it's not really what I wanted; but it was one of those things you do in relationships."

Accordingly, future research would do well to explore the various details and processes surrounding individuals' and couples' decisions to be monogamous or polyamorous. It would be useful to consider how partners leverage what Adam Isaiah Green[24] terms "sexual capital," based on their membership to particular groups, in their negotiations around sexual relationship structure. Overall, however, my findings offer evidence for the proliferation of queer relationship configurations in the postmodern era.

Resisting Queer Invisibility

Despite some scholars' claims that sociology might fruitfully move into a "post-queer" era,[25] 52%[26] of the cis women I interviewed self-identified as "queer."

Further, when offering a label to describe the sort of relationship that they had with their trans partner, 65%[27] of these relationships were described by participants as "queer." In the context of others' reported social misperceptions of these cis women as unremarkably heterosexual and/or part of a presumably unremarkably heterosexual couple, however, these queer identities and relationships were often elided. Many cis women described their fears of being perceived as "just like everyone else" by social others. In response, the cis women I interviewed described specific strategies for managing and resisting this (actual and potential) misrecognition and reasserting one's own identity as "queer" and/or counternormative.

Cis women's narratives, as discussed earlier in chapter 2, also revealed the extent to which some forms of normative resistance highlight sociopolitical and identity divisions *within* LGBTQ communities as well. As Trixie told me:

> A lot of my gay male friends and I talk about the difference between just gay people and queer people and, "Don't you hate when gay people are just gay and not queer?" And I guess what we mean by that is just . . . to me I guess it means that . . . someone identifying just as gay wants to assimilate somehow. . . . I know that's not necessarily true and I'm not judging anybody's identification at all. It's totally everyone's own business and I'm so in support of it. But, for me, when I identify as "queer," I feel like I'm also putting a message out there that my sexual orientation is not about assimilation to any sort of heterosexist ideal.

Trixie's narrative speaks to many participants' complicated negotiations of LGBTQ identification and disidentification when it comes to resisting normativity. Many strategies of normative resistance that participants described also resonated with Halberstam's[28] discussion of queer as "a mode of critique rather than a new investment in normativity or life or respectability or wholeness or legitimacy." Indeed, many of the cis women I interviewed saw their identities as feminist, femme, or queer as a form of embodied cultural critique that they enacted every day through their choices to resist normativity and cultural messages around who they should partner with and what their partnerships and families should look like. Just as some of the cis women I interviewed engaged in normative resistance as a queer survival strategy, they also articulated various strategies for carving out queer lives and families by becoming inventively pragmatic.

STRATEGIES OF INVENTIVE PRAGMATISM

Accessing Legally Recognized Marriage

Depending upon existing laws in their geographic area of residence, the cis women I interviewed often faced the unique circumstance of being able to have their marriage to a trans partner legally recognized if he obtained legal classification as male, something that was often *not* possible (across most of the United States when I was conducting interviews) for those in partnerships considered "same-sex." Recall a participant referring to this fact as an "amazing loophole" that "the Christian right hasn't figured ... out yet." Some participants insisted upon the pragmatic importance of having the option to access legal marriage with the hopes of broadening and expanding this institution for a broader diversity of couples. Terry described a contentious interaction she had with another member of the LGBTQ community upon announcing her upcoming marriage to her trans partner:

> This one [queer] woman put up this interesting analogy of how she saw getting married as selling out and [asked]: "If you could be a member of an exclusive club and go into that club and dine fabulously but your best friend, who is a different ethnicity, could not, how could you live with yourself if you went ahead and went into this club and dined fabulously?" And I said, "You know what? I would expect you to go in there and dine and bring me a plate." Don't be a martyr.... [I think you should] do what's right for you and if you can find a way to reach back and help everybody else, do it.

This analogy parallels the one discussed earlier by Toby, but the analysis and conclusion are starkly different. To Terry, marriage to a trans partner is a move *away from* ideologically motivated, punishing self-interest and may be a move toward LGBTQ community betterment (although she does not explicitly specify how or in which ways).

Like Terry, a small minority of cis women in the sample (10%) reported existing legal "same-sex/gay"[29] or "opposite sex/heterosexual"[30] marriages with their partners, while 28%[31] reported contemplating, discussing, and/or actively planning such legal unions and 22%[32] reported feeling neutral about the possibility of marriage. Cis women who self-identified as bisexual were more likely than any other group to report a desire to be legally married. Participants' endorsement of marriage, as a personal goal, increased along with the degree to which their trans partner was reportedly socially perceived as male, with those reporting that their partner was socially perceived as male "always" or "almost always" most likely to have a desire to marry. While only 2 cis women were actively raising children in their homes with their trans partner at the time of the interview, both were legally married to their trans partner. Future studies of trans families might usefully examine the degree to which the presence of children influences desire or propensity to legally marry.

Many cis women in the United States mentioned marriage as a gateway to accessing the material and social rights and privileges that accrue to those who are legally married, including (but not limited to) next-of-kin status, tax benefits, hospital visitation rights, legal parentage status, healthcare, and citizenship rights. As Lea told me: "This year we thought about okay, well, if you want your [transition] surgery then we can do the One-Plus-Adult. But we need some kind of life-changing event to allow us to put one or the other on the other one's insurance. So, what would that life-changing event be but marriage?" When Mel was asked if she had spoken with her partner about marriage, she responded:

> We've discussed it and our decision on whether to be married or not comes down to a case of protecting our rights as a couple. It usually comes in the context of, you know, would it help our tax situation or hinder our tax situation? If one of us were to be sick would we want to be sure to be able to sit with the other person in the hospital, to be the one that decisions about life support would be deferred to. . . . Is there something in the legal status of marriage that would make our lives a bit easier?

Mel, then, describes making future-oriented pragmatic assessments to consider the potential legal "what ifs" were injury or illness to befall her or her partner.

Cis women's reasons for accessing legal marriage were varied and complex, but most highlighted primarily instrumental and pragmatic (rather than emotional, romantic, or symbolic) factors. Anna directly connected her intention to marry with the ability to access certain material benefits and explicitly articulated the inner conflict that accessing such regulated social privileges entails:

> We made the decision really quickly. It was like, "Oh, I need healthcare." He was starting a new job, so if I was going to go onto his healthcare it should happen right away. So, it was like in a 3- or 4-day period we talked about getting married for the first time and then got married all in the same blink of an eye. I was aware though, during that time, of, "My God, this is something that I really don't completely believe in and never believed that I would do and I certainly wouldn't do it when . . . people who would like to get married can't because they're not legally able to."

June echoed this same sentiment: "There's a part of me that doesn't want to get married when there's so many people in the world that can't." Such complicated and fraught decision-making processes revealed participants' awareness that their decisions to access legal marriage were not similarly available at that time to other members of the LGBTQ community.

For Anna, whose marriage to her trans partner is legally recognized, her decision about whether or not to access marriage (a state and federally regulated institution) was imbued with awareness of its exclusionary and restrictive nature, while she aspired to secure present and future access to some of its associated benefits. Anna does not describe a desire connected to habituated romantic cultural ideals of marital love; rather, the focal point of Anna's decision-making process with her partner seems to be on pragmatic concerns: having healthcare. Indeed, participants' narratives frequently articulated the catch-22 nature of (and personal ambivalence toward) gaining access to an institution to which they may be both politically and ideologically opposed in order to access valuable and regulated economic, legal, and social benefits. Julie, for example, described marriage as "a bad institution" and stated that she thought that marriage should be "abolished." Yet Julie also admitted that she had once contemplated getting married in order to gain citizenship. These narratives frequently attested to the pragmatic concerns often fueling communication and decision making around accessing legal marriage.

Accessing Legally Recognized Parenthood

The pressing need for sociologists to consider the paradoxical sociolegal *invisibility* and *hypervisibility* of queer trans families is particularly highlighted when focusing on the issue of parenting. Take, for instance, the aforementioned international media firestorm that enveloped Thomas Beattie (a trans man who came to be known as "the pregnant man") and his wife Nancy Beattie in 2008 when they announced, on the *Oprah Winfrey Show* and in the pages of *People Magazine*, that Thomas was expecting the couple's first child.[33] While only 4%[34] of participants reported actively raising young children in their homes with their partners at the time of the interview, 12%[35] of participants reported current or former personal experiences with parenting, and 44%[36] of the remaining participants discussed intentions (many describing detailed plans) to become a parent in the future.

Participants discussed sociolegal challenges that they and their trans partner may face when considering the options available to them as parents. Rachel told me:

> We don't even know if we would be allowed to adopt a kid. He's a transsexual and gay people can't even adopt kids [in some states]. . . . People think trans people are even weirder than gay so who knows if that's even an option.

The dilemmas these couples face were sometimes met with frustration and discussion of the privilege that often accompanies cisgender heterosexual relationships. As Samantha stated: "I'm sort of angry that straight people have babies on accident and make it work. It makes me really pissed off. . . . We have to be more responsible because we can't just, like, have that. I'm sure they don't see it as a blessing, but I do."

The narratives of those who were currently parenting at the time of our interview also revealed important and potentially worrisome sociolegal dilemmas. For example, Maya and her partner have a legal, "opposite-sex/heterosexual" marriage in the United States. They are also recognized as the legal mother and father (respectively) of their infant daughter, to whom Maya gave birth. However, as Maya discussed:

> We are legally married . . . as long as no one contests it. . . . He's on the birth certificate and we're legally married [so] he's [our daughter's father

by] default. If you're legally married if something were to happen to me, [our daughter] goes to him automatically. However . . . my mother holds a trump card. In other words, if I were to die, she could conceivably potentially sue for custody saying that she's the nearest relative, not [my partner]. . . . There's this legal limbo we live in. . . . [In some states] we wouldn't be recognized as being legally married at all. He would never be recognized as [our daughter's] father.

Maya's family provides an example of how the marital paternity presumption, which is the legal assumption that children born to a legally married man and woman are that man's biological children, offers both a "trans loophole" for accessing legal parentage, as well as introduces instability insofar as such parentage may face legal challenges.[37]

Narratives like these provide striking examples of how the legal rights and privileges conveyed by marriage are often tenuous, at best, for some queer families. While Maya and her family may be considered social innovators, this innovation is dependent upon continuing familial and state recognition of both their marriage and their rightful and respective roles as mother and father to their child. As such, accessing parentage through legally recognized marriage for some of my participants could serve as a pragmatic, though not foolproof, safeguard for forming and protecting their trans families.

Accessing Reproductive Technologies

Technological advances in the biomedical sector are making parentage possible for a broader group of people in ways never before imagined.[38] A considerable number of participants in the sample (22%[39]) discussed—spontaneously and not under direct prompt—conversations they had with their trans partner about the possibility of retrieving and harvesting his eggs (among those whose trans partner had not had an oopherectomy, removal of the ovaries) for later fertilization and implantation into themselves or a surrogate. While almost all of these participants discussed this possibility as remote due to its present costliness, existing technologies radically shift possibilities for creating and forming families in the 21st century. Today, it is possible for cis women partners of trans men to give birth to their trans partner's biological children. While such procedures may not currently be common, they may become increasingly so as these novel reproductive technologies advance and become more affordable to consumers over time.

In the egg harvesting and donation scenario previously described, a trans man who has attained legal status as male might be simultaneously legally classified as a child's "legal father" and "biological mother," depending upon local jurisdiction and statutes, which vary widely.[40] Were the couple to separate, however, it might also be argued that the trans man was nothing more than an "egg donor," with no existing legal connection or rights to the child at all. Potential sociolegal dilemmas became further complicated as some cis women described their intention to choose a sperm donor, related to themselves or their partner, in order to maintain mutual genetic connection to the child. Martha talked to me about some of these complex and new sociolegal possibilities:

> I don't care to birth a child myself at this point in my life. . . . And he really wanted to. So, we talked about . . . if he's taking [testosterone] and then stops taking it, will he be able to get pregnant and how? And we would talk about, well, if we'd like a child that comes from both of us, we could use one of my brothers' sperm to impregnate him so we'd have a child that, hopefully, would look like both of us. . . . And then, also, how would this play out if he has transitioned further with testosterone and he can get pregnant and he looks very male? How's this gonna work with this person who identifies as male and possibly has had his sex changed on documents coming into a hospital pregnant as a man?

Existing technologies radically shift possibilities for creating and forming families in the 21st century. Yet these new possibilities engender complex sociolegal questions regarding who "counts" as a biological and/or or social mother, father, and parent.

As trans individuals, and the families they create with their partners, slowly become more socially visible within both mainstream and LGBTQ social life, they remain virtually unexplored within most social science research on the family. This study begins filling that gap by demonstrating the ways in which systemic structural forces work to constrain and discipline divergence from pathways of idealized, normatized family life even as they generate possibilities for new family forms. Cis women partners of trans men draw not only from contemporary understandings of what families were or are "supposed" to be, but also resist and reformulate some of these notions as well if doing so might prove personally and/or socially advantageous. The narratives explored in this chapter detail the ways in which contemporary notions of family work and do not work in the everyday lives of cis women partners of trans men and their families. These accounts also reveal the extent to which cis women partners of trans men actively evaluate and negotiate sociolegal notions and practices of "family," family structure, and family roles in ways that may court pragmatic advantage in the face of systematic structural and institutional barriers.

The cis women I describe in my research are negotiating new ways of constructing family forms, including those not strictly grounded in normative or nostalgic ideals for families and family life. I find that cis women partners of trans men often serve as social innovators, strategically and pragmatically negotiating system loopholes to access otherwise limited and regulated sociolegal institutions and structures (such as marriage and parentage) for their families that others within the "LGBTQ umbrella" were not able to similarly access at the time. Cis women partners of trans men face social realities that are not adequately explained or accounted for by existing sociological research focusing on the lives and relationships of either cis heterosexual women or lesbians, pointing to the growing necessity for research that accounts for a broader cross-section of queer lives and families.[41] Indeed, the negotiations of normative resistance and inventive pragmatism that I have uncovered hold relevance not only for families headed by cis women and trans men, but for a broad range of queer individuals and queer family types.

The families described herein present conceptual, social, legal, and political challenges that warrant closer attention. These narratives point to the ways in which queering families throws our current social and legal systems into delightfully perplexing disarray, blurring notions of both "opposite-sex" and "same-sex" legal marriage and parentage. The lives and choices of cis women partners of trans men are both transformative and fraught, pushing against and disrupting the contours of normativity from within powerful, interlocking social systems, communities, and institutions that push back and discipline in dynamic response. One possibility for expanding current social boundaries is to consider the many ways in which everyday people both fit into and push against these boundaries, sometimes encountering resistance and, at other times, changing or even imploding the very boundaries themselves. Despite holding the power to transform limiting normative social structures, queering families often involves considerable personal and interpersonal risk. In the next chapter, I detail the various contours of this risk in the form of social stigma, strain, and discrimination that cis women and their trans partners sometimes encounter, even within their own communities. I also explore the various sources of support upon which they draw to buffer these risks.

NOTES

1. See Rubin (1984).
2. See Rubin (1984).
3. Ingraham (1994:204)
4. See Jackson (2006:108).
5. See Rich (1980).
6. See Duggan (2002); Seidman (2005).
7. See Jackson (2006).
8. Karyotype refers to the exact chromosomal content of cells. Using staining techniques, it is possible to determine the chromosomal makeup of cells in the human body, including one's sex cells.
9. See Fausto-Sterling (2000).
10. See Meyerowitz (2002).
11. See Garfinkel (1967); Kessler and McKenna (1978).
12. See Currah, Juang, and Minter (2006); Kirkland (2006); Robson (2006); Meadow (2010, forthcoming).
13. See Robson (2006).
14. See Scott (1988).
15. See Ingraham (1999) for an analysis of the cultural romanticization of cisgender heterosexual marriage.
16. See Duggan (2002); Ward (2008).

17. n=12
18. See Pfeffer (2012).
19. See Duggan (1992).
20. Reported differences in power and status within relationships may call the mutuality of decisions to engage in an open or closed relationship into question, particularly in relationships that are open or closed for only one partner.
21. Eric Anderson's (2012) recent book, *The Monogamy Gap*, suggests that cheating, at least among men, emerges as a response to societal conditions that offer few alternatives to monogamy. An alternative social framework would situate negotiated polyamory as a viable, respectable, and nonstigmatized alternative, ostensibly reducing rates of cheating. For more on polyamorous relationship configurations within families, see Barker and Langdridge (2010) and Sheff (2011). For a comparative perspective on monogamous and nonmonogamous partnerships, see Wosick (2012).
22. See Jackson (2006) for more on heteronormativity.
23. See Anderson (2012); Green (2008); James (2010).
24. See Green (2013).
25. See Green (2002).
26. n=26
27. n=40
28. See Halberstam (2011:110–111).
29. n=1
30. n=4
31. n=14
32. n=11
33. See Albiniak (2008); Barkham (2008).
34. n=2
35. n=6
36. n=22
37. See Rosato (2006).
38. See Hare and Skinner (2008); Mamo (2007); Mamo and Alston-Stepnitz (2015); Thompson (2005).
39. n=11
40. For more on legal classifications, trans identity, and the law, see Cahill and Tobias (2007); Currah, Juang, and Minter (2006); Hare and Skinner (2008); Kirkland (2006); Meadow (forthcoming, 2010); Robson (2006); Spade (2011). See Cahill and Tobias (2007) and Smith (2009) for an overview of legal quandaries faced by lesbian and gay couples.
41. See Committee on the Status of Lesbian, Gay, Bisexual, and Transgendered (LGBT) Persons in Sociology (2002, 2009) for further discussion regarding inclusion of not only LGBTQ issues in sociology, but LGBTQ scholars as well. See also Gamson (2013) for an overview of existing and future research directions for sociology and queerness.

6

It Takes a Village, People

Social Strain and Support for Trans Partnerships and Families

When I asked cis women to talk to me about some of the struggles or challenges that they had experienced around the area of social support for themselves or their partners in the context of their relationship, they talked about finding it difficult to meet and connect with other cis women partners of trans men, being viewed as not *really* queer, losing family support, struggling financially through the cost of a partner's transition, and simply not fitting within the confines of most existing sexual identity classifications other than "queer." In this chapter, I offer an overview of some of the central areas of concern that interviewees voiced when it comes to finding support for themselves, their partners, and their families. Many of the themes across this chapter centrally address marginalization, exclusion, loneliness, social stigma, and potentials for discrimination and violence. On the other hand, the cis women I interviewed also spoke to me about key sources of support for both themselves, their partners, their partnerships, and their families; I detail these critical lifelines as well.

LIVING IN FEAR

Cis women I interviewed spoke about specific fears and concerns they held regarding their trans partners' safety and well-being. Indeed, these concerns are justified given that trans people face disproportionate risk for experiencing violence, abuse, suicide, and homicide.[1] Eva talked to me about discrimination her partner experienced in mainstream public spaces and everyday social interactions as he transitioned:

> There would be times when we would use a public restroom and if he would use the women's room, women would stare at him. One time a woman came up to us afterwards and yelled at him for being in the women's room.... I remember one time there was an issue of a parking spot and some teenage boy got in a fight with him and then realized he didn't even know what

the gender was of this person who he was fighting with. . . . He called him a "freak" or something like that. A lot of times people would call him a "fag" or a "dyke." So, they would sort of bring homophobia into it too.

These sorts of public interactions were described by some participants as having impacts that extended far beyond the interactions themselves. For example, when I asked Eva if she and her partner talked with one another when these sorts of interactions occurred, she told me:

> I feel like that's what a lot of our relationship was about. We processed it all the time. . . . He just always had a consistent sense of being in danger. He was always afraid for his safety and so I was always afraid for his safety. And so we spent a lot of time worrying about him and would he be okay, would people accept him, would he be safe when he's walking down the street late at night when people don't know: "What is this person? Who is this person?" We spent a lot of time on that. I think that it made us very dependent on each other. So, I think in some ways that increased the stress for both of us. It made me feel pretty isolated and lonely.

Other cis women I interviewed discussed an opposite response: carrying these experiences in individual silence and shame, even if the event had been experienced together, never discussing the emotional impact of these encounters because doing so simply felt too intense. I would argue that it makes sense to think of these sorts of fears and concerns with which many queer people and families grapple as a form of cultural violence. Living in fear of becoming the target of anti-trans and anti-queer stigma, hatred, or discrimination may exact a toll upon queer families and their members and hold the power to shape one's sense of personal safety, self-presentation, and interactions with others in the world.

Fears about a trans partner's well-being and safety were most pronounced among cis women who noted that their trans partner was *not* perceived always or most always as a man by others. In instances where trans men were not recognized as men but were, instead, viewed as gender-ambiguous by others, they reportedly faced greater social scrutiny by those outside LGBTQ community spaces. Some cis women I interviewed who were dating trans men of color—especially Black trans men—expressed particular concerns about their trans men partners being seen as predators, being socially avoided, or becoming targets for greater scrutiny by police.

TRANS EXCLUSION AND VIOLENCE WITHIN LGBTQ COMMUNITY SPACES

Because LGBTQ people may develop heightened cultural awareness of visual and interactive gender cues that signal gay, lesbian, and bisexual identities, some LGBTQ people may "read" or culturally misrecognize a trans man's masculinity as butch lesbian identity. This resulted, according to my interview participants, in servers and bartenders at LGBTQ establishments (or establishments where a staff member is LGBTQ) frequently referring to my interviewees and their trans men partners as "ladies." While the server or bartender may be attempting to formally recognize the queer identities of his or her patrons, and even make a "family" connection with them, this form of misrecognition was often described by the cis women partners I interviewed as demoralizing and embarrassing for some of their trans men partners, contributing to a sense of invisibility or even anxiety over their gender presentation.

Other misrecognition processes within LGBTQ social spaces carried particular social consequences as well. One set of trends that emerged in participants' accounts involved (a) explicit exclusion of trans people and their partners from primarily gay and lesbian social spaces and (b) intimidating and even violent interactions aimed toward "finding out" the "real" sex of those who are trans as they interact within primarily gay and lesbian social spaces.[2] About 1/3 of the cis women I interviewed described instances of being told by leaders of gay and lesbian organizations (or hearing through the grapevine) that their and/or their trans partner's presence was no longer welcome since their partner's transition.

Martha described making reservations at a lesbian bed and breakfast only to be told that she and her partner were no longer welcome upon the inn keeper learning of her partner's transition. Lynne described the exclusion of trans men from the yearly "dyke march" in her town. Kyla spoke about how her trans partner's own cis lesbian-identified sister would not acknowledge his trans identity:

> She refuses to acknowledge him as male. She refuses to acknowledge his new name that he's chosen for himself. He's had a nickname for several years now ... 6, 7, 8 years ... that was androgynous. And all of his friends over the last 5 or 6 years know him by the androgynous name and not by his given name. But his sister insists on calling him by his given name. He came out ... and announced his new name ... and asked for his friends and family to consider his given name to be dead and buried and henceforth to please call him by the name he had chosen or by his androgynous nickname. And his sister's just been making fun of that ever since.

Kendra spoke to me about a cis gay friend who refused to honor her partner's trans identity:

> I did have a friend who refused to call my partner his male name and use male pronouns. And he would still call us "lesbians." It was very upsetting for both of us because I was like, "Well, we're not lesbians and that's not how I choose to identify and that's definitely not how he chooses to identify. And you know this is his name now. It's been legally changed." We were both really upset that he just wouldn't recognize it, especially because this friend

of ours was a drag queen and we thought he would be the most accepting person of all. But it turns out he wasn't.

June, Samantha, and Kendra each relayed harrowing and eerily similar experiences that their trans partners had had in gay and lesbian bars. According to June: "He went out to a . . . lesbian bar . . . and they wanted him to prove that he was actually male. So, there was a lot of, 'Take your pants off and show me,' type of thing. They followed him into the bathroom and it was about an hour of harassment like that." Samantha told me: "He was going to the bathroom . . . and he was waiting for the stalls and . . . this old lesbian got up in face and was like, "Go use the other bathroom, we need this one more than you do. . . .' And she got really up in his face about it and he was like, 'I'm trans. I have to sit to pee.' And she was like, 'No, you're not. . . .' She actually ripped his shirt off to see." Kendra offered the following description about an incident in a gay bar:

> He almost got beat up that night. . . . He went to the women's restroom because he wasn't fully male and he didn't want gay guys to find out that he didn't have a penis; so, he chose to use the women's restroom that night. He was still fairly early into his transition and a guy followed him in there and watched him urinate and said, "Take off that binder. I don't know why you want to be a guy. . . ." Later, the guy lunged across the dance floor at my partner and, luckily, one of our friends pushed him out of the way.

In each of these instances, trans men were ultimately held accountable for others' recognition of them *as* men, social processes that could have frightening and even dangerous consequences, even within communities that had formerly served as safe havens from exclusion and discrimination.

EXCLUSION AND LACK OF SUPPORT FOR CIS WOMEN PARTNERS OF TRANS MEN

Not only were trans men kept on the periphery or excluded from some cisgender and transgender community spaces, but the cis women partners of trans men I interviewed also described facing exclusion and lack of support. Recall that, as detailed in Chapter 2, some cis women partners of trans men reported experiencing marginalization and invisibility within both cisgender lesbian and heterosexual communities. Cis women partners of trans men described feeling unwelcome in trans community spaces as well. Such experiences have also occasionally been discussed in autobiographical writings of trans men. For example, Green writes about an encounter at the International Foundation for Gender Education (IFGE) conference in Houston in 1992:

> The three or four female partners of FTMs who had also registered for the conference were asked to leave a workshop offered for partners of

transsexuals and cross-dressers because the wives of the MTF people felt that female partners of FTMs must be lesbians and therefore would not be able to sympathize properly with the difficulties faced by heterosexual women whose partners were changing their gender expression to female.[3]

Indeed, finding community may be quite challenging for some partners of trans people. A number of cis women talked to me about feeling isolated during the early stages of their partner's transition.

As Eva told me: "I remember that time [early transition] as being very lonely." As Robyn, whose trans partner's family had rejected him for his gender and sexual identity, said:

I think that I was already really having a hard time just coming out and being in my first queer relationship living in a smaller town, not really having much of like a social support system at all. And then on top of that he came out as trans and I didn't really know anything about what it was to be trans aside from researching it on the Internet. And I remember it was me who was researching all this stuff and calling all these support groups . . . and talking to all these people and trying to find somewhere for us to go to meet other people like him, or to meet hopefully other people that were partners. And I can just remember he was . . . coming out . . . going through a lot of depression. And I just remember feeling really, really alone and just isolated. I was constantly searching for people that were kind of like us or like him where I could find him some support. But I felt like it was kind of all on me to do that.

As discussed in Chapter 3, it was not uncommon for the cis women I interviewed to describe engaging in acts of both instrumental and emotional support connected to a partner's transition, even if they felt uncertain, afraid, anxious, or depressed. One of the challenges that interviewees expressed to me was that it was difficult for them to just feel anxious or sad because expression of those emotions might be perceived as a lack of support not only for one's trans partner and their transition, but for the trans community and trans identity in general. In this way, some cis women I interviewed described policing their own emotions and emotional displays or working to hide negative, ambivalent, or apprehensive emotions connected to a partner's transition from others, particularly their partners.

A central component of some cis women's fears or anxieties centered around becoming culturally invisible as queer and as a queer sexual subject. For some participants, losing recognition and cultural visibility (particularly within queer spaces) as a queer woman was something that they mourned. As Ellia discussed:

I felt weird when we're in public and there's a group of lesbians. . . . I'm completely invisible. I'm used to being checked out by the butch women and now I'm not. . . . There are times when I'll be standing around a group of lesbians and I feel awkward because I just look like a straight girl. They have no idea and . . . sometimes I just want to look at them and go, "Hey, I'm gay too!" even though that's totally weird. . . . When you're a gay couple out in public, other gay people sort of give you this . . . I don't know . . . nod. Not really a nod, but you know you're all in the club. And now, no club.

Ellia continued that it is not only the loss of queer recognition by other queer people that gives her pause, but her sudden acceptance among nonqueer people as well:

[Now] we're just [seen as] straight people. That's weird . . . I do notice when we're out older people will now be much more friendly to us . . . just talk-ing, smiling, being chatty. And if we were out before, not that they would be rude, but they would just sort of avoid us. . . . And now we're just an ador-able, straight, happy, engaged, or married (you know, they see the rings) [couple] . . . I get pissed because I think back and I get upset. Why was it not okay to be friendly to me and my partner when we were a lesbian couple? We were the same people before.

One of the dangers of being (mis)recognized as an unremarkably hetero-sexual couple, then, was the way in which it could ignite sudden awareness of privilege that one did not have at an earlier point in time, sometimes through social interaction as seemingly inconsequential and innocuous as a nod or a smile.

FINDING A CIS WOMEN PARTNERS OF TRANS MEN COMMUNITY

I asked the cis women I interviewed if they had a community of other partners of trans men to whom they could turn for advice and support. Lea responded: "I can't find them. . . . I wish I knew other women partners of F-to-Ms in trans relationships. That's the hardest thing I think—the isolation." When I asked Lea if she could talk to me a bit more about that sense of isolation as the partner of trans man she told me:

You know there's support groups for [my trans partner]. And there's sup-port [for him] in online communities galore. . . . I find it so frustrating that there's nothing for the partners or very, very little. And I'm a real-time per-son. I find it frustrating that we have very significantly different needs in terms of what to talk about. What's happening today with our identities? What happened yesterday when they had a boost in their T levels or some-thing? How are you reacting? How do you feel as a woman during this expe-rience? And the isolation is crazy because my queer and lesbian sisters don't want to really talk about it. They're still too freaked out by [my partner's transition] and what's happening. And my straight friends . . . it's sort of a freak show and they're just happy now that I look straight.

Feelings of isolation could be especially pronounced among those cis women who found themselves marginalized not only as cis women partners of trans men, but also for reasons connected to racial, class, or sexual identities. As Lilia told me:

> I feel like it's just kind of complicated. [I'm a] woman of color dating a White man, and I'm gender queer. So, I feel kind of isolated in that identity right now. . . . And, like, a lot of trans men here date other men, whether they be trans or nontrans men. . . . It would be nice to find women-identified folks who are dating trans men. . . . I haven't found any specific woman of color groups or anything where women of color are dating White trans men. . . . It would be nice if there was.

The Internet was often described as a central (though limited) method for connecting to similar others to transcend geographic boundaries.

Cis women also talked to me about having a trans partner who was "stealth" and the paradoxical challenges that a trans partner being recognized in accordance with his gender identity can pose for partners wishing to access or receive social support resources. The cis women I interviewed defined stealth as being perceived, socially, in accordance with one's gender identity and generally not informing others of one's transition and/or sex categorization at birth. While "going stealth" is not possible for all trans men, among those who are socially recognized as men in the world almost all of the time, there are many reasons for choosing to do so. Some of these reasons may be tied to employment or maintaining critical social relationships with those who may be transphobic or non-accepting of trans people. What this meant for the cis women partners of trans men who were stealth is that seeking sources of support for themselves could jeopardize their trans partner's ability to remain stealth.

As Nina told me, recalling her response to her trans partner's request that she not out herself as the partner of a trans man: " 'This is my experience that I really want to talk to this person about and you're asking me not to because it's outing you.' So that is when getting support isn't all that it could be for me; because people that I would turn to aren't people who know what I need support with." Finding other cis women partners of trans men could be quite challenging for cis women whose partner is almost always socially recognized as a man and who is not "out" as trans.

I asked Terry what her experience had been like in terms of finding other cis women partners of trans men with whom to network and dialogue:

> It's pretty hard [laughs]. It's been difficult. . . . [My partner] is stealth. He does not publicly identify as transsexual. And it's really hard to hook up with other people who identify that way, you know. You can't just walk up and say, "Oh, by the way, you're a really short guy . . . are you [trans]?" You

know, you can't! So, it's really been difficult to [connect with other partners] and there's not really a whole lot of Internet presence out there for this population either. . . . As far as anybody in my inner circle that is in the same situation as I am; I can't think of anyone off the top of my head.

June also spoke about how a trans partner's social recognition as a man holds consequences not only for one's own social recognition as queer, but for bracketing a partner's identity and social recognition as a man:

He came very strongly from the dyke community and now it seems like there's no place for him there. . . . Now when we're walking down the street, we know we're read as a hetero couple. And, for both of us, that's a little upsetting. So, we're trying. We're having this conflict now between how do we remain, keep him [laughs]. It's hard to explain. We don't always want to "out" him as trans to give me my queer identity and vice versa. Because as soon as you say, "Well, you know, I'm queer," they'll say, "Well, aren't you dating a guy?" And I'll say, "Yeah." And then as soon as I say, "He's trans," it sort of delegitimizes his male identity.

Cis women partners of trans men described often walking a tightrope double-bind when it comes to disclosures about their own and their partner's identity, faced with the decision to either be misrecognized themselves or to further marginalize their partner. While members of many marginalized communities experiencing stigma or significant challenges in the world may often turn to and find shelter in their families of origin, in my interviews I found evidence that this support is not always readily available for trans people and their partners.

FAMILIES AND LACK OF SUPPORT

Family support was described as particularly challenging for many cis women whose partners transitioned over the course of their relationship. For those participants who had been in a previously lesbian-identified relationship with their partner, having friends and family of origin become comfortable with that lesbian relationship was often described as far less challenging than announcing that a partner would be transitioning. Robyn told me about the process of coming out to her own friends and family:

It's more of like a concrete identity like, "I'm a lesbian, here's my female partner." Whereas when you're with a trans guy (especially because both my relationships started out as lesbian relationships) . . . both of my trans partners were introduced to my family and friends as my lesbian partner, by their birth names, female pronouns. And then [my family] had to go through that switch. . . . With my current partner, we had to go through that switch where he was re-introduced to all my friends and family members by a new name, [they were] asked to use new pronouns.

Some cis women struggled more than others around coming out to their family about their partner's transition, particularly those whose partners transitioned over the course of their relationship together. As Jodi explained:

> I used to talk about my partner with his female name and pronouns and then I stopped really saying anything specific. I just said, "Yeah, we this, we did that." And then I've started now using his name, but not the male pronouns. And I didn't say anything like, "Oh, I broke up with her." So, my poor father is probably really confused.

These language shifts could be challenging not only for families, but for cis women to keep track of as well. Many participants told me that the name and the pronoun that they used for their trans partner shifted depending on the context and audience, and that keeping track of which name or pronoun to use where, when, and with whom could be challenging and anxiety provoking.

When cis women met their trans partner during or after his transition, in some instances they reported that their families and/or friends were unaware that their partner was not a cis man. When I talked to Rachel about how she felt about her partner being perceived as a cis man (and she being perceived as part of an unremarkably cis heterosexual couple) she told me:

> Sometimes it's frustrating. . . . I work in the mall, so I deal with a lot of teenage kids and teenage kids say the most fucked-up stuff about people all the time. . . . We'll carry rainbow stuff or whatever and they'll be like dropping f-bombs [saying "fag"] and saying all this stuff like, "These queers . . ." or whatever. And usually I always felt like really comfortable with being like, "Okay, well, I'm queer." But with [my partner], [he] doesn't like other people and other co-workers to know because he just doesn't want to deal with harassment every day. So, I have to kind of temper my response because I can't just be like, "I'm a big raging queer." And then everybody's like, "Okay, then why are you dating this guy?" And then it raises questions. And my dad is a born-again Christian and I come out to him as queer and now he sees me in a solely heterosexual relationship. So, I have to deal with some of the kind of gloating from my dad: "I told you it was just a phase." And he likes my boyfriend so much that I don't want to jeopardize that for my boyfriend really. It's just complicated. . . . The everyday feeling of conflict. Not wanting to out him, but wanting to be able to celebrate my identity and stand up for people that need to be stood up for. . . . But I don't feel like I have the right to compromise his presentation or his safety or even just his emotional comfort to be able to come to the mall and not be looked at like a science experiment. . . . I had no idea how frustrating it would be until I was in the relationship.

When I asked Emily about her family's support of her relationship with her trans partner, she told me:

I've been out to them for years. They're not totally comfortable with the gay thing, but they don't mind me dating F-to-Ms because that means they can tell everyone I have a boyfriend. So, they kind of like it. But then again, they just don't tell a lot of people that my partner's trans and just let everyone assume we're straight. They're almost *more* comfortable with it in that sense. . . . In the past, I've had them never ask about a partner or something. They'll obviously know that I'm seeing someone and it will just never come up in conversation. They won't mention them or ask how they are or anything like that. . . . But now they ask about [my trans partner] all the time.

Some of the cis women I interviewed discussed their or their trans partner's parents' seemingly greater comfort with trans than with cis lesbian identity. This greater comfort emerged from being able to view their offspring as heterosexual or to present them in that way to others; though this could quickly change if they broached the topic of transition in any substantive way.

Transition-related body modification could be a particularly sore spot for some families. As Emma reported:

As soon as topics of physical changes came into discussion, [his mom] had a big problem with that. . . . She said, "I'm not sure if this identity is a phase for you. I want you to take more time. I want you to think about it." So, it was mainly around the physical changes. She said, "Why do you have to do this?" She's gotten better, much better since, in that she is supportive and accepting of his choices and his wants. But initially, you know, her perspective was, "If you have these surgeries, you are mutilating your body. You're my child, I love you as you are. And you were so happy as a lesbian, why is that not the case any more?" So, they still got along, they still spoke, but it became that they spoke less and they didn't speak as much about the transition stuff.

Some cis women reported that their trans partner delayed transition-related body modification, that they desired to pursue, at least in part due to fears about what his or her family members would think. Jodi relayed her own thinking about why taking the step to begin a medically facilitated transition may be so fraught for some trans men in its intersection with family dynamics:

If you do testosterone you can't go home and kind of ride the ambiguity train. You can't go home and pretend to be the daughter or the granddaughter and put up with it and still be loved by your family, you're just a little weird. If you start testosterone therapy and start growing facial hair and your voice drops, there's no going back. And so that has been, I think, a lot of the reason why he's held back from doing T.

Belinda told me: "In terms of me and my family and my friends, I was the only one who knew [he was trans], which was really isolating for both of us.... But I definitely remember that being his choice." In Bella's family, her parents knew that her partner was trans, but her grandparents and siblings did not. She said: "My whole family uses male pronouns but most of my family doesn't know that he's trans because they wouldn't be very accepting of that."

June told me that about half of her family knew about her partner's trans identity and the other half did not, assuming that he was a cis rather than trans man. I asked her if that had posed any challenges for her in terms of her relationships with her partner or other family members. She told me:

> There's part of me that's frustrated because I can't discuss where he is in his transition, especially when he's taking hormones and all these changes are happening. I kinda wanna discuss that with people and I know that my mom still feels a little uncomfortable about it. And that upsets me. But in terms of the rest of my family, I'm not too close with the rest of my family and they don't need to know.

Drea told me that her partner was not out as trans to any of the members of his own family, despite the fact that "He totally binds and packs in front of his family. They realize what his body looks like." She also told me that he seems more comfortable (with regard to his gender identity) in the presence of *her* family than when he is with his own family. As she told me:

> I refer to him as "he" to all of [my family] when I see them and introduced him as "my boyfriend" when he met them. When he hangs out with [my] side of the family, when he comes to family functions and stuff, it's a lot more comfortable for him because he can be himself more than [with] his own family, so it's very nice.

The fact that one side of the family knows about her partner's trans identity (and uses the appropriate gender pronouns), and the other side does not, has other consequences for the couple and their life together. Drea told me that it has made the possibility of getting married seem like such a logistical nightmare that they have simply pushed plans to marry into the future: "I think it's something we both kind of think about and we wish we could do in the future. I wish we could do it sooner but I don't really see it happening."

Some cis women spoke to me about their own family's attempts to actively withdraw support and to deny, lie about, or reject the relationship that they have with their trans partner. As Tiffany told me:

> I think that my family has never had an instance of support. They are mad every time they hear that I'm spending time with him. He needed a place to go last Thanksgiving because his dorms close, but it was too short of a time [for him] to go [to his] home. So, I let him stay in my dorm. But they were

completely against him coming to Thanksgiving dinner, which would have just been my parents and my grandmother. They are completely against him even being with me and completely against seeing a future with the two of us together. They won't even let me tell my grandma that I have someone I'm seeing. Any time he is mentioned in a conversation, my mother has fashioned it so that he is a gay biological male and a friend of mine. She won't let me clarify it, that I'm actually with him. . . . I had previously been in a relationship with biological men who were physically abusive to me. And my parents ended up realizing they were physically abusive to me. They were, amazingly, never against those relationships. But the moment they found out I was with my [trans] partner, who isn't abusive to me and who does everything he can for me, the minute they found out his biological identity, it became a problem.

A number of cis women spoke to me about how acceptance in a trans partner's family of origin was often mixed, with some of the greatest barriers to full acceptance coming in the form of refusing (or feeling unable to) adopt the correct pronouns (such as "he," "him," "ze,"[4] or "hir"), using different family role identifiers (such as referring to one's trans family member as "son," "grandson," "uncle," or "brother" rather than "daughter," "granddaughter," "aunt," or "sister"), and not using their trans partner's chosen name when referring to him. As Tiffany remarked when discussing her partner's family's issues with using the correct pronoun and terms:

I think he worries too much about it when they slip up. It's just ingrained in their memories that this is how their child was. They used to have a son and a daughter, so it's hard to reprogram your brain from having a son and a daughter to having a son and a son. And I think that he worries too much about them slipping up being some hidden idea that they're not supportive of him rather than it's just a really hard transition for them.

In other families, incorrect pronoun and name usage weren't mere accidents, but intentional barbs.

Gail discussed how her trans partner's lesbian sister refused to acknowledge her own brother as trans and insisted on continuing to use incorrect pronouns and his birth name rather than chosen name. Lynne talked to me about the women in her trans partner's family. All had dark facial hair that they regularly shaved or removed in other ways. Her trans partner's refusal to remove his own facial hair was one of the first signals to his family of his gendered atypicality, and one that made them deeply uncomfortable. This story was particularly compelling as it illustrated the blurred lines between sex, gender, embodiment, and socialization processes.

Some cis women spoke to me about becoming a personal sounding board for their partner's feelings about family members slipping on correct pronouns, names, or relationship designators. As Emily told me:

He would get really frustrated about it. He wasn't somebody who would kind of take things like that in stride. He was like, "This is how I see myself, this is how the rest of the world should see me and why they would slip up I don't know." [He was] not really seeing the fact that your family, who have known you your whole life, are going to slip up. It's just sort of a normal thing. I'd try to make him see that, but it often wouldn't go through. He would get like, "They should just know and accept it!" He would get pretty stubborn about it a lot of the time. . . . It was something we would argue over.

In some instances, cis women found themselves mediating family interactions around a partner's transition even more directly. Kendra spoke to me about a critical interaction she had with her trans partner's mother over the telephone early in his transition:

I think, at first, his mother felt like I was the reason that he was transitioning. Like I put it in his head or something to do it. And I had a conversation about it with her one evening when she called to talk to him and she just kind of broke down on the phone about everything that was happening. And I told [her], "I really don't want you to think that I'm the reason this is happening. You know, yes, I'm being supportive and open to it. But that doesn't mean that I don't have my own issues with it." I think that was important for her to hear. She didn't realize that she wasn't the only person that was having a problem with it that was close to him.

The cis women I interviewed spoke to me about how family members mixing pronouns could create confusing social situations. In some instances, a trans partner was "out" through local news media and had become somewhat recognized or visible as a trans person in their small town, yet one's trans identity was not openly spoken about in the context of family.

Jodi told me about a family interaction wherein her partner became so frustrated by his grandmother refusing to use the correct pronouns and his chosen name that he began to refer to her as "Stanley,"[5] refusing to address her using the name she knew and preferred. Despite his grandmother's stony response, this game of turnabout helped him shift responsibility for maintaining respectful and positive family relationships back to those who refuse or seem unable to accept a trans family member's gender identity. When I asked Lynne to describe her partner's interactions with his own family members, she told me:

He has a single mom who he's very close with. But she has had a very hard time with his transition and was still referring to him as "she" and referring to him with his female given name. And we went and spent about a week with her and she called him "she" the whole time and called him his given name the whole time and that was very, very frustrating for him.

Eliza talked to me about how the process of coming out to one's family as trans could often be a multistage process that involved telling various family members in a coordinated fashion. In some instances, trans partners chose not to ever come out to particular members of their family. As Kyla told me: "He didn't come out to anybody else but me until after his father died because he didn't want to break his father's heart."

Interestingly, the growing visibility of family members "coming out" as gay or lesbian may serve to open pathways for family disclosures about one's identity as trans. As Eliza said:

> My partner's younger brother came out as gay a couple years ago. [His parents] used to be much more conservative than they are now. So, they're just like, "You know what, we don't need any books. We love you. We might not understand it all; but we will and we'll work on this." So, they're very supportive. But at the same time, they're sort of having difficulties with pronouns, changing pronouns, changing names, and terms like "son" don't feel right to them yet. They have to be comfortable too before we tell their parents [her trans partner's grandparents], so it's this whole long chain.

Despite growing mainstream awareness of transgender identity and experience, some cis women spoke to me about making a decision not to disclose a partner's trans identity to family members because of the burden of education that often accompanies such decisions. As Kyla stated quite simply and clearly: "I'm not really interested in educating my family." The work involved in educating one's family about the language, experiences, and politics of being transgender may be considered yet another form of under-recognized emotion work or kin work in which trans people and their partners often engage.[6]

Kyla told me that the amount of work that would be required to educate her family, whose members are not particularly savvy about transgender issues, was simply more than she felt willing or able to undertake in the context of her busy life. Teresa also spoke about a trajectory of educating her family, around issues connected to gender and sexuality, since first coming out as a lesbian:

> When I started dating masculine women, [my family] all kind of had a problem around it because they were all kind of like, "Well, it's okay that you're a lesbian. But we would rather you date someone who looks like you. Why are you not dating someone real pretty?" That was really a process and I spent a lot of time explaining, especially to my sister and my dad, about why I wasn't attracted to women who looked like me, why that didn't mean that I wanted to be with a man, and why it wasn't okay for them to say, "Why don't you just date a man?" So, that was really a process. And when I started dating [my trans partner], we basically had a family meeting about it and we talked about things. And I had talked to them about transgender stuff before because I started educating myself and then educating others. I was

doing a lot of speaking things as a trans ally at a lot of conferences. I was reading books, I was really trying to wrap my head around trans [issues]. So, I know I had conversations with my parents about it but I don't think they thought I would date someone that was transgender. So, that was really a process and we had to have a big conversation about it but generally they love [my partner] and they're supportive. They're unconditional.

Despite ultimately unconditionally accepting Teresa and her trans partner, Teresa described that their pathway to this acceptance was not without occasional stumbling points or roadblocks along the way:

They were very confused about how they were going to explain [my partner's transgender identity] to other people. How they were going to explain it to the rest of our family, who knew me as a lesbian, that now I have a boyfriend. I basically told them that I would rather they not try to explain [his] gender. I would rather them just say, "[Teresa] has a boyfriend, she still identifies as gay." "[Gay]'s" the term that they use because that's what they're most comfortable with. And he's comfortable with the term "queer," so they use that. So, I said, "You can tell them that, or you can tell them that I changed my mind." Really, it doesn't matter to me because I don't see those members of my family often enough. I don't have a close relationship with many of them . . . so it's not important to me that they understand my current relationship, quite honestly. And I don't think it would feel good to try to explain it to them, so I just haven't. There are a few aunts that I've definitely had great conversations with, so it kind of depends on how close I am with the person in my family as to whether or not I'm going to explain it.

In this way, one of the methods that cis women partners of trans men used to diminish the possibility of stigmatizing responses or lack of support from friends and family was to manage disclosures about a trans partner's identity and to selectively disclose only to those deemed relatively safe or open to education around trans issues.

Further, cis women described making very careful decisions about disclosing a partner's trans identity to their family based on their own assessments of the likely future of their relationship with their trans partner. If interviewees felt that their partnership may be short-lived, they often did not even broach the topic of a partner's trans identity with friends or family. As Michele told me:

[My partner] is not out [as trans] to my family. That is a decision that I've made because of [my partner's] issues around commitment and that my family . . . even more so than [his] family . . . will try very hard to understand what being trans means. And it will be difficult for them. And they will worry about their daughter. And I want to make sure before I ask them to do that. And when I do ask them to do that, they will need to do that in order to have a relationship with me. I want to make sure that [my partner] is going to be somebody who is in my life long term.

In addition to participants making decisions about disclosures based on their assessments of family members' openness and supportiveness and the likelihood of the partnership continuing, participants also described navigating "coming out" as the cis partner of a trans man when they had previously come out as lesbian, and helping their families to understand the differences between these identities.

Some cis women discussed how their families had worked very diligently to accept their identities as lesbian and subsequently felt unsure about how to then understand their loved one's relationship with a trans man. As Lynne told me: "The only person [in my family] that knew was my mom. And I think she was confused and saddened and depressed. I think she was just coming to a point where she was beginning to accept that I was queer. And then I started this next oil on the fire or whatever." Samantha also had the experience of achieving some measure of acceptance from her family after coming out as lesbian, only to have this acceptance challenged when a partner transitioned. This acceptance, Samantha told me, had never been easy. As she described it: "I grew up Catholic and very Republican and I went to Catholic schools all my life. When I came out as a lesbian when I was 16 it was like the first thing they did was put me in therapy to try to change me. It's always been a fight."

I asked Samantha to tell me more about how she was managing disclosures to her family around her partner's trans identity as they planned a wedding. She had told me that her mother was particularly uncomfortable with her partner's transition. Samantha said:

I was like, "Well, hey, this is your opportunity! Just tell everybody I'm straight and they can all come to the wedding. I don't care." She said, "But it's not like that." She's dead set to tell everybody that he's "really" a woman. But he's not. And I know that and he knows that and his family knows that and our friends know that. Why can't she get it? It's not just her. It's everybody in my entire family. It's been really awful and really awkward. I have a younger brother who's . . . 10 years younger than me. I'm not allowed to speak [to him] about my partner as my partner, he's my "roommate," which is silly. And I have really pushed at letting that in and it's then refused. I'm not allowed to talk about it. It makes things really complicated. If she could just get over the fact that his body is female, it would make things easier for her. Even though I know I'm not straight, if it would de-complicate things for her, I would be fine with her thinking of me that way.

I asked Samantha to talk to me about the amount of time and energy she had been investing in managing her relationship with her family in the context of her partner's transition and disclosures around it. Her response was heartbreaking:

It's been really hard because me and my mom were best friends. She was the only person in the world that got me. And even when things were really fucked up and really hard, she was always constantly there. She was my rock. And I'm ... starting to pull away more. While I try to keep her as my mother figure, as my rock she has sort of crumbled under the pressure. ... Since I was with my partner while he was still female-identified, my stepfather knows that he used to be a girl. So, he sees it as a lesbian relationship and [my mom] chose to not explain the whole trans thing, just to leave it at that. And so that really complicates things. ... So, I put a lot of energy into it. A lot of tears and a lot of everything. It really has just come down to the fact that I had to choose. I had to choose between my family and my partner, and I chose my partner. And so that was really hard, but we all make choices like that. ... I don't really have much of a connection with anybody in my family anymore because of it and it's made it really hard.

Nina was one of a number of cis women I interviewed who told me that support from their families was a somewhat tricky area to talk about because they tended not to discuss their relationship with their families. Moreover, Nina's account of her previously supportive yet now fractured family relationships, as a direct result of her partnership with a trans person, highlights the tremendous social ignorance and stigma around trans identities.

Some of the cis women I interviewed had learned from prior interactions, often when first coming out as lesbian or with a same-sex partner, that their family members were uncomfortable having such discussions. What this meant on a day-to-day basis is that they rarely received open or active criticism of their relationships, but that there was a silence surrounding the relationship or their sexual identity. As Ani remarked: "My family is not actively supportive. They are not like, 'Why are you doing this fucked up thing with your life?' Although sometimes I think that they think that, they have the sense not to say it. But that doesn't mean that they are supportive." As Nina remarked: "It's not like there is an active criticism with my relationship, it is just totally absent from conversation." Nina told me that her mother not knowing about her partner's trans identity will become increasingly stressful for her as she and her partner contemplate moving geographically closer to family:

It's stressful to have to pay attention to what pronouns I use with my mom or trying to say his girl name because it is weird for me to say it. ... We both want to move closer to our families in the near future ... and if my mom comes to visit any time soon, like, he looks really different from last time that she saw him. So, those things are kind of stressful just thinking about. If [we] want to live around my parents like we're talking about in the next 2 years, they need to know soon. ... So, it is stressful in those ways.

Other cis women described a sort of curious "forgetting" among family members to whom they had previously disclosed their queer identity or partnership with a trans man. I asked Veronica how her interactions with her dad had been after she came out to him: "He just never brought it up again and has completely ignored it by the things that he says." When I asked her what sorts of statements made it clear that he had somehow "forgotten" about her coming out, Veronica told me that he often makes mention of her "finding a husband" or makes statements about "when you're married with kids." It was clear to Veronica that he was not envisioning her potential future husband as trans.

Other interview participants told me that they viewed disclosures about their partner's trans identity to their family of origin as a nonissue for another reason— namely, that no one *should* care about a person's trans identity. Maya said:

In my family, the only one that knows about him [being trans] is my mother. When we got married, we didn't feel the need to tell because he identifies as male, presents as male, is male. So, therefore, there was no need to tell. It's a part of his personal business. There's nothing to tell. It doesn't make any difference in his relationships with people, or shouldn't at least. But he's able to do that because he passes. He doesn't *have to* put it out there. . . . I know it makes it easier on our relationship because he's not having to deal with it every day except when he wants to. So, it's on *his* terms when he gets to be out about being trans. . . . So, I think in that respect I feel good because he doesn't have to deal with transphobia very often. It's safer because you know there are people who really do not like . . . they hate transsexuals even more than gay people. Because at least they don't feel that gay people are deceiving them. A lot of people feel that transgender people are being deceptive and so, therefore, are somehow offending them. So, when he's out and about at night or whatever by himself, I don't worry as much. It made it a little bit easier dealing with my family because we didn't have to deal with that issue. I'm not out to my family. I have a don't ask, don't tell policy with the rest of my family. So, my mother knows about my identity, but nobody else does in my family. . . . It's not a secret as much as I don't feel like it's an issue that affects them. Like my sexuality and his gender identity or my gender identity or whatever. In the same way I don't go to my cousin and say, "Well, I'm a woman." It's the same thing. I don't come at it from a heterosexist or a normative gender approach. There's no "normal" gender.

Maya's trans partner's ability to go stealth in the world, to be recognized by others as unremarkably male, afforded her and her partner the privilege to *not* disclose her partner's trans identity to unsafe or unsupportive friends and family if they did not wish to do so. Of course, not all trans people have the ability or desire to be recognized in this way.

Marisol spoke to me about the ways in which family members and their perceived acceptance (or lack thereof) could play an active role in a partner's decisions around transition, even from afar. Marisol's partner's family primarily lives in the Middle East. As she told me:

He talked about wanting to transition a lot. . . . He would talk about how much he wanted to start taking testosterone and how much he wanted top surgery. He was never ever interested in any phalloplasty; bottom surgery didn't concern him at all. He really wanted top surgery and he really wanted to start taking testosterone. But he was afraid of his family's reaction and how long he would be able to hide it from his family. And I tried to be supportive without trying to push him one way or another. But there was a point about a year and a half into our relationship where I was finally like, "You bring this up constantly and it's obviously something that you want to do. You can't live in fear of what your family's going to think your whole life. If you want to do it then you need to do it."

Marisol's partner did end up pursuing both testosterone and top surgery despite his worries about his family's potentially negative response. Familial rejection of a trans member may take both overt and covert forms. Kendra told me about an encounter she had with her partner and his grandmother:

His grandmother is the only grandparent that is still living and she is trying, I guess, to be supportive of us. She's the stereotypical older person where she's set in her ways and she doesn't know how to deal with that and still love her grandchild. We went to visit her and she was kind of embarrassed of us in that she took us almost an hour away to go eat dinner because she didn't want any of her friends to see us. She pretty much just said, "Well, we're going to go here and eat because I don't want my friends to see you. I don't want to have to explain to them who you are because, frankly, I'm embarrassed." It was nice that she was honest about it, but it was kind of heartbreaking at the same time. Like, how can you really say that you're accepting us [when] we're going an hour away to eat dinner because you're embarrassed of the fact that your friends might see us?

During this same visit, Kendra and her partner also noticed that his grandmother had hidden away all family photos containing his image prior to transition. She had quite literally erased his earlier existence from her home. Kendra said: "Both his mother and grandmother had expressed to me that they felt like their daughter and granddaughter was killed in some kind of violent accident and that she no longer existed." While struggling around stigma or lack of support from friends and family was a potent stressor and strain described by some of the cis women I interviewed, perhaps even more challenging were experiences where they felt unsupported even by their trans partner.

TRANSITION AS A POTENTIALLY PARTNER-ISOLATING PROCESS

Jamison Green has written about the transition process and the impact it may have on interpersonal relationships. Green describes transition as a lifelong process that may have particularly intense moments (often near the beginning) involving seeming self-centeredness or even narcissism on the part of some trans people. He writes to make this period more comprehensible to others who have not experienced it firsthand:

> Once we have begun hormone treatment, the power of these biochemical substances plunge us into adolescence, creating or recreating all the transitional mood swings, confusion, timidity, and bravado that society expects in teenagers but has no way of interpreting or accommodating in adult behavior. There is also the inevitable fascination with our physical body as it changes right before our eyes into something to which we finally feel connected and of which we want to be proud. We may also share a sense of freedom in wearing clothing of choice, the ability to experience psychologically satisfying sexual interaction for the first time, being recognized at last as a member of the gender category in which we feel most comfortable, and the sense of doing something for ourselves rather than always trying to please others. It is this euphoria, self-interest, or self-satisfaction that leads others to criticize us for being horribly self-centered. Many of us have spent much of our pre-transition lives trying to please others in order to fit in, or to compensate for our own internalized sense of incompleteness or inappropriateness, so accusations of self-centeredness seem doubly wounding, surrounded as we are in the U.S. with meta-messages about the positive ramifications of self-indulgence.[7]

Green's writing here directly addresses some of the unsupportive criticisms that have been launched at trans people: that their life choices are selfish or self-centered. It usefully highlights the privileges that cisgender people have that they often take for granted on a daily basis, chief among them the ability to be seen and recognized in accordance with their own most deeply held sense of self.

What has been less carefully addressed in research and writing on trans experience, however, is the impact that the intense focus placed on an individual during some points of transition may have upon a partner, other members of a family, or the partnership and family dynamic itself. Some partners of trans men report that their partner's self-absorption during certain time periods across transition seriously impacted the quality, and even the possible continuation, of their relationships. In his writing, Matt Kailey urges trans men to remain cognizant of people and relationships outside of themselves and their bodies, even during heightened periods connected to transition:

> My advice to transpeople is to listen, listen, and listen some more. Your friends and family, and especially your spouse or partner, need to be heard, they need to have their feelings and fears recognized and acknowledged by you, and they need some downtime, some time away from the transition ... Many transmen, regardless of age, go through a period of adolescent thought and behavior brought on by body changes and the unfamiliar and overpowering sensations of testosterone. It levels out eventually, and the frightening thrill of change, the rabid sexual desires,

and the adolescent silliness dissolve into real life. You still have to make a living and pay bills. You still have to interact with people in the world. You still have responsibilities, the expectations of others, and the day-to-day requirements of whatever life you have established for yourself.[8]

Aimed toward trans people themselves, this passage explicitly considers the impact that some aspects of transition may have upon partners and family members, urging trans individuals to be mindful of their transition as a relational aspect of daily life.

Also difficult for some cis women partners of trans men to navigate is the sense that while transitioning is certainly an individual's choice, its consequences are often relational, and being excluded from decision-making processes around transition may feel disempowering and confusing. Consider the following quotation from Minnie Bruce Pratt:

In the crowded bar when I put my head on your shoulder, with your arm around me, people stared at us. Curious to be so conventional in dress and to draw so much attention. Something too intimate and queer about how we do maleness and femaleness together in public. Perhaps it's easier for you to slip through if you're not with me. One glance and you're a gay man to them, or a slightly ambiguous boy. But when you're with me, I see their eyes flicker: "If he's gay, why is he with her? Why is she with him? If they are two women, why do they look so much like a woman and a man? What are they up to?"[9]

In this passage, maleness and femaleness and heterosexuality and homosexuality are something that is "done," something produced and read through the dyadic relationship of bodies in relation to one another. The social intelligibility of each person, each body, emerges out of this relationality. In making what are often asserted to be very personal and autonomous choices about sex and gender, however, partners of trans individuals may come to feel shut out of a series of decisions in which they often have a deeply vested interest.

Some partners and family members of trans people discuss feeling that their loved one has made the choice to become someone totally different from who they were, someone they may no longer even recognize.[10] Cooper Lee Bombardier, a trans man, begins an essay with a list of things a cis person might say to urge a trans person they care about not to transition, including pleas about how they love the trans person's body just as it is and how they are afraid of what the transition will mean in terms of how their own sexual orientation is read by others when in association with the trans person. Sailor Raven, writing in the same anthology as Bombardier, responds quite differently to her partner's impending transition:

You said last night that you're sorry, that you have this perfectly good body that you can't seem to really live in. I said, baby it's not your fault. This is

some trick played on you, bringing you out into the world in someone else's
form and expecting you to find your own or live in a trap for yourself all
your life. A body owned and confined.[11]

Indeed, reactions to transition surely run the gamut from fear, anger, and dis-
couragement to excitement, understanding, and encouragement—sometimes
within the very same partnership.[12]

Given that transition decisions are ones that will substantially alter not only
the form and structure of one's body, but the form and structure of one's identity
and identity in relation to others, it is perhaps surprising that partners do not
figure more centrally in discussions of transition. This is especially the case considering that trans narratives often discuss the emotional labor, physical work,
money, and time that partners may invest in terms of learning about transition
options, managing family relationships, providing emotional support, paying
for transition-related medical supplies and procedures, providing postsurgical
aftercare, and advocating for trans rights.[13] Nevertheless, in a study by Rachlin[14]
on trans men's decisions about electing surgery, the only question that mentioned partners was an item that asked trans men if they had decided against
surgery because their partners were against it (no respondents indicated that this
was a factor).

Narratives from trans men also reveal that some clinicians and doctors may be
unprepared to communicate effectively with partners of trans men. In response
to research findings that trans men's relationship satisfaction was reduced
(though not significantly) after phalloplasty, Barrett[15] advocated that partners
be informed about realistic post-surgical expectations. According to Lev,[16] such
seemingly obvious considerations are, unfortunately, rare. Lev writes that partners and families have too often been considered difficult or burdensome to clinicians and doctors working with trans people, due to the fact that they often
express many concerns and ask lots of questions.

In the acknowledgment section of his book, Jamison Green makes the following declaration: "I want also to acknowledge the partners of transpeople,
particularly the present or former partners of transmen . . . for their ability to
love beyond conventional boundaries."[17] Patrick Califia[18] titles one of the chapters in his book, "The Invisible Gender Outlaws: Partners of Transgendered
People." Califia describes the numerous ways in which the partners of trans men
often receive little credit for the work that they do to support their partners and
advance trans politics and rights. Several narratives of trans men did, however,
highlight the important role partners played in their transition and lives. Raven
Kaldera, for example, writes:

My lover of seven years, now my wife . . . was the first person in my life not
only to support my gender transgressions 100% but to encourage me. She
sweet-talked me into growing out my beard, encouraged my masculinity,
let me wear the dick during sex, and held me through bouts of body dysphoria. She is a male-to-female transsexual, and she started dating me while

I was still in the denial stage. But she had me pegged long before I knew my own mind. Somehow she knew I was the man for her, even when I was wearing skirts. I've already thanked her, of course, and I continue to do so every day. Her I owe for knowing that no matter what I did with my flesh, someone would always desire me.[19]

These narratives underscore the critical though often invisible role that partners of trans people play in supporting their trans partners through transition and sometimes painfully stigmatizing social and familial interactions. While many partnerships certainly become stronger through the ongoing experience and process of transition, other partnerships struggle or end. Some of these struggles may be connected to transition, but it is critical not to reduce all relationship challenges to this singular source. In the next section, I consider another area of struggle that some cis women partners of trans men experience in the context of their partnerships and families: intimate partner violence.

INTIMATE PARTNER VIOLENCE

In a study of 20 cis women partners of trans men conducted by Nicola Brown,[20] 25%[21] of the sample reported experiencing some form of intimate partner violence. While these rates are undoubtedly disturbing and troublingly high, it is important to note that these rates parallel (and are even slightly lower than) those reported by cis women in heterosexual relationships with cis men and by cis women in lesbian relationships with cis women.[22] Within my sample, 6 cis women (12%) spoke about incidents that could be classified as intimate partner violence. Only 2 of these interviewees reported physical or sexual forms of violence and, in each instance, they were reporting on a past relationship. As such, it is likely that experiences of intimate partner violence were underreported in this sample, particularly in instances where the interviewee was currently involved in a relationship in which intimate partner violence was occurring.

Cis women who did report intimate partner violence described various types of abuse: emotional and psychological manipulation, verbal threats, sexual assault, hitting and slapping, pushing and pulling, throwing objects, and punching holes in walls. One participant told me that she had relatively little support for the sexual and physical abuse that she was experiencing during her relationship. One of the major reasons that she was cut off from her social support networks is because, at the time of the abuse, she was still in love and stayed with her partner, which made her feel embarrassed since she knew that her friends would tell her that she should leave. In another instance, an interviewee who had been slapped by her partner also discussed how his deepening voice after beginning testosterone contributed to the fear that she sometimes felt around him. She told me: "He's had to go to therapy for raising his voice now that his voice is deeper and bigger. He's been able to use that voice in a boom-ing context, which I finally had to say, 'Hey, no. You have this tool now that you can use against me and other women. You need to be aware of the power of that voice and how you utilize it'."

Living in a hostile environment, even without direct physical abuse, was described by participants who experienced it as extremely stressful. A partici-pant described exhausting arguments with her partner that could stretch out over hours:

> It used to be really hard. He used to be the kind of persona that would bottle everything up inside and then freak out and he would like punch holes in the walls and throw things. He was never violent towards me but he would just ... he had all this anger. And I was like, "You cannot manifest your negativity and anger. It's just not going to work." I was like, "I can't be with you if it's going to be like that." And he cared so much for me that he worked on that. [I asked: How did he work on that?] This is going to sound funny but we used to sit for hours and hours and hours and struggle for 1 sentence.... And I would be like, "Okay, what's the first word?" ... We would get blankets and pillows because we knew we were going to be there for hours. Not even kidding. And I would be like, "Well, what's the first word?" ...We trudged through it. We would go letter by letter by letter until he would finally voice what he was feeling.... We've worked really hard to get where we are.... Our communication is the best thing. We both really recognize how important it is and that's good. We both have our own savings accounts of course because that's the only smart thing to do, I think, in case anything goes wrong. If he turns out to be a wife beater, I'm going to want money to leave. And if I turn out to be a psycho, he's going to need to leave too.

While none of the cis women I interviewed described physically or sexually abusing their trans partner, an interviewee did describe pulling her partner's arm in an attempt to get him to sit back down during a conversation, and another described throwing objects at her partner, though she asserted that the objects never hit him.

Future research on social support and strain in cis women's partnerships with trans men would do well to include inquiries into the existence of inti-mate partner violence within these relationships, particularly to consider the ways in which societal and familial ignorance, stigma, strain, and discrimi-nation may contribute both to abusive relationship dynamics as well as limit institutional recognition and appropriately supportive responses to them. Given the social stigma and stereotypes around trans identity, it is also pos-sible that trans people and their partners may be less likely to disclose or report instances of intimate partner and intrafamily violence in order not to provide fodder for those who believe that these queer partnerships and families are inherently pathological.

SOCIAL SUPPORT NETWORKS AND COMMUNITIES
FOR TRANS PARTNERSHIPS AND FAMILIES

Despite participants reporting considerable struggles to find support within communities and families of origin and choice, the majority of cis women I interviewed told me that they had discovered or cultivated various forms of social support for their partnerships and families as well. Social support took on many different forms, but some of the most reportedly impactful was that expressed by one's own and one's trans partner's family of origin. The families of the cis women I interviewed and their partners were described as remarkably diverse in terms of how supportive they were around trans issues or for the couple's partnership in general. In some instances, the families of both the cis women I interviewed and their trans partner were tremendously supportive.

This support took many forms such as financial, emotional, situation-specific (e.g., support around a death, birth, or transition), and full inclusion in family events connected to holidays, vacations, or other special celebrations (such as weddings). In some instances of familial rejection, one partner's family provided a welcoming and safe space for both partners. The cis women I interviewed also spoke to me about how social support in their own or their partner's family shifted across time and context. In the following subsections, I consider some of the particular ways in which social support materialized for cis women and their trans men partners across families, friends, and community networks.

Material Support

Given the great cost of many transition-related pharmaceuticals and surgeries, the provision of financial support by others (and families of origin in particular) was often mentioned as both fiscally and symbolically critical. For those individuals and families willing and able to provide material support to assist with a trans person's transition-related medical care (such as hormones, therapy, or surgery), this act was often seen as a commitment beyond mere tolerance of trans identity, to one of trans acceptance and instrumental support. The cis women I interviewed described instances of financial support from small, non-recurring individual contributions, to ongoing loans or subsidies, and community-based fundraisers for large-scale medical costs.

For the trans partners of the cis women I interviewed, financial contributions from their families of origin were often viewed as the most personally affirming. When I asked Amber if her trans partner's family had been supportive of his transition, she told me: "Yes. They helped him raise money for surgery ... they helped pay his bills." For families who were not particularly wealthy, the provision of transition-related material support was viewed as particularly indicative of a positive relationship and trans acceptance. Ellia told me: "His parents paid for [top surgery] and they don't have a lot of money ... The surgery cost $7,000 ... and we didn't know what we were going to do. His parents said, 'You know, this is absolutely necessary for you and *we'll* pay for it'. That was amazing. We could not have done that without them."

In some instances, cis women described their own families of origin providing material support for their trans partner's transition-related medical procedures when other resources failed to materialize or simply were not enough. Kendra described her trans partner's increasing depression and her fears that he was becoming suicidal prior to his top surgery, which ultimately necessitated the couple's concerted search for material support to finance his top surgery. When Kendra discussed her partner's situation with her father, he agreed to co-sign on a loan with her trans partner so that he could borrow the $6,500 needed for his top surgery. In addition to this material act of support, Kendra's father took time off work, accompanied her at the hospital on the day of her trans partner's operation, sat with her while her trans partner was in surgery, and then provided aftercare assistance for her trans partner for several days. She also told me that her mother (who is divorced from her father) brought over snacks, movies, and magazines for her partner during his recovery at home. These forms of support could demonstrate to the cis women I interviewed, and their partners, that their trans partner was indeed seen as "part of the family," extending the network of available familial support far beyond their biological origins.

Friends and community members were also sometimes mentioned as sources of material support by the cis women I interviewed. As Selma told me:

> This last year has been almost impossible. Without the support of our friends we wouldn't have gotten through it. He is a union tradesman and since 9/11 there has been no work. I was out of work for a year this last year. We've had a lot of stressors on our relationship and I really give us a lot of credit for not ripping each other apart in the process. It would get the best of any couple regardless of where they were at or how they identified. Yeah, we've borrowed from all of our friends. They've all been there, are emotionally supportive, and truly our closest friends have been right there for us all year long and continue to be so.

As Selma's narrative highlights, it is important to remember that not all of the stressors and strains that cis women and trans men experience in their partnerships and families are directly related to a trans partner's family. Just as with any other family, people lose jobs, experience life-changing health events, and fall on bad times. The support of friends and family through some of these harrowing life events was described as critically important and sustaining.

Transition-Related Labor and Support

As detailed in Chapter 3, the medically necessary aftercare for some transition-related surgical procedures, with top surgery being among the most common, was an event and form of labor that many of the cis women I interviewed described.

In some instances, this aftercare brought families, friends, and communities together as cis women worked with their trans partner's family members, their own families of origin, and/or friends to provide postsurgical care. I asked Mel to talk to me about the support that she and her trans partner had in terms of providing home-based care following her partner's outpatient top surgery:

> For the first week, it was a combination of myself and [my partner's] mom and sister directly after [he] had surgery....We were picked up from the hospital ... by [my partner's] sister and we went up to where [his] parents are from and we were there for the first week. So, it was a combination of the 3 of us that were sort of primary caregivers for that week ... which was really nice to be able to share that. I mean no one fusses over their kid like a mom does. It was nice to have that weight or that responsibility of care shared among people who really cared for him and were dedicated to him. And then once we were back [where we live], [my partner] had a network of people, including a couple of other trans friends, who would sort of come by and say "Hi!" if I was out for the whole day or something like that. It's things like helping him get in and out of his clothing, helping him move around the house. It's all flooding back to me now. For the first bit he chose to sleep on the couch rather than the bed because sleeping in an upright position was much more comfortable. So, things like helping arrange bedding and making sure he was comfortable and helping him get in and out of bed and maybe helping him get to the washroom. Definitely getting him food and giving him sponge baths.

Even before partners, friends, and family members band together to provide postsurgical care, the cis women I interviewed talked to me about how gathering information about transition-related medical care was often a crowdsourced affair.

My interviewees discussed how the trans community banded together through the Internet to provide knowledge about the most affordable and competent doctors specializing in transition-related medical care and surgical procedures across the globe. Using Internet chat rooms, listserv, email, and at that time burgeoning social media sites (such as YouTube, Friendster, MySpace, LiveJournal, and Facebook), trans people and their partners exchanged information about hormones, top and bottom surgeries, support groups, therapists, doctors, clinics, financing, and fundraisers. This information flow was not only textual, but in the form of pictures and videos as well. Trans people and their partners quite literally hyperlinked their pathways to new embodiment and identity possibilities.

Crowdsourcing funds for transition-related medical care is just one way in which postmodern technologies (in this instance Internet-facilitated social media) provide not only information about available procedures, but the means through which to procure them as well. This is not to say that hormones and transition-related surgeries are now readily accessible to all; indeed, they are not. I observed through my interviews that crowdsourcing and drawing upon social support networks seemed most effective among the relatively privileged in my sample (those who were White, highly educated, and/or or middle-class) when it came to obtaining transition-related social support and funding for transition-related medical care.

In addition to providing information and potential funding around transition-related medical care, trans community social support networks were also galvanized for the purpose of providing procedural knowledge and expertise around the administration of hormones as well as the provision of aftercare following transition-related surgical procedures. These contributions ranged from bringing meals and providing support to primary caretaking and direct aftercare such as emptying drainage tubes and performing surgical wound care. As the recovery period progressed, trans community members were also enlisted to provide feedback about the healing process: from offering insights about whether incision sites were healing properly, to assessing the outcome of surgical results, to recommendations for scar-healing treatments and surgical revision procedures.

Trans community social support networks were mentioned as particularly valuable because the information and knowledge they offered extended beyond the abstract and was rooted in personal experience. In this way, this information was often seen as more trustworthy and accurate. On the other hand, some of the cis women who shared their stories with me discussed the potential for the support and feedback provided by trans community members to generate a comparative or competitive frame. In other words, in some instances cis women reported that their trans partners would compare their own embodied transition outcomes, both with hormones and surgical procedures, to those of their trans friends and community members. If a trans community member had a thicker beard, deeper voice, flatter chest, or less obvious scars, there was a potential for jealousy and a social hierarchy to emerge. Similarly, the cis women I interviewed sometimes compared their own provision of social support with those of other partners and community members, wondering if they were doing enough or providing support in the best possible way. Nevertheless, most of the cis women I interviewed indicated that their connections to trans community and to other cis women partners of trans men were vitally important. In addition to the Internet, other primary sites my interviewees described meeting partners of trans men like themselves were colleges and universities.

Colleges and Universities as Sites of Education and Support

Not only were colleges and universities the primary sites where many of the cis women in my sample met their trans partners, they were also some of the most-mentioned sites for the emergence of trans community and support. A considerable number of the cis women I interviewed, and their trans partners, were connected to a university or college-based social support or activist group that focused on the LGBTQ community, or even the trans community in particular. While the politics and membership of these groups could become contentious at times, they were frequently mentioned as spaces where the free exchange of information and support was facilitated and supported. Some trans-affirming faculty, therapists, nurses, clergy, social workers, and doctors were also mentioned as individual sources of support.

For many, simply being asked: "How are you and your partner doing?" made oneself, one's trans partner, and one's partnership feel both recognized and supported. Having basic knowledge about trans identities was also mentioned as a way to demonstrate one's support of trans individuals, partners, and families. As June mentioned:

> I think we've been fortunate, for the most part, to have a pretty good support system in terms of what [he went] through when he was transitioning. I guess, for me, I didn't realize there was such a big [support] group like that. I think being located within a university setting, he's been able to reach out and find people that he can talk to. So, I think that we've both been fortunate enough to have a solid group of people to go to.

Even in social contexts in which trans-specific supports and communities did not exist or were not accessible, the cis women with whom I spoke discussed the importance of that general recognition and support, simply being seen, recognized, and acknowledged.

In some instances, just being able to relay one's knowledge of another trans person and his partner or family could be seen as a way to connect and provide social support. As Robyn told me: "My really close buddy here . . . has known trans people before. She . . . knew this couple long before the partner transitioned. And now he's transitioned and they adopted a baby and they have a real nice stable relationship. Just sharing stories like that is really important." Some of the women I interviewed discussed that it takes a certain amount of bravery and courage to transition and to support someone who is transitioning.

Having that bravery and courage recognized as such by others in one's social network was seen as affirming by some, yet marginalizing by others. For some, being called "brave" or "courageous" conveyed an exceptionalism that could feel paradoxically disempowering. In these instances, some cis women talked about drawing inward and no longer seeking out social support. When I asked Terry how she became so self-reliant and why she distanced herself from trans-specific support, she told me: "Scar tissue. I got my feelers mashed too many times to take a risk anymore. . . . I am not willing to take a risk any more. I've got what I need. I have enough. The small circle that I have is enough. I don't need to surround myself." In this way, it was not necessarily the size of social support networks and communities that seemed to matter for participants as much as the quality, consistency, and dependability of their support.

Family Matters

Other forms of social support that were mentioned as particularly critical for trans people and their partners included others using the correct name and pronouns for trans partners, particularly among families of origin. Because families of origin are often the individuals in a trans person's life who have known them (and their name and gender categorization given at birth) the longest, it is sometimes most difficult for these individuals to transition, themselves, into using a different name or set of pronouns for their loved one.

Cis women talked to me about the importance of their family members truly seeing their trans partners as they wished to be seen. This sort of seeing was exemplified by Ellia, who relayed something her mother had told her that provided her and her partner with much comfort even as it also revealed potentially troubling insights into a parent's comfort with various members of LGBTQ communities:

> [My mother] said, "Well, when I first met him, I thought, 'He's not just a very butch lesbian, there's something else.'" And so she had started to research online and she had a book . . . like she was on to it before we told her. So, she has always said "he" and his name. I think it's even more comfortable for her that he's transgender instead of him just being a very masculine woman, which is so odd.

While Ellia describes this reaction as "odd," it makes sense if we consider the structuring power of conformity to gender norms and expectations. While a family member may be reticent to accept a partner whose gender identity and self-presentation seem at odds with normative expectations (e.g., identifies as a woman and is masculine in appearance), they may find it easier to accept when that seeming dissonance is reduced or absent (e.g., identifies as a man and is masculine in appearance). In some instances, the cis women with whom I spoke discussed their role as relationship facilitators, with their trans partner's own family of origin asking *them* how transition was going and how their partner was doing.

One aspect of postmodern partnerships and families is that members are often separated from one another through long distances, given the not-infrequent need for geographic relocation for the purposes of education or employment, as well as the fact that online dating provides unprecedented opportunities for individuals to find one another even if living across the world. Some of the cis women with whom I spoke discussed how social support could be provided by families even when living far away. Nina, whose own family lives far away, told me that the provision of support from her trans partner's family has been particularly critical since her own family is not near:

> His family is really consistent about phone calls and emails. They ask about me. They ask about his transition. They're generally really aware of what is going on in his life and my life because they communicate a lot. To me, that's a main source of support. My family is 2,000 miles away. So, a main source of support that we get from [my] family [pertains to questions like]: "Do you write me? Do you call me? Can I talk to you about this?" In those ways, they are very actively supportive. "Is there anything we can get you? Do you need

anything? How are you doing? How is [your partner's] transition? How is work coming along?" They are very supportive in the ways that they can be from far away.

In many ways, even the most relatively disengaged or distant forms of social support that families provided could serve as important symbolic indicators of their support for both trans identity and the queer partnerships and families the cis women I interviewed formed with their trans partners.

Being asked the same sorts of annoying, pesky, and sometimes intrusive questions that nontrans couples are frequently asked was often mentioned by my interview participants with a smile or chuckle. "When are you getting married?," for instance, was often described as a way for families to simultaneously acknowledge their understanding of a trans person's identity as well as the seriousness of the relationship between the cis women I interviewed and their trans partners. Even when this questioning revealed ignorance of the structural and institutional barriers that trans couples sometimes faced at this time when it came to legal recognition of their partnerships and families,[23] it could simultaneously express an understanding that these postmodern partnerships were not so different from the sorts of relationships and families they have always known insofar as they were, at their core, rooted in love, commitment, sacrifice, support, struggle, and family connections.

A number of the cis women I interviewed noted how comforting and reassuring it is that their communication with their own and/or their partner's family focuses largely on how each individual and the couple is doing across relatively mundane areas of life rather than focusing primarily or exclusively upon transition or trans-related issues. For some of the cis women I interviewed, the "sweet spot" was for trans identity to be acknowledged and supported by their families and loved ones, yet not constantly front and center or under close analysis. In other words, being a trans person or part of a trans partnership and family was critically important, but nowhere near the only (or even most) important aspect of their identities, partnerships, and families at all times and across all contexts. How well families and loved ones are able to understand this fact, and reflect it in the content of their communications, was often connected to when the cis woman met and began a relationship with her trans partner. For those individuals who began their relationship with their partner prior to (or early during) his transition, families were often described as being a bit slower to relate to the trans partner and the couple like any other.

In this way, some of these families may be said to have transitioned along with a trans person. They often went from viewing their family member's partner as a woman and the relationship as lesbian; their understanding of those identities and relationships transitioned over time. For those families who always knew their loved one's partner as a man or a trans man, and the relationship between them as (presumably) heterosexual, struggles not to centralize trans identity seemed less pronounced or protracted in cis women's descriptions.

Regardless of the timeline of how their relationships came to be, many cis women spoke to me about efforts that members of their communities and families had undertaken to better understand transgender identity and to accept trans people and their partners. As Jodi told me about her own mother:

> She watched *Transamerica*[24] on purpose because of my partner and the conversations we had about transgender [issues]. And she started really looking at it and thinking about it more. I'm her only child and she's real protective of me and she doesn't want anything hard for me. She wants everything to just be nice.

When I asked Judy to talk to me about whether or not she had received support for her relationship with her trans partner from her family, she told me:

> Yeah, the ones that I've come out and told have been really good and asked a lot of questions so they understood. Like, when I first told my father he was pretty short on the phone and wanted to get off the phone and I know that's him just going, "Okay, I need some time just to process." And it was very obvious that he had done some research just to educate himself. His wife's a nurse and they were looking online at stuff. And my sister and my brother, who I both told, again were really good at asking a lot of questions simply because they needed to understand.

When I asked Judy how her partner's family had reacted to the news of his transition, she said:

> They've actually been amazing. Like from the whole, "What did I do wrong with my child?" type thing and "You're my baby and you're always going to be my little girl," to now. . . . I mean, they live across the country so we see them twice a year. Last time when we were out there it was great. They were trying really hard to call him by his chosen name and the proper gender [pronouns] and made a point to correct themselves if they screwed up. So, it's been great.

Even among families that were generally supportive, cis women often spoke to me about their family's struggle, over time, to reconcile a trans person's identity or their loved one's sexual identity. Many of the cis women I interviewed revealed that these supportive responses were often accompanied by a great deal of work and education among all those involved.

Indeed, it would be fair to say that interest in, willingness to pursue, and commitment to expanding education around gender and sexual identities is a form of social support in and of itself offered by families of those who are trans or whose family member loves someone who is trans. These stories provide evidence that even in families that are initially unsupportive around trans issues, identities, and partnerships, it is possible to become more supportive and understanding over time with education and the commitment to work on strained relationships. It was not unusual for the cis women I interviewed to be actively involved in the education of family members (both their own and their trans partners') around issues connected to identity.

While a partner's trans identity could be a source of contention in some families, other cis women told me that their partner's trans identity was a relative nonissue. Margaret said:

> He's very out. I don't think one could get more out then he is. We went to my family reunion this weekend and he was completely stealth. Nobody knew he was trans except for the people who had been specifically told that he was trans. Not that he or I would have hidden it from people, but it was just this sort of nonissue.

I pushed Margaret a bit on her response and asked her if she ever felt like she had to manage information about her partner's trans identity when it came to relationships with her friends or family members. Margaret told me:

> No, I don't bother. I don't care who knows. If it comes up it comes up and it's out there and then we answer questions. If it doesn't come up, it just doesn't come up. I think probably the only people we've intentionally *not* told are my grandparents and simply because my grandfather is mostly deaf and it would involve yelling lots of really private kinds of words. And my grandmother, you know, she wouldn't understand unless we gave her a couple beers. I think we've protected them from it but simply because it would be way too complicated to try to explain it and not because we have any reservations about anyone knowing.

Experiences like Margaret's challenge the dominant cultural narrative that disclosures around trans identity must always be highly fraught, difficult to manage, and contentious.

The cis women I interviewed told me that it could sometimes be easier to find support, understanding, and acceptance for their identities and partnerships among their friends than among their families. As Veronica, whose mother still assumes that her daughter is in an unremarkably cis heterosexual relationship, told me:

> With friends that I've had before college, he knows all of them. And if anything, they just ask questions. They are really fine with [his trans identity]. They don't slip up with pronouns. They don't say, "Oh, you're in a lesbian relationship." They understand. They take it for face value and they've been wonderful. I'm not yet out to my mom about the situation, but my mom happens to really love [my partner]. So, that's something. . . . I actually had a really big anxiety dream about it the other day. I really want her to know

and [my partner] wants her to know. I just can't seem to do it yet. But she's pretty much the only important person that I haven't told this to yet.

Friends were described as more willing and eager to ask questions, while families sometimes clammed up, acting as if disclosures around trans identity had never happened (even when they had) and simply not discussing the issue.

Eliza described her approach of correcting strangers' and family members' misgendering of her trans partner. Both her and her partner's family were described as generally supportive, understanding, and accepting, and Eliza spoke about her family's path toward that eventual acceptance and understanding of her trans partner and the relationship she has with him:

Depending on the situation, if [strangers] are "reading" my partner as female, he might address it at that moment with them and just be like, "Oh, I'm actually trans," or something like that. With family, I think we've been more open about sort of trying to correct them as gently as possible and understanding that they've got their own unique sort of path and journey to go through to better understand it.

While acceptance and support were gradual or hesitant for some families, this was not true of all. A partner's trans identity was, for the families of some of the cis women I interviewed, simply not much of an issue at all and did not stand as a barrier to support and acceptance for the partner or partnership. When I asked Ellia whether or not she felt supported by her family, she replied:

They're just very loving of us both. My family just absolutely loves him and his family has just taken me in. Both of our families are very welcoming for us both. We got engaged 4 or 5 months ago and our families were so excited. My mother offered to pay for the wedding, which she never would have done if she didn't support the relationship. She's not the, "You should just get married!" type. She's very excited about the marriage. Our families have just been so amazing through this whole thing.

Some interviewees also told me that even if a trans partner's family struggled with his transition, this did not mean that they automatically rejected or failed to accept the cis woman partner or their partnership.

Emma was one of the cis women I spoke with who told me that her partner's family had truly struggled to use the correct pronouns, name, and relationship terms after he began his transition. Despite these challenges, however, Emma described her trans partner's family as a tremendous source of social support for her, personally:

Nothing changed about the way that they treated us as a couple when the transition happened. From the day that I met them, they completely welcomed me in and continued to do so and were very, very supportive and loving, affectionate, very inclusive. We were always welcome at holidays and whenever we wanted, really, on weekends. They always wished that they could see both of us more often. With his family there was never an occasion where they expressed that they only wanted to see him and that I should stay behind. It was always the 2 of us, I was very welcomed.

For some, family transitional moments also held the power to transform familial lack of support to support.

After Maya and her trans partner had a baby, some formerly resistant members of her partner's family came to respect his role as a man and a husband vis-à-vis his role as a new father. As Maya told me:

One thing that's happened really recently is [my husband's] family really rallied around the birth of [our daughter]. It really has brought his family, in large part, in line and [brought] a level of acceptance [for my husband] that I don't think he's really ever felt from them. We went to show her off to them a couple weekends ago and they were all calling him "dad" and just really very affirmative in a way that he hasn't felt from them . . . ever, really. It was funny because his brother, who does not acknowledge [him] at all, was there for a little bit and he wouldn't talk to [him] at all. He talked to me, held [our daughter], I mean [my husband] would directly ask him a question and he wouldn't even look at him much less answer him. His mother actually called and apologized for that and his uncle said that he thought the brother acted like a jerk and that we were good parents. And that was the first time that they actively supported him like that. Although they did not confront the brother. They didn't say, "Hey, you're being a jerk. Stop acting like that."

In this instance, while the birth of their daughter could not transform the hearts and minds of *all* of her husband's family members, moving them from hostility to support, it was able to positively transform *some* of these critical family relationships and dynamics. In this way, support and acceptance in the lives of many cis women and their trans partners could often be understood as incremental and dynamic rather than all-or-none and static.

NOTES

1. National Coalition of Anti-Violence Programs (2014). These risks are particularly pronounced for trans women of color, who experience the highest rates of murder and homicidal violence.
2. See Weiss (2004) for an overview of existing transphobia (and biphobia) within lesbian and gay communities in the United States.
3. See Green (2004:74).
4. "Ze" and "hir" are pronouns that are preferred, by some, to existing binary forms of gender identification and self reference.

5. This name has been changed to a pseudonym to protect participant confidentiality.
6. See Hochschild (1979, 1989) for more on emotion work.
7. See Green (2004:207).
8. See Kailey (2005:109, 121).
9. See Pratt (1995:85).
10. See Devor (1997).
11. In Diamond (2004: 50–51).
12. See Martino (1977) and Green (2004), respectively.
13. See, for example, Boenke (1999); Khosla (2006); Martino (1977); Pratt (1995).
14. See Rachlin (1999).
15. See Barrett (1998).
16. See Lev (2004).
17. See Green (2004: xi).
18. See Califia (1997).
19. In Nestle, Howell, and Wilchins (2002:159).
20. See Brown (2007).
21. 5 out of 20 participants.
22. See Breiding, Smith, Basile, Walters, Chen, and Merrick (2014).
23. For example, if a trans partner's legal sex marker had not or could not be changed to male on their birth certificate given restrictions in their state of birth, this precluded their ability to enter into a legal marriage with their cis woman partner in states that restricted legal marriage to those between 1 man and 1 woman. Even in states allowing for broader diversity in legal marriage (for example, legal recognition of "same-sex marriage"), many families failed to consider that entering into what would be considered a "same-sex marriage" could symbolically and legally invalidate a trans person's gender identity.
24. See Tucker (2005).

Conclusion

Toward Broader and More Inclusive Notions of Family in the 21st Century

On April 24, 2015, I sat in my office working on final edits of the first full draft of the book you're now holding in your hands. I left my office around 10 p.m. to get back home to watch the Diane Sawyer special I had DVRed from earlier that evening. In an exclusive 2-hour interview, Caitlyn Jenner came out to the world as a trans woman. I had watched my Facebook news feed explode with status updates critiquing and celebrating this very public disclosure. Notably, the episode was quite centrally focused on Jenner's family throughout. Their fears, anxieties, rejection, support, and pride were conveyed in various complicated ways that shifted across time and from member to member. Importantly, Jenner's interview shifted some (though certainly not all) of the common cultural narrative around trans identity and experience. She made it clear that transition most often is not a singular event, a single point in time, or even a constellation of specific medical procedures or surgeries. Instead, Jenner made it clear that this was a transition stretching across 30 or more years. The next day, news sources reported that the interview was seen by some 16.9 million viewers across the world.[1]

I thought about just how much had changed in the world since Oprah Winfrey's exclusive interview with Thomas Beatie 7 years earlier, almost to the day. Since that time, legal recognition for other types of queer families has swept across the land as same-sex marriage became legal across most of the country. Leaders of the Michigan Womyn's Music Festival, often noted for its "womyn born womyn intention" (which many viewed as exclusionary to trans women), announced that 2015 would be the last year the festival would be held.[2] Increasingly, parents are making the choice to support their trans kids, even working to facilitate their transitions.[3] Transgender people may now obtain a United States passport with a name and sex marker that is consonant with their gender identity. Trans students have been granted protection from discrimination in schools based on new rulings on Title IX, a federal law that protects students from discrimination based on their sex.[4] I also cannot help but notice just how much more positive and open the public response to Jenner's very public trans coming out story seemed compared to Beatie's, almost less spectacular despite the fact that Jenner is surely at the center of one of the most infamous celebrity families in the media eye. In 2016, as I make final edits on the final draft of this book, I note that many now seem much more aghast at Jenner's outspoken Republican stances than at her gender identity, suggesting that trans people are still expected to conform to narrow ideologies or a pre-specified set of liberal beliefs since their very identities are often viewed as emblematic of radical liberal politics.

Yet just as the world seems to change, so much stays the same. Trans people, particularly trans women of color, continue to face some of the highest rates of abuse, suicide, and homicide among all groups.[5] Trans people still fight for the right to use the restroom and wear the prom clothing that aligns with their gender identity in schools across the country. There is a growing backlash against trans rights and access to basic needs and resources that has emerged following the Supreme Court's legal recognition of same-sex marriage in the United States in 2015.[6] Trans people and their partners and families continue to be misrecognized and rendered simultaneously socially invisible and hypervisible. Trans people and their partners and families also struggle through a legal quagmire.

Paradoxically, the expanded legal rights granted to same-sex cisgender couples over recent years may only serve to further complicate how trans people, their partners, and their families are legally recognized in relation to one another. Many trans people continue to find transition-related hormones and medical procedures inaccessible due to their high cost and exclusion from insurance coverage. Those trans people who do not wish (or are unable) to pursue binary gender classifications, who use hormones, and who have transition-related surgeries are often marginalized both within cisgender and transgender communities. In the 21st century, trans people and their partners continue to grapple with stigma, discrimination, and exclusion not only from strangers and social institutions, but from their friends, families, and communities as well.

The experiences and perspectives of the 50 cis women partners of trans men appearing in the narratives woven throughout this book urge us to reconsider the complicated interface between individual versus structural accounts for inequalities in everyday life. Attending to the relational identity and emotion work processes in which many cis women partners of trans men engage, I have highlighted the complex tensions that often accompany their queer identities and families as they interface with social systems, institutions, and structures in the postmodern era. Cis women partners of trans men, and their relationships, are often accused of parroting cis heteronormativity. In other instances, they are cast as homonormative by those who misunderstand their relationships as lesbian.

Standing as a corrective to these overly simplistic assessments, I have discussed the powerful social, legal, and medical systems that structure normative social-relational practices such as marriage and parenting. Doing so allows us to more fully consider the ways in which life choices are often compelled not only by normalizing social-structural forces, but by strategic planning and pragmatism as well. I have also suggested that we might usefully challenge the assumption that those in relationships with trans people must have relationships that are somehow *more* transgressive or counternormative than other types of relationships. As Suzanne Kessler and Wendy McKenna[7] note, the prefix "trans" in "transgender" does not necessarily refer to the "transcendence" or "transformation" of gender or gender normativity, and to assume that it does is to minimize decades of empirical scholarship, referenced throughout each of the chapters in this book, testifying to the rigidity and recalcitrance of the socially structuring gender binary in our society.

Assertions that trans people and their partners should be more transgressive than their cisgender counterparts also fail to consider the ways in which identity choices are socially embedded, strategic, and constrained. We might approach questions about whether the relationships between cis women and trans men reflect a radical subversion of cultural normativity, or mirror and repackage cultural normativity, with some degree of critical suspicion. Such questions implicitly suggest that the onus of responsibility for radically reconfiguring gendered power relations ultimately lies with a numerical and marginalized social minority. Instead, we might question whether or not the relationships between cis women and cis men—a clear numerical majority in our culture—currently reflect radical subversion of cultural normativity. Reframing and reorienting the analysis to the normative center highlights the responsibility that those with relative privilege hold with regard to enacting social change, resisting stultifying normativity, and reconfiguring relationships of power.

Sociologist and gender theorist Raewyn Connell[8] argues that it is ultimately in the best interests of those who are committed to gender equality to recognize the "belonging" of trans people within the social identity groups that correspond to their gender identity. In this way, Connell urges a fundamental shift in how we approach studies of transgender social actors. Rather than focusing on transgender social actors' accomplishment of gender through "passing," we might focus, instead, on the interactional processes whereby *we all* act as judges of the gender order as we recognize or reject others as "belonging" to (or rightful members of) particular gender and sexual identity categories and groups. In essence, we might hold a mirror up to society in order to see a reflected image of a numerical majority choosing to either reproduce and maintain gender binaries and biologically essentialist notions of sex, or to challenge them. A central task for understanding transgender identity pivots upon recognition of the potential social solidarity between cis and trans people. As Connell notes: "It requires us to think of social embodiment as an active, changing historical process, not as a matter of fixed categories for bodies."[9]

Perhaps we might work to develop greater insight into the ways in which we are *all* performing and co-creating identities. As sociologist Leila Rupp notes: "Knowing how identities are created, institutions established, communities built, and movements mobilized, we learn from the margins what the center looks like."[10] We could work on our sociological imaginations by learning to approach the normative as "strange" in order to more clearly observe often taken-for-granted assumptions that (re)produce normative social structures and their attendant forms of regulation and oppression. The work of challenging oppression requires greater collective solidarity among social actors who inhabit, incidentally or intentionally, various social identity groups: "To sociologists, the contestation of gender hierarchy is fundamentally a collective process; it is not likely to be understood as a matter of individual gestures or dissent. Contestation as a social struggle requires some base of solidarity, of mutual support."[11]

The importance of queer (mis)recognition processes lies, at least in part, in destabilizing notions of the presumed "naturalness" and fixed perpetuity of identities (such as sex, gender, sexuality, race, and class), dogged belief in which reinforces and reproduces the hierarchical social order. The stories of the cis women I interviewed reveal some of the understudied ways in which the supposedly "natural" and stable links between sex, gender, and sexuality are under perpetual social challenge, flux, and maintenance, particularly in this postmodern era. The (mis)recognition processes these cis women have described hold the potential not only to constrain and make certain people, relationships, and families (in)visible, but also to more generously and broadly inscribe the parameters of identity and social group membership, even as they challenge the surety and boldness with which these very lines of demarcation are drawn.

Tensions imbue cis women's narratives about identity, revealing how they work to both embrace and resist normative gender and sexual identities in the context of the queer relationships and families they have built with trans men. For example, cis women discussed feeling less afraid of homophobic violence in their lives when they are perceived, socially, as part of a cisgender heterosexual couple. They talked about older people smiling at them when they are walking down the street holding hands with their trans partner. They discussed being able to legally marry and adopt children if their partner's legal sex status changes, and even having parents and other family members express relief that they have "finally" settled down with a man.

But cis women also spoke to me about how these forms of privilege carry a hefty price tag. They spoke about the work involved to manage disclosures about who knows their partner's gender history and who does not. They also spoke about feeling invisible as queer within queer spaces and trapped in a liminal place with regard to community, which could be particularly true for the cis women of color I interviewed. In these liminal spaces, you are not fully a part of any particular group and your own sexual identity and community membership may be largely determined by your partner's gender identity and other people's (mis)recognition of it. You are the cis woman partner of a trans man; you are queer because you are not straight and you are not lesbian. In this way, these narratives from cis women partners of trans men reveal some of the constraining contingencies of relational identity politics in the 21st century. Yet this was not the full story. Despite these constraints, the cis women I interviewed relayed the various ways in which they resisted and developed inventive and pragmatic strategies for resisting their own cultural erasure and dependence on another for identity and queer visibility. They spoke about their investments in social justice, contributions to trans communities and politics, and commitments to feminism and queer family and community building.

The 50 cis women I interviewed entrusted me with some of the most private, exciting, painful, transformative, and fraught aspects of their lives. Mostly feminist, they were not particularly eager to detail perceived inegalitarian divisions of household labor and emotion work within their relationships when these sorts of imbalances existed. Yet they did; and they offered explanations for these inegalitarian divisions in ways that made sense to them, or as they thought would make sense to me, in the context of their life circumstances. When I have presented these findings, many have focused on the perceived inegalitarian/stereotyped divisions of household labor and emotion work in these families rather than on the social processes and contexts that drive explanations for these perceived inegalitarian and/or stereotyped divisions of labor.

Rather than demonstrating that these couples "are just like every other heterosexual couple," or a modern-day "Ozzie and Harriet," I highlight the particular ways in which this group of cis women employ individualist, choice-based, and free-will explanations for inequality. This is a powerful finding, particularly in the context of these cis women's feminist identities, highlighting enduring inconsistencies between personal politics, political ideologies, and everyday lived experience. It also serves as an example of the ways in which Third Wave feminist politics, in practice, may actually obscure and/or impede certain pathways to women's empowerment. In this way, pathways to gender and sexual liberation may sometimes be derailed by the very politics and social movements that initially served as their engine. Rather than abandoning the entire enterprise, my findings suggest that postmodern feminist politics might usefully draw on the commitment to understanding oppression and privilege as intersectional in order to more deeply consider the tangled interface between individual agency and structural constraints.

Further, the narratives that my interview participants shared with me revealed how accessing certain social institutions, such as marriage and adoption, is under constant legal scrutiny and threat, destabilizing the queer partnerships and families my participants were working to create. These perspectives ultimately add to debates surrounding marriage by introducing dizzying social and legal permutations of "same-sex" and "opposite-sex" marital possibilities and social realities. I argue that these tensions, and the structural instabilities upon which these relationships are constructed, are what truly establish them as "queer," even in the face of, at times, perceived normativity. In other words, no matter how normative particular couples may appear, their relationships (and the identities of some of their members) are under constant threat of being legally and socially challenged, diminished, and invalidated by their families, the legal system, and sometimes even members of their own communities.

The cis women I interviewed often expressed profound enthusiasm and gratitude that someone had decided to systematically study their lives, perspectives, and experiences. Jodi said: "I'm just really glad you're doing this. Trans issues, in general, are underrepresented. . . . SOFFAs[12] are even more underrepresented. So, it's really thrilling to [be interviewed]." Martha concurred: "I thank you very much because I don't have this opportunity very often. . . . I thought, how great is that that I get to talk about my relationship? It doesn't happen very often. I appreciate it." Emily offered a clear and simple question that expressed the sentiments of most participants: "How come there's nothing from our side?"

Ani described the critical, yet often invisible, experiences and work of cis women partners of trans men as "behind the scenes." Ellia told me: "There's definitely an outlet for the trans person themselves. But when this was all happening, I had nothing. And so I always thought, 'God, I wish somebody would do something about that; that would be such an amazing resource for people.'" Marisol said:

> I really wish there was more stuff for female partners of trans men to read, more resources . . . it's really difficult to find that. And it's like I really think you covered a whole lot of ground here and the whole reason that I wanted to participate is because of exactly that. I want there to be information for people to find and people to be able to read about other people's experiences, whether they're experiencing something similar or not, just to find *some* sort of reflection of what they're going through.

Furthermore, cis women spoke about how having such resources could assist them in educating their trans partners about the struggles they may encounter in their partnerships. Ellia said:

> If [only] I could have given my boyfriend a book or something and [said]: "Read this; this puts into better words what I'm going through." Because I would get so emotional and so wrapped up . . . at times that I felt like [I wasn't] actually communicating with [him about] what's going on in my mind.

In this way, the narratives in this book may begin to expand these resources not only for cis women in partnerships with trans men, but for trans men as well.

This research also serves as a critical adjunct (and, in many instances, corrective) to the primary contemporary source of information on trans lives and communities: the media. As one of the interviewees for this study, Mel, told me: "God bless Oprah, 'cause I think [my parents] saw a couple of Oprah episodes [on trans people]. I think my mom's response was, 'Oh yes . . . I read about that in Maclean's.' Every little bit helps, I think, every little bit of information [helps]."[13] Participants frequently mentioned Jerry Springer-style depictions of trans people and the stigmatizing and stereotyped nature of such portrayals. Participants discussed fears about their partner's physical safety that deepened upon watching films based on the lives of trans people who have been physically assaulted and/or murdered (such as *Boys Don't Cry* and *Soldier's Girl*). Mel said:

> I went through a period of terror when I first got with him and he would go out alone. [Fear] that something would happen to him, like *Boys Don't Cry* action, like he was going to be raped and killed. And I felt really protective

of him which, now looking back, was kind of natural and also kind of fucked up because he's an adult.

Even mainstream films featuring gay and lesbian characters were mentioned as producing feelings of fear or worry among some of my research participants. As Lily told me:

> Honestly, I keep getting scared and terrified that something bad is going to happen to me . . . when *Brokeback Mountain* came out, everyone acted like that was the sum total of the queer experience . . . as if getting beaten up is normal and having an invisible life is normal and it's just part of it . . . this is what happens. I've been walking around so scared.

I hope that a contribution of this project is that others become aware not only of the struggles, but of the full, rich, rewarding, and diverse experiences that trans people and their partners may have and that their partnerships and families may create in the 21st century.

While the goal of much sociological research on minority groups is to produce information that can inform research on majority populations, it was also critical to me, as a feminist sociologist, to produce information about an understudied minority group so that this population could have access to a resource reflecting their lives, experiences, and perspectives. Mel told me:

> I'm so curious to hear about the other people who have participated in the study. I'm sure you're getting an amazing breadth of opinions and positions. It's one thing that can be so hard for people to understand who aren't a part of the trans community, just how great of a diversity of opinions and views there are within the trans community.

This book on the experiences and perspectives of cis women partners of trans men, and the partnerships and families they co-create, only *begins* to represent and explore the rich diversity and complexity of these (trans)formative relationships and families, situating them at the center of social analysis and inquiry rather than the periphery. As the rise of Caitlyn Jenner's visibility and political controversies exemplify, we have much left to learn about these diverse communities that resist monolithic description or characterization.

In a *New York Times* op-ed, Jennifer Finney Boylan (2000, May 12), a trans woman married to a cis woman, asks the question: "Is my marriage gay?" This is a question many trans people and their partners were asking as same-sex couples fought for, and attained, access to legally-recognized marriage. Boylan relates the complex and contradictory intersections of gender, sexuality, and the law as she discusses the case of a trans woman in Texas:

> Mrs. Littleton [a trans woman whose nontrans husband died], while in San Antonio, Tex., is a male and has a void marriage; as she travels to Houston, Tex., and enters federal property, she is female and a widow; upon traveling

to Kentucky she is female and a widow; but, upon entering Ohio, she is once again male and prohibited from marriage; entering Connecticut, she is again female and may marry; if her travel takes her north to Vermont, she is male and may marry a female; if instead she travels south to New Jersey, she may marry a male.

At the time of my interviews, this human drama was being played out, in conceptually dizzying permutations, across America.

One of my participants, living in Ohio, relayed a similar story about her trans partner's struggle to have the sex designation on his legal documentation changed from "female" to "male":

He has a Massachusetts driver's license. In Massachusetts, they require you to change your birth certificate [in order to change the sex designation on the driver's license]. But he was born in New York and it's difficult in New York to change your birth certificate. I guess they need pretty explicit documentation and part of what they require is bottom surgery.[14]

Other cis women told me about how their trans partners had to strategically wait to change their legal status to male so that they could have certain medical procedures (such as hysterectomy) covered by insurance since the increasingly technologically mediated bureaucracy of the insurance industry simply fails to recognize a hysterectomy as a possible operation for a patient coded as legally male in their computer systems. Similarly, cis women also spoke to me about trans partners whose testosterone prescription was not covered by insurance until they changed their legal status to male, which is quite literally impossible to do legally in some states.

Other important legal and social questions continue to emerge in this context of burgeoning queer partnerships and families as legal rights expand and sometimes contract: "Am I my partner's husband or wife?" "Am I my child's father or mother?" "Am I a widow or a widower?" "Should/can we get married as a same-sex or an opposite-sex couple?" The answer to each of these questions ultimately holds the power to grant or restrict access and membership to various social and legal communities, benefits, and resources.

In this book, I have engaged with aspects of cis women's relationships with trans men that many would consider explicitly non- (or counter-) normative; for example, the relatively high rates of reported consensual polyamory (nonmonogamy) among my sample participants. More than 25% of my sample reported polyamorous rather than monogamous relationship structures, a finding that aligns with recent work by Adam Isaiah Green[15] on gay and lesbian couples who access legal, same-sex marriage. I would argue that this finding complicates the assertion that the fight for marriage equality was predominantly a normative, assimilationist goal. I also contend that describing these queer partnerships and families as normative, even when cis women and their trans men partners access potentially normatizing social institutions such as marriage and parenting, may be preliminary and misguided. Indeed, these marital and parenting arrangements are under frequent legal contestation, often placing families under tremendous tension, strain, and uncertainty.

Despite the fact that individuals are becoming increasingly more aware and accepting of nonnormative gender and sexual identities over time, those who are lesbian, gay, bisexual, transgender, and queer continue to report familial rejection on the basis of their nonheterosexual or non-cisgender identities and partnerships.[16] In the world of sports, "home" often signifies the space or territory within which a person is considered safe or free from attack. For some LGBTQ people, however, home can feel anything but safe. In the face of historical and ongoing familial rejection, LGBTQ people have always adopted and forged social support networks of families of choice ("chosen family") and extended kinship networks. Indeed, some of the cis women I interviewed described their chosen family as their "real family," prioritizing healthy social support over biological ties in their everyday lives.

As I listened to the stories of cis women who detailed stories of family rejection, both by their trans partners' families and sometimes their own, what I came to recognize most profoundly is that *all* families are ultimately families of choice. Researchers of the family would do well to shift normative analyses of biological families, or families of origin as they are most often termed, to consider the social processes by which they ultimately choose and reject their own kin. When families of origin reject their own members, aren't they, too, actively involved in the construction of a family of choice, wherein only those members who conform to certain normative expectations may be welcomed, supported, and considered family? As Judith Stacey writes in her essay, "Good Riddance to 'The Family,'" "Family sociologists should take the lead in burying the ideology of 'the family' and in rebuilding a social environment in which diverse family forms can sustain themselves with dignity and mutual respect."[17]

The experiences my interview participants described articulate complex tensions between fitting in and chafing against, wanting to blend in and wanting to stand out. By attending to the contradictory forces that compel people as they engage in everyday life activities, in the context of potentially extraordinary life circumstances, we might develop a more nuanced analysis of postmodern partnerships and queer family life that is less driven by the need to circumscribe it as either normative or counternormative, conforming or revolutionary. If we begin, instead, to approach people's lives and experiences with a critical appreciation of the pragmatic, context-specific, and strategic aspects of particular relationship and family dynamics and social processes, we begin to do justice to their complexity, richness, and diversity.

NOTES

1. See Hibberd (2014).
2. See Ring (2014).

3. See Meadow (2011).
4. See Transgender Law Center (2014).
5. See Lombardi, Wilchins, Priesing, and Malouf (2002); National Coalition of Anti-Violence Programs (2014).
6. June 26, 2015, Supreme Court case decision on Obergefell v. Hodges.
7. See Kessler and McKenna (2003).
8. See Connell (2009).
9. See Connell (2009:108).
10. See Rupp (2006:9).
11. See Connell (2009:109).
12. This is an acronym that stands for "significant others, friends, family, and allies."
13. It should be noted, however, that Oprah's coverage of trans issues has also been critiqued as sensationalistic and essentializing.
14. Governor Andrew Cuomo eliminated the surgical requirement for legal sex designator changes to birth certificates for those born in the state of New York in June 2014. However, there is a surgical requirement that remains for citizens born in New York City, which maintains a separate birth certificate records system from the rest of the state. See Allen (2014) for additional media coverage of this policy change.
15. See Green (2008).
16. Research suggests that trends toward familial rejection of trans members may be particularly pronounced for trans women of color. See Koken, Bimbi, and Parsons (2009). Additional research would do well to consider structural and institutional supports both for trans women of color and their families.
17. See Stacey (1993:547).

APPENDIX

NOTE ON METHODS

The study on which this book is based stemmed from Institutional Review Board-approved dissertation work conducted at the University of Michigan from 2005–2009. All data for this project were collected from 2005–2007. I developed my interview protocol by drawing from existing sociological research with non-trans heterosexual, lesbian, and gay families.[1] My protocol was also informed by an exhaustive review of existing autobiographical, biographical, clinical, and academic writing on the experiences of trans men that existed at that time. The entire interview protocol follows this Note on Methods in the Appendix. In addition to drawing from the substantive thematic content of existing sociological work on the family, I also created interview questions that would allow me to tap into reports of gendered interactions and dynamics. More specifically, I drew upon symbolic interactionist,[2] ethnomethodological,[3] and phenomenological[4] approaches, through which I understand gender as a social accomplishment arising across repeated social interactions and work to consider how individuals make meaning of gender through their everyday experiences.

In order to do this, I created an interview protocol and used techniques for "probing" that encouraged participants to explain their perceptions, observations, and interactions in great detail.[5] The interview protocol could be divided into 6 broad thematic areas: (a) gender and sexual identities of self and partner, (b) experiences with a trans partner's gender transition, (c) friends and family support and strain, (d) community and social support and strain, (e) relationship form and structure, and (f) language, sexuality, and the body.

In my recruitment materials (the text of these materials follows), I specified that I wanted to interview self-identified women who had been in a current or former relationship with a trans man for at least 3 months. I was able to offer participants $20 in exchange for their time and willingness to participate in an interview, which was anticipated to last between 1 and 2 hours. In southeastern lower Michigan, I visited local LGBTQ social centers and groups, leaving recruitment materials on billboards and in lobbies. I sent emails and listserv posts to online social support and community sites targeting the transgender community and their significant others, friends, families, and allies (SOFFAs). I also asked the participants I successfully recruited to contact other women in their communities who might be candidates for participation in the study. Because the contemporary transgender community has established a substantial online presence and network of social support resources,[6] drawing samples using the Internet and word-of-mouth (generally referred to as Internet-based purposive social network sampling)[7] can be a particularly effective strategy for reaching this population.[8]

I decided to use both in-person and telephone interview formats so that I would be able to reach a broader cross-section of women partners of trans men. Across all interviews, I endeavored to notice and mention pauses, silences, expressions of discomfort, subject changes, inconsistencies, and seemingly irreconcilable aspects of participants' narratives, asking participants to consider and remark upon these where appropriate. With the informed consent of participants, I digitally audio recorded all interviews, using a digital audio recorder in face-to-face interviews and call recording software (Pamela) for interviews conducted over the telephone (voice-over-Internet-protocol using Skype). Interviews were transcribed verbatim, shortly after they were recorded, by a paid, professional transcriptionist whom I trained to be familiar with the various terms that participants used. The transcriptionist also signed a confidentiality agreement. Participants were asked to choose pseudonyms for themselves during the interview. I created pseudonyms for those participants who chose not to provide their own. I reviewed all transcripts to assure fidelity to the audio recordings. All potentially identifying materials were kept under locked and/or password-protected storage.

In order to analyze research interviews, I imported all transcripts into qualitative analysis software (NVivo). Qualitative analysis software primarily assists with the organization and systematic aggregation and sorting of large amounts of qualitative data. Interview transcripts were, on average, just over 40 pages of single-spaced text each, which resulted in over 2,000 pages of interview text across all 50 research interviews conducted for the project. I was also able to import research memos into NVivo, which allowed me to pair my interview and research observations with interview transcripts for each participant. In analyses of interview transcripts, I approached participants' narratives not as unequivocal recounting of social events or facts, but as *accounts*[9] of such events that present a mixture of what happened, how participants felt about what happened, and partial perspectives that often reflect various personal and interpersonal motivations for telling a story or recounting an event in a particular way.

I generated memos for each interview, which allowed me to record my impressions of the interview and the participant, as well as to note emergent themes or links to existing theory and empirical literatures. I coded for approximately 50 demographic variables for the interviewees, their partners, and the relationship itself. In an open coding process, I generated approximately 200 themes and subthemes, which were subsequently narrowed down and focused. I conducted axial (or matrix) coding, which allowed me to sort various themes and

subthemes by attributes such as participant, partner, or relationship demographics. This allowed me to generate more nuanced and grounded theoretical analyses as well as thickly descriptive accounts.[10]

INTERVIEWING ABOUT SENSITIVE ISSUES SUCH AS SEX

Because many of the cis women I interviewed provided detailed sensitive information about the sexual practices in which they engage with their partner, I am
sometimes asked to discuss if I used particular strategies to put research participants at ease around such sensitive topics. Discussing explicit sexual practices
with this population is particularly challenging given the potential for exploitation that often surrounds those gender and sexual identities considered "alternative" or marginal in some way. I wanted to gather candid and detailed information
about sex and sexual practices from this group because I would have wanted to
collect such information from any group with which I was gathering detailed
information about romantic partnerships and families. The utter lack of information and perspectives provided directly by cis women partners themselves presented a critical gap in knowledge, while information *about* these relationships,
sexual and otherwise, began to proliferate from other sources (e.g., clinicians,
trans men).

As I began to hear information from cis women partners of trans men about
sexual interactions that they found to be complicated, wonderful, confusing, or
transcendent, these narratives deserved further exploration. The most critical
components of obtaining direct and candid narratives about sex and sexuality
from the cis women I interviewed, in my estimation, involved the following 6
components: (a) interviewees' stated belief that the dearth of available and candid first-person accounts of sex and sexuality, specifically from other cis wom-
en's perspectives, made their own sexual relationships with their trans partner
more challenging as they sometimes felt they were entering uncharted territory;
(b) interviewees' stated belief that dissemination of knowledge about their sexual
experiences and perspectives with their trans partners could be illuminating to
other trans people and their partners; (c) commitment to following the language
of participants, using and mirroring back the terms they used, including terms
for body parts and sexual interaction, with openness and without hesitation or
discomfort; (d) reminders to participants that they did not have to answer any
question they felt uncomfortable answering or could take a break or stop the
interview whenever they needed or chose, without negative consequence; (e)
comfort with participants' open expression of sadness, anger, and embarrass-
ment during the interview and; (f) attention to maintaining rapport and respect
for interviewees at all points during and following the interview.

Being ever mindful of the importance of continuous consent emerged as a critical component of my approach toward participants and interviews. I was particularly taken aback when a participant sheepishly responded to my request for
information about the sexual relationship that she had with her trans partner.

She said: "Do I have to answer that?" She seemed reticent to even ask, almost apologetic. Methodologically (and ethically) speaking, having a commitment to continuous consent meant that it was important to me to be very attentive to verbal and nonverbal communication that could indicate discomfort among participants in both face-to-face and telephone interviews. Some of those indicators of discomfort included crying or sniffling, sighing, long pauses, shifting in a chair, breaking eye contact, becoming jittery, fiddling with clothing or accessories, shifting the topic, nervous laughter, and a trembling voice. These sorts of moments can serve as an indicator to the researcher to pause for a moment and check in with a participant to ask if they are okay, would like to take a break, or have a drink of water. I took these moments as cues to ask if participants needed a tissue, if they would like to skip a question or a section of questions, or if they would like to stop recording the conversation and go off the record.

EPISTEMOLOGY, METHODOLOGY, "TRUTH," AND "REALNESS": RESEARCH MISREPRESENTATION

It is my view that approaches toward studying trans identities, partnerships, and families may be considered particularly suspect whenever they invoke science and technology to argue against the "truth" or "realness" of trans men, trans women, and the family forms and structures they create with their partners. While it might be expected that such claims often derive from conservative or antifeminist critics, a number of self-identified radical feminist scholars have offered similar arguments. As Wilchins writes:

> It's particularly intriguing to hear charges of Realness coming from lesbians and feminists. Barely 100 years ago suffragettes were not considered to be "real women" because they shunned passivity to invade men's social prerogatives. Only 40 years ago, lesbians were accused of not being "real women" because they didn't want to marry men and become mothers. Twenty years ago femmes were ridiculed for not being "real lesbians" because they looked like straight women—yet another kind of displacement that ceded femininity to heterosexuality.[11]

In part to counter both "false consciousness" claims and the discursive abstraction of the transsexual subject, sociologist Henry Rubin advocates for the use of a "methodological hybrid" of genealogy and phenomenology in the study of transgender and transsexual subjects.[12] Rubin posits that using phenomenology in conjunction with discursive genealogy would allow researchers to better understand the lives and experiences of transgender and transsexual people as active subjects and in their own words.

No matter how carefully we work to reflect our participants' lives and experiences, we sometimes have shockingly little control over how these narratives may be taken up by others and for what purposes. While I was working on this book, I learned that some of my own published research on cis women partners of trans men had been cited extensively by Sheila Jeffreys, a trans-exclusionary radical feminist, in her latest work.[13] Within this text, Jeffreys frequently misgenders the partners of my research participants as women and refers to them as "transgenders" or "female-bodied transgenders."[14] Jeffreys poaches verbatim quotations from my research participants and frequently writes "[*sic*]" in instances where participants use "he" or "him" to refer to their trans partners. When Jeffreys does use pronouns such as "he" or "him" to refer to the trans partners of my research participants, it is always surrounded by shudder quotes. These editorial gestures reveal Jeffrey's appraisal of trans men's illegitimacy as men. In one instance, Jeffreys describes the gender identities of the partners of my research participants as "carefully constructed myths."[15] Jeffreys cherry picks my data for quotes to bolster her claims about the hurtful potential of gendered (and especially transgender) identities, omitting most context, particularly that which does not square with her claims.

Rather than engaging directly with Jeffreys' claims that trans individuals are not "real" men and women, or that delighting in masculinity, femininity, and butch or femme gender expression is inherently antifeminist, I am increasingly more invested in asking the question: Why do people like Sheila Jeffreys get to decide? More precisely, through which processes do any of us obtain the cultural authority to adjudicate *realness* when it comes to sex, gender, and sexual identities, and to what ends and consequences? How do any of us become real or legitimate members of the groups to which we stake our claims? When the experiences and perspectives of trans people, their partners, and families are ridiculed or erased, their words and self-identifications violently replaced without their consent, all in the name of feminism, the consequences extend far beyond the ideological.

Jeffreys and recent social media debates over her (and similar) work should serve as a cautionary tale to feminist scholars who approach gender and gendered identities as inherently harmful. Such approaches deny the very lives and identities of those whose stories may provide useful lessons and insights about not only the dangers and pitfalls of gender, but also its nuances, pleasures, and potentials—if we will recognize and listen to them. Gender can surely hurt, but, as a growing body of research[16] on transgender suicide and homicide attests, social exclusion, revilement, and erasure can kill.

RECRUITMENT TEXT

Do you self-identify as a woman? Have you been in a romantic relationship with a transman/ftm-identified person for at least three months (either currently or in the past)? Are you at least 18 years of age? Do you want to make $20 chatting about it? I am a doctoral student in Sociology at the University of Michigan and I am conducting a research project on the romantic relationships of self-identified women (of all sexual orientations) who are partnered with transmen/ftms. I will be conducting

1–2 hour interviews with participants to discuss issues connected to your and your partner's identity, relationship, and sources of support. These interviews will be scheduled at mutually-convenient times and conducted either on the University of Michigan campus, at a location of our mutual convenience, or via telephone. Each participant will receive $20 per interview. If you feel you might be eligible for this study, and are interested in participating, please contact Carla at (XXX) XXX-XXXX or cpfeffer@umich.edu. This research project has been reviewed for compliance with federal regulations for human participants and approved.

INTERVIEW PROTOCOL

Gender and Sexual Identities of Self and Partner

1) Can you briefly tell me about your identity in terms of how you gender identify?
2) Can you tell me about your identity in terms of your sexual orientation?
3) And what about your partners' identity in terms of gender identification?
4) How does your partner identity in terms of sexual orientation?
5) What pronoun(s) do you and your partner use for your partner's gender?
6) What pronoun(s) do strangers, friends and family tend to use when referencing your partner's perceived gender?
7) Does your partner generally "pass" as male/a man in public?
   IF YES OR NO→How does this make you feel? How does it make your partner feel?
   IF YES→Why is it, do you think, that your partner generally successfully passes as male in public?
   IF NO→Why is it, do you think, that your partner generally does not successfully pass as male in public?
8) Have you had any conflicts or struggles between your gender and sexual identity and those of your partner?
9) Has your understanding and experience of your own gender or sexual identity changed since being with a transman/ftm-identified person?
   PROBE IF YES→If so, how and what are your feelings about this?
10) As far as you know, has your partner's gender or sexual identity changed since being with you?
    PROBE IF YES→If yes, how and what are your feelings about this?
11) How do you conceptualize the relationship that you have with your partner in terms of sexual orientation?
12) Do strangers, friends or family ever misperceive your relationship (in terms of sexual orientation and/or gender)?
    IF YES→How do you process the situation (both individually and as a couple) when that happens? What do you do?

Experiences with a Trans Partner's Gender Transition

13) Has your partner transitioned?
     IF YES→Were you in the relationship when your partner transitioned?
     IF YES→Can you describe the process undertaken, your role in it (if
          you had one) and your feelings about this transition.
     IF NO→Can you tell me a bit more about how your partner made the
          choice and how you feel about it?
     IF NO→GO TO Q14
14) Is your partner currently in the process of transitioning?
     IF YES→Can you tell me a bit about what is happening, what is your
          role in this process (if you have one) and how you feel about it?
     IF NO→GO TO Q15
15) Is your partner considering transitioning?
     IF YES→Do you know what do they intend to do? What is your
          anticipated role in the process (if any) and how do you feel about it?
     IF NO→Have you spoken with your partner about the decision not
          to transition? What are the reasons for not transitioning?
16) Is there any discrepancy between how you and your partner talk
     about your partner's gender identity and how you feel about it?
17) Is there any discrepancy between how you and your partner talk
     about sexual orientation and how you feel about it?
18) How do you experience your partner's maleness/male identity? Is this
     identity ever challenged or in question?

Friends and Family Support and Strain

19) Do your friends and family know about your relationship?
     IF YES→What pronoun(s) does your and your family, your partner's
          family and friends tend to use when referencing your partner's
          gender?
     IF NO→Can you tell me more about why friends and family don't
          know about your relationship?
20) IF FRIENDS/FAMILY KNOW OF RELATIONSHIP→Are your
     friends and family generally supportive of your relationship with
     your partner?
     Can you give some examples of support and non-support?
21) Are there any other transgender-identified people in your or your
     partner's family?
22) Is your partner "out" as transgender to family, friends and
     coworkers?
     IF PARTNER IS NOT "OUT"→How are these situations handled?
     IF PARTNER IS NOT "OUT"→Has there ever been a "pronoun
          "slip"? IF YES→What happened?

Community and Social Support and Strain

23) Do you and/or your partner participate within the LGBT social and political community?
Why or why not?
Are there any tensions in your participation within the LGBT community?

24) Do you and/or your partner feel connected to the transgender community?

25) Do you and your partner have transgender friends?

26) Do you have any friends who have transgender partners?

27) Have you noticed any tensions or rifts among and between various types of transgender-identified people (ftms, mtfs, those who transition and those who don't, those who identify as trans and those who don't, feminists and non-feminists)?

28) Have you ever had any interactions with social workers in the context of your relationship as therapists, counselors, health professionals, etc.?

29) What are some sources of support that you have for this relationship? Are they enough? Do you wish for more? If yes, what might you wish existed?

30) Have you experienced any harassment or discrimination due to your or your partner's gender or sexual identity? PROBE FOR DETAILS

31) How do you feel your relationship with your partner "fits in" to the social structure (or not)?

32) How do you and your partner deal with harassment, discrimination or feeling like you don't fit?

33) What effect do you think these stressors have on your relationship and on your life?

34) Do you think that you and/or your partner have special strengths due to your or your partner's gender or sexual identity? PROBE

35) What do you feel are the unique strengths of your relationship with your partner?

Relationship Form and Structure

36) [FOR THOSE WHO REPORT BEING IN A HETEROSEXUAL RELATIONSHIP NOW AND IN THE PAST]:
How is your heterosexual relationship with your ftm partner similar to and different from heterosexual relationships you have been in with men who are not ftm?
Do you miss anything from your heterosexual relationships with men who were born male?

[FOR THOSE WHO REPORT BEING IN A HETEROSEXUAL
RELATIONSHIP NOW AND LESBIAN RELATIONSHIPS IN
THE PAST]:

How is your heterosexual relationship with your ftm partner similar
to and different from lesbian relationships you have been in?

Do you miss anything from your lesbian relationships?

[FOR THOSE WHO REPORT BEING IN A LESBIAN
RELATIONSHIP NOW]

Is your partner aware that you think of your relationship as lesbian?

IF YES→What does your partner think about this?

IF NO→Why does your partner not know and how does this make
you feel?

[FOR THOSE WHO REPORT PREVIOUS LESBIAN
RELATIONSHIPS ONLY]

Would you consider dating a man who had been born male? Would
you consider dating other ftms?

37) Do you and your partner consider yourself married? Do you want to
be married?

38) Do you and your partner each play certain roles in your
relationship?

IF YES→What are the roles in your relationship and how flexible
are they?

39) IF PARTNERS LIVE TOGETHER→Can you tell me a little bit about
how housework is divided? [Probe specific tasks using Carrington]

40) Do you and/or your partner have any children?

IF YES→Probe for more information

IF NO→Have you and your partner had any discussions about the
topic of having and/or raising children. What are your thoughts
and feelings on this issue?

IF YES→Adopt or not?

Who would have the kids?

Have you thought about the legal stuff?

Language, Sexuality, and the Body

41) What sort of language do you and your partner use to describe:
you (girlfriend, wife, partner)
your partner (boyfriend, girlfriend, husband, wide, partner)
your relationship (heterosexual, queer, transgender)
your sex (female)
your partner's sex (female, male)
your gender (woman, lady, female, girl, tomboy, femme, butch)
your partner's gender (man, male, transgender, genderqueer,
genderfluid, boi)

your sexual identity (bisexual, queer, lesbian, heterosexual)

your partner's sexual identity (bisexual, gay, lesbian, heterosexual)

your body parts (soft, tomboy, feminine, masculine)

your partner's body (soft, tomboy, hard, masculine, feminine)

your partner's breasts (if they have them)

your partner's genitals

your partner's menstrual cycle (if partner still has one)

the sexual practices with which you both engage (mutually and/or independent from one another)?

42) What is your comfort level with this language?

43) Do you and your partner have an understanding that your relationship is monogamous or polyamorous? Is this understanding implicit or has it been explicitly discussed?

44) Does your partner's body image or experience intersect or shape feelings that you or your partner have about your own body?

45) Are there certain issues that are considered off-limits to discuss or areas that you avoid in order to maintain certain understandings about sex, gender, bodies, sexuality, identity, etc.?

46) How do you and/or your partner think your partner's gender identity came to be?

47) How do you and/or your partner think your gender identity came to be?

48) What else should I be asking about the experiences and lives of the women partners of transmen/ftms?

Table 1 PARTICIPANT BRIEF DEMOGRAPHICS BY PSEUDONYM

Pseudonym	Age	Race or Ethnicity	Country	State/Province
Abigail	28	White	USA	California
Amber	19	White	Canada	Ontario
Ani	21	White, Jewish	USA	Ohio
Anna	48	White	USA	California
Belinda	24	White	Canada	Ontario
Bella	18	White	Canada	Ontario
Charlene	24	White	Canada	Ontario
Donna	47	White	USA	Florida
Drea	28	White	USA	Illinois
Eliza	25	White	Canada	Nova Scotia
Ellia	24	Latina	USA	New Mexico
Emily	23	White	Canada	Ontario
Emma	22	White	Canada	Ontario
Eva	29	White	USA	New York
Frieda	28	White	Canada	Ontario

Pseudonym	Age	Race or Ethnicity	Country	State/Province
Gail	28	White	USA	California
Jodi	38	White	USA	Colorado
Josie	31	White, Jewish	USA	Washington
Judy	27	White	Canada	British Columbia
Julie	30	White, Polish citizen	USA	Washington
June	21	White	Canada	Ontario
Kendra	21	White	USA	Ohio
Kyla	45	White	USA	Michigan
Lea	37	White	USA	Michigan
Lilia	22	Irish, Native American, Black	USA	California
Lily	26	White, Jewish	USA	Florida
Linda	22	White	Australia	Sydney
Lynne	35	White	USA	California
Margaret	29	White	USA	Massachusetts
Marisol	32	White	USA	New Mexico
Martha	25	White	USA	Massachusetts
Maya	30	White	USA	California
Mel	28	White	Canada	Ontario
Michele	32	White	USA	Michigan
Nina	25	White, Latina	USA	California
Polly	40	White	USA	New York
Rachel	27	White	USA	Ohio
Robyn	24	White, Jewish, Native American	USA	Ohio
Sage	21	White	Canada	Ontario
Samantha	20	White	USA	Michigan
Selma	43	White	USA	Michigan
Susan	23	White	USA	Tennessee
Tabitha	33	White, Jewish	USA	California
Teresa	24	White	USA	Maine
Terry	35	Black	USA	Michigan
Tiffany	20	White	USA	Massachusetts
Toby	50	White	USA	Michigan
Trixie	27	White	USA	Indiana
Veronica	21	White	USA	New York
Willow	51	White	USA	California

Box 1

Demographic Characteristics of Participant Sample[a]

Participants (N=50)

Geographic Residence
   United States (n=37)
      California (n=9); Michigan (n=7); Ohio (n=4); Massachusetts (n=3);
      New York (n=3); Florida (n=2); New Mexico (n=2); Washington (n=2);
      Colorado (n=1); Illinois (n=1); Indiana (n=1); Maine (n=1);
         Tennessee (n=1)
   Canada (n=12)
      Ontario (n=10); British Columbia (n=1); Nova Scotia (n=1)
   Australia (n=1)
      New South Wales (n=1)

Sex and Gender Identity
   "Female" (n=50)
   "Femme"(n=14); Gender Transgressive/Masculine (n=1)

Age
   Mean = 29 yrs.
   Range = 18–51 yrs.

Race / Ethnicity
   White (n=45); Multiracial (n=3); Black (n=1); Latina (n=1)

Sexual Orientation
   "Queer" (n=25); "Lesbian" or "Dyke" (n=11); "Bisexual" (n=7);
   "Bisexual/Queer"(n=2);"Heterosexual" (n=2);"Pansexual/Omnisexual"(n=1);
   "Undefined" / "Unsure" (n=2)

Educational Attainment
   Some HS (n=1); HS Diploma / GED (n=1); Some College (n=17); BA (n=16);
   Master's (n=10); Doctorate (n=2); Refusal / No Data (n=3)

Household Income (at time of interview)
   < $25K/yr (n=11); $25–50K/yr (n=12); $50–75K/yr (n=3); $75–100K/yr (n=1);
   >100K/yr (n=2); Refusal / No Data (n=21)

Parental Status
   Never parented/served as a guardian (n=44)
   Previous experience with parenting/guardianship (n=4)
   Currently parenting/guardian to children at home (n=2)
   44% of participants without parenting experience reported intentions and/or
   plans to parent a child in the future.

[a] All demographic characteristics reported herein are based on sample participants' self reports.

Box 2

DEMOGRAPHIC CHARACTERISTICS OF PARTICIPANT SAMPLE'S TRANSGENDER PARTNERS[a]

Transgender Partners of Participants (N=61)

Sex and Gender Identity
   Female (n=60); Intersex (n=1)
   "Man" (n=36); "Trans" or "Genderqueer" (n=25)

Age
   Mean = 27 yrs.
   Range = 13[b]–60 yrs

Race / Ethnicity
   White (n=46); Multiracial (n=11); Asian (n=1); Black (n=1);
   Native American (n=1); "Unsure" or "Unknown" (n=1)

Sexual Orientation
   "Queer" (n=29); "Heterosexual" (n=20); "Heterosexual But Bi-Curious" (n=5)
   "Bisexual" (n=5); "Gay" (n=1); "Undefined" / "Unsure" (n=1)

Education
   Some HS (n=2); HS Diploma / GED (n=6); Some College (n=19); BA (n=19);
   Master's (n=6); Doctorate (n=1); Refusal / No Data (n=8)

Transition Status
   Takes testosterone (n=42)
   Wants to take testosterone (n=14)
   Had "top surgery"[c] (n=23)
   Wants "top surgery"[c] (n=36)
   Had "bottom surgery"[d] (n=5)
   Wants "bottom surgery"[d] (n=21)
   Average time elapsed since beginning transition = just over 2 yrs.

Social Perception of Gender
   Reported frequency a trans partner is perceived, socially, as male:
   Almost Always / Always (n=38)
   Frequently (n=6)
   Occasionally (n=10)
   Rarely / Never (n=6)
   Refusal/ No Data (n=1)

a = all demographic characteristics reported herein are based on sample participants' self reports
b = a younger participant reporting on a past relationship
c = includes bilateral radical mastectomy or reduction mammaplasty with or without chest-wall recontouring
d = includes hysterectomy, oopherectomy, salpingectomy, metaoidioplasty, scrotoplasty, and/ or phalloplasty

Box 3

Demographic Characteristics of Participant Sample's Relationships[a]

Relationships with Transgender Partners (N=61)

Relationships and Relationship Status
Partnered with a trans man at the point of interview (n=42)
Not partnered with a trans man at the point of interview (n=8)
Median elapsed time since relationship's end = 3.8 yrs.
Number of reported relationships with a trans man:
1 (n=40); 2 (n=9); 3 (n=1)

Relationship Duration

Mean = 2.2 yrs.
Range = 3 mos. – 11 yrs

Cohabitation

Cohabitated during relationship (n=38)
Mean duration of cohabitation = 1.5 yrs.
Did not cohabit during relationship (n=23)

Marital Status

Legally-recognized "opposite-sex" marriage (n=4)[b]
Engaged to legally marry as an "opposite-sex" couple (n=4)[c]
Legally-recognized same-sex marriage (n=1)[d]

Relationship "Type" or "Label"

Participants' reports of relationship "type" with trans partner
"Queer" (n=30)
"Heterosexual" or "Straight" (n=11)
"Undefined" (n=2)
"Queer-Straight" (n=2)
"Bisexual" (n=1)
"Lesbian" (n=0)
Refusal / No data (n=15)

---

a = all demographic characteristics reported herein are based on sample participants' self reports
b = all in the United States
c = 3 in the United States and 1 in Canada
d = in Canada

Table 2 HOUSEHOLD LABOR CATEGORIES AND SUBCATEGORIES

Feeding Work	House Work	Kin Work	Consumption Work
Cooking	Clean Bathroom	Child Care	Car Care
Grocery Shopping	Decorating	Correspondence	Managing Bills
Knowledge of	Doing Dishes	(Telephone and	Driving
Tastes	Dusting	Written)	
	Clean Floors	Doctor	
	Garbage	Appointments	
	Home Repairs	(Attending)	
	Do Laundry	Doctor	
	Lawn Care	Appointments	
	Tidying	(Scheduling)	
	Clean Windows	Pet Care	
		Transition-Related	
		Care	

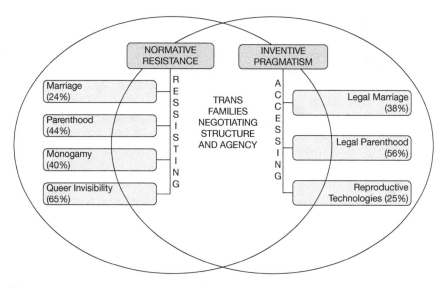

Figure 1

NOTES

1. See Blumstein and Schwartz (1983); Carrington (1999); DeVault (1991, 1999); Hochschild (1979, 1989); Oakley (1974).
2. See Goffman (1959, 1976, 1977). I also see my approach as one informed through accounts of gender/sexuality social construction, performativity, and phenomenology across a broad range of discourses and disciplines. For some of the

central influences, see Butler (1990, 1993, 2004), Friedman (2013), Foucault (1976), Salamon (2010); Swarr (2012); and Warner (1991).

3. See Garfinkel (1967); West and Zimmerman (1987).
4. See Rubin (1998); Schütz (1967).
5. Geertz (1973) describes this method as eliciting "thick description."
6. See Shapiro (2010).
7. See Patton (1990).
8. See Mustanski (2001), Rosser, Oakes, Bockting, and Miner (2007), and Shapiro (2004) for additional researcher accounts of the effectiveness of accessing gender and sexual minority populations using these recruitment strategies.
9. For additional information on the "accounts" framework and analytic approach, see Harvey, Weber, and Orbuch (1990); Heritage (1984); Scott and Lyman (1968).
10. See Charmaz (2006), Geertz (1973); Glaser and Strauss (1967, 1987), and Strauss and Corbin (1990) for excellent overviews of grounded theory, qualitative analysis and methods, and "thick description" approaches.
11. See Nestle, Howell, and Wilchins (2002:42).
12. See Rubin (1998:279). See also Ahmed (2006) for an overview of the critical analytic potentials in queer phenomenology. See Salamon (2010) for an extended phenomenological analysis of trans embodiment. See also Shrage (2009) for an excellent collection of philosophical perspectives on trans identity and embodiment.
13. See Jeffreys (2014).
14. See Jeffreys (2014:114).
15. See Jeffreys (2014:118).
16. See Clements-Nolle (2008); Jauk (2013); Westbrook and Schilt (2014).

REFERENCES

Ahmed, Sara. (2006). *Queer phenomenology: Orientations, objects, others*. Durham, NC: Duke University Press.

Albiniak, Paige. (2008, April 08). Pregnant man scores ratings highs for Oprah. *Broadcasting and Cable,*. Retrieved from http://www.broadcastingcable.com/article/93796Pregnant_Man_Scores_Ratings_Highs_for_Oprah.php

Alexander, Jonathan, and Karen Yescavage. (Eds.). (2003). *Bisexuality and transgenderism: InterSEXions of the others*. New York, NY: Harrington Park Press.

Allen, Jonathan. (2014, June 05). New York drops surgery rule for changing sex on birth certificate. *Reuters*. Retrieved from http://www.reuters.com/article/2014/06/05/us-usa-transgender-newyork-idUSKBN0EG2FK20140605

Allen, Mariette Pathy. (2003). *The gender frontier*. Heidelberg, Germany: Kehrer Verlag.

Alegría, C. Aramburu. (2010). Relationship challenges and relationship maintenance activities following disclosure of transsexualism. *Journal of Psychiatric and Mental Health Nursing* 17:909–916.

Alegría, Christine Aramburu, and Deborah Ballard-Reisch. (2013). Gender expression as a reflection of identity reformation in couple partners following disclosure of male-to-female transsexualism. *International Journal of Transgenderism* 14(2):49–65.

Althusser, Louis. (1971). *Lenin and philosophy, and other essays* (Ben Brewster, Trans.). London, England: New Left Books.

Ames, Jonathan. (Ed.). (2005). *Sexual metamorphosis: An anthology of transsexual memoirs*. New York, NY: Vintage.

Anderson, Eric. (2012). *The monogamy gap: Men, love, and the reality of cheating*. New York, NY: Oxford University Press.

Anderson, Jane. (Director). (2003). *Normal* [Film]. United States: HBO Films.

Anderson-Minshall, Diane, and Jacob Anderson-Minshall. (2014). *Queerly beloved: A love story across genders*. Valley Falls, NY: Bold Strokes Books.

Arnold, Chris. (Director). (2012). *Trans* [Film]. United States: RoseWorks.

Ault, Amber. (1996a). Ambiguous identity in an unambiguous sex/gender structure: The case of bisexual women. *The Sociological Quarterly* 37(3):449–463.

Ault, Amber. (1996b). The dilemma of identity: Bi women's negotiations. In Steven Seidman (Ed.), *Queer theory/sociology* (pp. 333–361). London, England: Blackwell Publishers.

Atkins, Dawn. (1998). *Looking queer: Body image and identity in lesbian, bisexual, gay, and transgender communities.* Binghamton, NY: Haworth Press.

Barker, Meg, and Darren Langdridge. (2010). *Understanding non-monogamies.* New York, NY: Routledge Research.

Barkham, Patrick. (2008, March 27). "Being a pregnant man? It's incredible!" *The Guardian.* Retrieved from http://www.guardian.co.uk/lifeandstyle/2008/mar/28/familyandrelationships.healthandwellbeing

Barrett, James. (1998). Psychological and social function before and after phalloplasty. *International Journal of Transgenderism* 2(1):1–13.

Baur, Gabrielle. (2002). *Venus boyz* [Film]. United States: Clockwise Productions.

Baus, Janet W., Dan Hunt, and Reid Williams. (Directors). (2012). *Cruel and unusual* [Film]. United States: Reid Productions.

Beatie, Thomas. (2008). *Labor of love: The story of one man's extraordinary pregnancy.* Berkeley, CA: Seal Press.

Bellwether, Miranda. (2010). *Fucking trans women: A zine about the sex lives of trans women* (Issue 0). CreateSpace Independent publishing Platform. Retrieved from: https://www.createspace.com/4397843

Benjamin, Harry. (1966). *The transsexual phenomenon.* New York, NY: Julian Press.

Berliner, Alain. (Director). (1997). *Ma vie en rose* [Film]. United States: Sony Pictures Classics.

Bernardes, Jon. (1999). We must not define "the family"! *Marriage and Family Review* 28(3-4):21–44.

Bernstein, Mary, and Renate Reimann. (Eds.). (2001). *Queer families queer politics: Challenging culture and the state.* New York, NY: Columbia University Press.

Bettcher, Talia Mae. (2014). When selves have sex: What the phenomenology of trans sexuality can teach about sexual orientation. *Journal of Homosexuality* 61(5):605–621.

Bianchi, Suzanne M. (1995). The changing economic roles of women and men. In Reynolds Farley (Ed.), *State of the union: Americans in the 1990s* (pp. 107–154). New York, NY: Russell Sage.

Bianchi, Suzanne M., Melissa A. Milkie, Liana C. Sayer, and John P. Robinson. (2000). Is anyone doing the housework? Trends in the gender division of household labor. *Social Forces* 79(1):191–228.

Biblarz, Timothy J., and Evren Savci. (2011). Lesbian, gay, bisexual, and transgender families. *Journal of Marriage and Family* 72(3):480–497.

Bischof, Gary H, Bethany L. Warnaar, Mark S. Barajas, and Harkiran K. Dhaliwal. (2011). Thematic analysis of the experiences of wives who stay with husbands who transition male-to-female. *Michigan Family Review* 15(1):16–34.

Bishop, Katelynn. (2016). Body modification and trans men: The lived realities of gender transition and partner intimacy. *Body & Society* 22(1):62–91.

Bittman, Michael, Paula England, Liana Sayer, Nancy Folbre, and George Matheson. (2003). When does gender trump money? Bargaining and time in household work. *American Journal of Sociology* 109(1):186–214.

Blanchard, Ray. (2005). Early history of the concept of autogynephilia. *Archives of Sexual Behavior* 34(4):439–446.

Blank, Hanne, and Raven Kaldera. (Eds.). (2002). *Best transgender erotica.* London, England: Circlet Press.

Blumer, Markie L. C., Mary S. Green, Sarah J. Knowles, and April Williams. (2012). Shedding light on thirteen years of darkness: Content analysis of articles pertaining to transgender issues in marriage/couple and family therapy journals. *Journal of Marital & Family Therapy* 38(1):244–256.

Blumstein, Philip, and Pepper Schwartz. (1983). *American couples: Money, work, sex.* New York, NY: William Morrow.

Boenke, Mary. (Ed.). (1999). *Trans forming families: Real stories about transgendered loved ones.* Imperial Beach, CA: Walter Trook.

Bornstein, Kate. (1994). *Gender outlaw: On men, women, and the rest of us.* New York, NY: Routledge.

Bornstein, Kate. (1998). *My gender workbook: How to become a real man, a real woman, the real you, or something else entirely.* New York, NY: Routledge.

Brill, Stephanie A., and Rachel Pepper. (2008). *The transgender child: A handbook for families and professionals.* San Francisco, CA: Cleis Press.

Boucher, Michel. J. (2011). "Do you have what it takes to be a real man?" Female-to-male transgender embodiment and the politics of the "real" in *A Boy Named Sue* and *Body Alchemy.* In Elwood Watson and Marc Edward Shaw (Eds.), *Performing American masculinities: The 21st-century man in popular culture* (pp. 192–231). Bloomington, IN: Indiana University Press.

Boyd, Helen. (2007). *She's not the man I married: My life with a transgender husband.* Berkeley, CA: Seal Press.

Boyd, Helen. (2003). *My husband Betty: Love, sex, and life with a crossdresser.* Berkeley, CA: Seal Press.

Boyd, Nan Alamilla. (1999). The materiality of gender: Looking for lesbian bodies in transgender history. In Dawn Atkins (Ed.), *Lesbian sex scandals: Sexual practices, identities, and politics* (pp. 73–82). Binghamton, NY: Haworth Press.

Boylan, Jennifer F. (2000, May 12). Is my marriage gay? *The New York Times,* p. A27.

Brake, Elizabeth. (2012). *Minimizing marriage: Marriage, morality, and the law.* New York, NY: Oxford University Press.

Breiding, Matthew J., Sharon G. Smith, Kathleen C. Basile, Mikel L. Walters, Jieru Chen, and Melissa T. Merrick. (2014). *Prevalence and characteristics of sexual violence, stalking, and intimate partner violence victimization—National Intimate Partner and Sexual Violence Survey, United States, 2011.* Atlanta, GA: Division of Violence Prevention, National Center for Injury Prevention and Control, Centers for Disease Control and Prevention.

Brown, George R. (1998). Women in the closet: Relationships with transgendered men. In Dallas Denny (Ed.), *Current concepts in transgender identity* (pp. 353–371). New York, NY: Garland Publishing.

Brown, Mildred L., and Chloe Ann Rounsley. (1996). *True selves: Understanding transsexualism: For families, friends, coworkers, and helping professionals.* San Francisco, CA: Jossey-Bass.

Brown, Nicola R. (2005). *Queer women partners of female-to-male transsexuals: Renegotiating self in relationship* (Doctoral dissertation). Retrieved from ProQuest Dissertations and Theses database. (UMI No. 1079667931)

Brown, Nicola R. (2007). Stories from outside the frame: Intimate partner abuse in sexual-minority women's relationships with transsexual men. *Feminism & Psychology* 17(3):373–393.

Brown, Nicola R. (2009). "I'm in transition too": Sexual identity renegotiation in sexual-minority women's relationships with transsexual men. *International Journal of Sexual Health* 21(1):61–77.

Brown, Nicola R. (2010). The sexual relationships of sexual-minority women partnered with trans men: A qualitative study. *Archives of Sexual Behavior* 39(2):561–572.

Brydum, Sunnivie. (2015). The true meaning of the word "cisgender." *The Advocate*. Retrieved from http://www.advocate.com/transgender/2015/07/31/true-meaning-word-cisgender

Bullough, Bonne, Vern L. Bullough, and James Elias. (1997). *Gender blending.* Amherst, MA: Prometheus Books.

Burana, Lily, Roxxie, and Roxxie Linnea Due. (1994). *Dagger: On butch women.* Pittsburgh, PA: Cleis Press.

Burrill, Katkryn G. (2001). Queering bisexuality. *Journal of Bisexuality* 2(2-3):95–105.

Butler, Judith. (1990). *Gender trouble: Feminism and the subversion of identity.* New York, NY: Routledge.

Butler, Judith. (1993). *Bodies that matter: On the discursive limits of "sex."* New York, NY: Routledge.

Butler, Judith. (2004). *Undoing gender.* New York, NY: Routledge.

Cahill, Sean, and Sarah Tobias. (2007). *Policy issues affecting lesbian, gay, bisexual, and transgender families.* Ann Arbor, MI: University of Michigan Press.

Calavita, Kitty. (2000). The paradoxes of race, class, identity, and "passing": Enforcing the Chinese Exclusion Acts, 1882–1910. *Law & Social Inquiry* 25(1):1–40.

Califia, Patrick. (1997). *Sex changes: The politics of transgenderism.* San Francisco, NY: Cleis Press.

Califia, Patrick. (2000, June 20). Family values: Two dads with a difference—Neither of us was born male." *The Village Voice.* Retrieved from http://www.villagevoice.com/2000-06-20/news/family-values/

Cameron, Loren. (1996). *Body alchemy: Transsexual portraits.* San Francisco, NY: Cleis Press.

Carrington, Christopher. (1999). *No place like home: Relationships and family life among lesbians and gay men.* Chicago, IL: University of Chicago Press.

Charmaz, Kathy. (2006). *Constructing grounded theory: A practical guide through qualitative analysis.* Thousand Oaks, CA: Sage Publications.

Chivers, Meredith L., and J. Michael Bailey. (2000). Sexual orientation of female-to-male transsexuals: A comparison of homosexual and nonhomosexual types. *Archives of Sexual Behavior* 29(3):259–278.

Clements-Nolle, Kristen. (2008). Attempted suicide among transgender persons: The influence of gender-based discrimination and victimization. *Journal of Homosexuality* 51(3):53–69.

Cogan, Jeannie C. (1999). Lesbians walk the tightrope of beauty: Thin is in but femme is out. In Jeanine Cogan and Joanie Erickson (Eds.), *Lesbians, Levis, and lipstick: The meaning of beauty in our lives* (pp. 77–90). New York, NY: Haworth.

Cole, Sandra S. (1998). The female experience of the femme: A transgender challenge. In Dallas Denny (Ed.), *Current concepts in transgender identity* (pp. 373–390). New York, NY: Garland Publishing.

Committee on the Status of Lesbian, Gay, Bisexual, and Transgendered (LGBT) Persons in Sociology. (2002, July 16). *Report on the status of gay, lesbian, bisexual, and transgender persons in sociology.* Retrieved from American Sociological Association website: http://www2.asanet.org/governance/glbtrpt.html

Committee on the Status of Lesbian, Gay, Bisexual, and Transgendered (LGBT) Persons in Sociology. (2009, May 28). *Report on the status of gay, lesbian, bisexual, and transgender persons in sociology.* Retrieved from American Sociological Association website: http://www.asanet.org/about/Council_Statements/GLBT%20Status%20 Cmte%20Rpt%20(Aug%202009).pdf

Connell, Raewyn. (2009). Accountable conduct: "Doing gender" in transsexual and political retrospect. *Gender & Society* 23(1):104–111.

Connell, Raewyn (1987). *Gender and power.* Sydney, Australia: Allen and Unwin.

Coolidge, Martha. (Director). (2000). *If these walls could talk 2* (segment "1972") [Film]. United States: HBO.

Coontz, Stephanie. (1992). *The way we never were: American families and the nostalgia trap.* New York, NY: Basic Books.

Corvino, John, and Maggie Gallagher. (2012). *Debating same-sex marriage.* New York, NY: Oxford University Press.

Cram, Bestor. (1997). *You don't know dick: The courageous hearts of transsexual men* [Film]. United States: Northern Light Productions.

Cromwell, Jason. (1999). *Transmen and ftms: Identities, bodies, genders, and sexualities.* Urbana, IL: University of Illinois Press.

Cummings, Mark A. (2006). *The mirror makes no sense.* Bloomington, IN: AuthorHouse.

Currah, Paisley, Richard M. Juang, and Shannon P. Minter. (2006). *Transgender rights.* Minneapolis, MN: University of Minnesota Press.

Currah, Paisley, and Susan Stryker. (Eds.). (2014). Special Issue: Postposttranssexual: Key concepts for a 21st century transgender studies. *Transgender Studies Quarterly* 1(1-2):1–302.

Cvetkovich, Ann. (2003). *An archive of feelings: Trauma, sexuality, and lesbian public cultures.* Durham, NC: Duke University Press.

Damaske, Sarah. (2011). *For the family? How class and gender shape women's work.* New York, NY: Oxford University Press.

Davidmann, Sara. (2014). Imag(in)ing trans partnerships: Collaborative photography and intimacy. *Journal of Homosexuality* 61(5):636–653.

Davis, Kate. (Director). (2001). *Southern comfort* [Film]. United States: Q-Ball Productions.

Denzin, Norman K. (1989). *Interpretive interactionism.* Newbury Park, CA: Sage.

Deutsch, Francine M., Amy P. Kokot, and Katherine S. Binder. (2007). College women's plans for different types of egalitarian marriages. *Journal of Marriage and Family* 69(4):916–929.

DeVault, Marjorie L. (1991). *Feeding the family: The social organization of caring as gendered work.* Chicago, IL: University of Chicago Press.

DeVault, Marjorie L. (1999). Comfort and struggle: Emotion work in family life. *Annals of the American Academy of Political and Social Science* 561(1):52–63.

Devor, Aaron. (1989). *Gender blending: Confronting the limits of duality.* Bloomington, IN: Indiana University Press.

Devor, Aaron. (1993). Sexual orientation identities, attractions, and practices of female-to-male transsexuals. *Journal of Sex Research* 30(4):303–315.

Devor, Aaron. (1997). *FTM: Female-to-male transsexuals in society.* Bloomington, IN: Indiana University Press.

Diamond, Morty. (2004). *From the inside out: Radical gender transformation, ftm and beyond.* San Francisco, CA: Manic D Press.

Diamond, Morty. (2007). Trans entities: The nasty love of Papí and Wil *[Film].* United States: Morty Diamond Productions.

Diamond, Morty. (2011). *Trans/love: Radical sex, love and partnerships beyond the gender binary.* San Francisco, CA: Manic D. Press.

Dickey, Robert, and Judith Stephens. (1995). Female-to-male transsexualism, heterosexual type: Two cases. *Archives of Sexual Behavior* 24(4):439–445.

di Leonardo, Micaela. (1987). The female world of cards and holidays: Women, families, and the work of kinship. *Signs* 12(3):440–453.

Dixon, Jan and Diane Dixon. (Eds.) (1991). *Wives, partners, and others: Living with cross-dressing.* Waltham, MA: International Foundation for Gender Education.

Dozier, Raine. (2005). Beards, breasts, and bodies. *Gender & Society* 19(3):297–316.

Duggan, Lisa. (1992). Making it perfectly queer. *Socialist Review* 22(1):11–31.

Duggan, Lisa. (2002). The new homonormativity: The sexual politics of neoliberalism. In Russ Castronovo and Dana D. Nelson (Eds.), *Materializing democracy: Towards a revitalized cultural politics* (pp. 175–194). Durham, NC: Duke University Press.

Duncombe, Jean, and Dennis Marsden. (1993). Love and intimacy: The gender division of emotion and emotion work. *Sociology* 27(2):221–241.

Edelman, Elijah A., and Lal Zimman. (2014). Boycunts and bonus holes: Trans men's bodies, neoliberalism, and the sexual productivity of genitals. *Journal of Homosexuality* 61(5):673–690.

Ellis, Kelly M., and Karen Eriksen. (2002). Transsexual and transgenderist experiences and treatment options. *Family Journal—Counseling and Therapy for Couples & Families* 10(3):289–299.

Elson, Jean. (2004). *Am I still a woman? Hysterectomy and gender identity.* Philadelphia, PA: Temple University Press.

Emerson, Shirley. (1996). Stages of adjustment in family members of transgender individuals. *Journal of Family Psychotherapy* 7(3):1–12.

Epstein, Steven. (1994). A queer encounter: Sociology and the study of sexuality. *Sociological Theory* 12(2):188–202.

Erhardt, Virginia. (2007). *Head over heels: Wives who stay with cross-dressers and transsexuals.* Binghamton, NY: Hawthorn Press.

Erickson, Rebecca J. (1993). Reconceptualizing family work: The effect of emotion work on perceptions of marital quality. *Journal of Marriage and the Family* 55(4):888–900.

Erickson, Rebecca J. (2005). Why emotion work matters: Sex, gender, and the division of household labor. *Journal of Marriage and Family* 67(2):337–351.

Faccio, Elena, Elena Bordin, and Sabrina Cipolletta. (2013). Transsexual parenthood and new role assumptions. *Culture, Health & Sexuality: An International Journal for Research, Intervention, and Care.* Retrieved from http://dx.doi.org/10.1080/13691058.2013.806676

Farquhar, Clare. (2000). "Lesbian" in a post-lesbian world? Policing identity, sex and image. *Sexualities* 2(3):219–236.

Fausto-Sterling, Anne. (1992). *Myths of gender: Biological theories about women and men.* New York, NY: Basic Books.

Fausto-Sterling, Anne. (2000). *Sexing the body: Gender politics and the construction of sexuality.* New York, NY: Basic Books.

Feinberg, Leslie. (1993). *Stone butch blues: A novel.* New York, NY: Firebrand.

Feinberg, Leslie. (1999). *Trans liberation: Beyond pink or blue.* Boston, MA: Beacon Press.

Flax, Jane. (1990). Postmodernism and gender relations in feminist theory. In Linda J. Nicholson (Ed.), *Feminism/Postmodernism* (pp. 39–62). New York, NY: Routledge.

Fleming, Michael, Bradford MacGowan, and Daryl Costos. (1985). The dyadic adjustment of female-to-male transsexuals: A comparison. *Archives of Sexual Behavior*
14(1):47–55.

Fleming, Michael, Daryl Costos, and Bradford MacGowan. (1984). Ego development
in female-to-male transsexual couples. *Archives of Sexual Behavior* 13(6):581–594.

Flores, Andrew R., Jody L. Herman, Gary J. Gates, and Taylor N. T. Brown. (2016).
How many adults identify as transgender in the United States? Los Angeles, CA: The
Williams Institute

Foucault, Michel. (1976). *The history of sexuality. Volume I: An introduction.* New York,
NY: Vintage Books.

Franklin, Kolbe. (2014). Gender labor, assimilationism, and transformative practices: The relational negotiations of cisgender women and their transgender men
partners. *Sociology Compass* 8(6):648–659.

Friedman, Asia. (2013). *Blind to sameness: Sexpectations and the social construction of
male and female bodies.* Chicago, IL: University of Chicago Press.

Frisco, Michelle L., and Kristi Williams. (2003). Perceived housework equity, marital
happiness, and divorce in dual-earner households. *Journal of Family Issues* 24(1):51–73.

Gabb, Jacqui. (2004). Critical differentials: Querying the incongruities within research
on lesbian parent families. *Sexualities* 7(2):167–182.

Gamson, Joshua. (1995). Must identity movements self-destruct? A queer dilemma.
Social Problems 42(3):390–407.

Gamson, Joshua (1998). *Freaks talk back: Tabloid talk shows and sexual nonconformity.*
Chicago, IL: University of Chicago Press.

Gamson, Joshua. (2000). Sexualities, queer theory, and qualitative research. In Norman
K. Denzin and Yvonna S. Lincoln (Eds.), *Handbook of qualitative research* (2nd ed.)
(pp. 347–365). Thousand Oaks, CA: Sage.

Gamson, Joshua. (2013) The normal science of queerness: LGBT sociology books in the
twenty-first century. *Contemporary Sociology: A Journal of Reviews* 42(6):801–808

Gamson, Joshua, and Dawne Moon. (2004). The sociology of sexualities: Queer and
beyond. *Annual Review of Sociology* 30:47–64.

Garfinkel, Harold. (1967). *Studies in ethnomethodology.* Englewood Cliffs,
NJ: Prentice Hall.

Gauthier, DeAnn K., and Nancy K. Chaudoir. (2004). Tranny boyz: Cyber community
support in negotiating sex and gender mobility among female to male transsexuals.
Deviant Behavior 25(4):375–398.

Geertz, Clifford. (1973). Thick description: Toward an interpretive theory of culture.
In Clifford Geertz (Ed.), *The interpretation of cultures: Selected essays* (pp. 3–30).
New York, NY: Basic Books.

Ghaziani, Amin. (2011). Post-gay collective identity construction. *Social Problems*
58(1):99–125.

Gillespie, Peggy. (Ed.). (1999). *Love makes a family: Portraits of lesbian, gay, bisexual, and transgender parents and their families.* Amherst, MA: University of
Massachusetts Press.

Girschick, Lori B. (2008). *Transgender voices: Beyond women and men.* Hanover,
NH: University Press of New England.

Glaser, Barney G., and Anselm Strauss. (1967). *The discovery of grounded theory.*
Chicago, IL: Aldine.

Glazer, Nona Y. (1990). The home as workshop: Women as amateur nurses and care providers. *Gender & Society* 4(4):479–499.

Glazer, Nona Y. (1993). *Women's paid and unpaid labor: The work transfer in health care and retailing.* Philadelphia, PA: Temple University Press.

Goffman, Erving. (1959). *The presentation of self in everyday life.* Garden City, NY: Doubleday.

Goffman, Erving. (1976). Gender advertisements. *Studies in the Anthropology of Visual Communication* 3(2):69–154.

Goffman, Erving. (1977). The arrangement between the sexes. *Theory & Society* 4(3):301–331.

Green, Adam I. (2002). Gay but not queer: Toward a post-queer study of sexuality. *Theory and Society* 31(4):521–545.

Green, Adam I. (2007). Queer theory and sociology: Locating the subject and the self in sexuality studies. *Sociological Theory* 25(1):26–45.

Green, Adam I. (2008). *Same-sex marriage: Lesbian and gay spouses marrying tradition and change.* Paper presented at Annual Meeting, American Sociological Association, Boston, MA.

Green, Adam I. (2013). *Sexual fields: Toward a sociology of collective sexual life.* Chicago, IL: University of Chicago Press.

Green, Jamison. (2004). *Becoming a visible man.* Nashville, TN: Vanderbilt University Press.

Green, Jamison. (1999). Look! Don't!: The visibility dilemma for transsexual men. In Kate More and Stephen Whittle (Eds.), *Reclaiming genders* (pp. 117–131). London, England: Cassell.

Greenstein, Theodore N. (2000). Economic dependence, gender, and the division of labor in the home: A replication and extension. *Journal of Marriage and the Family* 62(2):322–335.

Grzanka, Patrick R., Katherine H. Zeiders, and Joseph R. Miles. (2016). Beyond "born this way?" Reconsidering sexual orientation beliefs and attitudes. *Journal of Counseling Psychology* 63(1):67–75.

Guberman, Nancy, Éric Gagnon, Denyse Côté, Claude Gilbert, Nicole Thivièrge, and Marielle Tremblay. (2005). How the trivialization of the demands of high-tech care in the home is turning family members into para-medical personnel. *Journal of Family Issues* 26(2):247–272.

Gupta, Sanjiv. (1999). The effects of transitions in marital status transitions on men's performance of housework. *Journal of Marriage and Family* 61(3):700–711.

Gurvich, Susan Ellen. (1991). *The transsexual husband: The wife's experience* (Unpublished doctoral dissertation). Texas Women's University, Denton, TX.

Halberstam, Jack. (1998). Transgender butch: Butch/ftm border wars and the masculine continuum. *GLQ: A Journal of Lesbian and Gay Studies: The Transgender Issue* 4(2):287–310.

Halberstam, Jack. (2005). *In a queer time and place: Transgender bodies, subcultural lives.* New York, NY: New York University Press.

Halberstam, Jack. (2011). *The queer art of failure.* Durham, NC: Duke University Press.

Hale, C. Jacob (1998). Consuming the living, dis(re)membering the dead in the butch/ ftm borderlands. *GLQ: A Journal of Lesbian and Gay Studies: The Transgender Issue* 4(2):311–348.

Hall, Radclyffe. (1929). *The well of loneliness.* New York, NY: Covici Friede.

Hansbury, Griffin. (2005). The middle men: An introduction to the transmasculine identities. *Studies in Gender and Sexuality* 6(3):241–264.

Haraway, Donna. (1985). A cyborg manifesto: Science, technology, and socialist-feminism in the late twentieth century. *Socialist Review* 80:65–108.

Hare, Jan, and Denise Skinner. (2008). "Whose child is this?" Determining legal status for lesbian parents who use assisted reproductive technologies. *Family Relations* 57(3):365–375.

Harris, Cheryl I. (1993). On passing: Whiteness as property. *Harvard Law Review* 106:1707–1091.

Harris, Laura, and Elizabeth Crocker. (Eds.). (1997). *Femme: Feminists, lesbians, and bad girls*. New York, NY: Routledge.

HARPO Studios. (2008). *Oprah Winfrey Show: Trivia*. Retrieved from: http://www.oprah.com/oprahshow/The-Oprah-Winfrey-Show-Trivia.

Harvey, John H., Ann L. Weber, and Terri L. Orbuch. (1990). *Interpersonal accounts: A social psychological perspective*. Cambridge, MA: Basil Blackwell.

Harvey, Kara. (2008). *The other side of metamorphosis: An exploratory study of how partners of transsexuals experience transition* (Master's thesis, Department of Sociology, Illinois State University). Retrieved from http://ir.library.illinoisstate.edu/mts/4

Hausman, Bernice L. (1995). *Changing sex: Transsexualism, technology, and the idea of gender*. Durham, NC: Duke University Press.

Haworth, Gwen. (Director). (2007). *She's a boy I knew* [Film]. Canada: Shapeshifter Films.

Heath, Melanie. (2012). *One marriage under God: The campaign to promote marriage in America*. New York, NY: New York University Press.

Henig, Robin Marantz. (2014). Transgender men who become pregnant face social, health challenges. *National Public Radio Health Blogs*. Retrieved http://www.npr.org/blogs/health/2014/11/07/362269036/transgender-men-who-become-pregnant-face-health-challenges.

Henry, Astrid. (2004). *Not my mother's sister: Generational conflict and third-wave feminism*. Bloomington, IN: Indiana University Press.

Heritage, John. (1984). *Garfinkel and ethnomethodology*. Cambridge, MA: Polity Press.

Heywood, Leslie, and Jennifer Drake. (1997). *Third wave agenda: Being feminist, doing feminism*. Minneapolis, MN: University of Minnesota Press.

Hibberd, James. (2014, April 25). Bruce Jenner interview delivers massive ratings for ABC. *Entertainment Weekly Online*. Retrieved from http://www.ew.com/article/2015/04/25/bruce-jenner-interview-ratings

Hines, Sally. (2006). Intimate transitions: Transgender practices of partnering and parenting. *Sociology* 40(2):353–371.

Hochschild, Arlie. (1979). Emotion work, feeling rules, and social structure. *American Journal of Sociology* 85(3):551–575.

Hochschild, Arlie. (1989). *The second shift: Working parents and the revolution at home*. New York, NY: Viking.

Hollibaugh, Amber. (1997). Gender warriors: An interview with Amber Hollibaugh. In Laura Harris and Elizabeth Crocker (Eds.), *Femme: Feminists, lesbians, bad girls* (pp. 210–222). New York, NY: Routledge.

Hollibaugh, Amber. (2000). *My dangerous desires: A queer girl dreaming her way home*. Durham, NC: Duke University Press.

Holstein, James A., and Jaber F. Gubrium. (1999). What is family? Further thoughts on a social constructionist approach. *Marriage and Family Review* 28(3-4):3–20.

Howey, Noelle, and Ellen Samuels. (Eds.). (2000). *Out of the ordinary: Essays on grow-ing up with gay, lesbian, and transgender parents*. New York, NY: St. Martin's Press.

Hutson, David. (2010). Standing out/fitting in: Identity, appearance, and authenticity in gay and lesbian communities. *Symbolic Interaction* 33(2):213–233.

Huyssen, Andreas. (1990). Mapping the postmodern. In Linda J. Nicholson (Ed.), *Feminism/Postmodernism* (pp. 234-280). New York, NY: Routledge.

Iantaffi, Alex, and Walter O. Bockting. (2011). Views from both sides of the bridge? Gender, sexual legitimacy, and transgender people's experiences of relationships. *Culture, Health & Sexuality* 13(3):355–370.

Ingraham, Chrys. (1994) The heterosexual imaginary: Feminist sociology and theories of gender. *Sociological Theory* 12(2):203–219.

Ingraham, Chrys. (1999). *White weddings: Romancing heterosexuality in popular cul-ture*. New York, NY: Routledge.

International Foundation for Gender Education. (1988). *Transsexualism: A collection of articles, editorials, and letters on the subject of male-to-female and female-to-male transsexualism edited from the tv-ts tapestry journal, issues 39–52*. Wayland, MA: International Foundation for Gender Education.

Jackson, Stevi. (2006). Interchanges: Gender, sexuality and heterosexuality: The com-plexity (and limits) of heteronormativity. *Feminist Theory* 7(1):105–121.

James, Scott. (2010, January 29). Many successful gay marriages share an open secret. *New York Times* A17A.

Jauk, Daniela. (2013). Gender violence revisited: Lessons from violent victimization of transgender identified victims. *Sexualities* 16(7):807–825.

Jeffreys, Sheila. (2014). *Gender hurts: A feminist analysis of the politics of transgender-ism*. New York, NY: Routledge.

Johnson, Carol. (2002). Heteronormative citizenship and the politics of passing. *Sexualities* 5(3):317–336.

Johnson, Jordan, and Becky Garrison. (2015). *Love, always: Partners of trans people on intimacy, challenge, & resilience*. Oakland, CA: Transgress Press.

Joslin-Roher, Emily, and Darrell Wheeler. (2009). Partners in transition: The transition experience of lesbian, bisexual, and queer identified partners of transgender men. *Journal of Gay and Lesbian Social Services* 21(1):30–48.

Kailey, Matt. (2005). *Just add hormones: An insider's guide to the transsexual experi-ence*. Boston, MA: Beacon Press.

Kamo, Yoshinori. (2000). He said, she said: Assessing discrepancies in husbands' and wives' reports on the division of household labor. *Social Science Research* 29(4):459–476.

Kan, Man Yee, Oriel Sullivan, and Jonathan Gershuny. (2011). Gender convergence in domestic work: Discerning the effects of interactional and institutional barriers from large-scale data. *Sociology* 45(2):234–251.

Kane-DeMaios, J. Ari., and Vern L. Bullough. (Eds.). (2006). *Crossing sexual boundar-ies: Transgender journeys, uncharted paths*. Amherst, NY: Prometheus Books.

Katz, Jonathan Ned. (1976). *Gay American history: Lesbians & gay men in the U.S.A.: A documentary history*. New York, NY: Thomas Y. Crowell.

Kenagy, Gretchen P., and Chang-ming Hsieh. (2005). The risk less known: Female-to-male transgender persons' vulnerability to HIV infection. *AIDS Care* 17(2):195–207.

Kennedy, Elizabeth Lapovsky, and Madeline D. Davis. (1993). *Boots of leather, slippers of gold. The history of a lesbian community*. New York, NY: Penguin.

Kennedy, Randall. (2002). *Interracial intimacies: Sex, marriage, identity, and adoption.* New York, NY: Random House.

Kennedy, Pagan. (2007). *The first man-made man: The story of two sex changes, one love affair, and a twentieth-century medical revolution.* New York, NY: Bloomsbury.

Kessler, Suzanne J. (1998). *Lessons from the intersexed.* New Brunswick, NJ: Rutgers University Press.

Kessler, Suzanne, and Wendy McKenna. (1978). *Gender: An ethnomethodological approach.* New York, NY: John Wiley and Sons.

Kessler, Suzanne, and Wendy McKenna. (2003). Who put the "trans" in transgender? Gender theory and everyday life. In Suzanne LaFont (Ed.), *Constructing sexualities: Readings in sexuality, gender, and culture.* Upper Saddle River, NJ: Prentice Hall.

Khosla, Dillon. (2006). *Both sides now: One man's journey through womanhood.* New York, NY: Tarcher/Penguin.

Kimport, Katrina. (2014). *Queering marriage: Challenging family formation in the United States.* New Brunswick, NJ: Rutgers University Press.

Kirkland, Anna. (2006). What's at stake in transgender discrimination as sex discrimination? *Signs* 32(1):83–111.

Kockott, Götz., and Eva-Maria Fahrner. (1988). Male-to-female and female-to-male transsexuals: A comparison. *Archives of Sexual Behavior* 17(3):539–546.

Koken, Juline A., Bimbi, David S., and Parsons, Jeffrey T. (2009). Experiences of familial acceptance–rejection among transwomen of color. *Journal of Family Psychology* 23(6):853–860.

Kotula, Dean. (2002). *The phallus palace.* Los Angeles, CA: Alyson Books.

Krieger, Susan. (1983). *The mirror dance: Identity in a women's community.* Philadelphia, PA: Temple University Press.

Kroska, Amy. (2003). Investigating gender differences in the meaning of household chores and child care. *Journal of Marriage and Family* 65(2):456–473.

Kurdek, Lawrence A. (2001). Differences between heterosexual non-parent couples and gay, lesbian, and heterosexual parent couples. *Journal of Family Issues* 22(6):727–754.

Kurdek, Lawrence A. (2006). Differences between partners from heterosexual, gay, and lesbian cohabiting couples. *Journal of Marriage and Family* 68(2):509–528.

Kurdek, Lawrence A. (2007). The allocation of household labor by partners in gay and lesbian couples. *Journal of Family Issues* 28(1):132–148.

Lee, Tracey. (2001). Trans(re)lations: Lesbian and female to male transsexual accounts of identity. *Women's Studies International Forum* 24(3-4):347–357.

Leli, Ubaldo, and Jack Drescher. (Eds.). (2004). *Transgender subjectivities: A clinician's guide.* Binghamton, NY: Haworth Medical Press.

Lenning, Emily, and Carrie L. Buist. (2013). Social, psychological and economic challenges faced by transgender individuals and their significant others: Gaining insight through personal narratives. *Culture, Health & Society* 15(1):44–57.

Lev, Arlene I. (2004). *Transgender emergence: Therapeutic guidelines for working with gender variant people and their families.* New York, NY: Routledge.

Lev, Arlene Istar. (2010). How queer! The development of gender identity and sexual orientation in LGBTQ-headed families. *Family Process* 49(3):268–290.

Levitt, Heidi M., Elisabeth A. Gerrish, and Katherine R. Hiestand. (2003). The misunderstood gender: A model of modern femme identity. *Sex Roles* 3(3-4):99–113.

Lewins, Frank. (2002). Explaining stable partnerships among ftms and mtfs: A significant difference? *Journal of Sociology* 38(1):76–88.

Lief, Harold I., and Lynn Hubschman. (1993). Orgasm in the postoperative transsexual. *Archives of Sexual Behavior* 22(2):145–155.

Link, Aaron Raz, and Hilda Raz. (2007). *What becomes you*. Lincoln, NE: University of Nebraska Press.

Lombardi, E. L., Riki Anne Wilchins, Dana Priesing, and Diana Malouf. (2001). Gender violence: Transgender experiences with violence and discrimination. *Journal of Homosexuality* 42(1):89–101.

Lothstein, Leslie M. (1983). *Female-to-male transsexualism: Historical, clinical, and theoretical issues*. Boston, MA: Routledge & Kegan Paul.

Mac, Amos, and Rocco Kayiatos. (Eds.). (2009). *Original Plumbing Magazine*. Retrieved from: http://www.originalplumbing.com

Mamo, Laura. (2007). *Queering reproduction: Achieving pregnancy in the age of technoscience*. Durham, NC: Duke University Press.

Mamo, Laura, and Eli Alston-Stepnitz. (2015). Queer intimacies and structural inequalities: New directions in stratified reproduction. *Journal of Family Issues* 36(4):519–540.

Marcus, Jana. (2011). *Transfigurations*. Aptos, CA: 7 Angels Press.

Martin, Biddy. (1996). *Femininity played straight: The significance of being lesbian*. New York, NY: Routledge.

Martino, Mario. (1977). *Emergence: A transsexual autobiography*. New York, NY: Crown.

Mason, Michelle E. (2006). *The experience of transition for lesbian partners of female-to-male transsexuals* (Doctoral dissertation). Retrieved from ProQuest Dissertations and Theses database. (UMI 1394648401)

McCauley, Elizabeth A., and Anke A. Ehrhardt. (1980). Sexual behavior in female transsexuals and lesbians. *The Journal of Sex Research*, 16(3):202–211.

Meadow, Tey. (2010). "A rose is a rose": On the production of legal gender classifications. *Gender & Society*, 24(6):814–837

Meadow, Tey. (2011). "Deep down where the music plays": How parents account for childhood gender variance. *Sexualities* 14(6):725–747.

Meadow, Tey. (forthcoming). Law's boundaries and the challenge of transgender. In Craig J. Calhoun and Richard Sennett (Eds.), *Edges*. New York, NY: New York University Press.

Meier, Stacey Colton, and Christine M. Labuski. (2013). The demographics of the transgender population. In Amanda Baumle (Ed.), *International Handbook on the Demography of Sexuality* (pp. 289–327). New York, NY: Springer.

Meyerowitz, Joanne. (2002). *How sex changed: A history of transsexuality in the United States*. Cambridge, MA: Harvard University Press.

Middlebrook, Diane Wood. (1998). *Suits me: The double life of Billy Tipton*. New York, NY: Houghton Mifflin.

Mills, C. Wright. (1959). *The sociological imagination*. New York, NY: Oxford University Press.

Minnotte, Krista L., Daphne P. Stevens, Michael C. Minnotte, and Gary Kiger. (2007). Emotion-work performance among dual-earner couples: Testing four theoretical perspectives. *Journal of Family Issues* 28(6):773–793.

Mock, Janet. (2012, July 9). Trans in the media: Unlearning the "trapped" narrative & taking ownership of our bodies. *Writings and reflections by Janet Mock*. Retrieved from http://janetmock.com/2012/07/09/josie-romero-dateline-transgender-trapped-body/

Moon, Dawne. (2008). Culture and the sociology of sexuality: It's only natural? *The Annals of the American Academy of Political and Social Science* 619(1):183–205.

Moore, Mignon R. (2008). Gendered power relations among women: A study of household decision-making in lesbian stepfamilies. *American Sociological Review* 73(2):335–356.

Moore, Mignon R. (2011). *Invisible families: Gay identities, relationships, and motherhood among Black women.* Berkeley, CA: University of California Press.

Moore, Mignon R. (2013). LGBT sexuality and families at the start of the twenty-first century. *Annual Review of Sociology* 39(1):491–507.

More, Sam Dylan. (1998). The pregnant man—an oxymoron? *Journal of Gender Studies* 7(3):319–328.

Morris, Ken. (2002). We were there: Female-to-male transsexuals in the Civil War. In Dean Kotula (Ed.), *The phallus palace* (pp. 147–156). Los Angeles, CA: Alyson Publications.

Munt, Sally R. (Ed.). (1998). *Butch/femme: Inside lesbian gender.* London, England: Cassell.

Muska, Susan, and Greta Olafsdottir. (Directors). (1998). *The Brandon Teena story* [Film]. United States: Bless Bless Productions.

Mustanski, Brian S. (2001). Getting wired: Exploiting the Internet for the collection of valid sexuality data. *Journal of Sex Research* 38(4):292–301.

Namaste, Ki. (1994). The politics of inside/out: Queer theory, poststructuralism, and a sociological approach to sexuality. *Sociological Theory* 12(2):220–231.

Namaste, Viviane. (2000). *Invisible lives: The erasure of transgender and transsexual people.* Chicago, IL: University of Chicago Press.

Nataf, Zachary I. (1996). *Lesbians talk transgender.* London, England: Scarlet Press.

National Coalition of Anti-Violence Programs. (2014). *Lesbian, gay, bisexual, transgender, queer, and HIV-affected hate violence in 2013.* New York, NY: National Coalition of Anti-Violence Programs.

Nelson, Maggie. (2015). *The Argonauts.* Minneapolis, MN: Graywolf Press.

Nestle, Joan. (1992). *The persistent desire: A femme-butch reader.* Boston, MA: Alyson Publications.

Nestle, Joan, Clare Howell, and Riki A. Wilchins. (2002). *Genderqueer: Voices from beyond the sexual binary.* Los Angeles, CA: Alyson Books.

Newton, Esther. (1984). The mythic mannish lesbian: Radclyffe Hall and the new woman. *Signs* 9(4):557–575.

Nicholson, Linda. (Ed.). (1990). *Feminism/Postmodernism.* New York, NY: Routledge.

Noble, Jean Bobby. (2006). *Sons of the movement: FtMs risking incoherence on a post-queer cultural landscape.* Toronto, Canada: Women's Press.

Nuttbrock, Larry A., Walter O. Bockting, Sel Hwahng, Andrew Rosenblum, Mona Mason, Monica Macri, and Jeffrey Becker. (2009). Gender identity affirmation among male-to-female transgender persons: A life course analysis across types of relationships and cultural/lifestyle factors. *Sexual and Relationship Therapy* 24(2):108–125.

Nyamora, Cory M. (2004). *Femme lesbian identity development and the impact of partnering with female-to-male transsexuals* (Doctoral dissertation). Retrieved from ProQuest Dissertations and Theses database. (UMI No. 766113091)

Oakes, Guy. (1995). Straight thinking about queer theory. *International Journal of Politics, Culture, and Society* 8(3):379–388.

Oakley, Ann. (1974). *The sociology of housework.* New York, NY: Random House.

O'Hartigan, Margaret Deirdre. (2002). Alan Hart. In Dean Kotula (Ed.), *The phallus palace*. (pp. 157–166). Los Angeles, CA: Alyson Publications.

O'Keefe, Tracie, and Katrina Fox. (Eds.) (2003). *Finding the real me: True tales of sex and gender diversity*. San Francisco, CA: Jossey-Bass.

O'Keefe, Tracie, and Katrina Fox. (Eds.) (2008). *Trans people in love*. New York, NY: Routledge.

Ong, Maria. (2005). Body projects of young women of color in physics: Intersections of gender, race, and science. *Social Problems* 52(4):593–617.

Park, Shelley M. (2013). *Mothering queerly, queering motherhood: Resisting mono-maternalism in adoptive, lesbian, blended, and polygamous families*. Albany, NY: SUNY Press.

Patterson, Charlotte J. (2000). Family relationships of lesbians and gay men. *Journal of Marriage and the Family* 62(4):1052–1069.

Patton, Michael Q. (1990). *Qualitative evaluation and research methods*. Newbury Park, CA: Sage.

Peddle, Daniel. (Director). (2005). *The aggressives* [Film]. United States: 7th Art Releasing.

Peirce, Kimberly. (Director). (1999). *Boys don't cry* [Film]. United States: Fox Searchlight Pictures.

Pepper, Rachel. (2012). *Transitions of the heart: Stories of love, struggle, and acceptance by mothers of transgender and gender variant children*. Berkeley, CA: Cleis Press.

Perez, Martin A., Eila C. Skinner, and Beth E. Meyerowitz. (2002). Sexuality and intimacy following radical prostatectomy: Patient and partner perspectives. *Health Psychology* 21(3):288–293.

Pfeffer, Carla A. (2008). Bodies in relation—bodies in transition: Lesbian partners of trans men and body image. *Journal of Lesbian Studies* 12(4):325–345.

Pfeffer, Carla A. (2009). *(Trans)formative relationships: What we learn about identities, bodies, work and families from women partners of trans men* (Doctoral dissertation). Retrieved from ProQuest Dissertations and Theses database. (UMI No. 3382326)

Pfeffer, Carla A. (2010). "Women's work?" Women partners of trans men doing housework and emotion work. *Journal of Marriage and Family* 72(1):165–183.

Pfeffer, Carla A. (2012). Normative resistance and inventive pragmatism: Negotiations of structure and agency among transgender families. *Gender & Society* 26(4):574–602.

Pfeffer, Carla A. (2014a). "I don't like passing as a straight woman": Queer negotiations of identity and social group membership. *American Journal of Sociology* 120:1–44.

Pfeffer, Carla A. (2014b). Making space for trans sexualities. *Journal of Homosexuality* 61(5):597–604.

Pfeffer, Carla A. (Ed.). (2014c). Trans sexualities [Special issue]. *Journal of Homosexuality* 61(5):597–780.

Pierson, Frank. (Director). (2003). *Soldier's girl* [Film]. United States: Bachrach/Gottlieb Productions.

Pitts, Victoria. (2000). Visibly queer: Body technologies and sexual politics. *The Sociological Quarterly* 41(3):443–463.

Plummer, Ken. (2003). Queers, bodies and postmodern sexualities: A Note on revisiting the "sexual" in symbolic interactionism." *Qualitative Sociology* 26(4):515–530.

Ponse, Barbara. (1978). *The social construction of identity and its meanings within the lesbian subculture*. Westport, CT: Greenwood Press.

Ponterotto, Joseph G. (2006). Brief on the origins, evolution, and meaning of the quali-
    tative research concept "thick description." *The Qualitative Report* 11(3): 538–549.

Powell, Brian, Catherine Bolzendahl, Claudia Geist, and Lala Carr Steelman. (2010).
    Counted out: Same-sex relations and Americans' definitions of family. New York,
    NY: Russell Sage Foundation.

Pratt, Minnie B. (1995). *S/he.* New York, NY: Firebrand Books.

Preves, Sharon. (2003). *Intersex identity: The contested self.* New Brunswick, NJ: Rutgers
    University Press.

Preves, Sharon E. (2002). Sexing the intersexed: An analysis of sociocultural responses
    to intersexuality. *Signs* 27(2):523–556.

Prosser, Jay. (1998). *Second skins: The body narratives of transsexuality.* New York,
    NY: Columbia University Press.

Queen, Carol, and Lawrence Schimel. (Eds.). (1997). *PoMoSexuals: Challenging
    assumptions about gender and sexuality.* San Francisco, CA: Cleis Press.

Rachlin, Katherine. (1999). Factors which influence individual's decisions when con-
    sidering FTM genital Surgery. *International Journal of Transgenderism* 3(3):1–12.

Rachlin, Katherine. (2002). FTM 101: Dispelling myths about the invisible and the
    impossible. In Dean Kotula (Ed.), *The phallus palace* (pp. 3–19). Los Angeles,
    CA: Alyson Publications.

Rashid, Mamoon, and Muhammad Sarmad Tamimy. (2013). Phalloplasty: The dream
    and the reality. *Indian Journal of Plastic Surgery* 46(2): 283–293.

Raymond, Janice. (1979). *The transsexual empire: The making of the she-male.* Boston,
    MA: Beacon Press.

Rees, Mark N. A. (1996). *Dear sir or madam: The autobiography of a female-to-male
    transsexual.* New York, NY: Cassell.

Reger, Jo. (2005). *Different wavelengths: Studies of the contemporary women's move-
    ment.* New York, NY: Routledge.

Rich, Adrienne. (1980). Compulsory heterosexuality and lesbian existence. *Signs*
    5(4):631–660.

Richman, Kimberly D. (2014). *License to wed: What legal marriage means to same-sex
    couples.* New York, NY: New York University Press.

Ring, Trudy. (2014, April 21). This year's Michigan Womyn's Music Festival will be the
    last. *The Advocate.* Retrieved from http://www.advocate.com/michfest/2015/04/21/
    years-michigan-womyns-music-festival-will-be-last

Risman, Barbara J. (Ed.). (2015). *Families as they really are.* New York, NY: W.
    W. Norton.

Robson, Ruthann. (2006). Reinscribing normality? The law and politics of transgen-
    der marriage. In Paisley Currah, Richard M. Juang, and Shannon P. Minter (Eds.),
    Transgender rights (pp. 299–309). Minneapolis, MN: University of Minnesota Press.

Roen, Katrina. (2001). Transgender theory and embodiment: The risk of racial margin-
    alisation. *Journal of Gender Studies* 10(3):253–263.

Roen, Katrina. (2002). "Either/Or" and "both/neither": Discursive tensions in trans-
    gender politics. *Signs* 27(2):501–522.

Rogers, Mary F. (1992). They all were passing: Agnes, Garfinkel, and company. *Gender
    & Society* 6(2):169–191.

Rosato, Jennifer L. (2006). Children of same-sex parents deserve the security blanket
    of the parentage presumption. *Family Court Review* 44(1):74–86.

Rosser, B. R. Simon, Michael J. Oakes, Walter O. Bockting, and Michael Miner. (2007). Capturing the social demographics of hidden sexual minorities: An Internet study of the transgender population in the United States. *Sexuality Research and Social Policy: Journal of NSRC* 4(3):50–64.

Rosskam, Jules. (Director). (2006). *Transparent* [Film]. United States: Frameline.

Rosskam, Jules. (Director). (2008). *Against a trans narrative* [Film]. United States: Frameline.

Rowniak, Stefan, Catherine Chesla, Carol Dawson Rose, and William L. Holzemer. (2011). Transmen: The HIV risk of gay identity. *AIDS Education and Prevention* 23(6):508–520.

Rubin, Gayle S. (1984). Thinking sex: Notes for a radical theory of the politics of sexuality. In Carole S. Vance (Ed.), *Pleasure and danger: Exploring female sexuality* (pp. 267–319). Boston, MA: Routledge & Kegan Paul.

Rubin, Gayle S. (1992). Of catamites and kings: Reflections on butch, gender, and boundaries. In Joan Nestle (Ed.), *The persistent desire: A femme-butch reader* (pp. 466–482). Boston, MA: Alyson Publications.

Rubin, Henry. (1998). Border wars: Phenomenology as method in trans studies. *GLQ: A Journal of Lesbian and Gay Studies: The Transgender Issue* 4(2):263–281.

Rubin, Henry. (2003). *Self-made men: Identity and embodiment among transsexual men*. Nashville, TN: Vanderbilt University Press.

Rudd, Peggy J. (1999). *My husband wears my clothes: Crossdressing from the perspective of a wife* (2nd ed.). Katy, TX: PM Publishers.

Rudd, Peggy J. (2000). *Crossdressers: And those who share their lives* (2nd ed.). Katy, TX: PM Publishers.

Rupp, Leila J. (2006). Everyone's queer. *Organization of American Historians Magazine of History* 20(2):8–11.

Sabatello, Maya. (2011). Advancing transgender family rights through science: A proposal for an alternative framework. *Human Rights Quarterly* 33(1):43–75.

Salamon, Gayle. (2010). *Assuming a body: Transgender and rhetorics of materiality*. New York, NY: Columbia University Press.

Samons, Sandra L. (2009). Can this marriage be saved? Addressing male-to-female transgender issues in couples therapy. *Sexual and Relationship Therapy* 24(2):152–162.

Sanger, Tam. (2007). *Desiring difference? Transpeople's intimate partnerships and the cultural construction of gender and sexuality* (Unpublished doctoral dissertation). The Queens University of Belfast, Northern Ireland.

Sanger, Tam. (2010). *Trans people's partnerships: Towards an ethics of intimacy*. New York, NY: Palgrave Macmillan.

Schilt, Kristen. (2006). Just one of the guys: How transmen make gender visible at work. *Gender & Society* 20(4):465–490.

Schilt, Kristen. (2010). *Just one of the guys? Transgender men and the persistence of gender inequality*. Chicago, IL: University of Chicago Press.

Schilt, Kristen, and Elroi Windsor. (2014). The sexual habitus of transgender men: Negotiating sexuality through gender. *Journal of Homosexuality* 61(5):732–748.

Schilt, Kristen, and Laurel Westbrook. (2009). Doing gender, doing heteronormativity: "Gender normals," transgender people, and the social maintenance of heterosexuality. *Gender & Society* 23(4):440–464.

Schleifer, David. (2006). Make me feel mighty real: Gay female-to-male transgenderists negotiating sex, gender, and sexuality. *Sexualities* 9(1):57–75.

Schofield, Scott Turner. (2008). *Two truths and a lie.* Ypsilanti, MI: Homofactus Press.

Scholinski, Daphne. (1997). *The last time I wore a dress.* New York, NY: Riverhead Books.

Schrock, Douglas P., Emily M. Boyd, and Margaret Leaf. (2008). Emotion work in the public performances of male-to-female transsexuals. *Archives of Sexual Behavior* 38(5):702–712.

Schütz, Alfred. (1967). *Phenomenology of the social world.* Evanston, IL: Northwestern University Press.

Schwartz, Pepper, Brian J. Serafini, and Ross Cantor. (2013). Sex in committed relationships. In Amanda K. Baumle (Ed.), *International handbook on the demography of sexuality* (pp. 131–165). New York, NY: Springer.

Scott, Joan Wallach. (1988). *Gender and the politics of history.* New York, NY: Columbia University Press.

Scott, Marvin B., and Stanford M. Lyman. (1968). "Accounts." *American Sociological Review* 33(1):46–62.

Scott-Dixon, Krista. (Ed.). (2006). *Trans/forming feminisms: Trans-feminist voices speak out.* Toronto, Canada: Sumach Press.

Seidman, Steven. (1994). Queer-ing sociology, sociologizing queer theory: An introduction. *Sociological Theory* 12(2):166–177.

Seidman, Steven. (1995). Deconstructing queer theory or the under-theorization of the social and the ethical. In Linda Nicholson and Steven Seidman (Eds.), *Social postmodernism: Beyond identity politics* (pp. 116–141). Cambridge, England: Cambridge University Press.

Seidman, Steven. (2001). From identity to queer politics: Shifts in normative heterosexuality and the meaning of citizenship. *Citizenship Studies* 5(3):321–328.

Seidman, Steven. (2005). From polluted homosexual to the normal gay: Changing patterns of sexual regulation in America. In Chrys Ingraham (Ed.), *Thinking straight: New work in critical heterosexuality studies* (pp. 39–62). New York, NY: Routledge.

Sennett, Jay. (2006). *Self-organizing men: Conscious masculinities in time and space.* Ypsilanti, MI: Homofactus Press.

Serano, Julia. (2007). *Whipping girl: A transsexual woman on sexism and the scapegoating of femininity.* Emeryville, CA: Seal Press.

Serano, Julia. (2013). *Excluded: Making feminist and queer movements more inclusive.* Berkeley, CA: Seal Press.

Shapiro, Eve. (2004). "Trans"cending barriers: Transgender organizing on the Internet. *Journal of Gay and Lesbian Social Services* 16(3-4):165–179.

Shapiro, Eve. (2010). *Gender circuits: Bodies and identities in a technological age.* New York, NY: Routledge.

Sheff, Elisabeth. (2011). Polyamorous families, same-sex marriage, and the slippery slope. *Journal of Contemporary Ethnography* 40(5):487–520.

Sheldon, Jane P., Pfeffer, Carla A., Petty, Elizabeth M., Fedbaum, Merle, and Jayaratne, Toby E. (2007). Beliefs about the etiology of homosexuality and about the ramifications of discovering its possible genetic origin. *Journal of Homosexuality* 52(3-4):111–150.

Shrage, Laurie J. (Ed.). (2009). *"You've changed": Sex reassignment and personal identity.* New York, NY: Oxford University Press.

Simmons, Jeremy. (Director). (2005). *TransGeneration* [Film]. United States: Sundance Channel.

Smith, Anna Marie. (2009). Reproductive technology, family law, and the post-welfare state: The California same-sex parents' rights "victories" of 2005. *Signs* 34(4):827–850.

Smock, Pamela J. (2000). Cohabitation in the United States: An appraisal of research themes, findings, and implications. *Annual Review of Sociology* 26:1–20.

Solomon, Andrew. (2012). *Far from the tree: Parents, children and the search for identity.* New York, NY: Scribner.

Soloway, Jill. (Director). (2014). *Transparent* [Film]. United States: Amazon Studios.

Spade, Dean. (2011). *Normal life: Administrative violence, critical trans politics, and the limits of law.* Brooklyn, NY: South End Press.

Squires, Catherine R., and Daniel C. Brouwer. (2002). In/Discernible bodies: The politics of passing in dominant and marginal media. *Critical Studies in Media Communication* 19(3):283–310.

Stacey, Judith. (1993). Good riddance to "The Family": A response to David Popenoe. *Journal of Marriage and Family* 55(3):545–547.

Stacey, Judith. (2011). *Unhitched: Love, marriage, and family values from West Hollywood to western China.* New York, NY: New York University Press.

Stein, Arlene. (1997). *Sex and sensibility: Stories of a lesbian generation.* Berkeley, CA: University of California Press.

Stein, Arlene, and Ken Plummer. (1994). "I can't even think straight": "Queer" theory and the missing sexual revolution in sociology. *Sociological Theory* 12(2):178–187.

Steinbock, Eliza. (2014). On the affective force of "nasty love." *Journal of Homosexuality* 61(5):749–765.

Steinbugler, Amy C. (2012). *Beyond loving: Intimate racework in lesbian, gay, and straight interracial relationships.* New York, NY: Oxford University Press.

Stoller, Robert. (1975). *Sex and gender, volume II: The transsexual experiment.* New York, NY: Aronson.

Stone, Amy L. (2012). *Gay rights at the ballot box.* Minneapolis, MN: University of Minnesota Press.

Stone, Sandy. (1991). The "empire" strikes back: A posttranssexual manifesto. In Julia Epstein and Kristina Straub (Eds.), *Body guards: The cultural politics of gender ambiguity* (pp. 280–304). New York, NY: Routledge.

Strassberg, Donald S., Howard Roback, and Jean Cunningham. (1979). Psychopathology in self-identified female-to-male transsexuals, homosexuals, and heterosexuals. *Archives of Sexual Behavior* 8(6):491–496.

Strauss, Anselm L. (1987). *Qualitative analysis for social scientists.* Cambridge, England: Cambridge University Press.

Strauss, Anselm L., and Juliet M. Corbin. (1990). *Basics of qualitative research: Grounded theory procedures and techniques.* Thousand Oaks, CA: Sage.

Stryker, Susan, and Stephen Whittle. (Eds.) (2006). *The transgender studies reader.* New York, NY: Routledge.

Sullivan, Lou. (1980). *Information for the female-to-male.* San Francisco, CA: The Janus Information Facility.

Sullivan, Lou. (1990a). *From female to male: The life of Jack Bee Garland*. Boston, MA: Alyson Publications.

Sullivan, Lou. (1990b). *Information for the female to male cross dresser and transsexual*. Seattle, WA: Ingersoll Gender Center.

Sullivan, Oriel. (2011). An end to gender deviance neutralization through housework? A review and reassessment of the quantitative literature using insights from the qualitative literature. *Journal of Family Theory and Review* 3(1)1–13.

Swarr, Amanda Lock. (2012). *Sex in transition: Remaking gender and race in South Africa*. Albany, NY: SUNY Press.

Tabatabai, Ahoo, and Annulla Linders. (2011). Vanishing act: Non-straight identity narratives of women in relationships with women and men. *Qualitative Sociology* 34(4):583–599.

Taormino, Tristan. (Ed.). (2011). *Take me there: Trans and genderqueer erotica*. Berkeley, CA: Cleis Press.

Taylor, Charles. (1992). *Multiculturalism and "the politics of recognition."* Princeton, NJ: Princeton University Press.

Taylor, Verta, and Nancy E. Whittier. (1992). Collective identity in social movement communities: Lesbian feminist mobilization. In Aldon D. Morris and Carol McClurg Mueller (Eds.), *Frontiers in social movement theory* (pp. 104–129). New Haven, CT: Yale University Press.

Tesene, Megan. (2011). *Transforming lives: Exploring the impact of transitioning on female-to-male transpersons and partners of female-to-male transpersons* (Master's thesis). Department of Sociology, University of Northern Iowa.

Theron, Liesl, and Kate L. Collier. (2013). Experiences of female partner of masculine-identifying trans persons. *Culture, Health & Sexuality* 1(15):62–75.

Thompson, Charis. (2005). *Making parents: The ontological choreography of reproductive technologies*. Cambridge, MA: Massachusetts Institute of Technology.

Tompkins, Avery B. (2011). *Intimate allies: Identity, community, and everyday activism among cisgender people with trans-identified partners* (Doctoral dissertation). Retrieved from ProQuest Dissertations and Theses database. (UMI No. 3454427)

Tompkins, Avery B. (2014). "There's no chasing involved": Cis/trans relationships, "tranny chasers," and the future of a sex-positive trans politics. *Journal of Homosexuality* 61(5):766–780.

Transgender Law Center. (2014, April 29). *Big news: DOE guidance says transgender students protected under federal law*. Retrieved from http://transgenderlawcenter.org/archives/10249

Tresniowski, Alex. (2008, April 14). He's having a baby. *People* 69(14):54–60.

Treut, Minika. (Director). (1999). *Gendernauts: A journey through shifting* [Film]. Germany: Hyena Films.

Tucker, Duncan. (Director). (2005). *Transamerica* [Film]. United States: Belladonna Productions.

Turner, Victor. (1969). *The ritual process: Structure and anti-structure*. Ithaca, NY: Cornell University Press.

Uekrongtham, Ekachai. (Director). (2004). *Beautiful boxer* [Film]. Thailand: GMM Pictures Co.

United States Census Bureau. no date. *Current Population Survey (CPS) definitions*. http://www.census.gov/cps/about/cpsdef.html.

Valerio, Max Wolf. (2006). *The testosterone files: My hormonal and social transformation from female to male.* Emeryville, CA: Seal Press.

Valocchi, Stephen. (2005). Not yet queer enough: The lessons of queer theory for the sociology of gender and sexuality. *Gender & Society* 19(6):750–770.

Vanderburgh, Reid. (2012). The story of Diana and Daniel and Mary. *International Journal of Childbirth Education* 27(4)32–36.

Veale, David, Sarah Miles, Sally Bramley, Gordon Muir, and John Hodsoll. (2015, March 2). Am I normal? A systematic review and construction of nomograms for flaccid and erect penis length and circumference in up to 15,521 men. *BJU International.* Retrieved from http://onlinelibrary.wiley.com/doi/10.1111/bju.13010/abstract

Veale, Jamie F. (2014). Evidence against a typology: A taxometric analysis of the sexuality of male-to-female transsexuals. *Archives of Sexual Behavior* 43(6):1177–1186.

Vidal-Ortiz, Salvador. (2002). Queering sexuality and doing gender: Transgender men's identification with gender and sexuality. In Patricia Gagné and Richard Tewksbury (Eds.), *Advances in gender research (volume 6): Gendered sexualities* (pp. 181–233). New York, NY: Emerald Group Publishing.

Vidal-Ortiz, Salvador. (2008). Teaching and learning guide for: Transgender and transsexual studies: Sociology's influence and future steps. *Sociology Compass* 2(2):799–807.

Volcano, Del Lagrace, and Jack Halberstam. (1999). The drag king book. London, England: Serpent's Tail.

Walby, Kevin. (2012). *Touching encounters: Sex, work, and male-for-male Internet escorting.* Chicago, IL: University of Chicago Press.

Walters, Suzanna Danuta. (2014). *The tolerance trap: How god, genes, and good intentions are sabotaging gay equality.* New York, NY: New York University Press.

Ward, Jane. (2008). *Respectably queer: Diversity culture in LGBT activist organizations.* Nashville, TN: Vanderbilt University Press.

Ward, Jane. (2010). Gender labor: Transmen, femmes, and the collective work of transgression." *Sexualities* 13(2):236–254.

Warner, Michael. (1991). Introduction: Fear of a queer planet. *Social Text* 29(4):3-17.

Warner, Michael. (1993). *Fear of a queer planet: Queer politics and social theory.* Minneapolis, MN: University of Minnesota Press.

Warren, Carol A. B. (2014). Gender reassignment surgery in the 18th century: A case study. *Sexualities* 17(7):872–884.

Watson, Mary Ann. (Director). (2009). *Becoming me: The gender within* [Film]. United States: Films Media Group.

Weiss, Jillian T. (2004). GL vs. BT: The archaeology of biphobia and transphobia within the US gay and lesbian community. *Journal of Bisexuality* 3(3):25–55.

Wentling, Tre, Kristen Schilt, Elroi Windsor, and Betsy Lucal. (2008). Teaching transgender. *Teaching Sociology* 36(1):49–57.

West, Candace, and Don H. Zimmerman. (1987). Doing gender. *Gender & Society* 1(2):125–151.

Westbrook, Laurel, and Kristen Schilt. (2014). Doing gender, determining gender: Transgender people, gender panics, and the maintenance of the sex/gender/sexuality system. *Gender & Society* 28(1):32–57.

Whisman, Vera. (1996). *Queer by choice: Lesbians, gay men, and the politics of identity.* New York, NY: Routledge.

Whitehead, Jaye Cee. (2013). Sexuality and the ethics of body modification: Theorizing the situated relationships among gender, sexuality, and the body. *Sexualities* 16(3/4):383–400.

Whitley, Cameron T. (2013). Trans-kin undoing and redoing gender: Negotiating relational identity among friends and family of transgender persons. *Sociological Perspectives* 56(4):597–621.

Whittle, Stephen. (2000). *The transgender debate: The crisis surrounding gender identities*. Reading, UK: Garnet Publishing.

Wilchins, Riki A. (1997). *Read my lips: Sexual subversion and the end of gender*. New York, NY: Firebrand.

Williams, Colin J., Martin S. Weinberg, and Joshua G. Rosenberger. (2013). Trans men: Embodiments, identities, and sexualities. *Sociological Forum* 28(4):719–741.

Wolkomir, Michelle. (2009). Making heteronormative reconciliations: The story of romantic love, sexuality, and gender in mixed-orientation marriages. *Gender & Society* 23(4):494–519.

Wosick, Kassia R. (2012). *Sex love and fidelity: A study of contemporary romantic relationships*. Amherst, NY: Cambria Press.

Yogev, Sara, and Jeanne Brett. (1985). Perceptions of the division of housework and child care and marital satisfaction. *Journal of Marriage and the Family* 47(3):609–618.

Zamboni, Brian D. (2006). Therapeutic considerations in working with the family, friends, and partners of transgendered individuals. *The Family Journal: Counseling and Therapy for Couples and Families* 14(2):174–179.

Zelizer, Viviana A. (2005). *The purchase of intimacy*. Princeton, NJ: Princeton University Press.

Ziegler, Kortney. (2014, July 15). The peculiarity of Black trans male privilege. *The Advocate*. Retrieved from http://www.advocate.com/print-issue/current-issue/2014/07/15/peculiarity-black-trans-male-privilege.

Zimmerman, Don H. (1992). They were all doing gender, but they weren't all passing: Comment on Rogers. *Gender & Society* 6(2):192–198.

in understanding trans partnerships
and families, 14–18
Solomon, A., 14
Southern Comfort, 104
Squires, C.R., 77
SRS. *see* sex reassignment surgery (SRS)
Stacey, J., 193
"Standards of Care for Gender Identity
Disorders," 19–20
Standards of Care for the Health of
Transsexual, Transgender, and
Gender Nonconforming People
by WPATH, 31*n*
stealth
defined, xxxvi
Steinbugler, A., 71–72
*Still Black: A Portrait of Black
Transmen,* 76
Stone Butch Blues, 5
study methods, 195–197
Sullivan, L., 8–9, 36, 104
support
for cis women partners of trans men,
149–184
lack of, 152–154
from families
in interview protocol, 201
lack of, 156–167
for trans partnerships and families,
149–184
from colleges and universities,
176–177
labor-related, 174–176
material, 173–174
transition-related, 174–176
Swindler, W., 76

T. *see* testosterone (T)
T. Wood Pictures, 100
*Take Me There: Trans and Genderqueer
Erotica,* 100
Tambor, J., 18
Taormino, T., 100
Tea, M., 45, 79*n*
Teena, Brandon (*see also* Brandon,
Teena), 4–5

TERF. *see* Trans-Exclusionary Radical
Feminist
testosterone (T)
and insurance, 192
and menstrual cessation, 105–106
and orgasm, 128*n*
as defining manhood, 7, 16
celebrations, 61
cessation to achieve pregnancy, 13, 146
defined, xxxvi
effects, xxxv, 15–16, 61–62, 95–96,
103–107, 111, 114–115, 120, 123,
128*n*, 158, 168, 171
intramuscular injection of
in body transition, 92–93, 96,
103–107
purchase on the "black market," 36
social effects, 146, 166–167
use among butch-identified
lesbians, 23
use among trans partners of
interview participants, 108,
129*n*, 207*b*
Testosterone Male Syndrome ("TMS"), 106
The Aggressives, 18, 29*n*, 75, 81*n*
The Argonauts, 17
The Doctors, xxx*n*
"The Invisible Gender Outlaws: Partners
of Transgendered People," 170
"The Man with a Pussy," 127
"The Mom Who Fathered Her Own
Children," xix
The Monogamy Gap, 148*n*
*The Transsexual Empire: The Making of
the She Male,* 27*n*
The Well of Loneliness, xxiii
"the world's first pregnant man,"
xviii, 144
"thick description," xx–xxi
Third-Wave feminism, 48, 67, 79*n*, 81*n*,
94, 189
Tipton, B., xxiii, 4
Tipton, K., xxiii
"TMS" ("Testosterone Male
Syndrome"), 106
Tomkins, A.B., 57

CPSIA information can be obtained
at www.ICGtesting.com
Printed in the USA
BVHW04s0558250818
525407BV00001B/1/P